MW00426889

Praise for *Vindicating the Filioque*

"*Vindicating the Filioque* is a great scholarly work. Placing the *Filioque* debate in a historical context gives much-needed clarity to the old dispute of the so-called 'Greek' and 'Latin' traditions regarding the procession of the Holy Spirit. It is both patristic theology and ecclesiology. Fr. Crean provides the reader with an engrossing analysis of a diverse range of Church Fathers on the topic with a detailed analysis of Greek and Latin theological terms, showing how the teaching of the Fathers stands in relation to the Florentine definition. Examining the concept of ecumenicity embodied by the first seven councils, Fr. Crean shows how the Council of Florence meets any criteria accepted at the time by Greeks or Latins, vindicating the infallibility of its definitive teachings on matters of faith. As a Catholic priest of the Byzantine Rite, I consider this book to hold a special importance for rediscovering the theological heritage of the Eastern Catholic Churches and I recognize its important contribution to ecumenical dialogue. The good friar has offered us a clear exposition of '*fides orthodoxa*' regarding the Procession of the Holy Spirit."

REV. DR. YOSYP VERESH
Greek Catholic Eparchy of Mukachevo

"The Council of Florence is perhaps the greatest of all the Ecumenical Councils and Thomas Crean is its worthy expositor and champion. Its work and his is the antithesis of the ecumenism of ambiguity and compromise. Here is a scholasticism which goes *ad fontes* to drink deep of the sources of living faith at the fountains wrought for us by the Fathers of the Church. Here is the Latin tradition at its most self-confident but completely preoccupied with the need for reconciliation and reunion, with the indispensability to the life of the Church of the ancient and apostolic witness of Romania. This is the *κατάστασις* of the tragedy of Byzantium, the golden charter of reunion, which ensured that the last of the Palaiologoi could with clean hands and a pure heart make their final stand against a monstrous tyranny."

ALAN FIMISTER
Holy Apostles College and Seminary

VINDICATING THE *FILIOQUE*

VINDICATING THE *FILIOQUE*

The Church Fathers at the Council of Florence

Fr. Thomas Crean, O.P.

EMMAUS
ACADEMIC
Steubenville, Ohio
www.emmausacademic.com

EMMAUS
ACADEMIC
Steubenville, Ohio

A Division of The St. Paul Center for Biblical Theology
Editor-in-Chief: Scott Hahn
1468 Parkview Circle
Steubenville, Ohio 43952

Printed in the United States of America.

Library of Congress Cataloging-in-Publication Data applied for.
ISBNs: 978-1-64585-317-6 hardcover / 978-1-64585-318-3 paperback / 978-1-64585-319-0 ebook

Cover design by Allison Merrick
Layout by Laura Cruise and Allison Merrick
Cover woodcut: Concilie van Bazel; Concilium Basilian. Nuremberg Chronicles, 1493

Νέα Σιὼν ἡ Φλωρεντία ἐγένετο,
τοὺς πατέρας πάντοθεν συνάψασα πρὸς ἑαυτὴν
καὶ τὸν ἱερὸν ὅρον θεοφρόνως εἰς πᾶσαν γῆν ἐξαπέστειλεν,
πολλῇ θεολογίᾳ καὶ σοφίᾳ συνθεῖσα,
τὴν ὀρθόδοξον πίστιν κηρύττοντα.

Florence became a new Sion:
gathering the fathers to herself from all sides,
by divine counsel she sent forth into all the world the sacred dogma,
composed with much theology and wisdom,
proclaiming the orthodox faith.

—JOSEPH PLOUSIADENOS, *CANON OF THE 8TH SYNOD*
(ACROSTIC POEM)

To Alan and Colleen Fimister

Table of Contents

Acknowledgments

This book is the fruit of two unexpected and happy years spent studying and teaching at the Centre for Eastern Christian Studies at the International Theological Institute in Trumau, Austria. I should like to thank Fr. Yuriy Kolasa, the head of formation at the ITI, for issuing the invitation to go there, Dr. Alan Fimister for prompting it, and my then Dominican provincial, Fr. John Farrell, for encouraging me to accept it. My gratitude is also due to Fr. Yosyp Veresh, supervisor and friend, to Msgr. Larry Hogan, the president who welcomed me to the ITI, to Dr. Andrei Gotia for generously aiding me with his linguistic expertise, to Fr. Rupert Mayer, O.P., and Dr. Timothy Kelly, to the librarian of the abbey of Heiligenkreuz, and to my successive priors, Fr. Fabian Radcliffe (RIP) and Fr. David Rocks, for accepting my absence from the priory with equanimity. Finally, I should like to thank all the students whose company I was privileged to share during those two years, and in particular Brother Evagrius Hayden, O.S.B., for his unfailing kind and fraternal presence and manifold practical aid.

November 18, 2022
550th Anniversary of the death of
Cardinal Bessarion, Bishop of Nicaea

Acknowledgments

[illegible]

Abbreviations

AAS	*Acta Apostolicae Sedis*. Rome: Vatican Press, 1909–.
AG	*Quae supersunt actorum Graecorum Concilii Florentini. CFDS* vol. 5.
AL	Andreas de Santacroce. *Acta Latina Concilii Florentini. CFDS* vol. 6.
CCC	*Catechism of the Catholic Church*. London: Geoffrey Chapman, 1994.
CCSG	*Corpus Christianorum, Series Graeca*. Turnhout: Brepols, 1953–.
CCSL	*Corpus Christianorum, Series Latina*. Turnhout: Brepols, 1953–.
CFDS	*Concilium Florentinum: Documenta et Scriptores* [*CFDS*]. Edited by Georg Hoffman, Emmanuel Candal, Joseph Gill, Vitalien Laurent, et al. 11 vols. Rome: Pontifical Oriental Institute, 1940–1976.
CPG	*Clavis Patrum Graecorum*. Edited by M. Geerhard. 6 vols. Turnhout: Brepols, 1974–2003. Listing authors and works for *CCSG*, with authenticity rating.
CPL	*Clavis Patrum Latinorum*. Edited by E. Dekkers and A. Garr, 3rd edition. Steenbrugge: Brepols, 1995. Listing authors and works for *CCSL*, with authenticity rating.
DTC	*Dictionnaire de théologie catholique*. 15 vols. Paris: Letouzey et Ané, 1907–1951.

DH	Heinrich Denzinger. *Compendium of Creeds, Definitions and Declarations on Matters of Faith and Morals*. 43rd Latin–German edition. Edited by Helmut Hoping and Peter Hünermann. Latin–English edited and and translated by Robert Fastiggi and Anne Englund Nash. San Francisco: Ignatius Press, 2012.
EP	*Epistolae pontificiae ad Concilium Florentinum spectantes. CFDS* vol. 1. All citations from *EP* are from part 1 of 3, which is marked by Roman numeral.
Mansi	*Sacrorum conciliorum et decretorum nova et amplissima collectio*. 53 vols. Edited by John Mansi. Leipzig: H. Welter, 1759–1927.
*NPNF*1/ *NPNF*2	*Nicene and Post-Nicene Fathers of the Christian Church*, 1st and 2nd series. Edited by Philip Schaff and Henry Wace. Edinburgh: T. & T. Clark; New York: Christian Literature Company, 1899.
OAU	*Opera anti-unionistica Marci Ephesi*. Edited by Louis Petit. Rome: Pontifical Oriental Institute, 1977.
ODCC	*The Oxford Dictionary of the Christian Church*. Edited by Frank Cross and Elizabeth Livingstone. 3rd edition revised. Oxford: Oxford University Press, 2005.
ODDU	*Oratio Dogmatica de Unione. CFDS* vol. 7/1.
ODM	*Orientalia Documenta Minora. CFDS* vol. 3/2. Cited by document and page.
PG	*Patrologia Graeca*. 162 vols. Edited by Jacques Migne. Paris, 1857–1886. Cited by column within volume.
PL	*Patrologia Latina*. 221 vols. Edited by Jacques Migne. Paris, 1844–1864. Cited by column within volume.
SYR	*The Memoirs of Sylvester Syropoulos on the Council of Florence. CFDS* vol. 9.

NOTE: Unless English translations are cited as from published English-language volumes, they are original to this volume.

INTRODUCTION

DOES MANKIND NEED a new book on the *Filioque*? More than a hundred years ago, the ironical English Orientalist and Catholic priest Adrian Fortescue wrote: "One shudders to think what rivers of ink have flowed because of this question, since Photius's happy thought of making this grievance against us."[1]

Yet a curious change has taken place since Fortescue wrote, and especially in the last quarter century. Increasingly, and among theological writers of all denominations, one finds the conviction expressed that the age-old dispute was, after all, largely verbal.[2] At the same time, paradoxically, one also finds it often implied or stated by the same writers that the Catholic Church has misled her members for centuries by defining the *Filioque*;[3] whence also widespread calls to remove the incriminated term from the Creed. It is remarkable that in a recent collection of essays by authors writing from many Christian perspectives, for instance, none

1 Adrian Fortescue, *The Orthodox Eastern Church* (London: Catholic Truth Society, 1920), 372.

2 For a decent summary of trends among Catholic theologians, see Brian Daley, "Revisiting the *Filioque*, Part Two: Contemporary Catholic approaches," *Pro Ecclesia* 10, no. 2 (2001): 195–212.

3 G. K. Chesterton once remarked that a certain kind of student of comparative religion loves to insist that "Christianity and Buddhism are very much alike, especially Buddhism" (*Orthodoxy* [London: John Lane, 1909], 238). Many writers today apparently hold that, when it comes to the procession of the Holy Spirit, Catholicism and Orthodoxy are very much alike, especially Orthodoxy.

was willing to defend the account of the Holy Spirit's procession that has been peacefully held by all Western Christians time out of mind.[4]

The definition in 1439 by the Council of Florence of the dogma of the *Filioque* might seem to be an insuperable barrier for any Catholic theologian hoping to shift the meaning of "procession from the Son" into something more acceptable to Eastern Orthodox theology. Unsurprisingly, then, just as past decades have seen a tendency among Catholic theologians to tamper with the meaning of this dogma (to put the matter bluntly) and to deprecate the inclusion of the word itself in the Creed, so also have they seen a tendency to ignore or belittle the achievement and authority of the Florentine synod. A certain myth has thus come to obscure the true visage of that great council of unity.

The present work aims to counter all these trends. The dispute about the *Filioque* is not, and never has been, a mere quarrel about words: it is a disagreement about the most important of all subjects, God himself. According to a phrase sometimes attributed to the Synod of Rheims in 1148, "whatever is in God, is God" ("quidquid in Deo est, Deus est").[5] The spiration and procession of the Holy Spirit *is* God.[6]

Again, and in consequence, Catholics and Orthodox are not both right about the procession of the Holy Spirit. One side must be right

4 *Ecumenical Perspectives on the* Filioque *for the 21st Century*, ed. Myk Habets (London: Bloomsbury Academic, 2014).

5 The attribution is made, for example, in Ludwig Ott, *Fundamentals of Catholic Dogma* (Cork: Mercier, 1960), 69. The words do not appear literally in the Council's confession of faith, though they are found equivalently, especially in: "We believe and confess that only God the Father, Son, and Holy Spirit are eternal, and that there are no things at all in God that exist from eternity and that are not God, whether they be called relations or properties or singularities or unities or anything else" ("credimus et confitemur solum Deum Patrem Filium et Spiritum Sanctum aeternum esse, nec aliquas omnino res, sive relationes, sive proprietates, sive singularitates, sive unitates dicantur, vel alia huiusmodi, adesse Deo, quae sint ab aeterno, et quae non sint Deus" [Mansi, 21:713B]). St. Thomas expresses the same idea when he writes, "whatever is in God, is his essence"—"Quidquid in Deo est, est sua essentia" (*Scriptum super libros sententiarum Petri Lombardi*, bk. I, dist. 43, q. 2, a. 1, ad. 3, ed. Pierre Mandonnet and Maria Moos, 4 vols. [Paris: Lethielleux, 1929–1947]).

6 Hence, as Pope Pius XII recalled in the encyclical letter *Mystici Corporis*, the vision of this spiration is part of the essential beatitude of the saints in heaven: "In that vision it will be granted to the eyes of the human mind strengthened by the light of glory to contemplate the Father, the Son, and the divine Spirit in an utterly ineffable manner, to be closely present throughout eternity to the processions of the divine persons, and to be beatified with a joy like to that with which the holy and undivided Trinity is blessed" (§80; *AAS* 35 [1943]: 232: "Qua quidem visione, modo prorsus ineffabili fas erit Patrem, Filium divinumque Spiritum mentis oculis superno lumine auctis contemplari, divinarum Personarum processionibus aeternum per aevum proxime adsistere, ac simillimo illi gaudio beari, quo beata est sanctissima et indivisa Trinitas").

and the other wrong. My approach in this book is, I hope, ecumenical in the truest sense, in that I appeal to authorities and to a tradition that are recognized in common by both parties. The authorities are the Fathers of the Church, while the Tradition is that of the ecumenical council as a means by which the Spirit of God may instruct his people. Yet I write as a Catholic theologian convinced that, in ecumenical dialogue, a clear presentation of the Catholic claims is both required by honesty and also the only way to reach the goal of lasting unity. It was by a courteous but robust presentation of the dogma of the *Filioque* that the Latin participants at Florence, especially the Dominican provincial John de Montenero, were able under grace to effect a union that might have been lasting had it not been for the tragic accident of the Fall of Constantinople.

In recovering the achievement of the Council of Florence, I make use especially of the monumental series *Concilium Florentinum: Documenta et Scriptores*. These eleven volumes, published by the Pontifical Oriental Institute between 1940 and 1977, allow for a very full understanding of the Council in its preparation, sessions, and aftermath. Despite the pioneering work of the English Jesuit Joseph Gill in the 1950s and 1960s, insufficient use has been made of these volumes in showing how the Florentine council fulfilled both Western and Eastern ideas of an ecumenical synod. The present work seeks to remedy this omission.

This book falls into three parts. In the first, I study the understanding the Fathers of the Church had of the procession of the Holy Spirit, in each case comparing their doctrine with that of Florence. Although many other writers before me, of course, have surveyed the patristic evidence, I do not know of a work in English that does so with sufficient fullness. Either too few patristic quotations are adduced, or if they are multiplied, they are not analyzed with sufficient regard for their context.[7] A fresh

7 To take an extreme example, Fortescue "proves" that the Greek Fathers believed in the procession from the Father and the Son by means of a single quotation attributed to St. Athanasius, but not considered authentic by modern scholarship (*The Orthodox Eastern Church*, 380). I would except from my general allegation of insufficiency Martin Jugie's work *De Processione Spiritus Sancti*, but since this is available only in Latin and dates from 1936, it is not by itself able to deal with the modern crisis.

presentation and analysis of the patristic evidence is merited. While I have not sought to give a synopsis of the best contemporary literature on each of the Fathers, I refer to this scholarship to the extent that it seemed helpful for establishing the meaning of some disputed passage relevant to our question.[8]

In the second part, I shall examine the nature of an ecumenical council by looking at the witness of history and at authorities common to Catholics and Orthodox alike. In the third part, I turn to the Council of Florence itself and (if a presumptuous expression may be forgiven) vindicate it in the light of what has gone before.[9] Although my discussion—especially of the writing of the Fathers—necessarily requires close analysis of texts with reference to the original Latin and Greek, I have striven to make all my arguments accessible also to readers unfamiliar with these languages.

When Patriarch Philotheos of Alexandria heard of the happy termination of the Council of Florence, he wrote to Pope Eugenius IV in exultant terms. May the present work in some small way help others one day to echo the patriarch's words: "Now that the old schism and enmity have been cast aside, love and peace have been brought back, for a common mystical worship of almighty God."[10]

---

8 In some places, constrained by my own circumstances, I have quoted from Migne's *Patrologia* even when more recent editions of a given text are available, and I have sometimes likewise quoted from older rather than newer translations. But when a significant variant appears, I have referred to modern critical editions and contemporary scholarly discussion.

9 I shall not directly seek to justify the insertion in the Latin West of the word *Filioque* into the Nicene-Constantinopolitan Creed, though I fully accept the teaching contained in the Florentine decree of union that this insertion was made by the church of Rome *licite et rationabiliter*, "lawfully and with reasonable cause." I believe it will appear sufficiently from the present work why the word is today more necessary than ever.

10 *ODM*, 38:52.

Part I

The Procession of the Holy Spirit and the Fathers of the Church

CHAPTER I

THE 1995 STATEMENT ON THE *FILIOQUE*
An Ambiguous Clarification

Introduction

WHAT DOES CHRISTIANITY TEACH about the origin of the Holy Spirit? This question has long divided the two greatest Christian bodies: the Roman Catholic communion and the Eastern Orthodox communion. The Catholic Church teaches that the Holy Spirit "proceeds," that is, eternally comes forth, from the Father and the Son. This doctrine is called briefly the *Filioque*, the Latin word which means "and from the Son." The word *Filioque* accordingly appears in the creed used in the Roman rite of Mass, known as the Nicene-Constantinopolitan creed, after the two early Church councils where it was elaborated, Nicaea (325) and Constantinople I (381). The word itself, however, was famously placed into the Creed in the Latin-speaking West some time after the latter of these councils.[1] Eastern

[1] The history is obscure, but the Creed was perhaps first recited in this form by the Third Council of Toledo

Orthodox Christians, by contrast, who have retained the original form of this creed, speak of the Holy Spirit simply as proceeding from the Father, and at least from the time of Photios, patriarch of Constantinople in the ninth century, this has generally been understood to mean "from the Father alone," not also from the Son.[2] Over the centuries, official and unofficial representatives of the two sides have often attempted to reach an understanding over the question, most notably in the Italian city of Florence in the fifteenth century, but no enduring agreement has ever been achieved.[3]

The Statement and Its Reception

On the feast of St. Peter and St. Paul in 1995, Pope John Paul II preached a sermon in St. Peter's basilica in the presence of Patriarch Bartholomew of Constantinople that contained the following exhortation:

> The traditional doctrine of the *Filioque*, present in the liturgical version of the Latin *Credo*, [is to be clarified] in order to highlight its full harmony with what the Ecumenical Council of Constantinople of 381 confesses in its creed: the Father as the source of the whole Trinity, the one origin both of the Son and of the Holy Spirit.

On September 8 of the same year, the Pontifical Council for Promoting Christian Unity quoted this exhortation at the start of a document entitled *Greek and Latin Traditions regarding the Procession of the Holy Spirit*, referred to by some as the *Clarification*.[4] The pontifical council

in 589. The Creed itself was first placed into the rite of Mass used in Rome by Pope Benedict VIII in 1014. For a summary of the facts, see A. Edward Siecienski, *The Filioque: History of a Doctrinal Controversy* (New York: Oxford University Press, 2010), 68–69, 112–13.

2 Photios set forth his criticism of the *Filioque* in the work *On the Mystagogy of the Holy Spirit.*

3 However, the Union of Brest at the end of the sixteenth century happily achieved a lasting union between Rome and several Ukrainian eparchies (dioceses) on the basis of the Florentine decrees.

4 Many authors refer to this document as "the Clarification" or "the Clarification on the *Filioque*." The text appeared in the daily edition of *L'Osservatore Romano* on September 13, 1995, with the French original and

stated that its document presented "the authentic doctrinal meaning of the *Filioque*."[5]

Many voices in both the Roman Catholic and the Eastern Orthodox communions have enthusiastically welcomed this new document as solving the ancient dispute, or at least as being an important step toward a solution.[6] I shall consider their reasons in detail in a moment, but for now we may say that they argue that the two sides have been defending complementary, rather than contradictory, views on the mystery of the Blessed Trinity, and that the ancient disagreement is thus largely verbal and not substantial. They say that the so-called "Greek and Latin traditions" do not really disagree about the nature of the Blessed Trinity, but that a difference in the use of words—especially the difficulties of translating between the two languages—have given rise to a needless quarrel.

On the Catholic side, for example, the Spanish ecumenist Fr. Jean-Miguel Garrigues has stated that the pontifical council's document shows that the *Filioque* is, despite appearances, compatible with the Eastern Orthodox doctrine of procession "from the Father alone."[7] In this he has been followed by Dom Emmanuel Lanne of the bi-ritual abbey of Chevetogne, in Belgium.[8] Carl Krauthauser, likewise, holds that the document contains "a fuller expression of the dogmatic truth

an Italian translation. An English translation was published in the English weekly edition of *L'Osservatore Romano* dated September 20, 1995. My references are to the English translation found as: Pontifical Council for Promoting Christian Unity, "Traditions regarding the Procession of the Holy Spirit, " *Eastern Christian Journal* 2, no. 3 (1995): 35–46.

5 Pontifical Council for Promoting Christian Unity, "Traditions," 38. Avery Dulles, however, stated that "the Pontifical Council for Promoting Christian Unity . . . has no doctrinal authority" (*Magisterium: Teacher and Guardian of the Faith* [Naples, FL: Ave Maria University Press, 2007], 112).

6 Siecienski, *Filioque*, 211: "Reaction to the Roman document was, on the whole, very positive."

7 Jean-Miguel Garrigues, "A la suite de la clarification romaine: Le *Filioque* affranchi du 'Filioquisme,'" *Irenikon* 69 (1996): 189–212, at 211. Garrigues holds that there is therefore need of "an ecumenical re-interpretation of the confessions of faith of the Second Council of Lyon and of the Council of Florence," which two councils defined that procession of the Holy Spirit as being "from the Father and the Son." He does not, however, examine how such a reinterpretation might be reconciled with the solemn teaching of Vatican I that it is unlawful to say that with the progress of knowledge, a different meaning may be attributed to dogmas from that which the Church has understood and understands (DH no. 3043).

8 See Emmanuel Lanne, "La *Processio* dello Spirito Santo nella tradizione occidentale," *Nicolaus* 24, no. 1/2 (1999): 245–60, summarized in Jean-Yves Brachet and Emmanuel Durand, "La réception de la *Clarification* romaine de 1995 sur le *Filioque*," *Irénikon* 78, no. 1–2 (2005): 47–109, at 77–78.

about the eternal procession of the Holy Spirit" than is to be found in the conciliar definitions about the question made at the Second Council of Lyon (1274) and at the Council of Florence.[9] From Strasbourg, Anne-Marie Vannier argues that the document is a great step toward unity that must eventually lead to the suppression of the very word *Filioque* from the Latin Creed.[10] This may strike the reader as strange, since John Paul II had asked that the *harmony* between the Greek and Latin forms of the Creed be manifested, but the reason for it will become clearer in what follows.[11]

On the Orthodox side, Olivier Clement affirmed that the pontifical council's document was "admirably argued" and "could well mark the end of the quarrel over the *Filioque*."[12] Metropolitan John Zizioulas has likewise welcomed it as "an encouraging attempt to clarify the basic aspects of the *Filioque* problem and show that a rapprochement between West and East on this matter is eventually possible."[13] He praises in particular the document's claim that God the Father is the "sole principle" of the Holy Spirit. The Romanian Orthodox theologian-bishop Dumitru Popsecu considered the Catholic Church to be taking an important step forward by means of the *Clarification* toward the Orthodox doctrine.[14]

Indeed, it seems to have become almost a commonplace to say that the 1995 statement marks an advance toward agreement. The Canadian

---

9 Carl Krauthauser, "The Council of Florence Revisited," *Eastern Christian Journal* 4, no. 1 (1997): 141–54, at 154.

10 Anne-Marie Vannier, "L'apport de la Clarification sur le *Filioque*," *Revue des sciences religieuses* 75, no. 1 (2001): 97–112, at 98, 103.

11 The suggestion of suppressing the *Filioque* was not new: the Catholic theologians Yves Congar, Louis Boyer, and Hans urs von Balthasar had proposed the same thing (see chapter 3, "The Holy Spirit and the *Filioque*," in Matthew Levering, *Engaging the Doctrine of the Holy Spirit: Love and Gift in the Trinity and in the Church* [Grand Rapids, MI: Baker Academic, 2016]). Two Catholic theologians, Hans-Joachim Schulz (Professor of Ecumenical Theology at the Universiry of Wurzburg) and Waclaw Hryniewicz (Professor of Dogmatics at the University of Lublin), made the same proposal at a colloquium organized in Vienna in 1998 at the initiative of Cardinal Christoph Schönborn to study the pontifical council's document (see Brachet and Durand, "La réception").

12 Oliver Clement, "Liminaire [editorial]," *Contacts*, no. 48 (1964): 241–42.

13 John Zizioulas, "One Single Source: An Orthodox Response to the Clarification on the *Filioque*," Orthodox Research Institute, orthodoxresearchinstitute.org/articles/dogmatics/john_zizioulas_single_source.htm.

14 Dumitri Popescu, "Il problema del *Filioque*: ekporeusis e processio," *Nicolaus* 26, no. 1/2 (1999): 261–69 (summarized in Brachet and Durand, "La réception," 79–81).

Evangelical theologian David Guretzki, in a recent review of the state of the question, asserts that "even if it is granted that there was ambiguity in the Western tradition about a single source of deity in the Trinity, it should be evident that such ambiguity has given way to clarity in the last two decades," as a result of the Pontifical Council's work.[15] For its part, the North American Orthodox–Catholic Consultation, in an agreed statement sponsored by the United States Council of Catholic Bishops, believes that the 1995 document has shown that the Catholic Church was previously in error in regarding the Eastern Orthodox position as incompatible with her own. Like Garrigues, they recommend that "following a growing theological consensus," the condemnation of "those who presume to deny that the Holy Spirit proceeds eternally from the Father and the Son" issued by Lyon II should be declared to be "no longer applicable."[16] Apparently influenced by this widespread enthusiasm for the 1995 document, Cardinal Kurt Koch, the current president of the pontifical council that produced it, declared in 2018 that theological research has shown the historic disputes about the *Filioque* to have been largely verbal (*perlopiù problemi linguistici*), rather than substantial.[17]

The Proposed Harmonization

The burden of the present work is that such enthusiasm for the 1995 document of the pontifical council is misplaced. Far from considering it an ecumenical breakthrough, I shall argue that it presents a danger to the Catholic faith. This opinion is legitimate for a Catholic theologian, since the document, as already mentioned, is not a magisterial text. It is thus worth only what its arguments are worth. First, however, I must

15 David Guretzki, "The *Filioque*: Reviewing the State of the Question," in *Ecumenical Perspectives on the* Filioque *for the 21st Century*, ed. Myk Habets (London: Bloomsbury, 2014), 40–63, at 47.

16 North American Orthodox–Catholic Theological Consultation, "The *Filioque*: A Church-Dividing Issue? An Agreed Statement (October 25, 2003)," *St. Vladimir's Theological Quarterly* 48 (2004): 93–123. For the sponsorship of this body by the United States Council of Catholic Bishops, with an approving reference to the *Agreed Statement*, see usccb.org/news/2003/03-207.cfm.

17 The speech is available at www.christianunity.va/content/unitacristiani/en/cardinal-koch/2018/conferenze/conferenza-nel-dies-academicus-della-facolta-di-teologia-di-luga.html.

summarize the pontifical council's proposal for harmonizing the "Greek and Latin traditions."

The authors state that both the Greek Fathers and the Western tradition recognize God the Father as "the sole Trinitarian cause (αἰτία) or principle (*principium*) of the Son and of the Holy Spirit." When we come to look at the patristic texts, we shall see whether this is an accurate or a misleading statement. They also state that "the Holy Spirit . . . takes his origin from the Father alone (ἐκ μόνου τοῦ Πατρός) in a principal, proper and immediate manner."[18] Most importantly, they urge that:

> The doctrine of the *Filioque* must be understood and presented by the Catholic Church in such a way that it cannot appear to contradict the Monarchy of the Father nor the fact that he is the sole origin (ἀρχή) of the ἐκπόρευσις [procession] of the Spirit.[19]

How then do the authors think to preserve the dogma of the *Filioque* if they call the Father the "sole principle" of the Holy Spirit or the "sole origin of the procession [ἐκπόρευσις] of the Spirit"? They draw attention to the distinction between two Greek words, ἐκπορεύεσθαι and προϊέναι. Both words have commonly been translated into Latin by the single term *procedere*, and thence into other Western languages, again, by a single word: for example, into English as "proceed."[20] The Greek Fathers, the authors note, used the former term only for a relation of a divine person (normally the Holy Spirit, but occasionally also the Son) to God the Father, whereas the latter term was used of the Holy Spirit in relation both to the Father and to the Son. The *Filioque*

---

18 Pontifical Council for Promoting Christian Unity, "Traditions," 36.

19 Pontifical Council for Promoting Christian Unity, "Traditions," 38. Despite stating that "the Greek Fathers and the whole Christian Orient speak . . . of the 'Father's monarchy'" (36), the document gives no examples of such language. In ch. 7 (St. Gregory of Nazianzen), see the section on his "Oration 29 (Third Theological Oration)."

20 See, e.g., John 8:42: "Ἐγὼ γὰρ ἐκ τοῦ Θεοῦ ἐξῆλθον καὶ ἥκω"; the Vulgate reads, "Ego enim ex Deo processi et veni"; the RSV reads, "I proceeded and came forth from God." For John 15:26, the Greek text has "Τὸ πνεῦμα τῆς ἀληθείας ὃ παρὰ τοῦ πατρὸς ἐκπορεύεται"; the Vulgate has "Spiritum veritatis qui a Patre procedit"; the RSV has "the Spirit of truth who proceeds from the Father."

should therefore be understood with reference to the second word. They conclude: "The *Filioque* does not concern the ἐκπόρευσις of the Spirit issued from the Father as source of the Trinity, but manifests his προϊέναι (*processio*) in the consubstantial communion of the Father and the Son."[21]

What is meant by this last phrase? Here the *Clarification* becomes somewhat obscure:

> If in the Trinitarian order the Holy Spirit is consecutive to the relation between the Father and the Son, since he takes his origin from the Father as Father of the only Son, it is in the Spirit that this relationship between the Father and the Son itself attains its Trinitarian perfection. Just as the Father is characterized as Father by the Son he generates, so does the Spirit, by taking his origin from the Father, characterize the Father in the manner of the Trinity in relation to the Son and characterizes the Son in the manner of the Trinity in his relation to the Father: in the fullness of the Trinitarian mystery they are Father and Son in the Holy Spirit.[22]

In all this, the authors apparently are stating that (1) the hypostatic coming forth (ἐκπόρευσις) of the Holy Spirit, meaning his eternal coming forth as the third divine person, is from the Father alone, but that (2) the Holy Spirit may nonetheless be said to "proceed" (προϊέναι) from the Father and the Son because (a) the Father from whom the Holy Spirit comes is of necessity and from eternity the Father of the Son, and so (b) the Holy Spirit, by the very fact of coming from the *Father*, evokes or "characterizes" the Fatherhood of the Father, and hence the Sonship of the Son, and perhaps also because (c) the Holy Spirit evokes both the Father and Son by the very fact that he is consubstantial with them.

21 Pontifical Council for Promoting Christian Unity, "Traditions," 42.
22 Pontifical Council for Promoting Christian Unity, "Traditions," 43–44.

This, the authors indicate, is what is meant by saying of the Holy Spirit, *procedit Filioque* ("he proceeds also from the Son"), or with the Greek Fathers, προεῖσι ἐξ Υἱοῦ.[23]

Garrigues in his commentary seems to confirm this interpretation:

> Since the Spirit derives his origin from the Father as Father, he therefore comes forth (ekporeuomenos) from the Father alone through the one who characterizes the Father as Father, that is, through the Son, and he proceeds (procedit, proeïsi) from the Father and from the Son in the consubstantial communication of their unique divinity.[24]

The first part of this quotation appears to mean that the Holy Spirit is said to proceed (ἐκπορεύεται) from the Son not in the sense that the Son would be an active principle of the Holy Spirit, but because the Father from whom alone he issues is the Holy Spirit's source insofar as he is Father of the Son. For, the author asserts, the document teaches that the "one principle" of the Holy Spirit declared at Lyon II and Florence is "the Father of the Son."[25] The second half of the quotation is more obscure. One might imagine it to be saying that while the *person* of the Holy Spirit comes from the Father alone, *divinity* comes to the Holy Spirit through the joint action of the Father and the Son. Yet this would clearly be absurd: a divine person is not a "mold" into which the divine essence is then poured, as if the two were really distinct.[26] The author cannot mean this, and so presumably he simply means that in thus proceeding from the Father alone (who is nonetheless necessarily

---

23 Pontifical Council for Promoting Christian Unity, "Traditions," 37. This last expression they take to be equivalent to another expression found in the Greek Fathers, ἐκπορεύεται διὰ τοῦ Υἱοῦ, which they translate as "takes his origin from the Father by or through the Son."

24 Jean-Miguel Garrigues, "A la suite de la clarification romaine sur le *Filioque*," *Nouvelle revue théologique* 119 (1997): 321–34, at 322. According to Vannier, Garrigues was in fact one of the authors of the document ("L'apport," 102).

25 Garrigues, "A la suite," 321.

26 The Latin delegates insisted at Florence that to posit a real distinction between a divine person and the divine essence would be contrary to divine simplicity (*AG*, 414).

and eternally Father of the Son), the Holy Spirit is consubstantial to Father and Son.[27]

The authors of the document do affirm that there exists an eternal relation between the Son and the Holy Spirit other than that of consubstantiality. They seek to describe this relation more fully by the tradition, which they trace to St. Augustine, that sees the Holy Spirit as love, and thus as "the eternal gift of the Father to his beloved Son." There is, they say, "an eternal Trinitarian relationship through which the Spirit, in his mystery as Gift of Love, characterizes the relation between the Father, as source of love, and his beloved Son."[28] The meaning of this statement remains, again, somewhat obscure, but it does not tend to contradict the document's earlier statement that the Holy Spirit derives his ἐκπόρευσις from the Father alone.

A final point to note is the comment in the pontifical council's document on the teaching of Lyon II that "the Holy Spirit proceeds eternally from the Father and the Son, not as from two principles but as from one single principle." The authors affirm that this one principle cannot be the divine essence, on the ground that the Fourth Lateran Council taught that "the [divine] substance does not generate, is not begotten, does not proceed."[29] The significance of this claim will be explained below.

For now, we may say in summary that the document seeks to harmonize the "Greek and Latin traditions concerning the Holy Spirit" by placing great weight on the distinction between the two words ἐκπορεύεσθαι and προϊέναι, and by arguing from this distinction that

---

27 On the other hand, Krauthauser frankly tells us that the Holy Spirit has "hypostatic distinctiveness" from the Father alone, but receives the divine nature from the Father "with and through the Son," without going into the very necessary further explanations ("Council of Florence," 147).

28 Pontifical Council for Promoting Christian Unity, "Traditions," 46.

29 Pontifical Council for Promoting Christian Unity, "Traditions," 42. The definition of Lateran IV is given in DH no. 804. Someone might raise the objection that Lateran IV does not say that the divine essence does not *spirate*, only that it does not generate, is not begotten, and does not proceed. However, it is clear enough that this Council intended to say that none of the "notional acts" within the Holy Trinity—the acts that distinguish one divine person from another—can be attributed to the divine essence, even though it did not explicitly mention active spiration.

the Holy Spirit has some eternal relation to God the Father that he does not have to God the Son.

A Preliminary Critique

A curious feature of the pontifical council's document is that, although it mentions Lyon II and Lateran IV, it makes no reference to Florence, even though the "Greek and Latin traditions regarding the procession of the Holy Spirit" were discussed at that synod with a unique intensity.[30] It is hard to avoid a suspicion that the document's reticence is because the dogma of the procession was defined at Florence in both Greek and Latin with crystalline clarity, and that the Florentine teaching is not that which the authors of the 1995 document wished to communicate.

However that may be, the Catholic theologian is unfortunately obliged to criticize this document severely. Its claim that God the Father can be described as "the sole Trinitarian principle of the Holy Spirit" is at best dangerously misleading, and on the more natural reading of the words, simply false. The claim that the Father is the "sole origin of the ἐκπόρευσις of the Spirit" is, depending on how it is interpreted, either heretical or tautological. Its claim that the one principle from which the Holy Spirit proceeds cannot be the divine essence ignores a distinction long familiar to Catholic theology, a distinction without which the question of the *Filioque* remains wrapped in confusion. Finally, its attempt to characterize the eternal relation of the Son to the Holy Spirit confuses the second and third divine persons.

In this book, I seek to vindicate the dogma of the procession defined at Florence by reference to the Fathers of the Church, to the theory of ecumenical councils, and to the history of the Florentine synod itself. Nevertheless, it seems appropriate here to offer a summary critique

30 Yves Congar, for example, accepted that, at Florence, "the debate on the pneumatological question was both free and serious" (*I believe in the Holy Spirit*, vol. 3, Milestones in Catholic Theology [New York: Crossroad Pub. Co, 1997], 188).

of the pontifical council's document simply from the point of view of Catholic doctrine. This will explain why I believe that this document and the enthusiasm it has generated are a regression from and not an advance on the historic achievement of 1439.

Can God the Father Be Called "Sole Trinitarian Principle of the Holy Spirit"?

Lyon II condemned those "who presume to deny that the Holy Spirit proceeds eternally from the Father and the Son or who rashly assert that the Holy Spirit proceeds from the Father and the Son as from two principles and not as from one."[31] Likewise, the Council of Florence defined that:

> The Holy Spirit is eternally from the Father and the Son, and has his essence and His subsistent existence simultaneously from the Father and the Son, and proceeds eternally from each as from one principle and by a single spiration.[32]

It further defined that "that which the holy doctors and fathers said, that the Holy Spirit proceeds from the Father through the Son, is to be understood as meaning that the Son also is a cause, as the Greeks say, and a principle, as the Latins say, of the subsistence of the Holy Spirit, just as the Father is."[33]

The most natural reading of the pontifical council's document puts it in direct contradiction with this Catholic dogma.[34] To say

---

31 DH no. 850: "Qui negare praesumpserint, aeternaliter Spiritum Sanctum ex Patre et Filio procedere: sive etiam temerario ausu asserere, quod Spiritus Sanctus ex Patre et Filio, tamquam ex duobus principiis, et non tamquam ex uno, procedat."

32 DH no. 1300: "Spiritus Sanctus ex Patre et Filio aeternaliter est [ἐστί], et essentiam suam suumque esse subsistens [τὸ ὑπαρτικὸν αὐτοῦ εἶναι] habet ex Patre simul et Filiio, et ex utroque aeternaliter tamquam ab uno principio et unica spiratione procedit [ἐκπορεύεται]." See appendix 1 of the present volume for the full text. Bernard de Margerie argues convincingly that τὸ ὑπαρτικὸν εἶναι is equivalent here to "person," noting that the Greek Fathers never use the term ὕπαρξις to mean the common nature of the divine persons ("Vers une relecture du Concile de Florence, grâce à la reconsidération de l'Ecriture et des pères grecs et latins," *Revue thomiste* 86 [1986]: 31–81, at 36, with note 13).

33 DH no. 1300: "Id, quod sancti Doctores et Patres dicunt, ex Patre per Filium procedere Spiritum Sanctum, ad hanc intellegentiam tendit, ut per hoc significetur, Filium quoque esse secundum Graecos quidem causam, secundum Latinos vero principium subsistentiae Spiritus Sancti, sicut et Patrem."

34 Hence, as mentioned above, the North American Orthodox–Catholic Consultation has stated that the condemnation given by Lyon II should be abandoned.

that the Father is "the sole Trinitarian principle of the Holy Spirit" is incompatible with saying, as do Lyon II and Florence, that the Son also is a principle from whom the Holy Spirit has his "essence and subsistent existence." It is therefore not surprising that the 1995 document nowhere calls the Son a principle, "cause," or fount of the Holy Spirit.

The authors appeal to the authority of St. Thomas Aquinas to support them. After asserting that "the Holy Spirit therefore takes his origin from the Father alone (ἐκ μόνου τοῦ Πατρός) in a principal, proper and immediate manner," they claim in a footnote that Thomas employs these terms in the *Summa thelogiae* (*ST*) I, q. 36, a. 3, ad 1 and ad 2.[35] This claim is partly misleading, and partly false.

In this article of the *ST*, St. Thomas is asking whether one can say that the Holy Spirit proceeds "from the Father through [per] the Son." The first objection alleges that, if this were said, it would seem that the Holy Spirit would not proceed "immediately" from the Father, which would be unfitting. To this he replies:

> In every action, two things must be considered, namely the subject which acts [suppositum agens] and the power by which he acts [virtutem qua agit], as fire warms by means of heat. If therefore in the Father and the Son the power is considered by which they spirate the Holy Spirit, there is nothing intermediary [non cadit ibi aliquid medium]: for this power is one and the same. But if the spirating persons themselves are considered, in this way, since the Holy Spirit proceeds commonly [communiter] from the Father and the Son, the Holy Spirit is found to proceed immediately from the Father, insofar as he is from him; and mediately, insofar as he is from the Son [invenitur spiritus sanctus immediate a patre procedere, inquantum est ab eo; et mediate,

35 Pontifical Council for Promoting Christian Unity, "Traditions," 36n1.

> inquantum est a filio]. And thus he is said to proceed from the Father through the Son.[36]

The second objection in this article of the *ST* alleges that if the Holy Spirit proceeded from the Father through the Son, then he would proceed *more* from the Father than from the Son, citing the Scholastic adage "propter quod unumquodque, et illud magis." This phrase, derived from Aristotle's *Posterior Analytics*, is hard to translate, but it means that whatever is the reason why some other thing has some attribute, that reason itself possesses that same attribute in a higher degree. For example, a geometric axiom, which is the reason by which some conclusion is known to be true, is itself known more certainly than that conclusion. Thus the Father would seem to spirate the Holy Spirit more than the Son does, since to proceed through (*per*) the Son seems to mean that the Son has the power to spirate on account of (*propter*) the Father. St. Thomas replies in ad 2:

> If the Son received from the Father a numerically distinct power [aliam virtutem numero] for spirating the Holy Spirit, it would follow that he [the Son] would exist as a second, instrumental cause; and then the Holy Spirit would proceed more from the Father than from the Son. But numerically one and the same spirative power exists in the Father and in the Son: and so he proceeds equally from each. Yet sometimes he may be said to proceed principally or properly [principaliter vel proprie] from the Father, on account of the fact that the Son has this power from the Father.[37]

36 St. Thomas Aquinas, *Summa theologiae* [*ST*] I, ed. Institutum Studiorum Medievalium Ottavienses, 5 vols. (Ottawa: Studium Generalis Ordo Praedicatorum, 1941), q. 36, a. 3, ad 1.

37 *ST* I, q. 36, a. 3, ad 2.

These are the two texts on the basis of which the authors cite St. Thomas in support of their claim that "the Holy Spirit therefore takes his origin from the Father alone (ἐκ μόνου τοῦ Πατρός) in a principal, proper and immediate manner."

We can see that there is no justification for the claim that St. Thomas held that the Holy Spirit proceeds from the Father alone in an "immediate" manner. In fact, he says in the ad 1 something that contradicts this: the Holy Spirit can be said in one sense to proceed from the Father in an immediate manner, and in another sense in a "mediate" manner; while (as follows clearly from the same passage) he can be said to proceed from the Son *only* in an immediate manner, and in no sense in a mediate one. The authors have simply misunderstood this text. It would in fact be truer, though unsatisfactory, to represent Aquinas as saying that the Holy Spirit proceeds from the *Son* alone in an immediate manner.

As for the claim that the Holy Spirit proceeds from the Father alone in a "principal" and "proper" manner, the texts quoted show that this is misleading as a summary of St. Thomas's thought. First of all, "in a principal manner" is not a good translation" of *principaliter*, as I shall argue below.[38] Secondly, *principaliter* and *proprie* are not his preferred terms, simply ones for which, having found them in the tradition, he finds a justification ("although sometimes it may be said"; ["licet aliquando dicatur"]). Crucially, this justification is possible only on the understanding—not present in the pontifical council's document—that the Father and the Son possess numerically the same spirative power, in such a way that the Holy Spirit proceeds equally from both.

Is the Father the Sole Origin of the ἐκπόρευσις of the Holy Spirit?

As the document of the pontifical council explains, the term ἐκπόρευσις was often used by the Greek Fathers to refer to the coming-forth of the

[38] See the section "The Holy Spirit Proceeds *Principaliter* from the Father" in ch. 10 (St. Augustine).

third divine person.[39] There are no extant texts in which they certainly use this word or its cognates to accompany the phrase ἐκ (τοῦ) Υἱοῦ ("from or out of the Son"). The substantive theological implications of this fact cannot be known a priori. One must investigate the context in which these phrases occur, and also the use made by the same Fathers of other verbs and other phrases to describe the coming-forth of the Holy Spirit. This investigation will be pursued in the first of the three main sections of this book.

The authors of this document, however, assert on the basis of this Greek patristic usage that "he [the Father] is the sole origin (ἀρχή) of the ἐκπόρευσις of the Spirit."[40] This statement could be either a merely linguistic one or a substantive one: it could be simply a statement about the use of words or a statement about the Holy Trinity. They themselves do not distinguish these two possible meanings of their statement, though the tenor and slant of their document lead one to suppose that they intend the latter. If it is indeed a substantive statement about the Trinity, then it must mean that God the Father is the only divine person who is an active principle of the Holy Spirit. But this is contrary to the dogma defined at Lyon II and Florence. If it is merely a linguistic statement, then it means that the procession of the Holy Spirit is called ἐκπόρευσις only when it is considered in reference to the Father, not when it is considered in reference to the Son. But this Greek patristic usage cannot determine whether the Greek Fathers held, further, that the Holy Spirit has a relation to the Father different from that which he has to the Son. It could be that they held that he has the same relation to the Father as to the Son, but that, by reserving a special word to describe his relation to the Father, they intended to express the truth that it is because of the Father that the Son has the power to spirate. In a similar way, St. Thomas uses the word "mediately"[41] only to express

39 Pontifical Council for Promoting Christian Unity, "Traditions," 36.
40 Pontifical Council for Promoting Christian Unity, "Traditions," 38.
41 In the sense explained above.

the relation of the Father to the Holy Spirit, not to express the relation of the Son to the Spirit; and yet he does not think that the Father and the Son have different relations to the third Person. Once again, we cannot decide the meaning of the Greek Fathers a priori; we must study their texts.

This is why the document's claim that the Father is the sole origin of the ἐκπόρευσις of the Spirit is, according to Catholic dogma, either heretical or tautological. It is heretical, if it is taken to mean that the Holy Spirit draws his origin only from the Father as an active principle and not also from the Son; it is tautological if it is taken to mean that the word that is used only to describe the Holy Spirit's relation to the Father may be used in relation to the Father alone.

Can the One Principle from which the Holy Spirit Proceeds Be the Divine Essence?

We have seen above that the authors of this document state: "In the light of the [Fourth] Lateran Council, which preceded the Second Council of Lyon, it is clear that it is not the divine essence that can be the 'one principle' for the procession of the Holy Spirit."[42] They do not explain the significance of this claim, but it seems intended to undermine any attempt to attribute an identical role to the Father and the Son in the spiration of the Holy Spirit—for it is admitted on all sides that the Father and the Son possess the identical divine essence.[43]

Yet the teaching of Lateran IV does not imply, as the authors apparently suppose, that the divine essence cannot be *in any way* a principle of active spiration. To claim this would be to overlook the distinction already quoted from St. Thomas between "the one who acts" and "the power by which he acts." Both the one who acts and the power by which

42 Pontifical Council for Promoting Christian Unity, "Traditions," 42.

43 Hence Garrigues considers that the 1995 document frees the doctrine of the *Filioque* from what he calls *le filioquisme*. By this last term he means the view, which he traces to St. Anselm, that the "one principle" from which the Holy Spirit comes is a "non-personal common property": common to the Father and to the Son ("A la suite" [1996]).

he acts may rightly be called a "principle," a *principium*, since the act comes from both, though in different ways.[44] The teaching of Lateran IV concerning the proper subject to which generation, filiation, and procession may be attributed clearly refers to the former of these principles, since it goes on to conclude that the consequence of not attributing generation, filiation, and procession to the divine essence is that "there is distinction in *persons*." It leaves untouched the question of the power *by which* generation and procession occur.

St. Thomas explicitly draws attention to the double meaning of the word "principle" in the context of the Trinitarian processions. Discussing the "power of generation" and the "power of spiration" in God, he writes: "[Power] signifies a principle [principium]; not, indeed, in the way that an agent is called a principle, but in the way that that by which the agent acts [id quo agens agit] is called a principle."[45] The Greek bishop Bessarion,[46] writing two centuries later in defence of the Florentine dogma against Mark of Ephesus,[47] drew the same distinction. In the Holy Trinity, he explains, we may talk on the one hand of a "principle which or from which," τὸ ὅ or τὸ ἐξ οὗ, and on the other hand of a principle "through or by which," τὸ ᾧ.[48] An artist, he explains, is a principle in the former sense, while his artistic idea is one in the latter sense. Thus: the Father is the principle in the former sense for the generation of the Son; the Father and the Son together are in the same sense one principle for the spiration of the Holy Spirit;[49] the divine essence is in each case the principle in the

---

44 In the case of the Holy Trinity, of course, there is only a "distinction of reason" (that is, a distinction made by the mind), not a real distinction, between the subject who acts and the power by which he acts. See Ludwig Ott, *Fundamentals of Catholic Dogma* (Cork: Mercier, 1960), 69.

45 *ST* I, q. 41, a. 5, ad 1.

46 Bessarion (1403–1472) was bishop of Nicaea, active at the Council of Florence, and later made a Cardinal (see "Bessarion" in *ODCC*, at 196).

47 Mark was Bishop of Ephesus and chief anti-unionist speaker at the Council of Florence.

48 Bessarion, *Refutation of Mark of Ephesus* (*PG*, 161:164B).

49 St. Thomas affirms in *ST* I, q. 36, a. 4, ad 7, that the Father and the Son should be called one *spirator*, but two *spirantes*. The reason is that the former word, being a noun and hence more directly naming a form or essence, may be pluralized only when a plurality of essences is found, while the latter word, being an adjective, and more directly naming a subject as possessing some form, may be pluralized whenever there are more than one

second sense.[50] By ignoring these elementary and long-established distinctions, the authors of our document leave the question of the *Filioque* wrapped in unclarity.

Does the Father Spirate the Holy Spirit "as Father of the Son"?

We have seen that the pontifical council avoids all reference to the Son as a principle, source, or "cause" of the Holy Spirit. How then can the authors explain the Trinitarian order (τάξις): the fact that the Son is the second person and the Holy Spirit the third? They attempt to respond in some words mentioned above: "In the Trinitarian order the Holy Spirit is consecutive to the relation between the Father and the Son, since he takes his origin from the Father as Father of the only Son." A little further on, they add: "The Spirit does not precede the Son, since the Son characterizes as Father the Father from whom the Spirit takes his origin, according to the Trinitarian order."[51]

As I have suggested, this appears to mean that the Son is "involved" in the spiration of the Holy Spirit only in the sense that the Father, who alone spirates (being, we are told, "sole principle"), does so as Father of the Son.[52]

There are several problems with this explanation. First, it contradicts,

---

who possess it. Here he corrects his usage of the *Scriptum super sententiis* I, dist. 11, q. 1, a. 4, where he had defended the terminology of two *spiratores*.

50 Even more precisely, one could say that the divine essence is the *radical* principle *quo* of the spiration, while the *proximate* principle *quo* is the "spirative power," the divine essence as possessed by the Father and the Son; and that the principle "which or from which," what St. Thomas calls the *agens*, is the Father and the Son insofar as they are one in the act of spiration. (St. Thomas himself explains in *ST* I, q. 36, a. 4, ad 1, that they are one in spirating because they spirate by the act of love, and it is the nature of love to unify; but this goes beyond what is taught by the conciliar statements.) Similarly, Louis Billot wrote: "The Holy Spirit proceeds from the Father and the Son insofar as they are more than one, and insofar as they are one: more than *one subject* but *one in the relation of spiration*. But the duality of subject denotes only a condition, which according to our inadequate concepts is a precondition for there to be a Spirator; while the subsistent relation of spiration is formally the principle itself of the procession [Spiritus Sanctus procedit a Patre et Filio, in quantum sunt plures, et in quantum sunt unum: in quantum sunt *plures supposito*, in quantum sunt *unum relatione spirationis*. Sed dualitas suppositi signat tantum conditionem, quae secundum inadaequatos nostros conceptus praeexigitur ad rationem spiratoris. Subsistens vero relatio spirationis dicit formaliter ipsum principium processionis]" (*De Deo Uno et Trino: Commentarius in Primam Partem S. Thomae*, 7th rev. ed. [Rome: Gregorian University, 1926], 572; italics original).

51 Pontifical Council for Promoting Christian Unity, "Traditions," 43–44.

52 J.-M. Garrigues is explicit on this point: "He [the Holy Spirit] comes forth from the Father as Father, that is to say, in the latter's relation towards the Son of begetting [dans la relation d'engendrement de celui-ci au

or at least ignores, the express teaching of the Council of Florence that "the Son also is a cause, as the Greeks say, and a principle, as the Latins say, of the subsistence of the Holy Spirit, just as the Father is." Secondly, to say that the Holy Spirit comes forth from the Father strictly *as Father* would mean that the Holy Spirit is also a Son. The conclusion is inescapable, since the terms "Father" and "Son" are correlative.[53] Thirdly, the explanation does not, in fact, achieve what it wishes, which is to find an explanation for the Trinitarian τάξις. For, if the Father is the "sole origin" of Son and Holy Spirit, then just as the document says that "[the Holy Spirit] takes his origin from the Father as Father of the only Son," one might equally say that the Son takes his origin from the Father as "Spirator" of the only Spirit, thereby justifying a new Trinitarian order in which the Holy Spirit is second and the Son third.

The authors appeal in a footnote to the *Catechism of the Catholic Church* to justify their claim that "the Holy Spirit is consecutive to the relation between the Father and the Son, since he takes his origin from the Father as Father of the only Son":

> The Western tradition expresses first the consubstantial communion between Father and Son, by saying that the Spirit proceeds from the Father and the Son (*Filioque*). It says this, "legitimately and with good reason," for the eternal order of the divine persons in their consubstantial communion implies that the Father, as "the principle without principle," is the first

Fils]." He here goes so far as to write: "The *unum principium* of the Holy Spirit defined at Lyon II is the Father himself, the Father who is Father only in being the Father of the only Son" ("A la suite" [1996], 193–94).

53 Thus Aquinas writes very precisely in the *De potentia Dei*, q. 10, a. 4: "It does not belong to the Father as Father by reason of paternity to be the principle of the Holy Spirit, for in this way he is related only to the Son, and otherwise it would follow that the Holy Spirit was a Son [Esse autem principium spiritus sancti non convenit patri in quantum pater est, ratione paternitatis: sic enim non refertur nisi ad filium; unde sequeretur quod spiritus sanctus esset filius]" (*Quaestiones disputatae de potentia Dei*, ed. Raymundo Spiazzi [Turin: Marietti, 1953]). Jean Baptist Ku seems to have overlooked this point when he writes, in what is otherwise a very careful exposition of Aquinas's Trinitarian teaching: "Spiration formally belongs to the Father *as Father*" (*God the Father in the Theology of St. Thomas Aquinas*, American University Studies Series VII, Theology and Religion 324 [New York: Peter Lang, 2013], 257; italics original).

> origin of the Spirit, but also that as Father of the only Son, he is, with the Son, the single principle from which the Holy Spirit proceeds.[54]

However, this official English translation contains a small but crucial error. The correct translation of the last part of this quotation is: "*Seeing that he is* Father of the only Son, he is, with the Son, the single principle from which the Holy Spirit proceeds" ("quatenus Filii unici est Pater, cum Illo unicum esse principium ex quo, 'tamquam ex uno principio,' Spiritus procedit"). The official French version of this passage makes the same mistake, rendering it as "en tant que Père du Fils unique, Il soit avec Lui l'unique principe d'où procède l'Esprit Saint." These vernacular versions, by omitting one *est* and treating the conjunction *quatenus* as if it were the adverb *qua* thus unwittingly distort the sense of the Latin, which is rather: "Since the Father has an only Son—with whom therefore he has everything in common—he is with His Son the one principle of the Holy Spirit."[55] The *Catechism* is thus here the faithful echo of the Council of Florence and its teaching that the Son is, with the Father, the principle "from which" the Holy Spirit proceeds is incompatible with the use to which the authors of the pontifical council's document, misled by the erroneous translation, wish to put this paragraph.[56]

Finally, one may remark that the proposal to "solve" the *Filioque* "problem" in this way, by declaring that the Holy Spirit proceeds from the Father alone as Father of the Son, so far from being a breakthrough of

---

54 *CCC* §248: "Traditio vero occidentalis imprimis consubstantialem communionem inter Patrem et Filium affirmat, Spiritum ex Patre *Filioque* procedere dicens. Ipsa hoc "licite et rationabiliter" dicit, quia Personarum divinarum aeternus ordo in communione consubstantiali implicat Patrem, quatenus est "principium sine principio" primam originem esse Spiritus, sed etiam, quatenus Filii unici est Pater, cum Illo unicum esse principium ex quo, 'tamquam ex uno principio,' Spiritus procedit."

55 For similar examples of the use of the conjunction *quatenus* in this section of the *Catechism*, see, e.g., §§ 12, 31, 81, 86, 117, and 330.

56 Garrigues is likewise misled, seeing in this passage from the *Catechism* the beginning of "a separation of the *Filioque* from filioquism," a process completed to his satisfaction by the pontifical council's document ("A la suite" [1996], 193).

modern ecumenical dialogue, is at least seven hundred years old. Martin Jugie, in listing fifteen different explanations that have been given of the phrase διὰ τοῦ Υἱοῦ ἐκπορεύεται, attributes it to Gregory of Cyprus, patriarch of Constantinople from 1283 to 1289.[57]

[57] Martin Jugie, *Theologia Dogmatica Christianorum Orientalium ab Ecclesia Catholica Dissidentium*, vol. 2, *De Theologia Simplici, De Oeconomia, De Hagiologia* (Paris: Letouzey et Ané, 1933), 493–96.

CHAPTER 2

PROLEGOMENA TO THE STUDY OF THE FATHERS

The Authority of the Fathers

I DO NOT OFFER here a comprehensive account of the doctrine of the procession of the Holy Spirit during the patristic period, such as was written by Henry Swete[1] as long ago as 1876, and which has been attempted more recently by such authors as Yves Congar[2] and A. Edward Siecienski.[3] My intention is more narrow: to look at the witness of those saints of the patristic period who were revered in both Rome and Constantinople before the schisms of the ninth and eleventh centuries, and especially those who wrote at greater length about the Holy Spirit. For, at the Council of Florence in 1439, after long and inconclusive

1 Henry Barclay Swete, *On the History of the Doctrine of the Procession of the Holy Spirit: From the Apostolic Age to the Death of Charlemagne* (Cambridge: Deighton and Bell, 1876; rep. n.p.: Nabu, 2014).

2 Yves Congar, *I Believe in the Holy Spirit*, vol. 3, Milestones in Catholic Theology (New York: Crossroad, 1997).

3 A. Edward Siecienski, *The Filioque: History of a Doctrinal Controversy* (New York: Oxford University Press, 2010).

debates, the principle by which union was finally achieved was that these saints, the common Fathers of Eastern and Western Christendom, could not be in error about so fundamental a matter as the nature of the Holy Trinity and the relations between the three divine persons. Bishop Bessarion urged this principle before his fellow Greeks with great eloquence during his crucial *Oratio Dogmatica de Unione*, declaring that whoever denies it is no better than an unbeliever.[4] We refute the Gentiles, Bessarion remarked, by showing how their great doctors disagreed among themselves; we cannot accept that ours also contradicted each other on articles of faith unless we wish also to overthrow our own religion.[5] Likewise, the two principal disputants at that Council, John of Montenero and Mark of Ephesus, agreed that the testimonies of Sacred Scripture and "of the Fathers whom holy Church receives" were to be accepted as decisive.[6]

Bessarion noted that this was also how previous ecumenical councils had acted: they sought to establish truths of faith not by "syllogisms," but by the bare testimonies of earlier doctors.[7] I shall consider especially those saints who have been recommended by the earlier ecumenical councils themselves as sure guides to the mysteries of the Trinity and the Incarnation.[8] Thus, the Council of Chalcedon, in its first session, explicitly endorsed the writings of St. Gregory Nazianzen, St. Basil, St. Athanasius, St. Hilary, St. Ambrose, and St. Cyril of Alexandria.[9] The Second Council of Constantinople explicitly endorsed the writings of St. Athanasius, St. Hilary, St. Basil, St. Gregory Nazianzen, St. Gregory of Nyssa, St. Ambrose, Theophilus, St. John Chrysostom, St. Cyril of Alexandria, St. Augustine, St. Proclus of Constantinople, and Pope St. Leo I.[10]

---

4 *PG*, 161:555A.
5 *PG*, 161:552D.
6 *AG*, 252.
7 *PG*, 161:553C.
8 See appendix 2 of the present volume.
9 See *The Decrees and Canons of the Seven Ecumenical Councils*, ed. Henry Percival, *NPNF*2, 14:248.
10 Percival, *Decrees and Canons* (*NPNF*2, 14:303).

Chronological Order

It is common, in making a survey of the teaching of the Fathers on some theological question, to consider separately those of the East and those of the West. I shall not take this approach, as I do not want to reinforce the common opinion that there exists some fundamental difference between the ways the Holy Trinity as a whole and the procession of the Holy Spirit in particular have been conceived by Latin and by Greek theologians. The proposition that some such fundamental difference exists was put forward at the end of the nineteenth century by the theological historian Theodore de Régnon.[11] Frequently repeated in popular summaries of the Fathers since then, this postulate is now increasingly questioned. The Orthodox theologian David Bentley-Hart, for example, writes:

> I shall ignore altogether the venerable notion (first advanced by Theodore de Régnon), that the general tendency of Latin trinitarian reflection has always been to accord priority to the unity of God's nature or essence rather than to the plurality of the divine persons, while that of Greek trinitarian reflection has been the reverse. Not only do I find the sheer vastness of this assertion dauntingly imprecise; I find it utterly impossible to defend from the actual textual evidence of either East or West, ancient, mediaeval or modern.[12]

The Orthodox priest John Behr has suggested that the popularity of what he calls the "de Régnon paradigm" was due to the arrival in the West of "Russian orthodox émigré theologians, wanting to emphasise the distinctiveness of their own theological tradition and its superiority to

---

11 Theodore de Régnon, *Études de théologie positive sur la Sainte Trinité*, vol. 1 (Paris: V. Reteaux, 1892), 33.

12 David Bentley-Hart, "Metaphysics after Nicaea," in *Orthodox Readings of Augustine*, ed. George E. Demacopoulos and Aristotle Papanikolaou (Crestwood, NY: St. Vladimir's Seminary Press, 2008), 191–226, at 195.

that stemming from Augustine."[13] This paradigm is relevant to our question, since it is often suggested that the so-called Eastern approach, by beginning its Trinitarian reflection with God the Father, has emphasised his position as ἀρχή (source), and for that reason has been reluctant or unwilling to speak also of procession from the Son, while the so-called Western approach, by beginning its reflection with the divine essence has sought to understand how this essence could exist in more than one hypostasis, and for this reason embraced the *Filioque*.[14]

Instead of dividing the survey of the Fathers between East and West, therefore, I follow a simple chronological order, allowing each to appear in his distinctiveness, rather than as representatives of either an Eastern or a Western tradition. They themselves would doubtless have claimed to represent only the apostolic tradition. While differences of emphasis will certainly appear among these different ancient authors, these differences will not be a simple "binary opposition" between geographical regions.

Quotations and "Proof Texts"

Those who bring passages from the Fathers or from other authoritative sources in order to establish some thesis are sometimes accused of dealing in "proof texts." Taken literally, the accusation is a strange one. As in the other sciences, so also in theology, proof is what we seek. Yet the accusation can be just if it refers to brief quotations used without proper consideration of their context.[15] For example, if someone were simply to quote St. John Damascene's statement about the Holy Spirit ἐκ τοῦ Υἱοῦ τὸ Πνεῦμα οὐ λέγομεν ("We do not refer to him as from the Son") and claim that as proof that Damascene rejects the *Filioque*, this

[13] John Behr, "Calling upon God as Father: Augustine and the Legacy of Nicaea," in Demacopoulos and Papanikolaou, *Orthodox Readings of Augustine*, 153–66.

[14] Behr, "Calling upon God as Father, "195–96; Thomas F. Torrance, *The Trinitarian Faith: The Evangelical Theology of the Ancient Catholic Church* (Edinburgh: T. & T. Clark, 1988), 246.

[15] Thus André de Halleux deprecates the use by both sides of "anthologies of quotations that are always open to dispute, since they have been artificially separated from their context" (A. de Halleux, "Pour un accord oecuménique sur la procession de l'Esprit Saint et l'addition du *Filioque* au symbole," *Irenikon* 15 [1978]: 451–69, at 461).

would, I believe, be over-hasty.[16] For this reason I shall often include quite lengthy quotations from the Fathers, sometimes extending an extract even beyond what might seem necessary, in order to reassure the reader that the key quotations are presented with sufficient context.

Interpretations by Later Writers

Before we begin our survey, it seems useful to summarize the various interpretations that have been given by later writers of patristic passages that speak of the relation between the Son and the Holy Spirit. Thus alert to the daunting variety of possible interpretations that have been suggested, we shall perhaps approach these passages with a more discerning eye.

Already in the fifteenth century, Bessarion noted four ways in which Greek writers opposed to union with the Latins explained, in a sense other than that defined at the Council of Florence, Greek patristic references to the Holy Spirit coming through the Son.[17] First of all, since the Greek Fathers more often used verbs other than ἐκπορεύεται when they added the words διὰ τοῦ Υἱοῦ ("through the Son"), some people claim that only ἐκπορεύεται refers to the hypostatic or personal procession of the Holy Spirit, and that all other verbs when found with the phrase διὰ τοῦ Υἱοῦ refer to the distribution of the Holy Spirit's gifts and his temporal mission in the world.[18] Secondly, Bessarion explains, some say that the Holy Spirit is said to be "through the Son" not in the sense that the Son is a principle of the Spirit, but because "son" and "father" are relative terms, the notion of one implying the other. Hence, although the procession is from the Father alone, since one cannot think of the Father without thinking

16 *PG*, 94:831B.

17 Bessarion, *Declaration of Some Points Contained in the Dogmatic Oration* (*PG*, 161:612D–13C).

18 Bessarion composed this work entirely in Latin, for Latins; I use the Greek terms in order to bring out his thought, since he is referring to Greek writings.

also of the Son, the procession is said to be through the Son.[19] Thirdly, some claim that only the consubstantiality of the Father and the Son is designated by the phrase "through the Son." Fourthly, because some poets, "constrained by the requirements of metre," have very occasionally used the preposition διά metaphorically in the sense of the preposition μετά ("together with"), opponents of the *Filioque* argue that, in the same way, the Holy Spirit is said to proceed διὰ τοῦ Υἱοῦ only in the sense that he proceeds from the Father at the same time as and along with the Son.

Some five hundred years after Bessarion, the Assumptionist scholar Martin Jugie listed no less than fifteen possible theories that may be propounded about the meaning of the Greek patristic texts.[20] Although Jugie was concerned with the various explanations of the precise Greek phrase διὰ τοῦ Υἱοῦ ἐκπορεύεται, his list also serves as an account, perhaps exhaustive, of the possible explanations of any phrase, whether in Greek or Latin Fathers, that suggests some kind of dependence of the Holy Spirit on the Son.[21]

1. *Mere temporal relation.* The dependence of the Holy Spirit on the Son consists simply in the fact that Christ in his humanity, preeminently on the first Pentecost, sends forth the Holy Spirit from the Father.
2. *Temporal for the Son, eternal for the Father.* This is similar to 1, except for claiming that the phrase "he proceeds from the Father through the Son" refers to the eternal procession of the Holy Spirit in the first half of the phrase and the temporal act of sending by the incarnate Son in the second half. This explanation was given

[19] This appears to be at least part of the position of the pontifical council's document, discussed above.

[20] Martin Jugie, *Theologia Dogmatica Christianorum Orientalium ab Ecclesia Catholica Dissidentium*, 5 vols. (Paris: Letouzey et Ané, 1926–1935), 2:493–96.

[21] The reader will notice that some authors have sponsored more than one explanation.

by Neilos Kabasilas (ca. 1298–1363) and by Gregory of Cyprus (Patriarch of Constantinople from 1283–1289).[22]

3. *Temporal with eternal connotation.* The phrase "through the Son" denotes, as with 1 and 2, Christ's human act of sending the Holy Spirit on Pentecost and subsequently, but it also connotes the Son in his divinity as producing this same sending of the Holy Spirit. Gemistus Plethon argued thus.[23]

4. *Eternal procession, according to "grace and operation" only.* The Son is not a source of the person of the Holy Spirit, but of the latter's eternal energies. Jugie attributes this view to Gregory Palamas and "some moderns." It was accepted by the so-called "Palamite councils" at Constantinople of 1341, 1347, and 1351.[24] It has been put forward again recently by Theodoros Alexopoulos and perhaps by Bishop Hilarion Alfeyev.[25] The distinction between divine essence and supposed eternal divine "energies" or operations is not accepted by the Catholic Church.[26]

5. *Consubstantiality.* The phrase διὰ τοῦ Υἱοῦ simply means that the Holy Spirit is consubstantial with the Son: he draws his essence through the Son simply in the sense that he draws the same essence

22 Kabasilas taught Demetrios Kydones and authored a patristic *florilegium* against the *Filioque* (Marcus Plested, *Orthodox Readings of Aquinas*, Changing Paradigms in Historical and Systematic Theology [Oxford: Oxford University Press, 2012], 96–100).

23 Plethon was a lay peritus at the Council of Florence ("Gemistus Plethon, Georgius," *ODCC*, 662).

24 Siecienski, *Filioque*, 147.

25 Theodoros Alexopoulos, "The Eternal Manifestation of the Spirit 'Though the Son' (διὰ τοῦ Υἱοῦ) according to Nikephoros Blemmydes and Gregory of Cyprus," in *Ecumenical Perspectives on the* Filioque *for the 21st Century*, ed. Myk Habets (London: Bloomsbury Academic, 2014), 65–86; Hilarion Alfeyev, *Orthodox Christianity*, trans. Andrew Smith, vol. 2 (Yonkers, NY: St. Vladimir's Seminary Press, 2012), 433–35. However, it is not clear with Alfeyev whether the Son is supposed to transmit the "uncreated energies" eternally, or simply to bestow them upon the faithful in time.

26 A very similar distinction, perhaps the ancestor of Palamas's, was already rejected by St. Gregory Dialogos (Pope Gregory I), who wrote: "But we are to know that there were some persons, who said that even in that region of blessedness God is beheld indeed in His Brightness, but far from beheld in His Nature. Which persons surely too little exactness of enquiry deceived. For not to that simple and unchangeable Essence is Brightness one thing, and Nature another; but Its very Nature is to It Brightness, and the very Brightness is Nature [ipsa ei natura sua claritas, ipsa claritas natura est]" (*Moralia in Iob* 18, ch. 54.90 [*PL*, 76:93C–D], trans. John Henry Parker [London: J. G. F and J. Rivington, 1844]).

as the Son. This was proposed by Gregory of Cyprus and by many thirteenth-century writers.

6. *Inseparability.* The phrase διὰ τοῦ Υἱοῦ means that the Holy Spirit proceeds inseparably from the Son, never without the Son. George Scholarios used this argument.[27]

7. *Characterization of the Father.* The Son is mentioned because the Father is necessarily related to him: "through the Son" means "from the Father of the Son." This was also proposed by Gregory of Cyprus.

8. *Distinction of Persons.* The Son is mentioned in the procession of the Holy Spirit to emphasize that their persons are distinct. This was maintained by Mark Eugenikos and following him, by Scholarios.[28]

9. *Simultaneity.* On this view, διά is used to mean σύν, "at the same time as," and so describing the second procession as διὰ τοῦ Υἱοῦ simply indicates that the two processions are simultaneous. This argument was used by Gregory Palamas, Mark of Ephesus, and Scholarios.

10. *Posteriority.* Here, διά is used to mean "after," and so procession διὰ τοῦ Υἱοῦ would indicate that the procession of the Holy Spirit comes after that of the Son, at least in the sense that the Holy Spirit is called the third person and the Son the second. Scholarios also used this argument.

11. *Passage.* Διά refers to a mere "passage" of the Holy Spirit through the Son without the Son being a "cause" or true principle of the Holy Spirit's subsistence. This was perhaps the position of Theodore

27 Scholarios was a lay peritus at the Council of Florence and supporter of the union; he later changed his mind and became the first patriarch of Constantinople to receive an official mandate from the Turks ("George Scholarios," *ODCC*, 668–69).

28 Eugenikos was bishop of Ephesus and the chief anti-unionist speaker at the Council of Florence.

Muzalo.[29] It has no apparent meaning and perhaps results from the attempt to grasp spiritual things with the imagination, as if they were material ones.

12. *Eternal manifestation.* The Holy Spirit has his hypostasis from the Father alone yet is eternally "manifested" by the Son. This was the position of the Synod of Blachernae in 1285, presided over by Gregory of Cyprus. Again, without further explanation, it has no definite meaning.[30]

13. *Unity of principle.* The Father alone is the principle of the Holy Spirit, but the Son is mentioned to show that he has one and the same essence as the Father. Scholarios gave this explanation of "through the Son."

14. *Necessary condition.* The procession of the Son is a necessary condition for that of the Holy Spirit, even though the Son is not an active principle of the Spirit. The commission established by the Russian Synod to study the question in 1892 gave this explanation of the phrase "through the Son" to the Old Catholics.[31]

15. *True procession.* The Holy Spirit truly proceeds from the Son as one active principle with the Father. This is the dogma defined at Lyon II and Florence and has been accepted as the meaning of διὰ τοῦ Υἱοῦ by such Greek writers as John Bekkos (Patriarch of Constantinople, 1275–1282), Barlaam of Calabria (ca. 1290–1348), Demetrios Kydones (ca. 1324/5–1397/8), Manuel Kalekas (†1410), and Bessarion.[32]

29 Muzalo was a thirteenth-century writer.

30 One also finds a variant on this proposal according to which the expression "through the Son" is said to mean that the Holy Spirit is "manifested" *to* the Son. This proposal has been made by Metropolitan Daniel Cibotea of Moldavia (Jean-Yves Brachet and Emmanuel Durand, "La réception de la *Clarification* romaine de 1995 sur le *Filioque*," *Irénikon* 78, no. 1–2 [2005]: 47–109, at 72). Dumitru Popescu, for his part, proposes that the role of the Son is to manifest the Spirit to the Father (*verso il Padre*) (79). This suggestion borders on the mythological: does God the Father require an act of manifestation by the Son in order to know the Holy Spirit?

31 Siecienski, *Filioque*, 186–88.

32 Barlaam was a monk condemned in 1341 for his opposition to Palamism, but he later acknowledged papal

According to Jugie, explanations 1, 2, 5, and 9 have historically been most popular among opponents of the *Filioque*. In more recent times, however, some prominent Orthodox theologians have used some combination of interpretations 4 and 7 to explain the eternal relation between the Son and the Holy Spirit.[33] This is found in the writing of Vladimir Lossky (1903–1958), Dumitru Staniloae (1903–1993), Olivier Clément (1921–2009), Boris Bobrinskoy (b. 1925), and Theodoros Alexopoulos.[34] Jean-Miguel Garrigues appears in his earlier writing to sponsor what sounds like a combination of explanations 12 and 14, claiming that "in their incommunicable hypostatic name," the Son and the Holy Spirit are related only to the Father, whereas insofar as their hypostases manifest themselves by "enhypostazing the divine essence," the Son is a condition of the Holy Spirit's consubstantial communion.[35]

As mentioned above, argument 7, coupled with 5, appears to be sponsored by the 1995 document of the Pontifical Council for Christian Unity, *Greek and Latin Traditions regarding the Procession of the Holy Spirit*, considered in chapter 1, as well as by Garrigues in his later writing.

Jugie also provides a helpful summary of the ways in which antiunionist writers have interpreted those places in the Fathers where the Holy Spirit is said to be *from* the Son: *ex Filio*; *de Filio*; *a Filio*; ἐκ τοῦ Υἱοῦ; ἐξ Υἱοῦ.[36] Generally they have sought to understand such passages of the temporal mission of the Holy Spirit. If this is clearly not possible, they have tended to argue either that the texts are corrupt or that

authority and was made a bishop. Kydones was chief minister of three emperors and translator of some of St. Thomas Aquinas's works into Greek. Kalekas was a theologian who was exiled for his opposition to Palamism but died as a Dominican friar, and was also a translator of Boethius and St. Anselm, in 1410 (Plested, *Orthodox Readings of Aquinas*, 115–20).

33 It is, in fact, not clear that these are distinct explanations.

34 For Lossky, Staniloae, Clément, and Bobrinskoy, see Siecienski, *Filioque*,197–201. Alexopoulos is a contemporary scholar at the University of Bern.

35 Jean-Miguel Garrigues, *L'Esprit qui dit "Père!": l'Esprit-Saint dans la vie Trinitaire et le problème du* Filioque, Croire et Savoir 2 (Paris: Téqui, 1982), 75. It is not easy to understand what Garrigues means. Possibly he simply means that the Holy Spirit could not be said to be in communion with the Father and the Son if one did not think of the Father and the Son as "already" existing. But if so, it is not clear why the Son would be a condition for the Holy Spirit, rather than vice versa.

36 Jugie, *Theologia Dogmatica Christianorum Orientalium*, 2:499.

the reference is to one of the first fourteen of the fifteen interpretations already listed. There has, however, also been a willingness among some authors to say that the Latin Fathers may simply have erred. In regard to St. Augustine in particular, there has been since the nineteenth century a tendency among Orthodox writers to acknowledge that he taught the Florentine dogma.[37]

The Translation of *αἰτία*

The correct way of translating the Greek term *αἰτία* is a question that arises in connection with Trinitarian theology. It is often rendered as "cause." St. Thomas Aquinas observed that when the Greek saints spoke of one divine person as a "cause" of another, they intended simply to say that one person was the principle of another.[38] Effectively, he was saying that the term *αἰτία* does not have quite the same range of meaning as the late Latin term *causa*. Bessarion likewise, in his later clarification of his *Oratio Dogmatica de Unione*, written after he had become proficient in Latin, noted that the Greek term is used more broadly than the Latin one, inasmuch as it refers to any kind of "coming forth" of one from another without implying any inferiority or limitation in what comes forth.[39] For its part, Florence's Decree of Union explicitly identified the terms *αἰτία* and *principium* in connection with the spiration of the Holy Spirit.[40] Ἀιτία might therefore be rendered for purposes of Trinitarian theology as "principle," but then one would lack a distinctive translation of the other key Greek term, ἀρχή, which is itself normally translated into Latin as *principium* and into English as "principle." The word "cause" also has the advantage that it forms derivatives such as "causal," "causing," and "causative," whereas the term "principle" lacks such useful connected

37 Jugie, *Theologia Dogmatica Christianorum Orientalium*, 2:498.

38 St. Thomas Aquinas, "Against the Errors of the Greeks," in *Ending the Byzantine Greek Schism*, ed. James Likoudis, 2nd ed. (New Rochelle, NY: Catholics United for the Faith, 1992), 128.

39 *PG*, 161:611D–12D.

40 *Decrees of the Ecumenical Councils: From Nicaea I to Vatican II*, ed. Norman P. Tanner and Giuseppe Alberigo, 2 vols. (Washington, DC: Georgetown University Press, 1990), 1:527.

forms. I shall therefore leave the translation of αἰτία as "cause" where I find it in existing English versions of the Greek Fathers, and shall even sometimes use the term "cause" and its connected terms in my own sentences. In the latter case, I shall generally enclose the word in quotation marks to indicate that it is a partially improper usage.

ἐκπορεύεσθαι, προϊέναι, and *Procedere*

Mention has already been made in the introductory chapter of various Greek and Latin terms, in particular ἐκπορεύεσθαι, προϊέναι, *procedere,* and their derivatives and cognates. To avoid misunderstanding, it should be noted that none of these is by origin a technical word for speaking of the Holy Trinity. The word ἐκπορεύεσθαι, for example, while not a common word, is found in classical Greek with the sense "to go out, to go forth, to go away, to march out."[41] It is used in the Septuagint of words that come forth from the mouth of God (Ezek 33:30) and of the waters that issue from the threshold of the temple in Ezekiel's vision (Ezek 47:1). Similarly, in the New Testament, it is used of words coming from the mouth of God (Matt 4:4), of the sword that comes forth from the mouth of the Son of man (Rev 1:16), and of the waters that flow from the throne of God and of the Lamb (Rev 22:1).[42] Although these scriptural references do foreshadow the Trinitarian application of the word, they also show that it is not itself a "term of art" coined by theologians.[43] The words προϊέναι and *procedere* are common in classical Greek and Latin, respectively, with the meaning "to go forward, advance, go forth, proceed." The point of this observation is that to interpret the Fathers, we do not need to have in mind a precise or technical sense for these words; it is sufficient

---

41 *A Greek–English Lexicon: With a Revised Supplement*, ed. Robert Scott and Henry G. Liddell, 9th ed. (Oxford: Clarendon, 1996).

42 *A Patristic Greek Lexicon*, ed. G. W. H. Lampe (Oxford: Oxford University Press, 1969).

43 This point is also made by Jean Galot, "L'origine éternelle de l'Esprit Saint," *Gregorianum* 78, no. 3 (1997): 501–22, at 507.

to be aware of their ordinary sense so that we may determine from the context how exactly an author is using them.[44]

Garrigues has claimed that there is an innate difference of meaning between ἐκπορεύεσθαι and *procedere*, anterior to the use made of them by theologians. He states that the Greek verb signifies going out of something, and thereby becoming distinct from it, whereas the Latin verb means going out of something while remaining united to it, as a man who heads a procession remains attached to the place of origin by virtue of those who follow.[45]

Garrigues does not, however, offer any proof of this assertion, and it is not borne out by the examples of the verb ἐκπορεύεσθαι already given. The waters streaming from the threshold of the temple or from the throne of God can presumably be conceived as united to their source, and while an army that marches out from camp indeed becomes separated from its origin, if that is relevant for his thesis, the same action could be described in Latin by the verb *procedere*. Further proof that Garrigues's distinction is imaginary seems given by the fact that the Vulgate translates ἐκπορεύεσθαι with *procedere* in Matthew 4:4, John 15:26, and Revelation 22:1. Although it is often suggested that the Vulgate version of John 15:26 is not a perfectly adequate rendering of the Greek,[46] it becomes implausible to suggest that ἐκπορεύεσθαι and *procedere* denote two essentially different forms of emanation when the Vulgate uses the latter to render the former in a number of unrelated contexts. Words, after all, mean what people use them to mean.

---

44 Given that I shall often have occasion to refer to the Father's property of being "principle without principle" within the Trinity, it may be worth remarking with Bernard de Margerie that this attribute is not implied by the use of the word ἐκπορέυεθαι in classical or New Testament Greek ("Vers une relecture du concile de Florence, grâce à la reconsidération de l'Ecriture et des pères grecs et latins," *Revue thomiste* 86 [1986]: 31–81, at 74).

45 Garrigues, *L'Esprit qui dit "Père!,"* 97. He here proposes this distinction as part of his obscure claim that the Holy Spirit has his person from the Father alone but comes from the Father and the Son "in the communication of the consubstantial divinity that proceeds according to the order of the divine persons." Aidan Nichols also appeals to Garrigues's distinction in *Rome and the Eastern Churches: A Study in Schism* (Edinburgh: T. & T. Clark, 1992), 225.

46 I return to this question in ch. 17 ("Concluding Linguistic Remarks") in the section on ἐκπορεύεσθαι and *procedere*.

CHAPTER 3

SAINT ATHANASIUS

Introduction

St. Athanasius's teaching on the Holy Spirit and on his relation to the Son is found principally in the *Epistolae ad Serapionem*, written probably around the years 359–361, although other important material can be found in the so-called *Discourses against the Arians*, written perhaps during his second exile (ca. 339–346).

The main purpose of the *Letters to Serapion* was to defend the true divinity of the Holy Spirit against a mutant form of Arianism that was willing to accept the godhead of the second person of the Trinity but not that of the third. In refuting his opponents' position, St. Athanasius is naturally led to speak of the relation of the Son to the Spirit.[1]

[1] St. Athanasius, *The Letters of Saint Athanasius concerning the Holy Spirit*, trans. C. R. B. Shapland (London: Epworth, 1951); *Works on the Holy Spirit: Athanasius's Letters to Serapion on the Holy Spirit and Didymus's On the Holy Spirit*, ed. and trans. Mark DelCogliano, Andrew Radde-Gallwitz, and Lewis Ayres, Popular Patristics Series 43 (Yonkers, NY: St. Vladimir's Seminary Press, 2011). All citations are taken from Shapland and cited in main text parenthetically. Modern scholarship divides the work into three letters, rather than into four, but

As the Son Is to the Father, so Is the Holy Spirit to the Son

A recurring idea in the *Epistolae ad Serapionem* is that "as the Son is to the Father, so is the Holy Spirit to the Son." After having spoken about the divinity of the Son at length, the saint explains to his fellow bishop Serapion why he has taken this approach in a work that is supposedly about the Holy Spirit:

> It is natural therefore that I should have spoken and written first concerning the Son, that from our knowledge of the Son we may be able to have true knowledge of the Spirit. For we shall find that the Spirit has to the Son the same proper relationship as we have known the Son to have to the Father [ὅιαν γὰρ ἔγνωμεν ἰδιότητα τοῦ Υἱοῦ πρὸς τὸν Πατέρα, ταύτην ἔχειν τὸ Πνεῦμα πρὸς τὸν Υἱὸν εὑρήσομεν]. And as the Son says "all things whatsoever the Father hath are mine," so we shall find that through (διὰ) the Son all these things are in the Spirit also (3:1).[2]

A key word in this quotation is ἰδιότης. Literally it is "that which is proper" or "the quality of being characteristic." Hence, a very literal translation of the words given in Greek in the extract would be: "For we find, what sort of properness the Son has to the Father, the Spirit has this sort to the Son." Although the term ἰδιότης does not in itself contain the idea of "relationship," C. R. B. Shapland's translation above is suitable, given that it is speaking of what is characteristic of the Holy Spirit precisely "in reference to" (πρὸς) the Son. Less satisfactory is the translation of Mark DelCogliano: "For we will find that the way in which we know the Son belongs to the Father corresponds to the way

---

I keep here the older division because of citing Shapland's older translation. The authorship of all the letters is undisputed.

2 *PG*, 26:625A–B.

in which the Spirit belongs to the Son." This makes it appear as if something in our minds is being said to be equivalent to the relation of the third and second divine persons, whereas in fact *this relation itself* is equated to the relation of the second person to the first.

St. Athanasius, then, is saying that the Holy Spirit has the same relation to the Son as the Son has to the Father. He immediately explains that the relationship of the Son to the Father consists in the Son's having "all things whatsoever" (πάντα ὅσα) from the Father. He draws the conclusion that these same "things" are in the Holy Spirit by means of (διὰ) the Son. From the immediate context of this passage, which is that of the true divinity of the Son, these "things" must be the divine essence and all the divine attributes implied by it.[3]

The Holy Spirit Is Proper to the Son

Another recurring theme in the *Epistolae* is that the Holy Spirit is "proper to" or "belonging to" (ἴδιον) the Son. Arguing that his opponents are no better than the earlier Arians, he writes: "If they thought correctly of the Word, they would think soundly of the Spirit also, who proceeding from the Father and belonging to (ἴδιον) the Son is from him given to the disciples" (1.2). An apparently equivalent phrase to "proper to" is "proper to (or belonging to) the essence of." The saint writes: "If the Son, because he is of the Father, is proper to his essence, it must be that the Spirit, who is said to be of God, is in essence proper to the Son [ἴδιον εἶναι κατ' οὐσίαν τοῦ Υἱοῦ]" (1.25).[4] A little further on, he writes: " [The Holy Spirit] is distinct from things originate, proper to and not alien from the Godhead and essence of the Son; in virtue of which essence and nature he is of the Holy Triad" (1.27).

Yet to be proper to the Son does not imply, for St. Athanasius, *not*

[3] The Greek passage itself has no word that directly translates as "thing." πάντα ὅσα could be rendered as "whatever."

[4] *PG*, 26:588D–89A.

being proper to the Father—despite Sergei Bulgakov's claim that "St. Athanasius's doctrine of the Holy Spirit is not triadic but dyadic in nature, for it considers only the relation of the Holy Spirit to the Son."[5] For, the saint writes: "The Spirit is not a creature but proper to [ἴδιον] the essence of the Word and proper to [ἴδιον] God in whom he is said to be" (4.1). Nevertheless, he has a preference for naming the *Son* as the one to whom the Holy Spirit is proper: "The Spirit then is distinct from the creatures, and is shown to be proper to the Son, and not alien from God" (1.25). This is not because he thinks of the Holy Spirit as more proper to the Son than to the Father, but rather, it seems, because we first know him as proper to the Son, and thereby know him as proper also to the Father.[6]

The Holy Spirit Is the Image of the Son

We have seen that St. Athanasius establishes a general principle that "as the Son is to the Father, so is the Holy Spirit to the Son." He applies this in particular to the idea of the "image."[7] He first mentions a number of different metaphors or analogies that can give some idea of the relation between the Father and the Son: the fountain and the river, the light and its radiance, essence (ὑπόστασις) and expression (χαρακτήρ),[8] that of which an image is and the image itself. While the course of the argument implies that each of these pairs might be applied to the relation between the Son and the Holy Spirit, it is only the last pair that he uses explicitly for this purpose: "As the Son is in the Spirit as in his own image, so the Father is in the Son [Ὥσπερ γὰρ ἐν ἰδίᾳ εἰκόνι ἐστὶν ὁ Υἱὸς

---

5 Sergei Bulgakov, *The Comforter*, trans. Boris Jakim (Grand Rapids, MI: Eerdmans, 2004), 26.

6 Andrew Louth observes that it is an Alexandrian usage to speak of one *person* as ἴδιος to another, and that the Cappadocians used this adjective to refer to the distinctive *notes* of a divine person, for example, unbegottenness for the Father ("The Use of the Term Ἴδιος in Alexandrian Theology from Alexander to Cyril," *Studia Patristica* 19 [1989]: 198–202).

7 St. Gregory Thaumaturgos in the third century had already spoken of the Holy Spirit as the image of the Son (A. Edward Siecienski, *The Filioque: History of a Doctrinal Controversy* [New York: Oxford University Press, 2010], 36).

8 This derives from Hebrews 1:3.

ἐν τῷ Πνεύματι, οὕτω καὶ ὁ Πατὴρ ἐν τῷ Υἱῷ]" (1.20). He continues, in a passage of particular importance:

> As the Son is an only-begotten offspring, so the Spirit, being given and sent from the Son, is himself one and not many, nor one from among many but only Spirit. As the Son, the living Word is one, so must the vital activity and gift whereby he sanctifies and enlightens be one perfect and complete; which is said to proceed [ἐκπορεύεσθαι] from the Father because it is from [παρά] the Word, who is confessed to be from the Father, that it shines forth [ἐκλάμπει)] and is sent and is given. The Son is sent from the Father, for he says, "God so loved the world that he gave his only begotten Son." The Son sends the Spirit; "If I go away," he says, "I will send the Paraclete." The Son glorifies the Father, saying, "Father, I have glorified thee." The Spirit glorifies the Son, for he says, "he shall glorify me." The Son says, "the things I have heard from the Father speak I unto the world." The Spirit takes of the Son; "he shall take of mine," he says, "and declare it unto you." The Son came in the name of the Father. "The Holy Spirit," says the Son, "whom the Father will send in my name." But if in regard to order and nature the Spirit bears the same relation to the Son as the Son to the Father [τοιαύτην δὲ τάξιν καὶ φύσιν ἔχοντος τοῦ Πνεύματος πρὸς τὸν Υἱόν, οἷαν ὁ Υἱὸς ἔχει πρὸς τὸν Πατέρα], will not he who holds the Spirit to be a creature necessarily hold the same to be true also of the Son?" (1:20–21)[9]

Shapland suggests here that, in this passage, the words "the Spirit takes of the Son" refer only to the temporal mission of the Holy Spirit. But temporal mission and eternal relation seem hardly to be distinguished

---

9 *PG*, 26:576D–80B.

in this passage. For one thing, the immediate context of the passage is that of the "place" of the Holy Spirit in the Trinity, and his true divinity. Likewise, the passage itself begins with a reference to the eternal generation of the Son, not simply to his temporal mission. So it is not forcing the text to say that being an "image," for St. Athanasius, implies that the divine person who is an image, precisely because he is a *perfect* image, comes from the divine person of whom he is an image, in every possible way, both eternally and temporally.

Elsewhere, the *Epistolae* express the same idea by the terms "seal" and "form." By "sealing" rational creatures, the Holy Spirit gives them the form (μορφή) of the Son. The use of language is not entirely consistent: for example, in quoting Philippians 2, he says that the Son is "in the form of the Father" (3.3). Logically one might have expected him to say the Holy Spirit is "in the form of the Son." Instead he says that the Holy Spirit is the form of the Son. But the meaning is clear: as the Son possesses the whole nature of the Father, so the Holy Spirit possesses the whole nature of the Son.

Finally, he describes the Holy Spirit as an unction or anointing, and adds: "This unction is a breath of the Son [τὸ χρίσμα τοῦτο πνοή ἐστι τοῦ Υἱοῦ]" (3.4).[10] Since this expression is not developed by Athanasius, it is not possible to say that he is thinking, in using the word "breath," either specifically of the "breathing" of the Holy Spirit described after the resurrection in John 20 or of an eternal "breathing." But since he is simultaneously defending the divinity of the Holy Spirit and describing his work among Christians, it seems most reasonable to think that he intends the term "breath," like the term "image," to apply to both things.

10 *PG*, 26:628C.

The Holy Spirit Is Related to Both the Father and the Son

We have already seen, as part of a longer quotation, one sentence in which Athanasius describes the relation of the third divine person to the first two:

> As the Son, the living Word is one, so must the vital activity and gift whereby he sanctifies and enlightens [i.e., the Holy Spirit] be one perfect and complete; which is said to proceed [ἐκπορεύεσθαι] from the Father because it is from [παρά] the Word, who is confessed to be from the Father, that it shines forth [ἐκλάμπει] and is sent and is given. (1.20)

Following the usage of John 15:26, he uses the word ἐκπορεύεσθαι here and elsewhere only of the Holy Spirit's relation to the Father, and not of his relation to the Son.[11] But note why the Holy Spirit is said to "proceed" from the Father: it is because he "shines forth" from the Son, who is himself from the Father, that the Holy Spirit is said to proceed from the Father. This shows that Athanasius is far from thinking that it is only the Father who stands as a principle or "cause" of the Holy Spirit. In fact, if one were to limit oneself to this passage, one might suppose that it is only the *Son* whom he considers such a principle, and that the Father is a principle of the Holy Spirit only indirectly or in a manner of speaking. Thus, A. Edward Siecienski's remark that Athanasius never explicitly attributed the procession (ἐκπόρευσις) of the Spirit to the Son, though true as far as words go, is misleading inasmuch as it suggests that he did not think of the Son as a principle of the Holy Spirit's person.[12] Henry Swete's comment is more to the point: "It seems impossible to regard this ἔκλαμψις

[11] Shapland, *Letters*, 64n13.
[12] Siecienski, *Filioque*, 38.

(shining forth) of the Spirit from (παρά) the Word as implying less than an essential derivation."[13]

The slight difference between the way St. Athanasius conceives the Holy Spirit's relation to the Father and how the saint conceives his relation to the Son is suggested by a difference in prepositions: ἐκ for the Father and παρά for the Son.[14] While both words may be rendered as "from," the former has more the suggestion of an initial origin.[15] One exception to his general preference for παρά in regard to the Son occurs in 3.1 of the *Epistolae*, where, in describing Christ's gift of the Spirit to the apostles on the day of the resurrection, he writes: "He gives the Holy Spirit from himself [ἐξ αὐτοῦ]."[16] Clearly this text refers directly to the economic Trinity; yet as mentioned above, his style of writing leads one to suppose that he considers the divine missions as a prolongation in time of the eternal processions.

In 1.27 Athanasius again speaks as if the Holy Spirit were more directly related to the Son than to the Father: "It is obvious that the Spirit does not belong to the many, nor is he an angel. But because he is one, and, still more, because he is proper to the Word who is one, he is proper to God who is one, and one in essence with him." One might easily conclude that the Holy Spirit belongs to the Father only insofar as he, the Spirit, belongs to the Son. The idea that the Father is the sole principle of the Holy Spirit is alien to his thought.

Similarly, where he speaks of the Holy Spirit as *in* the Son, he writes: "The Spirit is not outside the Word, but being in the Word, through him is in God [ἐν τῷ Λόγῳ ὄν, ἐν τῷ Θεῷ δί αὐτοῦ ἐστιν]" (3.5).[17] This shows the same preference for understanding the Holy Spirit's divinity

---

13 Henry Barclay Swete, *On the History of the Doctrine of the Procession of the Holy Spirit: From the Apostolic Age to the Death of Charlemagne* (Cambridge: Deighton and Bell, 1876; rep. n.p.: Nabu, 2014), 92.

14 Theodore Campbell remarks that Athanasius does not often use ἐκ when speaking of the Holy Spirit's relation to the Son ("The Doctrine of the Holy Spirit in the Theology of Athanasius," *Scottish Journal of Theology* 27 [1974]: 408–40, at 436).

15 See the section on ἐκπορεύεσθαι and *procedere* in ch. 17 ("Concluding Linguistic Remarks").

16 *PG*, 26:625.

17 *PG*, 26:633A.

by his relation to the Son rather than by his relation to the Father, even though this latter is also affirmed.

Yet at other times our author so expresses the relation of the Holy Spirit to the Father and the Son that there is no suggestion of the Spirit's relation to the Son being the reason for his relation to the Father. Responding to the taunt that the Holy Spirit, if not a creature, must be either the brother of the Son or the grandson of the Father, he replies by a simple reassertion of the scriptural statements:

> The Spirit is not given the name of son in the Scriptures, lest he be taken for a brother; nor the son of the Son, lest the Father be thought to be a grandfather. But the Son is called Son of the Father, and the Spirit of the Father is called Spirit of the Son. (1.16)

One may add that, from this reply, it is clear that St. Athanasius did not hold a derivation of the Holy Spirit from the Father alone or from the Son alone. If he had held the first position, to have mentioned it would have been the obvious way of rebutting the suggestion that the Holy Spirit was a "grandson," while the second position would have rebutted the suggestion that he was a "brother." Taking neither alternative, he expresses himself in a way that suggests an equal relation to the first and second persons: "The Spirit of the Father is called Spirit of the Son."

Finally, we do not find in the *Epistolae ad Serapionem* an attempt to explain why the Holy Spirit is not a son. Instead, he reproves the irreverence that was inspiring these questions in his opponents:

> Seeing that the Spirit is of God and is said by Scripture to be in him ("the things of God none knoweth save the Spirit of God which is in him"), and that the Son has said, "I am in the Father and the Father in me," why have these two not the same name,

> but the one is Son, and the other is Spirit? If anyone asks such a question, he must be mad. For he is searching the unsearchable. (4.4)

Whereas later writers will attempt to distinguish the Son and the Holy Spirit by the fact that the former comes forth by γέννησις and the latter by ἐκπόρευσις, St. Athanasius treats "Son" and "Holy Spirit" as more basic names.[18] In this, his instinct was surely sound: "generation" and "procession" are understood by us in reference to the divine persons, and not *vice versa*.

Orationes adversus Arianos

The Eternal Relations

As is clear from the title, these three discourses of the *Orationes adversus Arianos* are directed against the deniers of the true divinity of God the Son.[19] The relation of the Son to the Holy Spirit is discussed in only one place.[20] Athanasius wishes to refute those who might claim that Christ only *participated* in the Spirit, as the faithful do. A rather lengthy quotation will enable us to grasp his reply:

> John then thus writes; "Hereby know we that we dwell in him and he in us, because he has given us of his Spirit." Therefore because of the grace of the Spirit that has been given to us, in him we come to be, and he in us; and since it is the Spirit of God, therefore through his becoming in us, reasonably are we, as having the Spirit, considered to be in God, and thus

18 Shapland, *Letters*, 184n8. Shapland mentions the *De Trinitate* ascribed to Didymus the Blind for an early example of an attempt to give γέννησις and ἐκπόρευσις epistemological priority over "Son" and "Holy Spirit." Shapland also points out that Athanasius does not have a special word to characterize the mode of derivation of the Holy Spirit in the way that γέννησις characterises that of the Son (183n15).

19 The "fourth discourse" is not considered authentic (*CPG*, 2:42).

20 Quotations are from Athanasius, Selected Works and Letters, trans. Archibald Robertson, *NPNF*2 vol. 4.

is God in us. Not then as the Son in the Father, so also we become in the Father; for the Son does not merely partake the Spirit, that therefore he too may be in the Father; nor does he receive the Spirit, but rather he supplies it himself to all; and the Spirit does not unite the Word to the Father, but rather the Spirit receives from the Word. And the Son is in the Father, as his own Word and Radiance; but we, apart from the Spirit, are strange and distant from God, and by the participation of the Spirit we are knit into the Godhead; so that our being in the Father is not ours, but is the Spirit's which is in us and abides in us, while by the true confession we preserve it in us, John again saying, "Whosoever shall confess that Jesus is the Son of God, God dwells in him and he in God." What then is our likeness and equality to the Son? Rather, are not the Arians confuted on every side? And especially by John, that the Son is in the Father in one way, and we become in him in another, and that neither we shall ever be as he, nor is the Word as we; except they shall dare, as commonly, so now to say, that the Son also by participation of the Spirit and by improvement of conduct came to be himself also in the Father. But here again is an excess of irreligion, even in admitting the thought. For he, as has been said, gives to the Spirit, and whatever the Spirit has, he has from the Word [αὐτὸς γάρ, ὥσπερ εἴρηται, τῷ Πνεύματι δίδωσι, καὶ ὅςα ἔχει τὸ Πνεῦμα παρὰ τοῦ Λόγου ἔχει].[21] It is the Spirit then which is in God, and not we viewed in our own selves; and as we are sons and gods because of the Word in us, so we shall be in the Son and in the Father, and we shall be accounted to have become one in Son and in

21 Some manuscripts have τὸ πνεῦμα instead of τῷ Πνεύματι, with the meaning "he gives the Spirit."

> Father, because that Spirit is in us, which is in the Word which is in the Father. (3:24–25)[22]

Here again the saint is speaking both of the economy of salvation and of the eternal relations that exist between the divine persons. The economy of salvation is in question when he speaks of our participation in the Holy Spirit. But in order to dispel the idea that Christ also merely participates in the Holy Spirit, he appeals to the eternal relations: "The Spirit does not unite the Word to the Father, but the Spirit receives from the Word." It is implausible to see the second part of this phrase as merely a reference to the temporal mission of the third person, since the first half of the phrase is plainly speaking of the immanent Trinity, in which the Word is related to the Father.[23] Therefore it is only reasonable to see the phrase used toward the end of this passage—"whatever the Spirit has, He has from the Word"—as also a reference to the immanent Trinity. Commenting on this passage, Yves Congar made a rather confused claim: "Athanasius does not speculate about the eternal intra-divine relationships but only speaks about them in the context of the activities of the divine persons within the economy of salvation."[24] In reality, while the saint refers constantly to the economy when speaking of the eternal relations of the persons, he does nonetheless speak of eternal relations and not simply of temporal missions. It would be surprising if he were not to do so: his intention both in the *Epistolae ad Serapionem* and in the *Orationes adversus Arianos* is to establish the eternal divinity of a divine person.

---

22 *PG*, 26:373A–76B.

23 The "immanent Trinity" means the Holy Trinity considered in itself without reference to creation; the "economic Trinity" means the Holy Trinity considered as acting in and thus "related" to creation.

24 Yves Congar, *I Believe in the Holy Spirit*, vol. 3, Milestones in Catholic Theology (New York: Crossroad, 1997), 25.

διά as Indicating an Efficient Cause

Another passage in the third of the *Orationes adversus Arianos* is of possible interest for understanding the relation of the Son and the Holy Spirit. He is speaking of the fact that the Father's acting through the Son implies that the Son is a true cause of what is done:

> For though the Father gives it, through the Son [διὰ τοῦ Υἱοῦ] is the gift; and though the Son be said to vouchsafe it, it is the Father who supplies it through and in the Son; for "I thank my God," says the Apostle writing to the Corinthians, "always on your behalf, for the grace of God which is given you in Christ Jesus." And this one may see in the instance of light and radiance; for what the light enlightens, that the radiance irradiates; and what the radiance irradiates, from the light is its enlightenment. So also when the Son is beheld, so is the Father, for He is the Father's radiance; and thus the Father and the Son are one. But this is not so with things originate and creatures; for when the Father works, it is not that any Angel works, or any other creature; for none of these is an efficient cause, but they are of things which come to be;[25] and moreover being separate and divided from the only God, and other in nature, and being works, they can neither work what God works, nor, as I said before, when God gives grace, can they give grace with Him. (3.13–14)[26]

This is relevant because it suggests that the saint would understand a spiration of the Holy Spirit from the Father *through* the Son as involving the same "causality" on the part of the Son as on the part of the Father.

---

[25] That is, they are creatures.

[26] *PG*, 26:349A–C; trans. Robertson in *NPNF2* vol. 4.

However, he does not draw this conclusion himself in this place, as it is not his subject, and as has been mentioned, he tends to use the preposition παρά rather than διά to express the Holy Spirit's relation to the Son.

The Father and the Son Act Indivisibly

Similarly, the following passage from the third oration also tends to support the idea of the Son as a "causal" principle of the Holy Spirit, even though St. Athanasius is certainly not teaching it expressly:

> The Godhead of the Son is the Father's; whence also it is indivisible; and thus there is one God and none other but He. And so, since they are one, and the Godhead itself one, the same things are said of the Son, which are said of the Father, except His being said to be Father: for instance, that He is God, "And the Word was God"; Almighty, "Thus says He which was and is and is to come, the Almighty"; Lord, "One Lord Jesus Christ"; that He is Light, "I am the Light"; that He wipes out sins, "that you may know," He says, "that the Son of man has power upon earth to forgive sins"; and so with other attributes. For "all things," says the Son Himself, "whatsoever the Father has, are Mine"; and again, "And Mine are Yours." (3.4)

A similar passage is found in the second oration: "As when the sun shines, one might say that the radiance illuminates, for the light is one and indivisible, nor can be detached, so where the Father is or is named, there plainly is the Son also" (2.41). Again, the reference is not to the procession of the third person, but in this case to the co-activity of the Father and Son in baptism. Still, it would be easy to make the argument that, in the spiration of the Holy Spirit, the Father "is" and "is named," and that therefore the Son must also be there, doing what the Father does. At any rate, it is hard to believe that so zealous a champion of Trinitarian orthodoxy would have made no exception of the Holy Spirit in such passages as these if he had held that God the Father were in fact the sole active principle of the spiration.

Undeveloped Hints

In a couple of places, the saint makes passing remarks that might have led to a more developed doctrine of the procession. Near the end of the second oration, he writes:

> The knowledge of Father through Son and of Son from Father is one and the same, and the Father delights in Him, and in the same joy the Son rejoices in the Father, saying, "I was by Him, daily His delight, rejoicing always before Him." And this again proves that the Son is not foreign, but proper to the Father's Essence. For behold, not because of us has He come to be, as the irreligious men say, nor is He out of nothing (for not from without did God procure for Himself a cause of rejoicing), but the words denote what is His own and like. When then was it, when the Father rejoiced not? But if He ever rejoiced, He was ever, in whom He rejoiced. And in whom does the Father rejoice, except as seeing Himself in His own Image, which is His Word? . . . And how too has the Son delight, except as seeing Himself in the Father? (2.82)

Since he refers to joy as springing from knowledge, and explains knowledge by reference to the first Trinitarian procession, one wonders whether he has the second procession in mind when he speaks of the divine joy. In this connection, we may note how this joy is attributed to both the first two divine persons: as the Father has delight in seeing himself in the Word, the Son delights in seeing himself in the Father. Although the holy doctor does not mention the Holy Spirit explicitly in this passage, there is arguably here an anticipation of that association of the Holy Spirit with the "affective life" in God that would later become established in Western theology.[27]

Contra Sabellianos

At the Council of Florence, Mark Eugenikos quoted the following passage from the *Contra Sabellianos* to prove that the archbishop of Alexandria had taught the procession from the Father alone:

> We are distinguished both from the Judaizers and from those who corrupt Christianity into Judaism by denying God from God and affirming that God is one in the same manner as the Jews; they do not say that the Father is the only God because he alone is unbegotten and the fount of divinity (μόνος πηγὴ θεότητος ὁ Πατήρ), but as being infecund, without a Son and living Word.[28]

The treatise is listed among the doubtful works of St. Athanasius.[29] However, even if it is authentic, the passage selected by Eugenikos can hardly disturb an adherent of the *Filioque*. Athanasius is not speaking in this passage about the Holy Spirit at all, let alone considering and rejecting a certain theory of his relation to the Son. The phrase that is used to describe God the Father, "the fount of divinity," poses no problem for a Catholic, as it is a natural way of referring to the "principle without principle" within the Trinity. Such was, however, the only argument that the chief anti-unionist speaker at Florence could offer from this saint.

27 The same association is suggested by Athanasius's use in his *De decretis Nicaenae Synodi* of a phrase taken from a letter of Dionysius, the third-century bishop of Rome, that the Holy Spirit "loves to be in [φιλοχωρεῖν] God" (*PG*, 25:464A).

28 *PG*, 28:97B–C.

29 *PG*, 28:93–94.

Summary and Conclusion

The purpose of St. Athanasius's writings on the Holy Spirit is not to define the nature of "procession" as opposed to "generation," nor therefore to distinguish the principle of generation from that of procession; it is rather to defend the full divinity of the third person. Nevertheless, one may discern his understanding of the procession from his description of the Holy Spirit's "place" in the Trinity, an account that I should venture to summarize in two propositions: (1) the Holy Spirit eternally draws all things from the Son just as and insofar as the Son draws all things from the Father, and yet (2) he is proper both to the Son and to the Father. Insofar as these two propositions require some further harmonization, this would be achieved by explaining that because the Son spirates the Holy Spirit only insofar as he is perfect Son, and therefore has the same substance and activity as the Father, the Father thus spirates the Holy Spirit equally with the Son, which is why the Spirit is "proper" to both. In other words, the doctrine of the Father and Son as "one principle," which is not present explicitly in St. Athanasius, would have completed the Trinitarian synthesis of the great bishop of Alexandria.

CHAPTER 4

SAINT HILARY

On the Trinity

St. Hilary of Poitiers wrote his twelve-volume treatise *De Trinitate* while exiled in Phrygia in the years 359–360.[1] It is principally a defence of the divinity of the Son, the doctrine for which he had been banished, but it contains several important passages on the origin of the Holy Spirit. We shall see that the question of the correct translation of his words frequently recurs. As his twentieth-century translator Stephen McKenna writes, "St. Hilary is . . . difficult to understand because he uses the same words to convey different meanings and

[1] Lewis Ayres has suggested that the first three books of the *De Trinitate* may have been drafted before this exile (*Nicaea and its Legacy: An Approach to Fourth-Century Trinitarian Theology* [Oxford: Oxford University Press, 2004], 180n33). For a summary of modern studies of the formation of Hilary's Trinitarian theology, see Marie Doerfler, "Entertaining the Trinity Unawares: Genesis XVIII in Western Christian Interpretation," *The Journal of Ecclesiastical History* 65, no. 3 (2014): 485–503, at 490n17. For a detailed discussion of the structure of *De Trinitate* and of the relation of this work to earlier works of Hilary, see Carl Beckwith, *Hilary of Poitiers on the Trinity: From* De fide *to* De Trinitate, Oxford Early Christian Studies (New York: Oxford University Press, 2008), esp. 71–147.

one must often puzzle over them for a long time before determining their significance in a particular context."[2]

Patre et Filio Auctoribus

The first passage of importance for our purpose occurs in book 2:

> Concerning the Holy Spirit I ought not to be silent, and yet I have no need to speak; still, for the sake of those who are in ignorance, I cannot refrain. There is no need to speak, because we are bound to confess Him, proceeding, as He does, from Father and Son [loqui autem de eo non necesse est, qui Patre et Filio auctoribus confitendus est]. For my part, I think it wrong to discuss the question of His existence. He does exist, inasmuch as He is given, received, retained; He is joined with the Father and the Son in our confession of the faith, and cannot be excluded from a true confession of Father and Son. (2.29)[3]

There is a difficulty about this translation by L. Pullan and E. Watson for the original Latin inserted. The verb "proceed" does not occur; a more literal translation of the phrase would be "who is to be confessed, the Father and the Son as the authors." McKenna translates it: "Him in whom we must believe together with the Father and the Son who begot [*sic*] Him." Yves Congar states without argument that the phrase "clearly points, not to a procession, but to the witness borne by

2 Hilary of Poitiers, *On the Trinity*, trans. Stephen McKenna, Fathers of the Church 25 (Washington, DC: Catholic University of America Press, 1954), xv. On the other hand, the nineteenth-century translators, L. Pullan and E. Watson affirm: "It is never safe to assert that Hilary is unintelligible. The reader or translator who cannot follow or render the argument must rather lay the blame upon his own imperfect knowledge of the language and thought of the fourth century" (*NPNF*2, 9:iii). Nevertheless, I shall argue that these latter translators have not always correctly interpreted Hilary's words.

3 The Latin text of St. Hilary's *De Trinitate* is taken from *CCSL* vols. 62 and 62a. Except where stated otherwise, translations are taken from *NPNF*2 vol. 9, with the punctuation sometimes slightly altered, though not so as to change the sense.

the Father and the Son."[4] Luis Ladaria likewise states that "the whole of the this passage is clearly 'economic' in its approach."[5] Watson and Pullan note that the phrase could be rendered "whom we are to confess on the testimony of the Father and the Son," hence referring not to the Holy Spirit's eternal origin, but to our knowledge of his existence. Their preference for the translation quoted above comes from the way that St. Hilary employs the ambiguous term *auctor* in the following passage from earlier in book 2:

> Certain teachers [the Arians] of our present day assert that the Image and Wisdom and Power of God was produced out of nothing, and in time. They do this to save God, regarded as Father of the Son, from being lowered to the Son's level. They are fearful lest this birth of the Son from Him should deprive Him of His glory, and therefore come to God's rescue by styling His Son a creature made out of nothing, in order that God may live on in solitary perfection without a Son born of Himself and partaking of His nature. What wonder that their doctrine of the Holy Ghost should be different from ours, when they presume to subject the Giver (*largitore*) of that Holy Ghost [that is, the Son] to creation, and change, and non-existence. Thus do they completely destroy the consistency and completeness of the mystery of the faith. They break up the absolute unity of God by assigning differences of nature where all is clearly common to Each; they deny the Father by robbing the Son of His true Sonship; they deny the Holy Ghost in their blindness to the facts that we possess Him and that Christ gave Him. (2.4)[6]

4 Yves Congar, *I Believe in the Holy Spirit*, vol. 3, Milestones in Catholic Theology (New York: Crossroad, 1997), 50.

5 Luis Ladaria, *El Espiritu Santo en San Hilario de Poitiers* (Madrid: Eapsa, 1977), 291.

6 In the last sentence of this passage, Watson and Pullan have "deny" rather than "are ignorant of," in accordance with the variant *negando* that appears in some manuscripts (see *PL*, 10:53B).

The Latin for the final phrase reads, "Patrem negando, dum Filio quod est filius adimunt; Spiritum sanctum nesciendo dum et usum et auctorem eius ignorant," and a more literal translation of the second (beginning "Spiritum sanctum") would be "denying the Holy Spirit in that they do not recognise His association [with the faithful] and His author." Although this is not clearly a reference to the eternal procession of the Holy Spirit, it does show St. Hilary using the term *auctor* in the sense of a principle whence the Spirit comes, at least as sent in time, as opposed to one on whose authority we believe in the Spirit. For this reason, Watson and Pullan see *De Trinitate* 2.29 as a reference to the *origin* of the Holy Spirit.

Their reasoning, however, is not wholly convincing. The fact that a writer uses a potentially ambiguous term in a clear sense in one place does not show that he will everywhere be using it in the same sense. The immediate context of 2.29 is our obligation to confess the existence of the Holy Spirit just as we confess the existence of the Father and the Son. So it is quite possible that *auctoribus* is being used to reinforce this obligation, pointing out how great the authority is that obliges us to the confession. It is of course also possible that St. Hilary had both meanings in mind more or less consciously and thought of them as correlatives—that the Father and Son are the ones to bear witness to the Holy Spirit precisely because he is from them. This is perhaps the most satisfactory interpretation, as it explains why Hilary did not make clear that he was using an ambiguous word in one sense rather than another.

At the end of 2.29, he writes:

> When they ask, Through Whom is He [the Holy Spirit]? To what end does He exist? Of what nature is He? If our reply displease them, when we say "Through whom are all things" [per quem omnia] and "From whom are all things" [ex quo omnia], and that He is the Spirit of God, the gift of the faithful; then let the apostles and prophets also displease them, who said of Him

> only that He was this, and finally, let the Father and the Son displease them.[7]

Along with Henry Barclay Swete, with the editor of Migne's *Patrologia Latina*, and with Ladaria,[8] but unlike McKenna, and also Watson and Pullan, I take the phrases *per quem omnia* and *ex quo omnia* not to state that all things are through and from the Holy Spirit, but that he himself is through the one through whom are all things, meaning the Son, and from the one from whom are all things, the Father. This interpretation is strongly supported by the fact that, at the start of this book 2, the saint writes: "God the Father is One, from Whom are all things; and our Lord Jesus Christ the Only-begotten, through whom are all things, is One; and the Spirit, God's Gift to us, Who pervades all things, is also One . . . the One Power from Whom all, the One Offspring through Whom all, the One Gift Who gives us perfect hope" (2.1). It is also supported by the fact that otherwise he would not in fact be answering the first question his interlocutors posed, "through whom is the Holy Spirit?" And since the question of these interlocutors is about the very nature of the Holy Spirit, we can infer that St. Hilary is teaching that the third person is eternally from the Father and through the Son. This in turn increases the likelihood that he included at least the idea of eternal derivation when saying in an earlier portion of 2.29 that the Holy Spirit was to be confessed *Patre et Filio auctoribus*.

"Egress of a Coexisting Being"

However, we must wait until book 8 to find an unambiguous reference to the eternal origin of the third divine person. This eighth book

---

7 My translation of the final sentence of 2.29: "Cum dicunt per quem sit, et ob quid sit, vel qualis sit; si responsio nostra displicebit dicentium, Per quem omnia, *et* ex quo omnia sunt, et quia Spiritus est Dei, donum fidelium; displiceant et Apostoli et Prophetae, hoc tantum de eo quod esset dicentes; et post haec Pater et Filius displicebit" (*PG*, 10:70A–B).

8 Henry Barclay Swete, *On the History of the Doctrine of the Procession of the Holy Spirit: From the Apostolic Age to the Death of Charlemagne* (Cambridge: Deighton and Bell, 1876; rep. n.p.: Nabu, 2014), 112; Ladaria, *El Espiritu Santo*, 291n7.

is dedicated to showing that the unity of the Father and the Son is one of nature and not only of will alone. One argument that Hilary uses to establish this conclusion is the relation of the Father and the Son to the Holy Spirit:

> The Father and the Son are one in nature, honour, power, and the same nature cannot will things that are contrary. Moreover, let them listen to the testimony of the Son as touching the unity of nature between Himself and the Father, for He says: "When that advocate has come, whom I shall send to you from the Father, the Spirit of truth who proceeds from the Father, He shall testify of me," of truth Who proceeds from the Father. Let the whole following of heretics arouse the keenest power of their wit; let them now seek for what lies they can tell to the unlearned, and declare what that is which the Son sends from the Father. He Who sends manifests His power in that which He sends. But as to that which He sends from the Father, how shall we regard it, as received or sent forth or begotten [quod a Patre mittit, quid intellegemus, utrum acceptum, aut dimissum, aut genitum]? For He necessarily signifies that what He is to send from the Father is some one of these [Nam horum necesse est unum aliquid significet, quod a Patre missurus est].[9] And He will send from the Father that Spirit of truth that proceeds from the Father [Et missurus a Patre est eum Spiritum veritatis, qui a Patre procedit];[10] there is now therefore no receiving, where the procession is shown to be [Iam ergo non est acceptio, ubi demonstrata processio est]. (8.19)

9 This sentence is my translation. Watson and Pullan render it as: "For His words that He will 'send from the Father' must imply one or other of these modes of sending." McKenna has: "That which He sent from the Father must mean one or the other of these things."

10 McKenna translates instead: "He Who proceeds from the Father will send that Spirit of truth from the Father." This also determines his translation of the next phrase.

This translation of the final phrase ("Iam ergo . . . processio est") is mine. Watson and Pullan render it as: "He [the Son] therefore cannot be the Recipient, since He is revealed as the Sender." But "He is revealed as the Sender" is hardly a translation of "ubi demonstrata processio est."

McKenna, by contrast, translates the phrase in question as, "hence, there is no longer an adoption where a procession is revealed," as if St. Hilary were simply arguing that the Son was not a son by adoption since he is said to proceed. This relies on his translation of the previous phrase as "He Who proceeds from the Father will send that Spirit of truth from the Father"; but it implies that Hilary is distorting the obvious meaning of the Scripture that he quotes, and would also be out of place in this part of book 8, where the author is attempting to show the unity of nature of Father and Son precisely by reference to their relation to the Holy Spirit.

Ladaria, by contrast, supposes that Hilary is seeking here to make more precise the relation between the Holy Spirit and the Father, and that the three participles *acceptum*, *dimissum*, and *genitum* name possible relations between them. Yet this supposition brings him into confusion: he states that *acceptum* refers to the Holy Spirit's receiving (*recibe*) from the Father and says that Hilary excludes this possibility, no doubt because of the words *non est acceptio*. But then he continues: "The Spirit does not only 'receive' from the Father, but also 'proceeds' from him."[11] In other words, Ladaria seems to both deny and affirm that Hilary speaks of the Holy Spirit receiving from the Father. As we shall see, Hilary does indeed speak of such a reception, while here he expressly states that *processio* excludes *acceptio*.

How shall we solve this puzzle? The best explanation seems to be that the participle *acceptum* refers not to reception of the Holy Spirit by the Son, nor to reception of the Holy Spirit from the Father, but to reception of the Spirit by the *creature*. That is, Hilary is asking whether

11 *Ladaria, El Espiritu Santo*, 301.

the Holy Spirit is simply a gift received in time (*acceptum*) or has rather an eternal existence, whether as *dimisssus* (sent forth) or as *genitus* (begotten). He then rules out the first possibility on the ground that a creaturely gift cannot be said to proceed from the Father—that is, come forth from the Father's substance. Logically, he continues:

> It only remains to make sure of our conviction on this point, whether we are to believe [in] an egress of a co-existent Being or a procession of a Being begotten [superest ut confirmemus in eo sententiam nostram, utrum in hoc consistentis egressionem an geniti processionem existimemus].[12]

As we shall see, he will exclude at the end of the treatise the suggestion that the Holy Spirit may be called begotten. Implicitly, then, in this present section, he contents himself with describing the Holy Spirit in rather general terms, as sent forth or "exiting" (*egressio*) from the Father, though as one who permanently exists (*consistentis*), not as coming into being.[13]

Receiving from the Father and from the Son

De Triniate 8.19 leads immediately to further investigation into the relation of the Holy Spirit to the other divine persons:

> I do not now find fault with people's freedom of understanding, by which they think of the Paraclete Spirit as from the Father or from the Son.[14] For our Lord has not left this in uncertainty, for after these same words, He spoke thus: "I have yet many things

12 McKenna translates: "Nothing remains but for us to corroborate our teaching on this point, whether we are to understand here the going forth of one who exists or the procession of one who has been born."

13 Ladaria remarks for his part that no parallel passage in Hilary's writings sheds light on the meaning of *egressio consistentis* (*El Espiritu Santo*, 301).

14 This sentence is my translation.

to say unto you, but you cannot bear them now. When He, the Spirit of truth, has come He shall guide you into all truth; for He shall not speak from Himself, but what things so ever He shall hear, these shall He speak; and He shall declare unto you the things that are to come. He shall glorify Me, for He shall receive of Mine and shall declare it unto you. All things whatsoever the Father has are mine: therefore said I, He shall receive of Mine, and shall declare it unto you." Accordingly, He receives from the Son, who is both sent by Him and proceeds from the Father. Now I ask whether to receive from the Son is the same thing as to proceed from the Father. But if one believes that there is a difference between receiving from the Son and proceeding from the Father, surely to receive from the Son and to receive from the Father will be regarded as one and the same thing [certe idipsum adque unum esse existimabitur a Filio accipere, quod sit accipere a Patre]. For our Lord Himself says: "Because He shall receive of Mine and shall declare it unto you. All things whatsoever the Father has are Mine: therefore said I, He shall receive of Mine and shall declare it unto you."

That which He will receive—whether it will be power, or excellence, or teaching [sive potestas, sive virtus, sive doctrina est]—the Son has said that it must be received from Him, and again He indicates that this same thing must be received from the Father. For when He says that all things whatsoever the Father hath are His, and that for this cause He declared that it must be received from His own, He teaches also that what is received from the Father is yet received from Himself, because all things that the Father hath are His. Such a unity admits of no difference, nor does it make any difference from whom that is received, which given by the Father is described as given by the Son. Is a mere unity of will brought forward here also? All things which the Father has are the Son's, and all things which

> the Son has are the Father's. For He Himself says, "And all mine are yours, and yours are Mine." It is not yet the place to show why He spoke thus, "For He shall receive of Mine," for this points to some subsequent time, when it is revealed that He shall receive [Futuri enim temporis significatio est, ubi accepturus ostenditur]. Now at any rate He says that He will receive of Himself, because all things that the Father had were His. Dissever if you can the unity of nature, and introduce some necessary unlikeness through which the Son may not exist in unity of nature. (8.20)

The first sentence of this extract is my own formulation, as the Latin is difficult to translate: "Neque in hoc nunc calumnior libertati intelligentiae, utrum ex Patre, an ex Filio Spiritum paracletum putent esse." Watson and Pullan render it as: "For the present I forebear to expose their licence of speculation, some of them holding that the Paraclete Spirit comes from the Father or from the Son." But this makes St. Hilary imply that it is a matter for criticism—albeit a criticism that he is not now going to pursue—to say either that the Holy Spirit comes from the Father or that He comes from the Son! It is possible that these translators mean us to understand that St. Hilary is not now going to bother describing the various details in which heretical systems differ among themselves, but the Latin itself hardly says that. McKenna renders the sentence: "Nor will I infringe upon anyone's liberty of thought in this matter, whether they may regard the Paraclete Spirit as coming from the Father or from the Son." However, this suggests a freedom to choose between two mutually exclusive positions, as if St. Hilary were saying that everyone is free to hold either that the Holy Spirit comes from the Father and not from the Son, or that he comes from the Son and not from the Father. The saint's meaning, rather, as is made clear by what follows, is that he will not criticize those who think of the Holy Spirit as from the Father or those who think of him as from the

Son, since the Lord has made it clear that he is from both, and so each thought is a true one.[15]

Yet what is it for the Holy Spirit to be from the Father and the Son, according to Hilary? It is for him to receive from the Father and from the Son; and this reception from each is "one and the same thing"—"idipsum adque unum." In saying, "that which He will receive—whether it will be power, or excellence, or teaching," Hilary does not of course mean to suggest that the Holy Spirit could receive one of these attributes without the other. He seems rather to be leaving open the question of which attribute is principally intended by Christ in this scriptural passage, content to insist that whatever the Holy Spirit receives he receives by one single reception from both Father and Son. This, he insists, is a necessary consequence of the truth that whatever the Father has the Son has also.

What are we to make of the unanswered question of whether to proceed from the Father and to receive from the Son differ? His hesitation here no doubt derives from an uncertainty about whether it is right to go beyond the explicit terminology of Scripture on so sublime a subject.[16] Nevertheless, he clearly affirms that the Holy Spirit has all that he has from both the Father and the Son, by a single donation.[17]

The saint raises the question of why the Holy Spirit is said to receive at some *future* time, but says that here is not the place to answer it: "Nondum loci est." Unfortunately, he does not return to it elsewhere. Is it possible that he would have said that "reception" refers not to the

---

[15] I cannot find any authority for McKenna's translation of *calumnior* as "infringe." St. Hilary is not saying that there are two parties, each of which *has* a right not to be prevented from thinking as it does, but that there are two forms of speech, each of which *is* right.

[16] It perhaps comes also from an awareness of the position of God the Father as the "first origin" within the Trinity, a position that one might wish to mark by reserving a unique word, such as "proceed," to express the relation of another divine person toward the Father.

[17] For this reason I do not agree with Jean-Miguel Garrigues's regret that St. Hilary's (alleged) distinction of procession and reception was too hesitant to affect later Latin tradition (*L'Esprit Qui Dit "Père!": l'Esprit-Saint dans la vie Trinitaire et le problème du* Filioque, Croire et Savoir 2 [Paris: Téqui, 1982], 70. Garrigues here has in mind his own theory that "proceed" and "receive" denote really distinct relations of the Holy Spirit to the other divine persons (see "A la suite de la clarification romaine sur le *Filioque*," *Nouvelle Revue Théologique* 119 [1997], 321–34).

Holy Spirit in his eternal existence, but just to future manifestations of the Spirit? The context of his words prevents us from supposing this. When he asked in 8.19, for example, whether we are to regard the Holy Spirit as begotten, or as having some other relation to His source, he was necessarily thinking of the eternal, personal existence of the Spirit and not simply of a manifestation of him to mankind. The fact that the word "begotten" is brought into consideration as a possible term shows that it is not simply the "economic" Trinity, but the "immanent" Trinity (as the foundation of the economy) which is in question.

"A Thing of One Nature"

Another significant passage occurs later in book 8 of Hilary's *De Trinitate*. Here the saint is arguing to the unity of nature of Father and Son from the unity of their Spirit, dwelling within the believer:

> Christ dwells in us, and where Christ dwells God dwells. And when the Spirit of Christ dwells in us, this indwelling means not that any other Spirit dwells in us than the Spirit of God. But if it is understood that Christ dwells in us through the Holy Spirit, we must yet recognise this Spirit of God as also the Spirit of Christ. And since the nature dwells in us as the nature of one substantive Being [cum per naturam rei natura ipsa habitet in nobis], we must regard the nature of the Son as identical with that of the Father, since the Holy Spirit Who is both the Spirit of Christ and the Spirit of God is proved to be a Being of one nature [res naturae esse demonstretur unius]. I ask now, therefore, how can They fail to be one by nature? The Spirit of Truth proceeds from the Father, He is sent by the Son and receives from the Son. But all things that the Father has are the Son's, and for this cause He Who receives from Him is the Spirit of God but at the same time the Spirit of Christ. The Spirit is a Being of the nature of the Son but the same

> Being is of the nature of the Father. He is the Spirit of Him Who raised Christ from the dead; but this is no other than the Spirit of Christ Who was so raised. The nature of Christ and of God must differ in some respect so as not to be the same, [only] if it can be shown that the Spirit which is of God is not the Spirit of Christ also. (8.26)

We may take the premise here as being that the Spirit of God and the Spirit of Christ are the same: the Holy Spirit, a "Being of one [non-complex] nature." This shows that the Father and the Son have the same nature, which is what St. Hilary wishes to establish. For any difference of nature between the Father and the Son would introduce some composition into the Holy Spirit, since he is of both, inasmuch as he proceeds from the Father and receives from the Son. In other words, the Holy Spirit has his one nature from Father and Son by a "proceeding and receiving," and his own unity is possible because of the unity of his principle.

Communication of the Divine Nature *ex Filio*

In book 9, St. Hilary returns to the text "He shall take of Mine," said by the Son concerning the Holy Spirit, and clearly understands it to refer to the communication of the divine nature, even though his direct intention, once again, is to prove the consubstantiality of the Father and the Son:

> He declares the unity of His nature as the only-begotten with the Father, by the unmistakeable words, "All things whatsoever the Father has, are Mine." There is no mention here of coming into possession: it is one thing for what He has to be external to

> His being [aliud est extrinsecus subsistenti sua esse];[18] another, for Him to exist in what He has, and Himself to be this [aliud est in suis adque ipsum se esse].[19] The former is to possess heaven and earth and the universe, the latter to be able to describe Himself by His own properties, which are His, not as something external and subject, but as something of which He Himself subsists. When He says, therefore, that all things which the Father has are His, He alludes to the divine nature, and not to a joint ownership of gifts bestowed. For referring to His words that the Holy Spirit should take of His [de suo], He says: "All things whatsoever the Father has, are Mine, therefore, said I, He shall take of Mine"; that is, the Holy Spirit takes of His [de suo] but takes also of the Father's: and if He receives of the Father's, He receives also of His [de suo]. *Nor does the Holy Spirit, who is the Spirit of God, take from creatures, as if He would seem to receive from them; for they are all of God [and not God Himself]. But not in such a way are "all the things which are the Father's [the Son's]" that [the Holy Spirit] should appear not also to receive from what is the Father's those things which He takes from the Son*; for all that the Father hath belongs equally to the Son. (9.7)

Here, for reasons to be discussed presently, the italicized material near the end is my own translation of the following Latin: "Neque enim de creaturis sumebat Spiritus sanctus, qui Dei Spiritus est, ut ex his videatur accipere, quia ea omnia Dei sunt. Sed non ideo omnia quae Patris sunt sua sunt: ut quod sumit ex Filio, ne etiam non de Patris [*sic*] sumere videretur."

St. Hilary intends here to show that when Christ said that all

---

18 Watson and Pullan translate: "to be the Possessor of things external to Him." Several variants occur in the manuscripts for *subsistenti*. The editor of Migne defends the reading *subsistentia*; see note (d) in *PL*, 10:339.

19 Watson and Pullan translate: "To be self-contained and self-existent." Some manuscripts have *idipsum* for *ipsum*. The editor of Migne notes that this variant, which he does not follow, would make Hilary's meaning clearer; see note (e) in *PL*, 10:340.

that the Father had was his, he was not referring to the possession of created things ("heaven and earth and the universe"), but of the divine nature. He does this by pointing out that these words of Christ were a prelude for speaking of what the Holy Spirit would receive. He next posits that the Holy Spirit does not receive created things, being the Spirit of God. He concludes that the things the Son receives from the Father, passing them on to the Holy Spirit, are the Father's own "things" by which the Father exists, not some external possessions: in other words, the divine nature. It thus emerges indirectly but clearly from this passage that the Son communicates the divine nature to the Holy Spirit, yet in such a way that in receiving from the Son, the Holy Spirit receives also from the Father.[20]

There are, admittedly, difficulties of translation in this passage. First, the sentence "neque enim de creaturis sumebat Spiritus sanctus, qui Dei Spiritus est, ut ex his videatur accipere, quia ea omnia Dei sunt" is rendered by Watson and Pullan as: "The Holy Spirit is the Spirit of God, and does not receive of a creature, but teaches us that He receives all these gifts, because they are all God's." McKenna has: "The Holy Spirit, who is the Spirit of God, did not receive anything from creatures, and this makes it clear that He received from those things which are wholly proper to God." These translators thus understand *ut* as introducing a result, and *ea* in the last clause to refer not to "creatures," but to "the things that are of God," in the sense of the divine nature and attributes. One difficulty with this reading is that it makes Hilary say that from the fact that the Holy Spirit does not take from creatures, we learn that he takes from God; yet where and how are we supposed to learn the former truth, independently of our knowing the latter truth? Another difficulty is that in the three immediately preceding occasions, Hilary has used the singular form of the adjective (*suo*) to denote what

20 There does not seem to be any significance in the difference of preposition whereby the Holy Spirit is said to receive *ex Filio* and *de Patris* (presumably this last phrase, ungrammatical as it stands, is an ellipsis for *de re/substantia Patris*).

the Holy Spirit receives from the Father and the Son; this interpretation would make him change abruptly to the plural. For these reasons, I agree with the editor of Migne in taking *his* and *ea* as referring to the plural noun used earlier in the sentence, which seems more natural.[21] Granted, one could argue that since *creatura* is a feminine noun, Hilary should have written *eae* not *ea*; but it is not unreasonable to suppose that he would use a neuter pronoun to refer to "created things in general." On this interpretation, *ut* is to be understood as having a concessive force: Hilary is saying that although the fact that "all things [i.e., all creatures] are of God" (see 1 Cor 11:12) might suggest to someone that the Holy Spirit would receive from some or all of these "all things," this is not in fact the case.[22]

The next sentence of the extract also raises difficulties: "Sed non ideo omnia, quae Patris sunt sua sunt, ut quod sumit ex Filio, ne etiam non de Patris sumere videretur." Watson and Pullan render this: "All things that belong to the Father are the Spirit's; but we must not think that whatever He received of the Son, He did not receive of the Father also." There are two objections to this rendering. First, it assumes that Hilary, having used a phrase taken from the Gospel ("quae Patris sunt sua sunt") in its literal sense, as a reference to what the Son has, without warning immediately uses it in a different sense, as a reference to what the Holy Spirit has. The other objection is that the first half of the sentence would have no logical connection with the second half: why should the Holy Spirit's having all the Father's things incline one to suppose, and thus require one to be warned against supposing, that he does not receive things from the Father because he receives things from the Son?

McKenna, for his part, translates the sentence: "Not everything, therefore, that belongs to the Father is His own, so that we are to

[21] See note (g) in *PL*, 10:340.

[22] It is likely that this text from St. Paul was in his mind, since Arians sometimes equivocally used it to allow them to say that they too believed that the Son was *ex Deo*.

believe that what He takes from the Son He does not also take from the Father." I find this incomprehensible.

However, none of these variant translations undermine the key point to which I want to draw attention: according to Hilary, the Son communicates the divine nature to the Holy Spirit, yet in such a way that in receiving from the Son, the Holy Spirit receives also from the Father.

Subsistence of the Holy Spirit through the Son

The bishop of Poitiers returns one last time to the relation between the Son and the Holy Spirit in the prayer to God the Father with which he concludes the last book of his great treatise:

> Thy Holy Spirit, as the Apostle says, searches and knows Thy deep things, and as Intercessor for me speaks to Thee words I could not utter; and shall I express or rather dishonour by the title "creature," the power of His nature, which subsists eternally, derived from Thee through Thy only-begotten [naturae suae ex te per unigenitum tuum manentis potentiam creationis nomine non modo eloquar, sed et infamabor]? Nothing, except what belongs to Thee, penetrates into Thee; nor can the agency of a power foreign and strange to Thee measure the depth of Thy boundless majesty. (12.55)

The phrase "which subsists eternally" is a rendering of the single word *manentis*. A more literal translation of "naturae suae manentis potentiam" might be "the power of his enduring nature" (McKenna leaves the word *manentis* untranslated, writing "the power of His nature"). In any case, the saint is clearly speaking of the Holy Spirit as he is in himself, and is saying that he has his divine nature from the Father through the Son. As Ladaria notes, "naturae suae manentis potentiam" shows that it is not simply the mission of the Holy Spirit to the world that is in question, but rather "the Spirit's whole being" ("todo el ser del Espiritu").[23]

Hilary continues his prayer:

> But I cannot describe Him, Whose pleas for me I cannot describe. As in the revelation that Thy Only-begotten was born of Thee before times eternal, when we cease to struggle with ambiguities of language and difficulties of thought, the one certainty of His birth remains; so I hold fast in my consciousness the truth that Thy Holy Spirit is from Thee and through Him [ex te per eum sanctus Spiritus tuus est], although I cannot by my intellect comprehend it. For in Thy spiritual things I am dull. (12.56)[24]

Distinction between Generation and Procession

St. Hilary does not enquire into the difference between generation and procession within God in order to understand why the Holy Spirit is not a Son. Indeed, he speaks in certain places as if there would be nothing to prevent the Holy Spirit from being called a Son. Thus, in *De Trinitate* 7.15, he writes that "only birth can bestow an equality of nature," and in 7.26: "We believe without any blasphemy that only the birth of the Son is similar to or equal to Him [the Father]." Again, in 12.51, he writes that "in the things of God, we confess nothing else except what is born and eternal."[25] However, in each case, the Holy Spirit is absent from the context; the saint is concerned, as he primarily is throughout the treatise, to uphold the true divinity of the Son. We

---

23 Ladaria, *El Espiritu Santo*, 306.

24 *PL*, 10:469B–70A. For a general discussion on the "limits of language" in the *De Trinitate*, see Tarmo Toom, "Hilary of Poitier's *De Trinitate* and the Name(s) of God," *Vigiliae Christianae* 64, no. 5 (2010): 456–79. Also note that McKenna does not translate the words *per eum* from the bracketed Latin, but rather writes simply, "Your Holy Spirit is from You." Migne does not mention any manuscript variations at this point, so it seems to have been simply an oversight. On the other hand, P. Smulders mentions in *CCSL* (62:52*) that a ninth-century manuscript of the *De Trinitate* has the variation *cum eo* ("with Him"). Speaking in general about this manuscript, and not with respect to this passage, he notes that it must be read with great caution (*caute omnino*).

25 These three lines are from McKenna's translation.

have seen that in 8.19 he raises the question of whether the Holy Spirit should be said to be begotten, or rather referred to by some other term. He answers this question (though without elaboration) at the end of the treatise in words addressed to the Father:

> As for me, it is certainly not enough to deny by means of my faith and voice that my Lord and God, your only-begotten Jesus Christ, is a creature. I will not even permit this name to be associated with your Holy Spirit, who has proceeded from You and been sent through Him. For I am scrupulous to speak rightly of all that is yours. Nor, because You alone are unborn and because, knowing that an only-begotten was born from you, I would not say that the Holy Spirit was begotten, will I ever say that He was created. (12.55)

While the first two sentences here are translated by McKenna, the last two are my own, with the last translating the following Latin: "Neque quia, te solum innascibilem et unigenitum ex te natum sciens, genitum tamen Spiritum sanctum non dicturus sim, dicam umquam creatum." McKenna renders this last sentence: "I will not say that the Holy Spirit was begotten, since I know that you alone are unborn and the only-begotten was born from You, nor will I ever say that He was created." This agrees substantially with my translation, although he leaves out the saint's implied statement that the temptation to call the Holy Spirit a creature arises from the impossibility of calling Him either begotten or unbegotten. Watson and Pullan, however, render it: "Nor, because I know that Thou alone art unborn, and the Only-begotten is born of Thee, will I refuse to say that the Holy Spirit was begotten, or assert that He was ever created." This gives the opposite sense, implying that St. Hilary would have called the Holy Spirit a Son. The Migne editor agrees with McKenna and notes that St. Hilary is expressly excluding the term *genitus* from the Holy Spirit.[26] Ladaria takes the same view.[27]

The *Opus historicum*

The *Opus historicum* is a collection of documents and commentaries describing the Arian controversies from the Council of Serdica in 343/4 to the time of St. Hilary's death around 368. While the authenticity of parts of the collection has been the subject of lively discussions in the past, particularly on account of what is said therein concerning the "Fall of Liberius," the *Opus* is generally accepted by modern scholars as Hilary's work.[28] The dates at which its various parts were composed or compiled is uncertain.[29] At one point, contrasting the Catholic and Arian accounts of the Trinity, St. Hilary writes:

> When they have with their irreligious and evil-speaking mouths torn the Son from the Father, making different substances of them, so that two separate principles are established, a third substance is assigned to the Spirit; so although the Father is in the Son and the Son in the Father, and the Holy Spirit receives from each [accipit ex Utroque], for the Spirit appears as the inviolable unity of this holy Trinity; yet the Trinity as explained by the heretics produces division. (*Opus Historicum*, 31; my trans.)[30]

---

26 See note (b) in *PL*, 10:469.

27 Ladaria, *El Espiritu Santo*, 305. Watson and Pullan's version seems not only theologically incorrect but also linguistically improbable. While it would be a possible translation of the phrase *neque . . . sim*, the *neque* could hardly at the same time also qualify *dicam umquam creatum*, as would be necessary for their translation to be correct.

28 See Hilary of Poitiers, *Preface to His Opus Historicum*, trans. P. Smulders with commentary, Supplements to *Vigiliae Christianae* 19 (Leiden: Brill, 1995), 23; see also "Hilary of Poitiers," in *ODCC*, 774.

29 See Hilary of Poitiers, *Preface to His Opus Historicum*, 17–23.

30 *PL*, 10:656B–C: "Ubi a diversis substantiis Filium a Patre impio et maledico ore disciderint, ut in separatis duobus adsistat auctoritas, tertia dinumeratur in Spiritu; ut cum sit Pater in Filio et Filius in Patre, et Spiritus Sanctus accipiat ex Utroque, in eo quod Spiritus exprimitur sanctae huius inviolabilis unitas [Trinitatis], haeretica parte parturiat Trinitas pronuntiata dissidium." This is the reading proposed in a footnote by the editor, which differs slightly from what is put in the body of the text. The differences do not affect our question.

This important passage has often been overlooked in accounts of St. Hilary's doctrine of the procession of the Holy Spirit.[31] Nevertheless, as Swete says: "There is but a step between the 'accipit ex Utroque' of this passage, and the 'ex Utroque procedit' which ultimately received the sanction of the Latin Church."[32] Of particular interest is the suggestion by the editor of Migne that the one *auctoritas* (i.e., the character of being a principle), which St. Hilary indicates as belonging to Father and Son, should be understood in relation to the Holy Spirit, so that Father and Son are here declared to be one principle of the third divine person. Although it is not certain that this is the meaning, since he could be thinking of them insofar as they are the principle of creation, this interpretation is plausible, since he immediately proceeds to mention the Holy Spirit. The passage thus also provides support for the understanding of *auctoribus* in 2.29 of *De Trinitate*, discussed above, as referring primarily to the derivation of the Holy Spirit rather than to the testimony by which we believe in him.

Summary and Conclusion

St. Hilary holds in the *De Trinitate* that the Father and the Son can be called *auctores* of the Holy Spirit (2.4). This term can be interpreted by what he teaches elsewhere in the same treatise: that, in regard to the eternal origin of the Spirit, the faithful are equally free to speak of him as *ex Patre* and as *ex Filio*, since the Saviour has not left the matter doubtful (8.20); that, even if the precise meaning of the word "proceed" is uncertain, the "receiving" from the Father is the same as that from the Son (8.20); that the Holy Spirit is from the Father and the Son insofar as they are one in nature (8.26); that he has from the Son those things by which the Father is God, yet not in such a way as not also to have them from the Father (9.73); that he and his nature subsist from the

31 For example, it is not mentioned by Congar or A. Edward Siecienski.

32 Swete, *On the History of the Doctrine of the Procession of the Holy Spirit*, 115.

Father through the Son (12.55–56); that he receives from each (*Opus Historicum*). I should therefore question A. Edward Siecienski's remark that "it remains unclear whether Hilary himself would have accepted the teaching of the procession of the Holy Spirit from the Father and the Son as from one principle."[33] This teaching appears to correspond well to the mind of the bishop of Poitiers, as does the further teaching of the Council of Florence that the procession may, without difference in meaning, be said to be either from or through the Son.[34]

---

33 A. Edward Siecienski, *The Filioque: History of a Doctrinal Controversy* (New York: Oxford University Press, 2010), 54.

34 See *Decrees of the Ecumenical Councils: From Nicaea I to Vatican II*, ed. Norman Tanner and Giuseppe Alberigo, vol. 1 (Washington, DC: Georgetown University Press, 1990), 526–27.

CHAPTER 5

SAINT BASIL THE GREAT

Introduction

THERE ARE TWO MAIN SOURCES for St. Basil's teaching on the Holy Spirit's relation to the Father and the Son: his treatise *De Spiritu Sancto* and his work *Adversus Eunomium*, in particular book 3. The authorship of a letter that touches on the same subject, number 38 in his collected letters, has long been discussed, since manuscript traditions attribute it both to him and to his brother St. Gregory of Nyssa.[1] In line with the more recent scholarship, I shall consider it among the latter's works.[2] Another letter concerning the Holy Spirit, long listed as number 8 in his works, is ascribed by modern scholarship to Evagrius Ponticus.[3] Finally, a phrase occurs in Homily 24 that was discussed at the Council of Florence.

1 Basil, *Letters 1–58*, trans. and ed. Roy Deferarri, Loeb Classical Library 190 (Cambridge, MA: Harvard University Press, 1926), 197.

2 John Behr, *The Nicene Faith*, vol. 2 (Crestwood, NY: St. Vladimir's Seminary Press, 2004), 419.

3 Evagrius, *Evagrius Ponticus*, ed. Augustine Casiday with introduction (New York: Routledge, 2006), 45.

The Russian theologian Sergei Bulgakov (1871–1944) declared: "For St. Basil the Great, the problem of the procession of the Holy Spirit from the Father only, or from the Father and the Son, simply does not exist in its later sense; and statements that seem to touch upon this question therefore do not refer to it at all."[4] Such a hermeneutical principle, however, cannot simply be assumed, but must be proved. The only way to test it is by a careful consideration of the relevant texts.

Adversus Eunomium

This treatise appears to have been written around 364 or 365. Eunomius was the bishop of Cyzicus in Asia Minor, and at the time the head of the so-called "heteroousian" party, who maintained that the Son was of another, and lesser, substance than the Father. As a natural consequence, he maintained also the inferiority of the Holy Spirit to the Son. Thus, in his response to Eunomius, St. Basil was thus led to elaborate his own doctrine of the Holy Spirit, particularly in the third and last book of the treatise. At the time of the Council of Florence, the treatise circulated with a fourth and fifth book, but they are not considered genuine by modern scholarship and will not be quoted in this section.[5]

The Son as Principle of the Holy Spirit

Toward the end of the second book, St. Basil is attacking Eunomius's contention that the Son was created by the Father, and the Holy Spirit by the Son. The saint writes:

> Isn't it clear to everyone that no activity of the Son is severed from the Father? That none of all the existing things that

4 Sergei Bulgakov, *The Comforter*, trans. Boris Jakim (Grand Rapids, MI: Eerdmans, 2004), 79.

5 Basil, *Against Eunomius*, trans. Mark DelCogliano and Andrew Radde-Gallwitz, Fathers of the Church 122 (Washington, DC: Catholic University of America Press, 2011), 33. Further quotations are taken from this translation by DelCogliano and Radde-Gallwitz, who translated from the critical edition prepared by Bernard Sesboue with Georges-Matthieu de Durand for *Basile de Césarée, Contre Eunome suivi d'Eunome apologie* (Paris: Cerf, 1982).

belong to the Son is foreign to the Father? For he says: "All that is mine is yours, and all that is yours is mine." So, then, how does Eunomius impute the cause [τὴν αἰτίαν] of the Spirit to the Only-begotten alone, and take the creating of the Spirit as an accusation against the Only-begotten's nature?[6] If he says these things to introduce two principles [ἀρχὰς] in conflict with one another, he will be crushed along with Mani and Marcion. But if he makes the beings depend on a single principle [μιᾶς ἔξαπτει τὰ ὄντα], that which is said to come into being from the Son [τὸ παρὰ τοῦ Υἱοῦ γεγενῆσθαι λεγόμενον][7] has a relationship with the first cause [πρὸς τὴν πρώτην αἰτίαν τὴν ἀνάφοραν ἔχει]. Hence, even if we believe that all things have been brought into being through God the Word, we nevertheless do not deny that the God of the universe is the cause of all.

How is it not an unmistakeable danger to separate the Spirit from God? On the one hand, the Apostle hands down to us that they are connected, saying now that he is the Spirit of God, now that he is the Spirit of Christ. For he writes: "If anyone does not have the Spirit of Christ, he does not belong to him." And again: "You have not received the spirit of the world, but the Spirit that comes from God." On the other hand, the Lord says, that he is the Spirit of truth—since he is himself the Truth—and that he "proceeds from the Father." But Eunomius, in order to diminish the glory of our Lord Jesus Christ, separates the Spirit from the Father and imputes him exclusively [διαφερόντως] to the Only-begotten in order to diminish his [Christ's] glory. (2.34)[8]

---

6 It would be an "accusation," as St. Basil explains just before this extract, since it would imply that the Son was less than the Father, being able to create only the Holy Spirit, whereas the Father could create the Son.

7 It would be better to translate the Greek phrase as "that which exists from the Son," as the Holy Spirit cannot be said to come *into* being, as if he came like creatures from non-being.

8 *PG*, 29:652A–C.

St. Basil does not object to Eunomius's holding that the Son is a principle of the Holy Spirit, but to the way in which he applies this principle. There are, he says, two ways to understand it: either the Son is the principle exclusively, διαφερόντως, or else he is in such a way that the Holy Spirit also has a relation to the first "cause," the Father. Only the second sense is acceptable, and since St. Basil explains this second sense by scriptural texts, we must assume that he himself holds it to be not only possible but true that the Holy Spirit is παρὰ τοῦ Υἱοῦ ("from the Son"). Even more than this, the word μιᾶς ("one") in this extract, agreeing as it does with the word ἀρχή ("principle") just before, seems intended to encompass both the παρὰ τοῦ Υἱοῦ, and the relation to the first "cause." In other words, St. Basil comes, as St. Hilary does around the same time, very close to the formulation that was later to become standard in the west, that the Father and Son are one principle of the Holy Spirit. The importance of this passage seems to have been overlooked by many who have written about St. Basil and the *Filioque*.[9]

Disputed Readings

The next passage to consider bristles with difficulties in regard to both authenticity and interpretation. I shall quote it first from the translation of Mark DelCogliano and Andrew Radde-Gallwitz:

> Eunomius says next that while he has learned on the authority of the saints that the Holy Spirit is third both in rank and in dignity [τῇ τάξει καὶ τῷ ἀξιώματι], he has come to believe on his own authority that the Holy Spirit is third in nature as well. Who are the saints who taught this? In what treatises have they expressed it? Has there ever been someone so audacious as to introduce innovations about the divine doctrines? If the Spirit is third in dignity and in rank, is there some necessity that he be

[9] It is not mentioned, for example, by Henry Barclay Swete, Yves Congar, or A. Edward Siecienski.

> third in nature as well? Perhaps the word of piety transmits that he is second to the Son in dignity [ἀξιώματι]. But we have not learned from the holy scriptures that a third nature is necessary. Nor do the preceding claims make it possible to infer such a conclusion.
>
> The Son is second to the Father in rank because he is from him. He is second to the Father in dignity because the Father is the principle and cause by virtue of which he is the Son's Father, and because we approach and access the God and Father through the Son. Even so, the Son is not second in nature, since there is one divinity in both of them. Likewise, it is clear that, even if the Holy Spirit is below [ὑποβέβηκε] the Son in both rank and dignity—something with which we too are in total agreement [ἵνα καὶ ὅλως συγχωρήσωμεν]—it is still not likely that he is of a foreign nature. (3.1)[10]

One can see immediately that something is awry with this translation: in the first paragraph, St. Basil is represented as saying that "perhaps" the Holy Spirit comes after the Son in "dignity," but in the second paragraph as saying simply that he certainly does. What is the explanation?

There are two textual problems with this passage, both of them discussed at the Council of Florence. Instead of the sentence in the first paragraph that runs, "perhaps the word of piety transmits that he is second to the Son in dignity," some ancient Greek manuscripts have the following passage: "The word of piety transmits that in dignity[11] he is indeed second to the Son, having his being from him and receiving from him and announcing to us and entirely[12] dependent upon this cause [Ἀξιώματι μὲν γὰρ δευτερόν τοῦ Υἱοῦ, παρ'αὐτοῦ τὸ εἶναι ἔχον, καὶ παρ'αὐτοῦ λαμβάνον καὶ ἀναγγέλλον ἡμῖν, καὶ ὅλως ἐκείνης τῆς αἰτίας

[10] *PG*, 29:653B–56A.

[11] I do not like the translation of ἀξίωμα as "dignity," but I retain it here to avoid further confusion.

[12] Or, "in sum"—see further in this section.

ἐξημμένον, παραδίδωσιν ὁ τῆς εὐσεβείας λόγος]." At the Council of Florence, not only the Greek manuscript of St. Basil used by the Latins but also four of the five manuscripts brought by the Greeks were found to have this latter passage, which so clearly affirms the Holy Spirit's origin from the Son. Bessarion, bishop of Nicaea, later related that, on returning to Constantinople, he examined all the manuscripts he could discover and found that all the older ones also had this passage, even though two of them had been defaced, one with a knife and another by having straw stuck over the offending words. He also stated that the passage could hardly have been forged by Latins, since not only they but not even Greeks themselves could have written so elegant a sentence, perfectly in keeping with St. Basil's style.[13] John of Montenero, the chief Latin speaker at Florence, also argued that St. Basil would not have made the hesitating statement attributed to him in the first version quoted ("perhaps the word of piety . . ."), when the Council of Chalcedon praised the accuracy of his doctrine.[14] The great Marist scholar Prudent Maran (1683-1762), whose treatise on St. Basil forms a preface to the Migne edition of this work, likewise remarks that it would be absurd for St. Basil to say that the Son is second to the Father in ἀξίωμα but doubt whether the same can be said of the Holy Spirit in regard to the Son, when in the treatise *De Spiritu Sancto* he says, as we shall see, that "the relation of the Spirit to the Son is the same as that of the Son to the Father."[15]

---

13 Bessarion, Letter to Alexios Lascaris (*PG*, 161:409A–10C). He also records here that the volume censored by means of straw had formerly been the possession of Demetrios Kydones, the fourteenth-century pro-unionist prime minister of Byzantium, who had added in the margin the words that had been covered over. Joseph, bishop of Methone, in his *Refutation of Mark of Ephesus*, recalls that, during one of the public sessions at Florence, a servant of the bishop of Nicomedia took John of Montenero's copy of the *Adversus Eunomium* in order to bring it to Mark Eugenikos, and stopped by an open window of the council hall in order surreptitiously to cut out the offending phrase, but that "the Spirit of truth stirred up a light breeze which caused the page to turn over" unnoticed by the servant, so that he cut out the wrong sentence (*PG*, 159:1048C).

14 *AG*, 331. The reference is to the third allocution to Emperor Marcian (Mansi, 7:461D–64A). We can add that such hesitation would be incompatible with the passage already considered at the end of book 2 of this work.

15 *PG*, 32:35D. Here he disagrees with the editors of Migne, who put the "non-*Filioque*" variants in the text itself of the *Adversus Eunomium*.

It may be argued against this, and it was so argued by Mark of Ephesus at Florence,[16] that St. Basil seems to be expressing uncertainty or even hostility toward the characterization of the Holy Spirit as "third" when he asks, "who are the saints who have taught this?" Bessarion's reply to this was that St. Basil is arguing not that there are no saints who have called the Holy Spirit "third," but that Eunomius is not in a position to bring forward their writings, since if he did so they would be evidently in opposition to his, Eunomius's, teaching on the inferiority of the Spirit.[17]

Georges-Matthieu de Durand, having made a thorough study of the manuscript tradition, concludes that "the two ms. traditions go back to a very early date, or at any rate to well before the controversy" (by this, however, he appears to mean the controversy of the second millennium, since according to the same author the manuscripts in question are not certainly older than the ninth century, when Photios made a charge of heresy against the *Filioque*).[18] It is somewhat surprising, therefore, that DelCogliano and Radde-Gallwitz, speaking of the disputed passage affirming the dependence of the Holy Spirit on the Son, baldly state in a footnote that "this text is not original to Basil," referencing Durand's article as their authority. A. Edward Siecienski states the passage was "apparently . . . an excerpt of Eunomius's added later," relying on a suggestion put forward by Michel van Parys.[19] Parys himself argues against

---

16 *AG*, 302–303.

17 *PL*, 161:411C. Here again there is a minor textual variation: some manuscripts have, at the end of the sentence that begins "who the saints are," the words "he cannot say," turning it from a question to a statement. Bessarion was perhaps using a manuscript of the second kind, while DelCogliano and Radde-Gallwitz appear to be using one of the former kind.

18 Georges-Matthieu de Durand, "Un passage du IIIe livre contre Eunome de S. Basile dans la tradition manuscrite," *Irenikon* 54 (1981): 36–52, at 52. Paul Fedwick concurs (*A Study of the Manuscript Tradition, Translations and Editions of the Works of Basil of Caesarea*, vol. 3, Corpus Christianorum, Bibliotheca Basiliana Universalis [Turnhout: Brepols, 1997], 629–30).

19 A. Edward Siecienski, *The Filioque: History of a Doctrinal Controversy* (New York: Oxford University Press, 2010), 281. See also Michel van Parys, "Quelques remarques à propos d'un texte controversé de Basile au concile de Florence," *Irenikon* 40 (1967): 6–14. Parys admits that his proposal is simply a hypothesis (13), whereas Siecienski mentions it as something almost certain. Alexander Alexakis authorizes himself on the basis of the same study by Parys to describe it as "beyond doubt" that the disputed passage is a Eunomian interpolation (Alexander Alexakis, "The Greek Patristic Testimonies Presented at the Council of Florence [1439] in Support of the *Filioque* Reconsidered," *Revue des études Byzantines* 58 [2000]: 149–65, at 156n24).

authenticity on the grounds that so clear an affirmation of procession from the Son would be unique in the Cappadocian Fathers and that the Greek term ὅλως would seem to go beyond orthodoxy, excluding procession from the Father. Yet, in response to this, it may be said first that the words under discussion go no further than the image of the three torches that we shall find in St. Basil's brother, Gregory of Nyssa; and secondly that the word ὅλως can be understood to mean "in short," summing up what has just been said. Yet, even if this word be translated as "wholly," it need not be taken as excluding the Father, but simply as denying that there could be any "part" of the Holy Spirit that was not from the Son.

To conclude the question: it seems that the manuscript evidence alone is unable to resolve the question of the authenticity of the text, while external evidence tends to favor authenticity, especially comparison with other passages from Basil.[20]

The second textual crux comes in the second paragraph of the extract. The Greek words ἵνα καὶ ὅλως συγχωρήσωμεν, translated above as "something with which we too are in total agreement," were not found in the manuscript of the Latin party at Florence, and Bessarion again says that they are a later addition.[21] One might wonder why such a discrepancy would have occurred, given that the words appear to strengthen the case *for* the origin of the Holy Spirit from the Son, for St. Basil in the same paragraph explains the Son's being second to the Father as a result of his coming from the Father. The answer is that the English translation given above is not the only possible one: one can also understand the Greek to mean "so that we might yield to them as far as possible." It is in this sense that it was understood at Florence.[22] In this case, if the phrase be authen-

20 The version of the text that teaches the dependence of the Holy Spirit on the Son was defended by Ladislaus Lohn in "Doctrina S. Basilii de processionibus divinarum Personarum," *Gregorianum* 10 (1929): 329–64, 461–500.

21 *PG*, 161:412B.

22 This alternative translation is perhaps better, insofar as it seems to do more justice to the conjunction ἵνα, "so that."

tic, St. Basil would be saying that "even if we were to say for the sake of argument that the Holy Spirit is below the Father and the Son in rank and dignity, he would still not be so in nature."[23] Maran argues in favor of the manuscript tradition that lacks the phrase, for the same reason as in the previous disputed passage: it would be suggesting a doubt that Basil elsewhere shows that he does not have.

There is a third textual dispute about a passage a little further on. St. Basil has been explaining, by reference to the angels and to the stars, how a difference in rank and dignity does not necessarily imply a difference in nature, and concludes, according to the translation of DelCogliano and Radde-Gallwitz: "Likewise, the same clearly holds true for the Holy Spirit, even if he is subordinate [ὑποβέβηκεν] in dignity and rank, as they claim [ὡς λέγουσιν]."[24] Here the controversy is about only the last phrase: the Latin manuscript at the council of Florence lacked the Greek words ὡς λέγουσιν. This leads once more to the question of whether St. Basil is giving his own thought or summarizing that of Eunomius and his followers without passing judgment on it. Once again, Maran argues that the teaching at the end of book 2 is incompatible with a real doubt in St. Basil's mind on this matter; deriving from Father and Son, the Holy Spirit is necessarily third in their regard.[25] It is possible, though, that here and in the previous passage it was simply the appropriateness of the word ὑποβέβηκε (literally, "he has gone below") about which St. Basil was uncertain, and not the Holy Spirit's being third "in dignity and rank."

The Movements of the Mind

Finally, it is worth mentioning one passage in this work that hints at a possible way of approach to the theology of the procession, one that St.

23 At Florence it seems to have been understood by everyone in the second way (*AG*, 313–17).

24 *PG*, 29:657C.

25 In the manuscript tradition, the three disputed passages are generally but not always found together either in their pro-*Filioque* or their anti-*Filioque* form (Durand, "Un passage").

Augustine was to follow two generations later. Faced with Eunomius's argument that since the Holy Spirit can properly be called neither unbegotten nor begotten, he must be a creature, St. Basil draws attention to our ignorance of many other things, an ignorance that should prevent presumptuous statements about God:

> But as for the very movements of our mind [αὐτὰ τὰ τοῦ νοῦ κινήματα], is it the nature of the soul to create or beget them? Who can say with precision? So, then, why is it shocking that we are not ashamed to confess our ignorance even in the case of the Holy Spirit, but we still render him the glorification for which there is ample testimony? (3:6)[26]

There is just a hint in these words that the "movements of the mind," taking the phrase "mind" in a broad sense, could furnish an analogy to help us gain some insight into the procession of the Holy Spirit and its difference from the generation of the Son. Neither here nor elsewhere, however, does St. Basil pursue this line of thought.

The Treatise *De Spiritu Sancto*

The immediate cause of this treatise was a request from his fellow bishop Amphilochius to explain the Trinitarian doxology used in the Church of Caesarea—"Glory be to the Father with [μετὰ] the Son with [σὺν] the Holy Spirit"—a form different from that used by Amphilochius in nearby Iconium, "Glory be to the Father through [διά)] the Son in [ἐν] the Holy Spirit." St. Basil, however, takes the opportunity to write an entire treatise on the Holy Spirit. The treatise is dated to the years 374 or 375.[27] I shall not attempt a summary of the whole work, but simply draw out some key assertions.

---

26 *PG*, 29:667B.

27 Basil, *On the Holy Spirit*, in Selected Works, trans. Blomfield Jackson, *NPNF2* vol. 8; Basil, *On the Holy Spirit*, trans. David Anderson (Crestwood, NY: St. Vladimir's Seminary Press, 1980); Basile, *Sur Le Saint-Esprit*,

The Holy Spirit Is to the Son as the Son Is to the Father

As part of their attempt to deny or cast doubt on the true divinity of the Holy Spirit, Basil's opponents were in the habit of saying that the Spirit was "numbered under" the Father and the Son (41). Basil first remarks that they have never made clear what they mean by this phrase. He then writes:

> Do you maintain that the Son is numbered under [ὑπαρισμεῖσθαι] the Father, and the Spirit under the Son, or do you confine your sub-numeration to the Spirit alone? If, on the other hand, you apply this sub-numeration also to the Son, you revive what is the same impious doctrine, the unlikeness of the substance, the lowliness of rank, the coming into being in later time, and once for all, by this one term, you will plainly again set circling all the blasphemies against the Only-begotten. To controvert these blasphemies would be a longer task than my present purpose admits of; and I am the less bound to undertake it because the impiety has been refuted elsewhere to the best of my ability. If on the other hand they suppose the sub-numeration to benefit the Spirit alone, they must be taught that the Spirit is spoken of together with the Lord [συνεκφωνεῖται τῷ Κυρίῳ] in precisely the same manner in which the Son is spoken of with the Father. The name of the Father and of the Son and of the Holy Ghost is delivered in like manner, and, according to the co-ordination of words delivered in baptism, the relation of the Spirit to the Son is the same as that of the Son to the Father [Ὡς τοίνυν ἔχει ὁ Υἱὸς πρὸς τοῦ Πατέρα, οὕτω πρὸς τὸν Υἱὸν τὸ Πνεῦμα]. And if the Spirit is co-ordinate [συντέτακται] with the Son, and the Son with the Father, it is obvious that the Spirit is also co-ordinate with the Father. (43)[28]

trans. Benoît Pruche, *Sources Chrétiennes* 17 *bis* (Paris: Cerf, 2002). Quotations are from Jackson's translation. All references are to sections, not to chapters or pages.

28 *PG*, 32:145D–48A.

The passage is directly concerned with the co-equality of the three divine persons, rather than with the origin of the Son and the Holy Spirit. The term συντέτακται, translated here as "co-ordinate with," indicates primarily this equality, both in itself and in our correct grasp of it. It is nonetheless striking to see the same idea in the Cappadocian Father as we found in the Alexandrian Athanasius: as the Son is to the Father, so the Holy Spirit is to the Son.

The Holy Spirit Is Conjoined to the Father and the Son

St. Basil writes:

> The greatest proof of the conjunction [συναφείας] of the Spirit with the Father and the Son is that He is said to have the same relation [οὕτως ἔχειν . . . ὡς] to God which the spirit in us has to each of us. "For what man," it is said, "knoweth the things of a man, save the spirit of man which is in him? even so the things of God knoweth no man but the Spirit of God." (40)[29]

The logic of the argument demands that he means by "God" both "the Father and the Son." If he were thinking of the Father alone, then the passage from St. Paul would not be "the greatest proof" of a conjunction of the Holy Spirit with the Son. Thus St. Basil is discerning here a single relation of the Holy Spirit to the Father and the Son, just as the human spirit has a single relation to the man whose spirit it is. It may be objected that the phrase ὁ Θεός ("God") in St. Basil is generally used to refer to the Father. While it is commonly so used when Basil wishes to refer to the Father as distinct from the other persons—ὁ Κύριος ("the Lord") being commonly used of the Son considered as a distinct person—this is no argument against its being used of the Father and the Son considered in their unity, as is apparently the case

---

29 *PG*, 32:144A.

here. On the other hand, it is not clear that he is speaking here of anything more than the consubstantiality of the Holy Spirit with the Father and the Son.

The Holy Spirit Is Joined to the Father through the Son

Elsewhere he will speak almost at the same time of a relation of the Holy Spirit to the Father *through* the Son and of a relation "to the Father and the Son." The following passage is the most explicit in the present treatise:

> One moreover is the Holy Spirit, and we speak of Him singly, conjoined as He is to the one Father through the one Son [δι' ἑνὸς Υἱοῦ τῷ ἑνὶ Πατρὶ συναπτόμενον], and through Himself completing the adorable and blessed Trinity. Of Him the intimate relationship [οἰκείωσιν] to the Father and the Son is sufficiently declared by the fact of His not being ranked in the plurality of the creation but being spoken of singly; for he is not one of many, but One. For as there is one Father and one Son, so is there one Holy Ghost. He is consequently as far removed from created nature as reason requires the singular to be removed from compound and plural bodies; and He is in such a way[30] united to the Father and to the Son as unity has affinity with unity [Πατρὶ δὲ καὶ Υἱῷ κατὰ τοσοῦτον ἥνωται, καθόσον ἔχει μονὰς πρὸς μονάδα τὴν οἰκειότητα]. (45)[31]

It is certain that St. Basil is speaking of the Trinity in itself, independently of the economy. It is in the Trinity as it exists eternally that the Holy Spirit is "conjoined" or "attached" to the Father by means of the Son. Again, the word "attached," along with the preposition διά ("by

[30] The original translator used the now-obsolete expression "in such wise."

[31] *PG*, 32:149C–52A.

means of"), shows that it is not simple consubstantiality that is in question, but something "dynamic."[32] It is thus highly misleading when Siecienski writes that Basil uses the expression διὰ τοῦ Υἱοῦ ("through the Son") to describe our coming to know God, while making no reference to a passage such as this.[33]

The latter part of this passage is difficult. The saint first offers an argument for the divinity of the Holy Spirit based on his unity. The idea seems to be that we know that the Holy Spirit, unlike any creature that could be conceived of, is not the kind of "thing" of which there could in principle be more than one, and hence he is not a creature. The last sentence of the passage is particularly interesting. In saying that the Holy Spirit is united to the Father and the Son in the way that unity has affinity with unity, the saint appears to be teaching that the Holy Spirit is united to the Father and the Son insofar as they are one, not insofar as They are two.[34] Since the uniting of the Holy Spirit with the other divine persons is not distinguished from his being "attached" to the Father through the Son, which in turn can refer only to his eternal existence, we are justified in saying that St. Basil here teaches, in different words, the derivation of the Holy Spirit from the Father and the Son as from one principle.

The Holy Spirit Is "Breath of God's Mouth"

Immediately after the passage just quoted, the saint continues:

> He is moreover said to be "of God"; not indeed in the sense in which "all things are of God," but in the sense of proceeding out of God [ἐκ τοῦ θεοῦ προελθόν], not by generation, like the

32 Moreover, the passage cannot be understood of some eternal "manifestation" of the Holy Spirit, distinct from his personal existence, since St. Basil explicitly says that he is speaking of the Holy Spirit insofar as He "completes" the Trinity.

33 Siecienski, *Filioque*, 40.

34 In the St. Vladimir's Press edition, Anderson translates: "He is united to the Father and the Son as unit dwells with unit."

> Son, but as the breath [Πνεῦμα] of His mouth.[35] But in no way is the "mouth" a member, nor the Spirit breath that can be dissolved; but the word "mouth" is used so far as it can be appropriate to God, and the Spirit is a substance having life, gifted with the supreme power of sanctification. Thus the close relation is made plain, while the mode of the ineffable existence is safeguarded. He is moreover styled "Spirit of Christ," as being by nature closely related [ᾠκειωμένον κατὰ τὴν φύσιν] to Him.[36] Wherefore "if any man have not the Spirit of Christ, he is none of His." He alone worthily glorifies the Lord [Christ], for, it is said, "He shall glorify me," not as the creature but as "Spirit of Truth," clearly shewing forth the truth in Himself, and as Spirit of wisdom, in His own greatness revealing Christ "the power of God and the wisdom of God." (46)[37]

St. Basil has in mind here Psalms 32:6: "By the word of the Lord the heavens were made and by the breath of his mouth all the stars." This metaphor or analogy is the closest that he comes to giving an account of the ἐκπόρευσις of the Holy Spirit and the manner in which it differs from generation. Is he thinking of the Father or of the Father and the Son when he speaks of "proceeding out of God" here? The scriptural verse itself suggests the Father, distinguishing as it does God, the Word, and the Breath. One might have expected the saint to identify the Son with "the mouth," given the preceding paragraph; but he does not do so, perhaps because of the lack of an explicit scriptural basis for this identification. However, as if unwilling to give the impression that only the Father is the one who breathes the Holy Spirit, he supplements the

35 Anderson, in the St. Vladimir's Press edition, uses the word "Father" in this sentence and the following one, where St. Basil simply speaks of the mouth of *God*.

36 Mark Eugenikos quoted this sentence in his principal speech at Florence and argued that St. Basil could not have expressed himself like this if he believed in the procession from the Son (*AG*, 374–75). He did not quote any other passage from St. Basil's treatise.

37 *PG*, 32:152A–C.

verse from the psalm with New Testament titles for the third person that "define" him in relation to the second.[38]

He then continues: "As Paraclete He expresses in Himself [ἐν ἑαυτῷ χαρακτηρίζει] the goodness of the Paraclete[39] who sent Him, and in His own dignity manifests the majesty of Him from whom He proceeded [τὴν μεγαλωσύνην ἐμφαίνει τὴν τοῦ ὅθεν προῆλθεν]." The almost unconscious way in which St. Basil passes from what belongs to the Holy Spirit by nature to what he performs as Paraclete strongly suggests that he takes for granted that the relations of the "economy" must perfectly reflect the eternal relations. The verb he uses for the Spirit's "expressing" the goodness of the Son recalls the use of the same word, "character," in the New Testament to describe the Son's relation to the Father (Heb 1:3). What of the statement that the Holy Spirit's dignity manifests the majesty of the one from whom he proceeded? In their commentaries on this point in the text, the translators are uncertain about whether to understand this as a reference to the Father or the Son. Blomfield Jackson leaves the question undecided; Benoît Pruche affirms that, in its literal sense, it is a reference to the Father. But this latter interpretation appears slightly forced; the saint has been speaking of the Son exclusively for several lines, and so, if he wished a reference to the Father to be understood, it would be more natural to name him in some unmistakeable way. Is he speaking of a temporal or an eternal procession? Since the same word, προῆλθεν, is used here as was used at the beginning of the paragraph, where it was certainly a reference to the eternal existence of the Holy Spirit, and since St. Basil makes no distinction between two different senses of the word, we are justified in seeing here also a reference to the

38 *PG*, 32:136C. One may also note that St. Basil makes no difference in meaning between προελθόν (the aorist form of προεῖσι) in this passage and ἐκπορεύεται, the word he uses in the same context in section 38, where he writes that "the Spirit of the mouth of God is the Spirit of truth who proceeds from the Father." This fact militates against the central argument of the 1995 document of the Pontifical Council for Promoting Christian Unity, that these two verbs, προεῖσι and ἐκπορεύεται, signify different relations of the Holy Spirit to the Father.

39 The St. Vladimir's Press edition puts in brackets the word "Father" at this point in the text. I do not know of any other interpreters who hold that the first Paraclete (the one who sends the Spirit) is the Father and not Christ.

eternal procession, even if the temporal mission is also implied. Once again, his manner of writing suggests that he takes for granted the correlation between what is eternal and what is temporal.

The Meaning of διά

We have already noted the saint's teaching that the Holy Spirit is "joined" to the Father through (διά) the Son. The meaning of the word διά as used by the Greek Fathers for the relation of the Son and the Holy Spirit was much later to become a matter of controversy. It is therefore worth considering a passage earlier in the treatise where the saint discusses the use of the preposition more generally. When creation is said to have been performed through (διά) the Son, he notes, this is not said as if the Father's creative activity is imperfect by itself, nor again as if the Son created in some lesser way. It rather indicates the unity of the will that passes from the Father to the Son, though remaining one will. Hence, "the expression 'through whom' contains a confession of an antecedent cause [προκαταρκτικῆς αἰτίας], and is not adopted in objection to the efficient cause [οὐκ ἐπι κατηγορίᾳ τοῦ ποιητικοῦ αἰτίου παραλαμβάνεται]" (21).[40] The relevance of this to the intra-Trinitarian relations is obvious. When St. Basil asserts that the Holy Spirit is joined to the Father through the Son, this implies that the Son is truly an "efficient cause," or in the usual Western terminology, a true principle in virtue of which the Holy Spirit is thus joined, while the Father is the first principle in the sense that it is from him that the Son is αἰτία ποιητική.

The Order of the Divine Persons Revealed by Their Working

At one point in the treatise, St. Basil makes explicit the way in which the working of the divine persons in the faithful reflects their eternal order. He does not speak precisely of a correspondence between the divine processions and the divine missions, however, but of one that

---

[40] *PG*, 32:105C.

exists between the processions and the knowledge engendered within us by their missions:

> When, by means of the power that enlightens us, we fix our eyes on the beauty of the image of the invisible God, and through the image are led up to the supreme beauty of the spectacle of the archetype, then, I ween, is with us inseparably the Spirit of knowledge, in Himself bestowing on them that love the vision of the truth the power of beholding the Image, not making the exhibition from without, but in Himself leading on to the full knowledge. "No man knoweth the Father save the Son." And so "no man can say that Jesus is the Lord but by the Holy Ghost." . . . It results that in Himself He shows the glory of the only-begotten, and on true worshippers He in Himself bestows the knowledge of God. Thus the way of the knowledge of God lies from One Spirit through the One Son to the One Father, and conversely the natural Goodness and the inherent Holiness and the royal Dignity extend [διήκει] from the Father through the Only-begotten to the Spirit. Thus there is both acknowledgement of the hypostases and the true dogma of the Monarchy is not lost. They on the other hand who support their subnumeration by speaking of first and second and third ought to be informed that into the undefiled theology of Christians they are importing the polytheism of heathen error. (47)[41]

Here is contrasted the knowledge of the Trinity with the Trinity in itself. In the former, the Holy Spirit enlightens us to know the Son, who as image grants us knowledge of the Father. In the latter, the divine nature (the "natural goodness and inherent holiness") passes from the Father through the Son to the Holy Spirit. Provided that one does not

[41] *PG*, 32:153A–C.

allow oneself to imagine this process in a material sense, as if the Son were a mere "place" through which the divine nature passes, it is clear that this implies that the Son is a principle of the Holy Spirit's possession of the divine nature. Since the Holy Spirit and the Son are real principles of the knowledge, it is natural to understand that the Father and the Son are real principles of the transmission of the divine nature. This passage, in fact, differs little from the disputed passage from book 3 of *Adversus Eunomium* already discussed: "The Holy Spirit has his being from the Son and receives from him and is, in short, dependent upon this principle" (3.1).

Homily 24

Mark Eugenikos, in his principal speech at Florence, quoted this passage from St. Basil's Homily 24, against Sabellians, Arians, and Eunomians:

> I acknowledge the Spirit as being with the Father, not as being the Father; I have received him as being with the Son, not as called Son; I perceive his relation [οἰκειότητα] with the Father, because he proceeds from the Father, and his relation with the Son, because I hear: "If anyone does not have the Spirit of Christ, he is not his."[42]

Eugenikos insisted that nothing could show more clearly than this passage that St. Basil would have rejected the dogma of the Latins, and that he taught that the Holy Spirit was related to the Son only by consubstantiality; if Basil had believed in a procession from the Son, this would have been the moment to mention it.[43] One may reply to this that the saint was intending to limit himself to scriptural expressions in order to argue with the greatest authority, and that his intention was

42 *PG*, 31:612BC.
43 *AG*, 375.

not to investigate the origin of the Holy Spirit, but to declare the real distinction of the divine persons. John of Montenero, in his response to Eugenikos, argued that the same passage told clearly in favor of the Latin position: since Basil explains relationship in regard to the Father by referring to the Holy Spirit's origin, it is reasonable to assume that he is also thinking of a relationship of origin when he compares the Holy Spirit and the Son.[44] It certainly seems true that if Basil had thought there was *no* relationship of origin between the Son and the Holy Spirit, it would have been natural to say so, to avoid giving a false impression.

Summary and Conclusion

Despite the difficulties of interpretation that we have encountered in this section, sufficient evidence remains that St. Basil would have accepted the Florentine definition of the *Filioque*. Both his words at the end of book 2 of *Adversus Eunomium* and his explanation of διά in *De Spiritu Sancto* show a belief that the Son is a true principle of the Holy Spirit, and that the Son has this from the Father. This belief is confirmed by other passages in the same treatise, and all these passages taken together provide the best criterion to judge of the authenticity of the disputed passages against Eunomius. The a priori hermeneutic principle quoted from Bulgakov at the beginning of this investigation into St. Basil does not appear to do justice to the facts.

44 *AL*, 220.

CHAPTER 6

SAINT EPIPHANIUS

Introduction

St. Epiphanius was born between the years 310 and 320 in Palestine and studied in Egypt. Afterward he founded a monastery in his homeland; around the year 366 he became bishop of Salamis in Cyprus, which see he ruled until his death in 402. His wide experience of the Eastern Church, therefore, as well as his well-known devotion to the cause of orthodoxy, make him an important witness for our question, while his two principal doctrinal works, the *Ancoratus* and the *Panarion*, afford a wealth of relevant passages.[1] In this section I shall not quote all such passages, but rather a representative sample.

---

1 Epiphanius, *Ancoratus*, trans. Young Richard Kim, Fathers of the Church 128 (Washington, DC: Catholic University of America Press, 2014); *The Panarion of St. Epiphanius, Bishop of Salamis: Selected Passages*, trans. Philip R. Amidon (New York: Oxford University Press, 1990); *The Panarion*, trans. Frank Williams (Leiden: Brill, 2013). Unless otherwise stated, translations for *Ancoratus* are from Kim and those for the *Panarion* are from Amidon. Kim dates the *Ancoratus* to the years 373–374; Amidon dates the *Panarion* to 374–376.

An Eternal Procession and Reception

St. Epiphanius frequently characterizes the Holy Spirit by the scriptural phrases "proceeding from the Father" and "receiving from the Son." Moreover, he does so in a way that can be understood only of the Holy Spirit's eternal, personal existence. Thus in the *Ancoratus* he writes:

> We do not say gods: [we say] God the Father, God the Son, God the Holy Spirit, and not gods. For there is no polytheism in God. But through the three names, the one divinity of the Father, Son and Holy Spirit [is indicated]. And there are not two sons: for the one Son is Only-begotten, and the Holy Spirit is the Spirit that is holy, the "Spirit of God," always existing with the Father and Son, not alien from God, but being from God, "proceeding from the Father" and "receiving from the Son." But the Only-begotten Son is incomprehensible, and the Spirit is incomprehensible, and from God, not alien from the Father and the Son. He is not a coalescence of the Father and the Son. But the Trinity is always of the same *ousia*,[2] neither another *ousia* besides the divinity, nor another divinity besides the *ousia*, but the same divinity and from the same divinity, the Son and the Holy Spirit. (6.9)

The Holy Spirit is God, possessing the one divinity, insofar as he proceeds from the Father and receives from the Son.

At other times, St. Epiphanius, having quoted the same scriptural phrases already mentioned, repeats the same idea by the use of prepositions. Sometimes he uses the preposition ἐκ, for example, in the *Ancoratus*:

---

2 Kim retains the Greek word in his translation.

Each of the names is mononymic [μονώνυμον[3]], not having a duplication. For the Father is Father and has no parallel, nor is he joined together with another father, so that there may not be two gods. And [the] Son is only-begotten, true God from true God, not having the name of Father, nor being alien from the Father, but existing as Son of the Father. He is only-begotten, that the "Son" may be mononymic; and he is God from God, in order that Father and Son may be called one God. And the Holy Spirit is one-of-a-kind, not having the name of "Son," nor having the name of "Father," but thus called Holy Spirit, not alien from the Father. For the Only-begotten himself says: "The Spirit of the Father," and "the one proceeding from the Father," and "he will receive from what is mine," in order that he may not be believed alien from the Father and the Son, but of the same *ousia*, the same divinity, divine Spirit, the "Spirit of truth," the "Spirit of God," the Spirit "Paraclete," called mononymically, not having a parallel, not being equated with some other spirit, not called by the name of the Son or being named with the naming of the Father, in order that the mononymic names may not be homonymic, except "God" in the Father, "God" in the Son, in the Holy Spirit, "of God" and "God." For the "Spirit of God," both Spirit of the Father and Spirit of the Son, is not according to some synthesis, as soul and body are in us, but is in the midst of Father and Son, from the Father and the Son [ἐκ τοῦ Πατρὸς καὶ τοῦ Υἱοῦ], third in naming. For it says, "Going forth, baptize in the name of the Father, Son and Holy Spirit." (8.1–7)[4]

Likewise in the *Panarion*:

---

3 Kim suggests that St. Epiphanius may have coined this Greek word, which is not attested in other authors. It could be translated "singular, unique name" (*Ancoratus*, 72n1).

4 *PG*, 43:29A–32A.

> There is one God, Father, Son and Holy Spirit. For the Spirit is forever with the Father and the Son—not brother to the Father, not begotten, not created, not the Son's brother, not the Father's offspring. He proceeds from the Father and receives of the Son and is not different from the Father and the Son, but is of the same essence, of the same Godhead, of the Father and the Son [ἐκ Πατρὸς καὶ Υἱοῦ], with the Father and the Son, forever an actual Holy Spirit—divine Spirit, Spirit of glory, Spirit of Christ, Spirit of the Father. (62.4.1)[5]

Elsewhere he uses the preposition ἐκ in relation to the Son and παρά in relation to the Father:

> If therefore "he proceeds from the Father" and "will receive from what is mine," the Lord says, just as "no one knows the Father except the Son, nor the Son except the Father," thus I dare to say that [no one knows] the Spirit except the Son from whom he receives and the Father from whom he proceeds. And [no one knows] the Son and the Father, except the Holy Spirit, the one who truly glorifies, the one who teaches all things, the one who bears witness concerning the Son, who is from the Father, who is of the Son [ὅ παρὰ τοῦ Πατρός, καὶ ἐκ τοῦ Υἱοῦ], the only guide of truth, expounder of holy laws." (*Ancoratus* 73.1–2)[6]

Mark of Ephesus argued at the Council of Florence that this text could be understood not of the Holy Spirit's hypostatic existence, but of his temporal mission: since the word ἐστιν ("is") was not found with the Greek words inserted in the extract above, we might understand some other verb, for example, "sent." His Latin interlocutor, John of Montenero, argued that where no other verb was implied by

5 *PG*, 41:1053D–56A.
6 *PG*, 43:153A.

the context, only the verb "to be" could be inserted, as indeed Young Richard Kim has done in this translation.[7] Perhaps a stronger argument in favor of Montenero's position is to point out the places already mentioned where "proceeding from the Father" and "receiving from the Son" can be understood only of the eternal existence of the Holy Spirit.

At other times, St. Epiphanius uses the preposition παρά in relation to both Father and Son:

> But someone will say: "Therefore, we say that there are two sons, and how is he only-begotten?" "No! Who are you, speaking against God?" For if he [the Father] calls the one from him "Son," and the Holy Spirit the one from both [τὸν Υἱὸν καλεῖ τὸν ἐξ αὐτοῦ, τὸ δὲ ἅγιον Πνεῦμα τὸ παρ'ἀμφοτέρων], *who being perceived by the saints by faith alone, as shining and illuminating, have a light-giving activity and make for themselves a harmony of light with the Father himself, for faith,*[8] listen, O man, because the Father is Father of the true Son, entire light, and [the] Son is [Son] of the true Father, light from light, not in appellation alone, as things which are made or created. And the Holy Spirit is the "Spirit of truth," third light from [παρά] the Father and the Son. But all the others [sons and spirits] are by adoption and by name, not similar to these in activity or power or light or notion. (*Ancoratus* 71.1–3)[9]

Thus, while he retains the scriptural language of proceeding (ἐκπορεύεσθαι) from the Father and receiving or taking (λαμβάνειν) from the Son, his own commentary on this language makes no

---

7 *AG*, 272.

8 The italicized content here is my own translation; the original Greek is: ἅ μόνον πίστει νοούμενα ὑπο τῶν ἁγίων, φωτεινά, φωτοδότα, φωτεινὴν τὴν ἐνέργειαν ἔχει, σύμφωνά τε πρὸς τὸν Πατέρα ποιεῖται φωτὸς πίστει. Kim has the incomprehensible translation "what alone is by faith being thought by the saints, that he is shining, illuminating, has illuminating activity, and makes a harmony 'of light' with the 'Father' himself," and then takes πίστει with the next sentence, beginning it "by faith listen."

9 *PG*, 43:148B.

distinction between the Holy Spirit's relations to the first two divine persons.[10] Likewise, the distinction between ἐκ and παρά seems to have no significance in his thought.

Finally in this section, we may note that as he speaks of the Holy Spirit as being from the Father and the Son, so also he speaks of him as from their essence:

> For the Spirit is forever with the Father and the Son—not brother to the Father, not begotten, not created, not the Son's brother, not the Father's offspring. He proceeds from the Father and receives of the Son, and is not different from the Father and the Son, but is of the same essence [ἐκ τῆς αὐτῆς οὐσίας], of the same Godhead, of the Father and the Son [ἐκ Πατρὸς καὶ Υἱοῦ], with the Father and the Son, forever an actual Holy Spirit—divine Spirit, Spirit of glory, Spirit of Christ, Spirit of the Father. For [scripture says], "It is the Spirit of the Father that speaketh in you," and, "My Spirit is in the midst of you." He is third in name but equal in Godhead, not different from the Father and the Son, bond of the Trinity, seal of the confession of it. (*Panarion* 62.4.1–2)[11]

"Of the same essence" here is somewhat misleading, as it suggests simple consubstantiality. Had St. Epiphanius wished to express this idea, he could have used the term ὁμοούσιος, which he uses of the Holy Spirit elsewhere in the *Panarion*.[12] In fact, the preposition ἐκ, especially when used in the phrase ἐκ Πατρὸς καὶ Υἱοῦ, denotes the eternal coming forth of the Holy Spirit.

---

[10] Martin Jugie remarks that the verb λαμβάνειν is more suited to describe the eternal procession than is ἐκπορεύεσθαι, since the former carries less suggestion of a movement *ad extra* (*De Processione Spiritus Sancti* [Rome: Facultas Theologica Pontificii Athenaei Seminarii Romani, 1936], 80–81).

[11] *PG*, 41:1053D–56A. The translation is Williams's.

[12] Kim, in his introduction to the *Ancoratus* (31), notes Epiphanius's use of ὁμοούσιος for the Holy Spirit, referencing *Panarion* 74.11.6–13.9.

The Holy Spirit as the Bond of the Trinity

In the seventh chapter of the *Ancoratus*, this passage occurs:

> The Spirit is the one proceeding from the Father and receiving from the Son, searching the depths of God, announcing the things of the Son in the world, sanctifying the saints through the Trinity, third in naming (since the Trinity is Father, Son, and Holy Spirit: for it says "going forth, baptize in the name of the Father, Son, and Holy Spirit"), seal of grace, bond of the Trinity [σύνδεσμος τῆς Τριάδος], not alien from the number, not separate from the naming, not a stranger from the gift. (7.1)[13]

According to Yves Congar, St. Epiphanius is the only one of the Eastern Fathers to speak of the Holy Spirit as "communion between the Father and the Son."[14] "Communion," however, suggests a definition of the Holy Spirit as a mutual exchange between the Father and the Son, which is not quite what Epiphanius says here. On the other hand, it is certainly significant that the bishop of Salamis "defines" the third person here with reference to the Father and the Son.

The Son as Breather and Fount of the Holy Spirit

Does Epiphanius ever speak explicitly of procession—ἐκπόρευσις—from the Son? There is one doubtful passage in the *Ancoratus*:

> The one who supposes that the Son, truly of the Father, is lacking the glory of the Father, rather dishonours [the Father]; instead of honour, he is being carried away by ignorance. So, as [the Son] reveals the Father, saying, "No one knows the Father if not

13 *PG*, 43:28A–B.

14 Yves Congar, *I Believe in the Holy Spirit*, vol. 3, Milestones in Catholic Theology (New York: Crossroad, 1997), 88.

> the Son, and no one knows the Son if not the Father," thus I dare to say that no one knows the Spirit if not the Father and the Son, from whom he [the Spirit] proceeds, and from whom he receives [Οὐδὲ τὸ Πνεῦμα τις οἶδεν, εἰ μὴ ὁ Πατὴρ καὶ ὁ Υἱὸς παρ᾽οὗ ἐκπορεύεται καὶ παρ᾽οὗ λαμβάνει]. (11.2–3)[15]

This passage also came under discussion at the Council of Florence. John of Montenero had a slightly different version from that just quoted. Instead of the Greek words inserted in the extract above, his copy read: Οὐδὲ τὸ Πνεῦμα οἶδε τις, εἰ μὴ ὁ Πατὴρ καὶ ὁ Υἱὸς ἀφ᾽οὗ λαμβάνει καὶ ἐκπορεύεται ("no one knows the Spirit if not the Father and the Son from whom he receives and proceeds"). Mark of Ephesus, on the other hand, had the same text as given in the extract.[16] While Mark's reading, which is that followed by Kim, as well as by the editors of Migne's *Patrologia Graeca*, can be understood to speak of a procession from the Son, it could also be understood—or so the bishop of Ephesus argued—as dividing the two verbs between Father and Son respectively. John's version, on the other hand, with its one singular pronoun, must refer either to a receiving and proceeding from the Son or to a receiving and proceeding from both Father and Son considered as one principle. If one were to suppose that the text had deliberately been changed, it seems more likely that it would have been changed to Mark's version by some scribe who wished to purge the reference to ἐκπόρευσις in relation to the Son. For, if a scribe in favor of the *Filioque* had made the change, altering Mark's version to Montenero's by removing the second παρ᾽οὗ,[17] why would he also have reversed the order of the verbs ἐκπορεύεσθαι and λαμβάνειν? Such a reversal would not have strengthened his position. On the other hand, an "anti-filioquist" scribe who had added a παρ᾽οὗ would have needed also to reverse the

---

15 *PG*, 43:36C.

16 *AG*, 256–57.

17 The variation between παρ᾽οὗ and ἀφ᾽οὗ does not seem significant.

verbs if they were to be attributed respectively to the Father and the Son. However, we cannot reach a certain conclusion—nor confidently attribute to St. Epiphanius the expression ἐκπορεύεται παρὰ τοῦ Υἱοῦ—on the strength of this isolated case.

Yet it is only the acceptance of this verbal expression by the saint that remains uncertain, not his acceptance of the doctrine that it enshrines.[18] The texts already quoted justify Henry Barclay Swete's comment that "it seems quite clear that [St. Epiphanius] regards the Son as being together with the Father, in the Unity of Their Consubstantial Life, the One Source and Origin of the Holy Ghost."[19] But there are other texts that, if possible, are even more decisive. In the *Ancoratus*, he speaks of the "breathing" of the Holy Spirit from the Father and the Son:

> Some people are accustomed, deciding wrongly and not thinking, to differentiate the reading in the saying, "All things came to be through him, and apart from him nothing came to be," while thus setting aside the literal meaning, to accept an opinion of blasphemy against the Holy Spirit. They err concerning the reading, and from the error of reading they stumble, being turned toward blasphemy. Thus the reading has: "All things came to be through him, and apart from him nothing came to be, that which has come to be in him," that is to say that if something has come to be, it came to be through him. Therefore the Father always was, and the Son always was; and the Spirit breathes forth from Father and Son [τὸ Πνεῦμα ἐκ Πατρὸς καὶ Υἱοῦ πνέει], and neither is the Son created nor is the Spirit created. But after Father, Son and Holy Spirit, all

18 Bernard de Margerie notes that there is nothing in St. Epiphanius to suggest that he thought that the verb ἐκπορεύεται could be used only in relation to the "principle without principle" ("Vers une relecture du concile de Florence, grâce à la reconsidération de l'Ecriture et des pères grecs et latins," *Revue thomiste* 86 [1986]: 31–81, at 38). He believes that this usage begins with Gregory Nazianzen (40).

19 Henry Barclay Swete, *On the History of the Doctrine of the Procession of the Holy Spirit: From the Apostolic Age to the Death of Charlemagne* (Cambridge: Deighton and Bell, 1876; repr., n.p.: Nabu, 2014), 97.

> things, created and originated, not existing at some point in time, came to be from Father and Son and Holy Spirit. (75.1–3)[20]

While the breathing is attributed here to the Holy Spirit himself, rather than to the Father and the Son, the two ideas are obviously correlative: if the Holy Spirit can be said to "breathe forth" from them eternally, they can be said to breathe him forth eternally.

In the *Panarion*, writing against the Ariomaniacs ("the mad Arians"), he considers their argument that there must be a difference of nature between Father and Son, because one is sender, the other sent. He replies:

> There is a sender and a sent, showing that there is one source of all good things, the Father; but next after the source comes one who—to correspond with his name of Son and Word, and not with any other—is one Source springing from a Source [πηγὴ ἐκ πηγῆς], the Son come forth, ever with the Father but begotten. "For with thee is the source of life." And to show the name of the Holy Spirit, "In thy light we shall see light," showing that the Father is light, the Son is the Father's light, and the Holy Spirit is light, and a Source springing from a Source, from the Father and the Only-begotten—the Holy Spirit [ἐκ τοῦ Πατρὸς καὶ τοῦ μονογενοῦς τὸ Πνεῦμα τὸ ἅγιον]. "For out of his belly shall flow rivers of living water springing up unto eternal life; but," says the Gospel, "he said this of the Holy Spirit." (69.54.1)[21]

The Son is here described as a "source" of the Holy Spirit not merely in his humanity, but insofar as he is "ever with the Father." Epiphanius also here reaches the doctrine of the Father and the Son as one principle of the Holy Spirit, though without quite expressly formulating it: the Holy

20 *PG*, 43:157A–B.
21 *PG*, 42:285C–D.

Spirit is described as a source springing not from two sources, but "from a source, from the Father and the Only-begotten."

Conclusion: The Value of St. Epiphanius's Testimony

Such testimony from an Eastern Father of the Church places opponents of the *Filioque* in a difficult position. A. Edward Siecienski writes:

> Whether he [St. Epiphanius] thought in terms of the Spirit receiving existence, consubstantiality, or temporal mission "from the Son" has been debated for centuries—the Latin West seeing in Epiphanius a clear witness to the *filioque* [sic], the East preferring to read these texts as references to the Spirit's missio (which he receives from Christ Himself). It must be admitted that Epiphanius's language allows for either reading, with scholars still divided over his precise meaning.[22]

I have already argued against the idea that the saint's language allows for either reading: he speaks of the Holy Spirit as from the Father and the Son, or proceeding and receiving, in contexts where the eternal nature of these relations is made clear.[23] Pace Siecienski, it is not only the "Latin West" that has so judged: Bessarion, metropolitan of Nicaea, after reading quotations from Epiphanius to the other Greek bishops at Florence, declared that he could see no way of denying that the saint considered the Son a "principle," αἰτία, of the Holy Spirit.[24] In modern times, Congar has acknowledged that St. Epiphanius "is clearly referring . . . to the intra-divine being" in the quotations of which I have given a representative sample.[25]

---

22 A. Edward Siecienski, *The Filioque: History of a Doctrinal Controversy* (New York: Oxford University Press, 2010), 45.

23 Again, it is impossible that the Holy Spirit should "receive consubstantiality" from the Son except by proceeding as a divine person from the Son.

24 Bessarion, *Oratio Dogmatica de Unione* (*PG*, 161:602B). In the Latin translation he made later, Bessarion was still more forthright: speaking of Epiphanius's and Cyril's writings, he asked, "what can be plainer or clearer than these?" (*PG*, 161:602C).

25 Congar, *I Believe in the Holy Spirit*, 27.

For such reasons, Sergei Bulgakov felt himself obliged, as it were, to repudiate St. Epiphanius as writing "imprecisely and primitively, without any theological sophistication." The Russian theologian declared: "To be sure, it is impossible to deny all connection between the immanent Trinity and the economic Trinity, but neither should one identify these relations, as St. Epiphanius does when he simply counts 'from Both,' from the hypostases of the Father and the Son."[26] In reply, I should simply note that, while none of the Fathers taken in isolation is infallible, the witness of St. Epiphanius to the apostolic doctrine concerning the origin of the Holy Spirit can surely not be rejected without rashness, given his devotion to the cause of tradition, and given the years of his episcopacy, running as it did from fifteen years before the First Council of Constantinople to more than twenty years afterward—the Council that concerned itself, more than any other of the first millennium, with the status of the third divine Person.

26 Sergei Bulgakov, *The Comforter*, trans. Boris Jakim (Grand Rapids, MI: Eerdmans, 2004), 82.

CHAPTER 7

SAINT GREGORY OF NAZIANZEN

Introduction

St. Gregory Nazianzen's teaching on the Holy Spirit is found in his various Orations, especially in the "Theological Orations," preached at Constantinople between the years 379 and 381.[1] As with his friend St. Basil, Gregory's principal concern in speaking of the Holy Spirit is to defend his true divinity, against both those who would simply deny it and those who, though at heart orthodox, had been so confused or discouraged by the heresies of the times that they were reluctant to confess it openly. The saint does not consider the relation of the Son and the Holy Spirit directly and of set purpose, and so his teaching on the subject has to be discerned carefully. Sergei Bulgakov comments somewhat sarcastically that "even Catholic

1 Gregory Nazianzen, Selected Orations, trans. Charles Browne and James Swallow, 203–435 in *NPNF2* vol. 7. All quotations of the Orations are taken from Browne and Swallow unless otherwise stated. In-text citations are to section numbers in the original text, not page numbers in the English edition.

theologians cannot find the *Filioque* in St. Gregory the Theologian except by drawing some suspect conclusions from his theses."[2] In this section I shall indeed be drawing some conclusions from what Nazianzen says; but I believe that the harmony that will be revealed as a result among his various Orations, especially in regard to some of their more obscure passages, will render these conclusions not suspect but convincing.

Oration 31 (Fifth Theological Oration)

This is the only one of the Orations expressly devoted to the doctrine of the Holy Spirit. St. Gregory's opponents, denying the divinity of the third person, offer this dilemma: either he is begotten or else he is unbegotten. In the first case he will be no different from the Son, in the second no different from the Father. In either case he will not be a distinct, divine hypostasis. Gregory answers by denying the adequacy of this division: to proceed is a third alternative in addition to being begotten or unbegotten. After quoting the scriptural phrase about "the Holy Spirit who proceeds from the Father," he goes on: "[The Holy Spirit], inasmuch as He proceeds from that source, is no creature; and inasmuch as He is not Begotten, is no Son; and inasmuch as He is between [μέσον] the Unbegotten and the Begotten is God" (8). Rather than explain here what he means by "between," he humorously anticipates his opponents' next question: "What then is procession? Do you tell me what is the Unbegottenness of the Father, and I will explain to you the physiology of the Generation of the Son and the Procession of the Holy Spirit, and we shall both of us be frenzy-stricken for prying into the mystery of God" (8). He continues more seriously:

2 Sergei Bulgakov, *The Comforter*, trans. Boris Jakim (Grand Rapids, MI: Eerdmans, 2004), 79.

> What then, they say, is there lacking to the Spirit which prevents His being a Son, for if there were not something lacking He would be a Son? We assert that there is nothing lacking—for God has no deficiency. But the difference of manifestation [τὸ δὲ τῆς ἐκφάνσεως . . . διάφορον], if I may so express myself, or rather of their mutual relations one to another [τῆς πρὸς ἄλληλα σχέσεως διάφορον], has caused the difference of their Names. For indeed it is not some deficiency in the Son which prevents His being Father (for Sonship is not a deficiency) and yet He is not Father. According to this line of argument there must be some deficiency in the Father in respect of His not being Son. For the Father is not Son, and yet this is not due to either deficiency or subjection of Essence; but the very fact of being unbegotten or begotten or proceeding has given the name of the Father to the First, of the Son to the Second, and to the Third,[3] Him of whom we are speaking, of the Holy Ghost. (9)[4]

Several points are worthy of note here. First, St. Gregory makes clear that when he speaks of the Son and the Holy Spirit being eternally "manifested," he does not mean anything other than the relation itself by which the Son and the Holy Spirit exist, each as a distinct divine person. For it is this very "manifestation"—of their persons—that causes the difference in their names.[5] Next, the Son and the Holy Spirit can be said to be distinct either in virtue of the distinction between generation and procession or in virtue of their relation to each other.[6] Finally,

3 The translation is slightly free here; St. Gregory does not use the ordinal numbers. This is a point of some (though secondary) importance, as the legitimacy of calling the Holy Spirit "third" was disputed at the Council of Florence between Mark of Ephesus and John of Montenero (*AG*, 317).

4 *PG*, 36:141B–44A.

5 See Frederick W. Norris, *Faith Gives Fullness to Reasoning: The Five Theological Orations of Gregory Nazianzen*, Supplements to *Vigiliae Christianae* 13 (Leiden: Brill, 1990), 193: "'Manifestation' appears to have no special technical meaning in this section. It simply means that the persons of the Trinity can be distinguished."

6 Although the translation given above suggests by the phrase "or rather" a preference for the latter reason of

whatever proceeding is, it establishes the name Holy Spirit, just as generating establishes the name Father. From this we can conclude that he is the Spirit of the one from whom he proceeds, just as the Father is the Father of the one whom he generates, and hence conversely that if he is by nature the Spirit of the Son, he also proceeds from Him.

That last argument might seem at first to be an example of the "fallacy of the consequent," as if I had argued that "if the Holy Spirit proceeds from a person, he is said to be of that person; but he is said to be of the Son; therefore he proceeds from the Son." This would be an invalid argument, akin to arguing that "if an animal can fly it has wings; but a penguin has wings; therefore a penguin can fly." The difference is that St. Gregory is telling us that procession is not just an attribute of the Holy Spirit: it *defines* the Holy Spirit (αὐτὸ . . . τὸ ἐκπορεύεσθαι . . . Πνεῦμα ἅγιον προσηγόρευσεν); and hence, to be the Spirit of the Son just is to proceed from the Son, just as to be the Father of the Son just is to generate the Son. The name "Holy Spirit," he is telling us, means "the Proceeder."

The suggestion that St. Gregory was a believer in the *Filioque* might seem to be undermined by the example of Adam, Seth, and Eve that he uses against those who allege that the Holy Spirit must be either begotten or not consubstantial. This illustration consists simply in pointing out that Eve was taken from the side of Adam, and, hence not begotten, and yet was just as consubstantial with Adam as Seth was (11). Henry Barclay Swete, in fact, says of this analogy: "The comparison must not be pressed, but it is scarcely consistent with any belief in a procession from the Son."[7] Without going so far as this, one might still ask why Gregory would choose such an illustration, which sheds no real light on the procession of the Holy Spirit, when one might have distinguished begetting from proceeding by saying that the principle of the former is

---

distinction, the Greek places the two reasons on equal footing, using the simple word ἤ ("or").

7 Henry Barclay Swete, *On the History of the Doctrine of the Procession of the Holy Spirit: From the Apostolic Age to the Death of Charlemagne* (Cambridge: Deighton and Bell, 1876; repr., n.p.: Nabu, 2014), 108.

one divine person, while the principle of the latter is two. Two answers present themselves. First, St. Gregory prefers to stay with the letter of Scripture, which in speaking of the procession of the Holy Spirit mentions only the Father; such prudence would be indicated in particular by the hostility of his opponents, ready to catch at any apparent novelty in his teaching. Secondly, his opponents are in the habit of making Catholics look ridiculous by asking whether the Holy Spirit is a grandson of the Father or a twin or a younger brother of the Son (7); to have said that procession was different from generation because the Holy Spirit came from two not from one would have offered a new avenue of attack for such minds who would have asked whether Father and Son were therefore like husband and wife, jointly producing an offspring.

Later in the same discourse, the holy bishop weighs several traditional analogies for the Trinity, finding them all unsuitable. The image of the "eye" or central part of a spring, the spring itself, and the river is unsuitable, as it seems to introduce change into the godhead (31); the image of the sun, the ray, and light might seem to make the Son and the Holy Spirit simple powers existing in the Father, and not themselves personal (32). But he does not object concerning either analogy that it would suggest that the Holy Spirit receives divinity through the Son; and so it is legitimate to suppose that he thought that the Holy Spirit did so receive divinity.

Oration 29 (Third Theological Oration)

This Oration was Nazianzen's first concerning God the Son. The defense of the Son's divinity leads to a discussion of how the unity of God is not undermined by Christian doctrine. The archbishop of Constantinople remarks first that there are three ancient opinions about the godhead, which he calls "anarchia," "polyarchia," and "monarchia," the first two being opinions entertained by pagans. He continues, in a difficult passage:

Monarchy is that which we hold in honour. It is, however, a Monarchy that is not limited to one Person,[8] for it is possible for Unity if at variance with itself [στασιάζον πρὸς ἑαυτό] to come into a condition of plurality; but one which is made of an equality of Nature and a Union of mind, and an identity of motion [ταυτότης κινέσεως], and a convergence of its elements to unity—a thing which is impossible to the created nature—so that though numerically distinct there is no severance of Essence. Therefore Unity having from all eternity arrived by motion at Duality, found its rest in Trinity [Διὰ τοῦτο μονὰς ἀπ' ἀρχῆς εἰς δυάδα κινηθεῖσα, μέχρι Τριάδος ἔστη]. This is what we mean by Father and Son and Holy Ghost. The Father is the Begetter and the Emitter [προβολεύς]; without passion, of course, and without reference to time, and not in a corporeal manner. The Son is the Begotten and the Holy Ghost the Emission [πρόβλημα]; for I know not how this could be expressed in terms altogether excluding visible things. For we shall not venture to speak of an overflow [ὑπέρχυσιν] of goodness, as one of the Greek philosophers dared to say as if it were a bowl overflowing, and this in plain words in his discourse on the first and second causes. Let us not ever look on this Generation as involuntary, like some natural overflow, hard to be retained, and by no means befitting our conception of Deity. Therefore let us confine ourselves within our limits, and speak of the Unbegotten and the Begotten and That which proceeds from the Father, as somewhere God the Word Himself saith. (2)[9]

St. Gregory calls only the Father the "Emitter" of the Holy Spirit, and not the Son. Does this imply a denial of the *Filioque*?[10] Looking at

8 This remark shows the falsity of the common claim that when the Greek fathers spoke of "monarchia" in respect of God, they were thinking only of God the Father. In ch. 1, on the 1995 document by the Pontifical Council for Promoting Christian Unity, see the section on "The Proposed Harmonization."

9 *PG*, 36:76B–C.

10 Mark of Ephesus adduced this as his first patristic text during his principal speech at Florence (*AG*, 66).

this passage alone, one might have supposed this, if it were not for the admittedly strange-sounding phrase that "Unity having from all eternity arrived by motion at Duality, found its rest in Trinity," or, as one might also translate it, "Unity, moved eternally into Duality, stands at last at Trinity."[11] St. Gregory appears to be seeking to express here something more than the truth that there are three divine persons owing to the generation and the procession. By using the nouns "Unity" and "Duality" he implies that what is signified by these words is the subject of, respectively, the "moving" and the "standing." In other words, the Unity, that is the Father, is "moved" into Duality by the begetting, while the Duality, that is the Father and the Son, stands at or takes its rest in the Trinity by means of the procession. As the Unity begets the second person, so the Duality spirates the third. Admittedly, this is an interpretation of Nazianzen's gnomic utterance; but it seems justified by his insistence at the beginning of the extract that when unity becomes plurality, the plurality then has one motion.

Oration 34: On the Arrival of the Egyptians

In this sermon, Nazianzen seeks to dispel the illusion that there can be any halfway point between being God in the full sense and being a creature:

> I find two highest differences in things that exist, viz., Rule and Service. . . . The Former is called God, and subsists in Three greatest, namely the Cause, the Creator and the Perfecter [αἰτίῳ, δημιουργῷ, τελειοποιῷ]; I mean the Father, the Son and the Holy Ghost. (8)[12]

[11] Norris renders it: "A one eternally changes to a two and stops at three" (*Faith Gives Fullness to Reasoning*, 246).
[12] *PG*, 36:248D–49A.

This is of importance as showing that, for St. Gregory, as for St. Basil, the words *αἰτία* or *αἴτιον* as used of the Father do not mean simply cause or principle, but rather "first cause" or "principle without principle." For, clearly creation—appropriated here to the Son—is also a form of causation. This allows us to have a proper understanding of what is said, according to the dominant manuscript tradition, a little later in the same oration: "All that the Father has belongs likewise to the Son except causality [πλὴν τῆς αἰτίας];[13] and all that is the Son's belongs also to the Spirit except his Sonship and whatever is spoken of him as to incarnation" (10). In this text, if indeed this be the correct reading, the saint would thus not be intending to deny that the Son could be a principle within the godhead, but that he is ever a principle without principle.[14]

Oration 25: In Praise of the Philosopher Hero

Oration 25 contains this passage:

> We do not call the Son unbegotten, for there is one unbegotten Father; nor do we call the Holy Spirit a Son, for there is one only-begotten, so that they may also have a unique divine thing, filiation for the former and procession but not filiation for the latter. We say that the Father is truly a Father, and much more truly indeed than those who have this name among us, first because He is Father in a proper and unique way, not as bodily things are; then because He is Father alone and not by conjunction with another; then because He is Father of an only one, that is, the only-begotten; then because He is Father only, not having been previously a son;

[13] The editor of Migne notes at this location that "not a few manuscripts read instead 'ἀγεννησίας,' that is the state of being unbegotten, or not from Another." A. Edward Siecienski does not notice this (*The Filioque: History of a Doctrinal Controversy* [New York: Oxford University Press, 2010], 42). See also *Discours 32–37*, ed. Claudio Moreschini (Paris: Cerf: Paris, 1985). In Oration 41, no. 9, the manuscript tradition is agreed that St. Gregory says that the Son has all that the Father has except for being unbegotten.

[14] Mark of Ephesus nevertheless made use of this text at the Council of Florence (*AG*, 377–78), and again in his *Encyclical to all Orthodox Christians* (*OAU*, 456–57).

> then because He is wholly and completely Father, which cannot be said of us; then because He is Father from the beginning with no afterwards. We call the Son truly a Son, because He is the only One, and is of the Only One, and is Son in a unique way, and is only a Son; for He is not also at the same time Father; and He is wholly and completely Son, and from the beginning, and never began to be Son; for the deity does not exist by change, nor by progress of deification, so that the Father might at some time cease to be Father, and He at some time cease to be Son. We call the Holy Spirit truly holy; for there is no other who is such or in the same way, nor does He have holiness as an addition, but He is holiness itself; nor does He become more or less, but with regard to time He has no beginning nor will He end. For not being created, and divinity, are common to Father and to Son and to Holy Spirit; being from the Father is common to the Son and the Holy Spirit. Being unbegotten is proper to the Father; generation, to the Son; and procession [ἔκπεμψις] to the Spirit (16).[15]

This is rather a tantalizing passage, in that having so eloquently spoken about the mutual relations of Father and Son, St. Gregory might be expected to speak about the Holy Spirit's relation to his principle. Instead, rather than explain why the word "Spirit" is truly said, he explains why "holiness" is truly said. This suggests that the doctrine of the procession lacked clarity, at least in the mind of his auditors. Can anything be inferred about his own doctrine of the procession? His words about what is common among divine persons do not allow us to do this, since the implicit principle of division he uses is whether a divine person comes from another, something that is affirmed to be common to Son and Holy Spirit and not to the Father. Had he made the principle of division whether or not a divine person has another

15 *PG*, 35:1221A–C (trans. mine).

coming from himself, then we would have had a clear statement of his doctrine of the procession of the Holy Spirit. However, something to our purpose may be discerned in what he says about the proper note of the divine persons. The Holy Spirit, he says, has procession as his proper mark. Yet the word for procession here is not the usual term, ἐκπόρευσις, but rather ἔκπεμψις, literally "sending out." Since this word normally refers to the temporal mission whose authors are explicitly stated in the New Testament to be both the Father and the Son, this suggests that he thinks of both the Father and the Son as the principle of the eternal hypostatic existence of the Holy Spirit.

Oration 39: On the Holy Lights

In this sermon, preached for the feast of the Epiphany, the saint is warning his hearers against the twin evils of Sabellianism and Arianism:

> The Father is Father, and is Unoriginate, for He is of no one; the Son is Son, and is not unoriginate, for He is of the Father. But if you take the word Origin in a temporal sense, He too is Unoriginate, for He is the Maker of Time, and is not subject to Time. The Holy Ghost is truly Spirit, coming forth [προιὸν] from the Father indeed, but not after the manner of the Son, for it is not by Generation but by Procession [ἐκπορευτῶς][16] (since I must coin a word for the sake of clearness); for neither did the Father cease to be Unbegotten because of His begetting something, nor the Son to be begotten because he is of the Unbegotten (how could that be?), nor is the Spirit changed into

16 Nazianzen here apparently invents the adverb. Siecienski misquotes it as ἐκπόρευσις (*Filioque*, 42), though the point is not very important. It is perhaps this passage that leads Bernard de Margerie to hold that Nazianzen first gives a technical sense to the word ἐκπορεύεσθαι and its cognates whereby it is used only of a relation to the Father ("Vers une relecture du concile de Florence, grâce à la reconsidération de l'Ecriture et des pères grecs et latins," *Revue thomiste* 86 [1986]: 31–81, at 40).

> Father or Son because He proceeds [ἐκπορεύεται], or because He is God—though the ungodly do not believe it. (12)[17]

What is St. Gregory excluding in the latter part of this quotation? In general, he is asserting that the three hypostases remain eternally distinct, each with his proper note. More specifically, he is asserting that the activity within the Trinity does not lead to a confusion between the principle and fruit of that activity. Thus the Father, the principle of generation, does not become begotten, like the fruit of that generation, the Son. Likewise, the Son does not become unbegotten, like the principle of generation, the Father. Even so, he concludes, the Holy Spirit, the fruit of the procession, does not become the Father or the Son. If we are to assign a logical structure to the passage, this can imply only that the Father and the Son are the principle of the Holy Spirit's procession. He is not simply denying that the consubstantiality of the persons removes their distinction, for in the last part of the extract he explains that *neither* the procession nor the *divinity* of the Holy Spirit confounds him with the Father or the Son.

A. Edward Siecienski claims that St. Gregory here distinguishes the ἐκπόρευσις of the Holy Spirit "from the more generalized 'coming-forth' [προϊεον] [*sic*] of both the Spirit and the Son."[18] In fact, all that he says is that the coming-forth of the Holy Spirit, and not that of the Son, is called ἐκπόρευσις.

Oration 40: On Holy Baptism

This sermon was preached on the day following Oration 39, to those who were about to be baptized. He exhorts the catechumens to remain true to the orthodox doctrine of the Trinity, telling them among, other things, not to give heed to those who cast doubt on the fittingness of the word "generation," as applied to the Son:

17 *PG*, 36:348B–C.
18 Siecienski, *Filioque*, 42.

> Do you fear to speak of Generation lest you should attribute anything of passion to the impassible God? I on the other hand fear to speak of Creation, lest I should destroy God by the insult and by the untrue division, either cutting the Son away from the Father, or from the Son the substance of the Spirit [ἀπὸ τοῦ Υἱοῦ τὴν οὐσίαν τοῦ Πνεύματος]. For this paradox is involved, that not only is a created life foisted into the Godhead by those who measure Godhead badly; but even this created life is divided against itself. For as these lowly earthly minds make the Son subject to the Father, so again is the rank [ἀξίας] of the Spirit made inferior to that of the Son, until both God and created life are insulted by the new Theology. (42)[19]

Why does St. Gregory speak here of the "substance of the Spirit" and not simply of the Spirit? It is perhaps because he wishes to show that the Holy Spirit pertains to the Son in virtue of the Spirit's substance, and not simply as an instrument adopted by the Son but extrinsic to the Son's own being. In any case, the fact that the substance of the Holy Spirit is presented as being in a relation to the Son analogous to that which the Son has to the Father certainly suggests (though again without saying explicitly) that as the Son comes from the Father, so the substance of the Spirit comes from the Son.

Oration 41: On Pentecost

In this Oration, where he is once more defending the divinity of the Holy Spirit, he writes:

> The Holy Ghost, then, always existed, exists, and always will exist. He neither had a beginning nor will He have an end; but He

[19] *PG*, 36:417C–20A.

> was everlastingly ranged with and numbered with the Father and the Son. For it was not ever fitting that either the Son should be wanting [ἐλλείπειν] to the Father, or the Spirit to the Son. (9)

Then after a passage detailing the divine attributes of the Holy Spirit, he summarizes his meaning:

> All that the Father hath the Son hath also, except the being unbegotten; and all that the Son hath the Spirit hath also, except the generation. And these two matters do not divide the Substance, as I understand it, but rather are divisions within the Substance [περὶ οὐσίαν]. (9)[20]

The first of these quotations indicates an eternal "having" or "possession" of the Holy Spirit by the Son analogous to the eternal "possession" of the Son by the Father. Since the only sense in which the Father can be said to "have" the Son rather than the Son "have" the Father is that the Son comes from the Father, it is reasonable to conclude that for the Son to "have" the Holy Spirit is for the Spirit to proceed from him. Again, given that we have seen St. Gregory teach in the Fifth Theological Oration that the mutual relations within the Trinity are the reason for the distinction of persons, we can conclude that the "possession" of the Holy Spirit by the Son is the reason for their personal distinction. We cannot therefore say that the Son's "possession" of the Holy Spirit presupposes that the latter has already been constituted in his hypostatic existence.

The second quotation could be appealed to by both defenders and opponents of the *Filioque*. If all that the Father has is the Son's except for being unbegotten, then active spiration must also be the Son's; on the other hand, if the Holy Spirit has all that the Son has except for

[20] *PG*, 36:441A–C.

having being generated, then active spiration cannot be the Son's, since it cannot be the Spirit's; and so the two halves of the statement seem to cancel each other out for our purposes. Yet a more careful consideration of the words may suggest something else. When the saint says that "all that the Father has, the Son has also, except the being unbegotten," he obviously intends us also to exclude from the Son that which is directly contrary to the notion of sonship: fatherhood. So the Son "lacks" not only the being unbegotten but also fatherhood. In the same way, then, when he says that all that the Son has the Spirit has also except for the being generated, we must also exclude from the Holy Spirit that which is directly contrary to the notion of being the Holy Spirit, meaning active spiration. So a careful reading of this text allows us to see in it a logic that implies the attribution of active spiration to the Son without the absurdity of its attributing active spiration to the Holy Spirit.

The Poems

Two passages from Nazianzen's poems may be considered. The first comes in the first of the "Moral Songs":

> The Holy Trinity is the first virgin. From the Father who has no principle, nor is impelled from outside (for He Himself is the path, the root and the principle of all), comes the Son, the King. . . . From the Son there does not come a beloved Son claiming like glory, for the Begetter is whole [i.e. there is only one], as is the Son, only of only; They go into one with the great Spirit [εἰς ἓν ἰόντε Πνεύματι σὺν μεγάλῳ], who goes from the Father as one who is like.[21]

The second passage comes in the doxology of the third of the "Dogmatic Songs": "Have mercy on us, have mercy, holy Trinity, going into One

[21] *PG*, 37:523A–24A (trans. mine). ἰόντε is dual.

from One. . . . one God from the Begetter through the Son into the great Spirit."[22]

It is difficult to draw definite theological conclusions from brief snatches of poetry. In the first extract, Nazianzen's predication of the same verb form (and that a verb of motion), ἰόντε, with regard to the Father and the Son, is perhaps noteworthy and seems to balance the explicit assertions that the Holy Spirit is from the Father and is not a Son of the Son. The second extract indicates that Gregory would have accepted the formulation διὰ τοῦ Υἱοῦ ἐκπορεύεται ("he proceeds through the Son"). More than that, one cannot say.

Summary and Conclusion

St. Gregory Nazianzen nowhere says explicitly that the Son is with the Father as the one principle of the Holy Spirit. Yet he says many things that, carefully considered, imply this. He says that the name "Spirit" comes by reason of procession, implying that he proceeds from any person whose Spirit he is (Oration 31); he considers analogies for the Trinity that suggest that the Holy Spirit receives divinity from the Son and finds no fault with them on this score (Oration 31); he says that there is a "motion" common to the "duality" by which it becomes a Trinity (Oration 29); he refers to the procession of the Holy Spirit by a word that normally refers to both the Father's and the Son's economic relation to the third person, the word ἔκπεμψις (Oration 25); he says that as the generation leads to no confusion between Father and Son, so the procession leads to no confusion between the Holy Spirit on the one hand and the Father and the Son on the other (Oration 39); he says that the substance of the Holy Spirit cannot be "cut away" from the Son (Oration 40); and he says that the Holy Spirit belongs eternally to the Son, and that the mutual relations of the persons are the reason for the distinction (Orations 41 and 31). So striking, in fact, is the way in

[22] *PG*, 37:632A (trans. mine).

which the saint implies the hypostatic procession from the Son without ever stating it that I am inclined to think that he acted thus by deliberate choice. Why he might have done so has already been suggested, when we considered Oration 31: a reluctance to give a new means of attack to his opponents, or a new cause of perplexity to those wavering between Eunomianism and orthodoxy. More generally it seems that he had in mind the principle that he formulated when explaining why the New Testament had not explicitly spoken of the Holy Spirit as God: "You see lights breaking upon us, gradually; and the order of Theology, which it is better for us to keep, neither proclaiming things too suddenly, nor yet keeping them hidden to the end" (Oration 31, no. 37).

CHAPTER 8

SAINT AMBROSE

Introduction

St. Ambrose's work *De Spiritu Sancto* was written around the year 381 as a treatise addressed to Emperor Gratian.[1] It is the first Latin treatise on the subject.[2] Its main purpose was to vindicate the true divinity of the third person of the Trinity. In the course of the treatise, as we shall see, the saint speaks in various places of the Holy Spirit as coming from the Father and the Son. Having considered some of these passages, A. Edward Siecienski writes: "The question remains whether for Ambrose the Spirit's procession from both Father and Son signified not only a temporal, but also an eternal relationship."[3] Siecienski professes

1 Ambrose, *On the Holy Spirit*, trans. H. de Romestin, 91–158 in *NPNF2* vol. 10. All translations of *De Spiritu Sancto* are taken from Romestin. This English translation has a fault in the numeration of the first book, since after section 134 it numbers the next section as 155, but no text is omitted from the translation.

2 Boniface Ramsey, *Ambrose*, The Early Church Fathers (London: Routledge, 1997), 52.

3 A. Edward Siecienski, *The Filioque: History of a Doctrinal Controversy* (New York: Oxford University Press, 2010), 58.

himself uncertain on this point: "Whether Ambrose himself would have accepted the doctrinal content implied by the later Latin teaching of the *filioque* [*sic*] remains unknown."[4] In this section, then, we shall look at such parts of the *De Spiritu Sancto* and of other works of the bishop of Milan as may help to resolve this doubt. Such resolution is the more important, insofar as St. Ambrose is one of only two Latin fathers of the Church to have been held out as models of orthodoxy by both the Council of Chalcedon and the Second Council of Constantinople.[5]

The Holy Spirit "Proceeds" from the Father and the Son

In book 1 of *De Spiritu Sancto*, as part of his response to those who imagine the Holy Spirit as a limited being, St. Ambrose explains that one should not think of him as being sent or proceeding in a spatial or bodily way: "Not as if from a place is the Spirit sent [mittitur], nor as if from a place does he proceed [procedit], when he proceeds from the Son" (1.119).[6] The terms *mitto* and *procedo* are not clearly distinguished here by the author, and up to this point in the chapter, it has been rather the idea of temporal mission that has prevailed. He continues, however, by drawing a comparison between the procession of the third person and that of the second, in such a way that we are obliged to say that he is thinking also of eternity, not only of time:

> Lastly, Wisdom so says that she came forth [prodiisse] from the mouth of the Most High, as not to be external to the Father, but with the Father; for "the Word was with God" and not only with God but also in God; for He says: "I am in the Father and the Father is in Me." But neither when He goes forth from the Father does He retire from a place, nor is He separated as a body

4 Siecienski, *Filioque*, 58.

5 See appendix 2 of the present volume ("Acts of Ecumenical Councils Approving by Name Certain Teachers of the Faith").

6 *PL*, 16:762B.

> from a body; nor when He is in the Father is He as if a body enclosed as it were in a body. The Holy Spirit also, when He proceeds from the Father and the Son [cum procedit a Patre et Filio], is not separated from the Father nor separated from the Son. For how could He be separated from the Father Who is the Spirit of His mouth? Which is certainly both a proof of His eternity [aeternitatis indicium], and expresses the Unity of this Godhead. (1.120)[7]

The juxtaposition of the passages from Proverbs and St. John's Gospel at the start of this extract shows that even if the words *prodire* and *procedit* here refer primarily to a temporal mission, they nevertheless presuppose an eternal relation. For the wisdom of God comes forth from the mouth of the most High in such a way as to be the Word who is with God. But the Word is said by St. John to be with God "in the beginning," from eternity. Ambrose thus seems to be putting in parallel the facts that neither the eternal nor the temporal coming-forth of the Son can separate him from the one from whom he comes forth. It is therefore natural to suppose that when he speaks of the Holy Spirit's not being separated from Father and Son when he proceeds from them, he likewise has in mind the Spirit's eternal relation to the first two persons, even if the word "proceeding" might denote primarily the temporal mission. Both Yves Congar and Siecienski seem to have missed this point.[8] Boniface Ramsey, speaking in general about Ambrose's doctrine of the procession, remarks that he "anticipates Augustine and thus goes contrary to the common Greek view, which was that the Spirit proceeded from the Father through the Son."[9] The first half of this statement is true, insofar as Ambrose appears to have originated the phrase *procedit a Patre et Filio*. The second half is

7 *PL*, 16:733A–B.

8 Yves Congar, *I Believe in the Holy Spirit*, vol. 3, Milestones in Catholic Theology (New York: Crossroad, 1997), 50; Siecienski, *Filioque*, 58.

9 Ramsey, *Ambrose*, 62.

unfortunate, both insofar as it supposes that there was only one way in which the Greek Fathers of the day expressed the procession and because it presupposes an incompatibility between the prepositions *a* and διά.

The Holy Spirit Receives from and through the Son

In book 2 of the treatise on the Spirit, St. Ambrose discusses two verses in St. John's Gospel that frequently recur in patristic discussions of the relation between Son and Holy Spirit, John 16:14–15. He has just been defending the doctrine that the Son knows all things, despite the passage in St. Mark's Gospel where the Son is said not to know the day of the end of the world. Ambrose continues:

> But if you are willing to learn that the Son of God knows all things, and has foreknowledge of all, see that those very things which you think to be unknown to the Son, the Holy Spirit received from the Son [de Filio]. He received them, however, through Unity of Substance [per unitatem substantiae], as the Son received from the Father. "He," says He, "shall glorify Me, for He shall receive of Mine and shall declare it unto you. All things whatsoever the Father has are Mine, therefore said I, He shall receive of Mine, and shall declare it unto you." What, then, is more clear than this Unity? What things the Father has pertain to the Son; what things the Son has the Holy Spirit also has received. (2.118)[10]

Although he does not develop the thought, as his principal intent here is to repel from the Son the charge of ignorance, the meaning is sufficiently clear: the Holy Spirit received his knowledge from the Son. That he is not using some kind of metaphor, but is speaking of the Holy Spirit's substantial knowledge that is one with his being, is made

---

[10] *PL*, 16:768B.

clear by the fact that the transmission is said to be "through the unity of substance." There is no way to understand these words of a temporal mission of the Holy Spirit.

Similar passages occur later in the same book. Summarizing some scriptural passages in which revelation is attributed to each divine person in turn, he writes:

> It has then been proved that like as God has revealed to us the things which are His, so too the Son, and so too the Spirit, has revealed the things of God. For our knowledge proceeds from one Spirit, through one Son to one Father; and from one Father through one Son to one Holy Spirit is delivered goodness and sanctification and the sovereign right [imperiale ius] of eternal power. (2.130)[11]

It is the same contrast drawn by St. Basil in his *De Spiritu Sancto*. Human knowledge travels in the opposite direction from the order of the divine persons. More important for our purposes is to note that a real communication of divine attributes, and therefore of the divine nature, is here being described. Clearly it is in eternity, and not in time, that the Holy Spirit receives his attributes.[12]

Shortly afterward, the saint is discussing the phrase used in John 16:13, "he will not speak of himself":

> What means, then, "He shall not speak from Himself"? That is, He shall not speak without Me; for He speaks the truth, He breathes wisdom. He speaks not without the Father, for He is the Spirit of God; He hears not from Himself, for all things are of God.

---

[11] *PL*, 16:759C.

[12] In passing we may note the fittingness of telling Emperor Gratian that the Trinity possesses the true *ius imperiale*.

> The Son received all things from the Father, for He Himself said: "All things have been delivered unto Me from My Father." All that is the Father's the Son also has, for He says again: "All things which the Father has are Mine." And those things which He Himself received by Unity of nature, the Spirit by the same Unity of nature received also from Him, as the Lord Jesus Himself declares, when speaking of His Spirit: "Therefore said I, He shall receive of Mine and shall declare it unto you." Therefore what the Spirit says is the Son's, what the Son has given is the Father's. So neither the Son nor the Spirit speaks anything of Himself. For the Trinity speaks nothing external to Itself.
>
> But if you contend that this is an argument for the weakness of the Holy Spirit, and for a kind of likeness to the lowliness of the body, you will also make it an argument to the injury of the Son, because the Son said of Himself: "As I hear, I judge"; and "The Son can do nothing else than what He sees the Father doing." For if that be true, as it is, which the Son said: "All things which the Father has are Mine," and the Son according to the Godhead is one with the Father, one by natural substance, not according to the Sabellian falsehood; that which is one by the property of substance certainly cannot be separated, and so the Son cannot do anything except what He has heard of the Father. (2.133–53)

This extract requires little comment. The Holy Spirit receives everything by unity of nature with the Son, as the Son does by unity of nature with the Father. What St. Ambrose seems to have primarily in mind when he says "all things" is wisdom or knowledge. Even if he is thinking also of the wisdom and knowledge which the Holy Spirit will himself inspire in the prophets and apostles (since he says, "he breathes wisdom"), his words directly refer to the wisdom that the Holy Spirit has in himself "by natural substance"; there is again no way to make this a reference only to a temporal mission of the Holy Spirit. The "hearing" of John 16:13 and the "receiving" of John 16:14–15 refer, for St. Ambrose, to the same eternal reality.

In book 3, the saint returns to this passage of St. John in conjunction with another from the same evangelist:

> If they are unwilling to allow that the Holy Spirit has all things which pertain to God, and can do all things, let them say what He has not, and what He cannot do. For like as the Son has all things, and the Father grudges not to give all things to the Son according to His nature [naturaliter], who gives[13] to Him that which is greater than all, as the Scripture bears witness, saying: "That which My Father has given unto Me is greater than all." So too the Spirit of Christ has that which is greater than all, because righteousness knows not grudging.
>
> So then, if we attend diligently, we comprehend here also the oneness of the Divine Power. He says: "That which My Father has given unto Me is greater than all, and no one is able to snatch them out of My Father's hand. I and the Father are One." For if we rightly showed above that the Holy Spirit is the Hand of the Father, the same is certainly the Hand of the Father which is the Hand of the Son, since the Same is the Spirit of the Father Who is the Spirit of the Son. Therefore whosoever of us receives eternal life in this Name of the Trinity, as he is not torn from the Father; so he is not torn from the Son, so too he is not torn from the Spirit.
>
> Again, from the very fact that the Father is said to have given to the Son, and the Spirit to have received from the Son, as it is written: "He shall glorify Me, for He shall take of Mine,

[13] Trans. mine. Romestin translates: "The Father grudges not to give all things to the Son according to His nature, having given to Him that which is greater than all," as if these were two distinct donations of the Father to the Son. I take St. Ambrose to be using the two scriptural phrases to refer to the same donation. The Latin is: "Nec invidet Pater quominus omnia naturaliter det Filio, qui dedit quod maius est omnibus."

> and shall declare it unto you"—which He seems[14] to have said rather of the office of distributing, than of the prerogative of Divine Power [quod de munere magis dispensationis videtur, quam de potestatis divinae iure dixisse], for those whom the Son redeemed the Spirit also, Who was to sanctify them, received—from those very words, I say, from which they construct their sophistry, the Unity of the Godhead is perceived, not the need of a gift. (3.113–15)[15]

Here the interpretation of John 16:14 is at first sight somewhat different. That which is given from the Son to the Holy Spirit is the elect, who cannot be torn away from the Spirit. This could seem to be a reference to a temporal mission, not to an eternal procession. But in fact the concluding words of the extract show that St. Ambrose is still thinking of the perfect possession of the divine nature by each of the three persons, which he takes to be proved against the heretics by these passages. So "all things" still seems to refer in the first place to the divinity, while the possession of the elect by each of the divine persons is thought of as a consequence of their possession of the divinity.

The Latin content inserted in the last paragraph of the extract seems to need some comment. I take it to be a reference to the "temporal" rather than the "eternal" possession by the divine persons: to their possession of the elect, not of the divinity. If so, St. Ambrose seems to mean that when the Holy Spirit is said to receive the elect from the Son, this does not imply that the Son loses his rights or his power over them, but simply that sanctification is appropriated to the Holy Spirit, as redemption is appropriated to the Son. A clearer, or at any rate more modern, translation of *munus dispensationis* might be "economic role."

Finally, we can note the saint's insistence that the Holy Spirit is at

---

14 Alternatively, and perhaps better, "which he is seen."

15 *PL*, 16:803C–4A.

one and the same time the "hand" of the Father and of the Son. Since the hand is united to the rest of the body as its principle, we can see here a sketch, though no more, of the notion of the Father and the Son as one principle of the Holy Spirit.

In his commentary on St. Luke's Gospel, St. Ambrose teaches the eternal origin of the Holy Spirit from the Son perhaps even more clearly. He is commenting on Luke 18:19—"no one is good but God alone"—and explaining why Christ is to be called "good":

> How is he not good, who was born from one who is good [ex bono natus]—"for a good tree brings forth good fruit"? How is he not good, since the goodness of the substance taken from the Father [bonitatis substantia assumpta ex Patre] has not become worse in the Son, since it has not become worse in the Spirit? For if the Spirit is good who received from the Son, he also must be good who passed on what was received [quod si bonus Spiritus qui accepit ex Filio, bonus utique et ille qui tradidit]. And since the Father is good, He is certainly also good who has all things which the Father has.[16]

Here again the saint is clearly speaking about the eternal relations of the divine persons, as shown by such words as *natus* and *substantia*. It is in this context that the Holy Spirit is said to have received from the Son. The verb *tradere*, used of the Son in respect to the Spirit, clearly presents the former as an active principle in regard to the latter.

The Holy Spirit as the Breath of the Mouth

Like the other Fathers, St. Ambrose, relying on the Psalms, speaks of the Holy Spirit as "breath of God's mouth," *Spiritus oris*. Does he offer

[16] *PL*, 15:1785C (trans. mine). The editor of Migne notes that the commentary on St. Luke was written after the *De Spiritu Sancto*, since the latter work is mentioned in the former (*PL*, 15:1527–28).

any explanation of this phrase? In *De Spiritu Sancto*, it is used but not explained:

> Nor, again, let it move you that he said "upon Him," for he was speaking of the Son of Man, because he was baptized as the Son of Man. For the Spirit is not upon Christ, according to the Godhead, but in Christ; for, as the Father is in the Son, and the Son in the Father, so the Spirit of God and the Spirit of Christ is both in the Father and in the Son, for He is the Spirit of His mouth. For He Who is of God abides in God, as it is written: "But we received not the spirit of this world, but the Spirit which is of God." (3.6)

The Holy Spirit's being the spirit or breath of God's mouth is given here as the reason for his being in both the Father and the Son. The thought is not explained: is the "mouth" thought of as something that Father and Son share, or could it be a reference to the Son directly? We may perhaps find further light if we turn to St. Ambrose's work *De Isaac et anima*, in which he comments eloquently on the opening verse of the Canticle of Canticles, "Let him kiss me with the kisses of his mouth":

> As if wounded with love, since she can no longer bear his delays, she turns to ask God the Father to send her God the Word, and to explain the reason why she is so impatient, she says: "Let him kiss me with the kisses of his mouth." She does not seek one kiss, but many, that she might fulfil her desire. For she who loves is not satisfied with one solitary kiss, but requires and wins many, and so endears herself more to her beloved. So indeed she was shown to be in the Gospel, for "she has not ceased," he said, "to kiss my feet, . . . and so many sins have been forgiven her, for she has loved much." Therefore this soul too desires many kisses of the Word, so that she may be enlightened with the light of divine knowledge. For this is the kiss of the Word, namely the light of sacred knowledge.

> For God the Word kisses us when he enlightens our heart, and the chief part of man, with the spirit of divine knowledge, which makes the soul, endowed with the nuptial pledge of charity, gladly exult, saying, "I opened my mouth and I drew the Spirit [duxi spiritum]." For a kiss is that by which lovers cleave to each other and enjoy a pleasant interior delight. Through this kiss the soul adheres to God the Word, through whom the Spirit of the one kissing is poured into her.[17]

St. Ambrose is surely thinking of the Holy Spirit in the last two sentences of this extract, particularly since the phrase "I drew the spirit," which he quotes from Psalms 118:131, is used by other patristic authors to refer to the third divine person (for example, St. Gregory of Nyssa, Letter 35, no. 4). Thus his identification of the Word as the one who kisses the bride, thus passing on the Spirit, suggests that he thinks of the Son as the "mouth" when, in the *De Spiritu Sancto*, he uses the scriptural phrase "spirit/breath of the mouth" to describe the Holy Spirit's eternal relation to Father and Son. This would at any rate be consistent with what has already been demonstrated above, that he speaks of the Holy Spirit as eternally both from and through the Son.

Finally, could we have in this passage of *De Isaac et Anima* at least an intimation of the doctrine of the Holy Spirit that was to be brought to light far more clearly by Ambrose's spiritual son, St. Augustine, according to whom the Holy Spirit is eternally breathed forth from the Father and the Son precisely in virtue of *love*? If we do, it would be St. Ambrose's most original contribution to the doctrine of the procession.

17 *PL*, 15:506A–C (trans. mine). The editor assigns this commentary to approximately the year 387 (*PL*, 15:501–502).

> [illegible] of God [illegible] which [illegible] heart, and the chief part of man, with the spirit [illegible] knowledge, which [illegible] endowed [illegible] the mortal [illegible] saying, "I opened my mouth and I drew the Spirit" [illegible] by which [illegible] and [illegible] pleasant [illegible] delight. Through this [illegible] God the Word, through whom the Spirit of the [illegible] is poured into hearts.

Ambrose is surely thinking of the Holy Spirit in the first two [illegible] Psalms [illegible] used [illegible] to refer to [illegible] for example [illegible] Word [illegible] the Spirit [illegible] Father and the Son [illegible] connection with what has already been said above that [illegible] Holy Spirit [illegible] through [illegible] doctrine of the Holy Spirit that was [illegible] Ambrose [illegible] according to [illegible] Father and the Son [illegible] Ambrose [illegible] doctrine of the procession.

[illegible]

CHAPTER 9

SAINT GREGORY OF NYSSA

Introduction

St. Gregory of Nyssa was engaged in the same defense of the divinity of the Holy Spirit as were the other two Cappadocian Fathers whom we have already considered. As with them, and perhaps even more explicitly, his doctrine of the relation between the Son and the Holy Spirit emerges mostly through his defense of this even more fundamental doctrine and can be discovered in various of his dogmatic and exegetical works. I shall consider his works in turn, though not necessarily in chronological order, since "most of Gregory's writings are extremely difficult to date."[1]

---

1 Johan Leemans, "Logic and the Trinity," in *Gregory of Nyssa: The Minor Treatises on Trinitarian Theology and Apollinarism. Proceedings of the 11th International Colloquium on Gregory of Nyssa*, ed. Volker Drecoll and Margita Berghaus (Leiden: Brill, 2011), 111–30, at 121.

The Letter to Ablabius

The Letter to Ablabius, also called somewhat awkwardly "On Not Three Gods," addresses the question of why the true divinity of Father, Son, and Holy Spirit would not imply that they are three deities.[2] It has been assigned to various dates between 379 and 388.[3] After arguing that nature as such cannot be multiplied, even maintaining that it would be more correct to speak of a plurality of those who "exhibit humanity" rather than of a plurality of men, he goes on:

> If, however, anyone cavils at our argument, on the ground that by not admitting the difference of nature it leads to a mixture and confusion of the Persons, we shall make to such a charge this answer;—that while we confess the invariable character of the nature, we do not deny the difference in respect of cause, and that which is caused, by which alone we apprehend that one Person is distinguished from another;—by our belief, that is, that one is the Cause and another is of the Cause [τὸ μὲν ἄιτιον πιστεὐειν εἶναι, τὸ δὲ ἐκ τοῦ ἀιτίου]; and again in that which is of the cause we recognize another distinction. For one is directly from the first Cause, and another by that which is directly from the first Cause [Τὸ μὲν γὰρ προσεχῶς ἐκ τοῦ πρώτου, τὸ δὲ διὰ τοῦ προσεχῶς ἐκ τοῦ πρώτου]; so that the attribute of being Only-begotten abides without doubt in the Son, and the interposition of the Son [τῆς τοῦ Υἱοῦ μεσιτείας], while it guards His attribute of being Only-begotten, does not shut out the Spirit from His relation by way of nature to the Father.[4]

2 Gregory of Nyssa, Selected Works and Letters, trans. William Moore and Henry Wilson, *NPNF*2 vol. 5. Quotations from St. Gregory's works are taken from this edition ("On 'Not Three Gods,' to Ablabius" on 331–36, not to be confused with another letter to Ablabius later in *NPNF*2 vol. 5), except for the Homily On the Lord's Prayer, or as otherwise stated.

3 Leemans, "Logic and the Trinity," 121–22.

4 *PG*, 45:133B–C.

St. Gregory here clearly maintains that the Father is the first principle of the Holy Spirit as of the Son. Does he also attribute "being a principle" to the Son, when he speaks of the Holy Spirit as being "by" or "through" the Son? Surely so, since he draws the contrast between being directly "of the first" and being "through the one who is directly of the first" in the context precisely of "causation": these two ideas are distinguished as two forms of "causation."[5] Again, he expressly says that it is only by "causation" that the persons of the Trinity are distinguished. He would thus be contradicting himself if he were to say that the Son and the Holy Spirit were distinct even though there was no difference in their "cause" or principle.[6]

Further light is shed on Gregory's understanding of the word διά as said in connection to the Holy Spirit and the Son in a passage earlier in the same letter:

> In the case of the divine nature we do not similarly learn that the Father does [ποεῖ] anything by Himself in which the Son does not work conjointly [οὗ μὴ συνεφάπτεται ὁ Υἱός], or again that the Son has any special operation apart from the Holy Spirit; but every operation which extends from God to the creation, and is named according to our variable conceptions of it, has its origin from the Father and proceeds through the Son, and is perfected in the Holy Spirit [ἐκ Πατρὸς ἀφορμᾶται καὶ διὰ τοῦ Υἱοῦ πρόεισι, καὶ ἐν τῷ Πνεύματι τῷ ἁγίῳ τελειοῦται].[7]

5 Giulio Maspero maintains that, in this way, St. Gregory succeeds better than his predecessors in characterizing what is proper to procession as distinct from generation ("The Fire, the Kingdom and the Glory: The Creator Spirit and the Intra-Trinitarian Processions in the *Adversus Macedonianos* of Gregory of Nyssa," in *Gregory of Nyssa: The Minor Treatises on Trinitarian Theology and Apollinarism. Proceedings of the 11th International Colloquium on Gregory of Nyssa*, ed. Volker Drecoll and Margita Berghaus [Leiden: Brill, 2011], 229–76, at 255).

6 Even Jean-Miguel Garrigues, who claims at one point that the Cappadocians see the Son's mediation as a mere "passive and absolutely non-causal condition" of the Holy Spirit, acknowledges a few pages later that Nyssa refuses to exclude all idea of causality from the Son's mediation (*L'Esprit Qui Dit "Père!": l'Esprit-Saint dans la vie Trinitaire et le problème du* Filioque, Croire et Savoir 2 [Paris: Téqui, 1982], 90 and 93).

7 *PG*, 45:125C.

This passage, of course, refers directly to God's work in creation, but it nevertheless shows that when he speaks of the Father acting through the Son, Nyssa understands the Son to be acting also. Any operation that proceeds from the Father through (διά) the Son is also worked by the Son: the verb *συνεφάπτεται* is literally to "lay hold of along with another person." If we combine this passage with the first one quoted from this letter (and there is nothing in Nyssa to suggest that we should not), then we must once again conclude that the spirating of the Holy Spirit, proceeding from the Father, is "worked" conjointly by the Son.

Contra Eunomium

Like his brother St. Basil, and in continuance of that saint's work, St. Gregory of Nyssa wrote against the Arian dogmatician Eunomius. His treatise *Contra Eunomium* is dated to the years 380–381.[8] Although the majority of Nyssa's treatise is a defense of the divinity of the Son, he also touches on the divinity of the Holy Spirit and his relation to the Son. One early passage in the work sheds a further light on the quotation from the Letter to Ablabius. A rather long extract will have to be given for the sake of sufficient context:

> We regard [the divine nature] as consummately perfect and incomprehensibly excellent yet as containing clear distinctions within itself which reside in the peculiarities of each of the Persons: as possessing invariableness by virtue of its common attribute of uncreatedness, but differentiated by the unique character of each Person. This peculiarity contemplated in each sharply and clearly divides one from the other: the Father, for instance, is uncreate and ungenerate as well: He was never generated any more than He was created. While this uncreatedness is common

[8] Anthony Meredith, *Gregory of Nyssa*, The Early Church Fathers (London: Routledge, 1999), 28.

> to Him and the Son, and the Spirit, He is ungenerate as well as the Father. This is peculiar and uncommunicable, being not seen in the other Persons. The Son in His uncreatedness touches the Father and the Spirit, but as the Son and the Only-begotten He has a character which is not that of the Almighty or of the Holy Spirit. The Holy Spirit by the uncreatedness of His nature has contact with the Son and Father, but is distinguished from them by His own tokens. His most peculiar characteristic is that He is neither of those things which we contemplate in the Father and the Son respectively. He *is* simply, neither as ungenerate, nor as only-begotten: this it is that constitutes His chief peculiarity. Joined to the Father by His uncreatedness, He is disjoined from Him again by not being "Father." United to the Son by the bond of uncreatedness, and of deriving His existence from the Supreme, He is parted again from Him by the characteristic of not being the Only-begotten of the Father, and of having been manifested by means of the Son Himself [ἐν τῷ δι' αὐτοῦ τοῦ Υἱοῦ πεφηνέναι]. Again, as the creation was effected by the Only-begotten [τῆς κτίτσεως διὰ τοῦ Μονογενοῦς ὑποστάσης], in order to secure that the Spirit should not be considered to have something in common with this creation because of His having been manifested by means of the Son, He is distinguished from it by His unchangeableness, and independence of all external goodness. (1.22)[9]

The "manifestation" of the Holy Spirit is apparently nothing else than His hypostatic procession, since it is that which makes him distinct from the Son: the Holy Spirit is manifested—that is, exists as an object of knowledge, simply by proceeding. Theodoros Alexopoulos's claim that St. Gregory is thinking of a manifestation to creatures is

---

9 *PG*, 45:336B–37A.

ruled out by the context, which is that of the eternal distinctions within the unchangeable godhead.[10] The saint is describing the same reality here as in the letter to Ablabius when he spoke of the Holy Spirit's being "through the one who is directly from the first." If not, this present text would not correspond to that letter, inasmuch as it would lack a reference to the Son in the Holy Spirit's hypostatic procession.

The final sentence of the extract is of particular importance. It recognizes that the Son's relation to the Holy Spirit is such that some people might wrongly see it as a particular instance of the Son's relation to creation, which he "effected" (literally, "which subsists through Him"). In anticipating this error, St. Gregory does not say the Son is not, in fact, a principle of the Holy Spirit and only a principle of creation, but rather insists on the Spirit's divinity. The obvious conclusion is that the Son is indeed a principle of the Holy Spirit, yet in the way in which one can be a principle of a divine person, not in the way in which he is a principle of creation. From this it follows that the term αἴτιον, used of God the Father in the Letter to Ablabius, means not simply cause, but first cause, or principle without principle, as we have argued is also true of the term as used by St. Basil and St. Gregory Nazianzen.[11]

Somewhat later in the same book, while explaining the impossibility of a temporal "before and after" in God, Nyssa says:

---

10 Theodoros Alexopoulos, "The Eternal Manifestation of the Spirit 'Through the Son' (διὰ τοῦ Υἱοῦ) according to Nikephoros Blemmydes and Gregory of Cyprus," in *Ecumenical Perspectives on the* Filioque *for the 21st Century*, ed. Myk Haberts (London: Bloomsbury Academic, 2014), 65–86, at 71.

11 See Yves Congar, *After Nine Hundred Years: The Background of the Schism between the Eastern and Western Churches* (New York: Fordham University Press, 1959), 31: "The word αἰτία signifies 'to proceed as from the first principle.'" For this reason, rather than saying with the Pontifical Council that the "Greek Fathers" spoke of "the monarchy of the Father," it would be more generally true to say that they taught His "monaitia" (even though the word itself was apparently not used, being not found in Lampe's *Patristic Greek Lexicon*, nor in Bauer's *Greek–English Lexicon*). We have seen how Nazianzen uses ἀρχή as a proper name for the *Son*, and that he uses the word μοναρχία to refer to the whole Trinity."

> If in this uncreate existence those wondrous realities, with their wondrous names of Father, Son, and Holy Ghost, are to be in our thoughts, how can we imagine, of that pre-temporal world, that which our busy, restless minds perceive in things here below by comparing one of them with another and giving it precedence by an interval of time? For there, with the Father, unoriginate, ungenerate, always Father, the idea of the Son as coming from Him yet side by side with Him is inseparably joined; and through the Son and yet with Him [δι' αὐτοῦ δὲ καὶ μετ' αὐτοῦ], before any vague and unsubstantial conception comes in between, the Holy Spirit is found at once in closest union [συνημμένως καταλαμβάνεται]; not subsequent in existence to the Son, as if the Son could be thought of as ever having been without the Spirit; but Himself also owning the same cause of His being [τὴν αἰτίαν ἔχειν τοῦ εἶναι], i.e. the God over all, as the Only-begotten Light, and having shone forth in that very Light, being divisible neither by duration nor by an alien nature from the Father or from the Only-begotten. (1.26)[12]

Consistently with the other Cappadocian Fathers, he again speaks of the Father as αἰτία; but we have seen that in Nyssa the preposition διά used of the Son also includes "causality." Also of significance is the phrase "through Him and yet with Him," which shows, if any further proof were needed, that διά is not used by St. Gregory as simply denoting a fellowship of the Son with the Holy Spirit. For, then there would have been no need to add μετά. Again, the "shining forth" of the Holy Spirit, in (ἐν) that light that is the Son, appears to be nothing other than his very procession, as it is given as the reason of his consubstantiality. What is the meaning of the preposition ἐν here? It suggests a "starting point" for the shining forth of the Holy Spirit. And when we remove

[12] *PG*, 45:368D–69A.

any material sense from this idea, there remains once more the meaning that the Son is a principle of that shining forth or procession.

In the same work we find the image of the three suns or lights, which further proves that the Holy Spirit's "shining forth" through or by the Son simply is his proceeding:

> Having taken our stand on the comprehension of the Ungenerate Light, we perceive that moment from that vantage ground the Light that streams from Him, like the ray co-existent with the sun, whose cause indeed is in the sun, but whose existence is synchronous with the sun, not being a later addition, but appearing at the first sight of the sun itself: or rather (for there is no necessity to be slaves to this similitude, and so give a handle to the critics to use against our teaching by reason of the inadequacy of our image), it will not be a ray of the sun that we shall perceive, but another sun blazing forth, as an offspring, out of the Ungenerate sun, and simultaneously with our conception of the First, and in every way like him, in beauty, in power, in lustre, in size, in brilliance, in all things at once that we observe in the sun. Then again, we see yet another such Light after the same fashion sundered by no interval of time from that offspring Light, and while shining forth by means of It yet tracing the source of its being to the Primal Light [*δι᾽ αὐτοῦ μὲν ἔκλαμπον· τὴν δὲ τῆς ὑποστάσεως αἰτίαν ἔχον ἐκ τοῦ πρωτοτύποῦ φωτός*]; itself, nevertheless, a Light shining in like manner as the one first conceived of, and itself a source of light and doing all that light does. There is, indeed, no difference between one light and another light, *qua light*, when the one shows no lack or diminution of illuminating grace, but by its complete perfection forms part of the highest light of all, and is beheld along with the Father and the Son, though counted after them, and by its own power gives

> access to the light that is perceived in the Father and Son to all who are able to partake of it. (1.36)[13]

Also of great interest is a passage where he seems to attribute not only the reality but also the name of "cause" to the Son in regard to the Holy Spirit. Explaining that if the terms "before" and "after" are used in regard to the three persons, it is without any idea of temporality, he writes:

> Because the existence of the Son is not marked by any intervals of time, and the infinitude of His life flows back before the ages and onward beyond them in an all-pervading tide, He is properly addressed with the title of Eternal; again, on the other hand, because the thought of Him as Son in fact and title gives us the thought of the Father as inalienably joined to it, He thereby stands clear of an ungenerate existence being imputed to Him, while He is always with a Father Who always is, as those inspired words of our master[14] expressed it, bound by way of generation to His Father's Ungeneracy. Our account of the Holy Ghost will be the same also; the difference is only in the place assigned in order. For as the Son is bound to the Father, and, while deriving existence from Him, is not substantially after Him, so again the Holy Spirit is in touch with the Only-begotten, Who is conceived of as before the Spirit's subsistence only in the theoretical light of a cause [κατὰ τὸν τῆς αἰτίας λόγον]. Extensions in time find no admittance in the Eternal Life; so that, when we have removed the thought of cause, the Holy Trinity in no single way exhibits discord with itself. (1.42)[15]

13 *PG*, 45:416B–D.
14 His elder brother, St. Basil.
15 *PG*, 45:464B–C.

The key phrase κατὰ τὸν τῆς αἰτίας λόγον literally means "according to the notion of the cause." William Moore and Henry Wilson remark that it would be possible to render it "by reason of a different kind of causation," though the one given in the extract is their preferred translation.[16] It is clear why this is so: the Holy Spirit's coming from the Father by a different kind of "causation" from the Son is not in itself a reason to think of the Son as existing before Him. On the other hand, the Son's being a "cause" of the Spirit is a reason why someone might suppose that the second person existed before the third; this explains why St. Gregory should wish to say that it is only as meaning "causality" that we can speak of the Son as "before." Yves Congar, however, after quoting this passage and the first passage quoted above from the letter to Ablabius, writes, apparently to summarize Nyssa's thought: "It is . . . hardly possible to deny that the Son played a part in the intra-divine existence of the Spirit, although that part was not of a causal nature."[17] I am unable to understand what Congar meant by this. Jean-Miguel Garrigues, for his part, translates κατὰ τὸν τῆς αἰτίας λόγον as "by reason of the only cause (the Father)."[18] This is an unnatural translation, since if the Father were the only "cause," there would be no explanation of how the Son was "before" the Holy Spirit. Finally, A. Edward Siecienski quotes this passage from *Contra Eunomium*, while two sentences later, as if interpreting Nyssa's thought, he writes that "the Spirit is not caused by the Son," but is simply a "presupposition" for his eternal manifestation.[19] Yet this is not what Nyssa says.

Before we leave the *Contra Eunomium*, it seems worthwhile to mention one other passage in which the Son and the Holy Spirit are considered together. In summarizing Eunomius's account of the origin

---

16 *NPNF2*, 5:100n6.

17 Yves Congar, *I Believe in the Holy Spirit*, vol. 3, Milestones in Catholic Theology (New York: Crossroad, 1997), 32.

18 Garrigues, *L'Esprit*, 112.

19 A. Edward Siecienski, *The Filioque: History of a Doctrinal Controversy* (New York: Oxford University Press, 2010), 44.

of the third person, St. Gregory writes: "He declares Him to be a work of both Persons; of the Father, as supplying the cause of his constitution, of the Only-begotten, as of the artificer of His subsistence" (1.16). While objecting to the description of the Holy Spirit as a work, and to the "subjection" that Eunomios attributes to him on account of his origin, Gregory does not oppose the idea of the Spirit's coming from Father and Son, but simply the denial of the equality of the three persons.

Letter to Peter

This letter has been attributed both to St. Gregory of Nyssa and to his brother St. Basil as Letter 38 of his collected letters.[20] Contemporary scholarship favors the former attribution.[21] The purpose of the letter is to explain the difference in meaning between the terms οὐσία and ὑπόστασις. Having explained that the three divine hypostases do not differ in such attributes as being uncreated and incomprehensibility, St. Gregory goes on to explain how they are distinct:

> There is a certain power subsisting without generation and without origination, which is the cause of the cause of all things. For the Son, by whom are all things, and with whom the Holy Spirit is inseparably conceived of, is attached to the Father. For it is not possible for anyone to conceive of the Son if he be not previously enlightened by the Spirit. Since then the Holy Ghost, from whom the supply of all good things for creation has its source, is attached to the Son [τοῦ Υἱοῦ μὲν ἤρτηται], and with

20 Basil, Letter 38, "to Gregory His Brother, on the difference between substance and person," in *Letters 1–58*, trans. and ed. Roy Deferrari, Loeb Classical Library 190 (Cambridge, MA: Harvard University Press, 1926), 196–227.

21 Gregory of Nyssa, Letter 35, "to Peter his own brother on the divine *ousia* and hypostasis," in *Gregory of Nyssa: The Letters*, trans. Anna Silvas, Supplements to *Vigiliae Christianae* (Leiden: Brill, 2007), 247–59. The question is still disputed, however; for a summary of recent scholarship, see Volker and Berghaus's preface in *Gregory of Nyssa*, xiv–xxi.

> Him is inseparably apprehended [συγκαταλαμβάνεται][22], and has His being attached to the Father as cause [τῆς δὲ τοῦ Πατρὸς αἰτίας ἐξημμένον[23] ἔχει τὸ εἶναι] from whom also He proceeds [ἐκπορεύεται]; He has this note of His peculiar hypostatic nature that He is known after the Son and together with the Son, and that He has His subsistence of the Father [ἐκ τοῦ Πατρὸς ὑφαστάναι]. The Son, who declares the Spirit proceeding from the Father through Himself and with Himself [Ὁ δὲ Υἱός, ὁ τὸ ἐξ τοῦ Πατρὸς ἐκπορευόμενον Πνεῦμα δι' ἑαυτοῦ καὶ μεθ'ἑαυτοῦ γνωρίζων], shining forth alone and by only-begetting from the unbegotten light, so far as the peculiar notes are concerned [κατὰ τὸ ἰδίαζον τῶν γνωρισμάτων], has nothing in common [οὐδεμίαν ... τὴν κοινωνίαν ἔχει] either with the Father or with the Holy Ghost. He alone is known by the stated signs. But God, Who is over all, alone has, as one special mark of His own hypostasis, His being Father, and His deriving His hypostasis [ὑποστῆναι] from no cause; and through this mark He is peculiarly known. Wherefore in the communion of the substance we maintain that there is no mutual approach or intercommunion of those notes of indication perceived in the Trinity [ἀσύμβατά φαμεν εἶναι καὶ ἀκοινώνητα τὰ ἐπιθεωρούμενα τῇ Τριάδι γνωρίσματα], whereby is set forth the proper peculiarity [ἡ ἰδιότης] of the Persons delivered in the faith, each of these being distinctly apprehended by His own notes. (4)

To draw out the most pertinent points: St. Gregory tells us that the Holy Spirit is "attached to" or united with the Son, that he is attached to the Father as his "cause" from whom he proceeds, and that he subsists from the Father. One crucial sentence is apparently ambiguous. According to the translation used above, which is Blomfield Jackson's, St. Gregory would be saying that the Holy Spirit proceeds "with and

[22] Deferrari translates this as "produced"; I cannot find any authority for this.

[23] Another possible reading is ἐξηρτημένον; the sense of the passage is not thereby changed.

through the Son," while Roy Deferrari, by contrast, relates the words δι' ἑαυτοῦ καὶ μεθ' ἑαυτοῦ to the participle γνωρίζων, translating "the Son, who through Himself and with Himself makes known the Spirit which proceeds from the Father."[24] In favor of the former is that it would be a kind of explanation of the earlier remark, that the Spirit is "attached" to the Son; in favor of the latter is the order of the words themselves, since the former sense would be better expressed by placing the words δι' ἑαυτοῦ καὶ μεθ' ἑαυτοῦ in front of ἐκπορευόμενον. The being "made known" must clearly from the context be a reference to the eternal relations, and not to the economy; like the equivalent term "manifested" in the *Contra Eunomium*, it appears just to mean "is known to exist," or perhaps better, "exists as an intelligible reality."

A little later, St. Gregory goes on:

> He who perceives the Father, and perceives Him by Himself, has at the same time mental perception of the Son; and he who receives [λάβων] the Son does not divide Him from the Spirit, but in consecution so far as order is concerned, in conjunction so far as nature is concerned [ἀκολούθως μέν, κατὰ τὴν τάξιν, συνημμένως δέ, κατὰ τὴν φύσιν], expresses the faith commingled in himself in the three together. He who makes mention of the Spirit alone, embraces also in this confession Him of whom He is the Spirit. And since the Spirit is Christ's and of God, as says Paul, then just as he who lays hold on one end of the chain pulls the other to him, so he who "draws the Spirit," as says the prophet, by this means draws to him at the same time both the Son and the Father. And if any one verily receives the Son, he will hold Him on both sides, the Son drawing towards him on the one His own Father, and on the other His own Spirit [καὶ εἰ τὸν Υἱὸν ἀληθινῶς τις λάβοι, ἕξει αὐτον ἑκατέρωθεν, πῆ μὲν τὸν ἑαυτοῦ Πατέρα, πῆ δὲ τὸ ἴδιον

24 Jackson's translation is included with Basil's letters in *NPNF*2, 8:137–41.

> Πνεῦμα συνεπαγόμενον]. For He who eternally exists in the Father can never be cut off from the Father, nor can He who worketh all things in the Spirit ever be disjoined from the Spirit. Likewise moreover He who receives the Father virtually receives at the same time both the Son and the Spirit; for it is no wise possible to entertain the idea of severance or division, in such a way that the Son should be thought of apart from the Father, or the Spirit disjoined [διαζευχθῆναι] from the Son. (4)

It might appear that St. Gregory in this second extract is talking about only the order in which we come to know about, or be enlightened by, the divine persons, not about the Trinity in itself. In fact, he is talking simultaneously about the eternal order of the divine persons and the way in which this order makes it impossible for the enlightened man to know one of the persons without the others. The eternal order and inseparability of the persons is the reason why the thought of one implies the thought of another: the sentence beginning "for he who eternally exists in the Father" is proof of this.

What does this passage teach about the relation between the Son and the Holy Spirit? The image of the chain seems to represent the Son as in the middle, with the Father and the Holy Spirit on either end. That by itself does not take us further than the previous quotation, with its statements that the Holy Spirit is "attached" both to Son and Father and that the Father is the αἰτία. The statement that the Son "draws" or brings to himself both the Holy Spirit and the Father is intriguing: it suggests a relationship involving activity, and even distinct activities of the Son in respect to the Father and in respect to the Holy Spirit. But more than this one cannot say: the thought remains undeveloped, hardly more than metaphorical.

Does this letter tend to support or oppose the *Filioque*? Opponents of the doctrine could point to phrases that might seem to be in their favor, in particular that the Holy Spirit is said simply "to have his subsistence from the Father." Yet this would be to overlook what is said about the Son "making known," γνωρίζων, the Spirit. Since for the Holy Spirit to be eternally made known simply is for him to proceed—since he does not first proceed and then afterwards become known—this letter does teach that the Son has an active role in the procession, even though it does not state expressly that he is one principle with the Father, nor does it use the word ἐκπόρευσις in reference to the Son.

De Spiritu Sancto adversus Pneumatomachos Macedonianos

This short work contains much that is germane to our purpose. It has been dated to the years 380 or 381.[25] Near the beginning, Gregory affirms the true divinity of the third person:

> We, for instance, confess that the Holy Spirit is of the same rank as the Father and the Son, so that there is no difference between them in anything, to be thought or named, that devotion can ascribe to a Divine nature. We confess that, save His being contemplated as with peculiar attributes in regard of Person, the Holy Spirit is indeed from God, and of the Christ [ἐκ τοῦ Θεοῦ ἐστι, καὶ τοῦ Χρίστου ἐστι], according to Scripture, but that, while not to be confounded with the Father in being never originated, nor with the Son in being the Only-begotten, and while to be regarded separately in certain distinctive properties, He has in all else, as I have just said, an exact identity with them. But our opponents aver that He is a stranger to any vital communion with the Father and the Son; that by reason of an essential variation He is inferior to, and less than they at every point; in power, in glory, in dignity, in fine in everything we ascribe to Deity. (2)[26]

[25] Maspero, "The Fire, the Kingdom and the Glory," 229.

[26] *PG*, 45:1304A–B.

The passage is clearly speaking of the Holy Spirit in his essence, not of his temporal mission. Words such as "rank," "divine nature," "essential variation," and "deity" leave no room for doubt on this point.

> The plea will not avail them in their self-defence, that He is delivered by our Lord to His disciples third in order, and therefore He is estranged from our ideal of Deity. Where in each case activity in working good shows no diminution or variation whatever, how unreasonable it is to suppose the numerical order to be a sign of any diminution or essential variation. It is as if a man were to see a separate flame burning on three torches (and we will suppose that the third flame is caused by that of the first being transmitted to the middle, and then kindling the end torch), and were to maintain that the heat in the first exceeded that of the others. (6)[27]

This image implies that the passing of the Holy Spirit "through" the Son involves a "causal" activity by the Son as well as the Father, since the second torch kindles the third. Not without reason does the editor of this passage in Migne's *Patrologia Graeca* comment that there could be "nothing clearer than this example of the three torches to support the dogma of the procession from each" person.[28] Giulio Maspero likewise writes that in this treatise, "Gregory . . . highlights the active role of the Son in the procession of the Spirit."[29]

The second passage that allows us to understand what St. Gregory means by teaching that the Holy Spirit is by nature τοῦ Χρίστου is this:

[27] *PG*, 45:1308A–B.

[28] See note 3 in *PG*, 45:1308: "Nihil evidentius hoc exemplo trium lucernarum est pro dogmate de processione ab utroque."

[29] Maspero, "The Fire, the Kingdom and the Glory," 258–59.

> The Son is, to begin with, because of qualities that are essentially holy, that which the Father, essential Holy, is; and such as the only-begotten is, such is the Holy Spirit; then again, He is so by virtue of life-giving, of imperishability, of unvariableness, of everlastingness, of justice, of wisdom, of rectitude, of sovereignty, of goodness, of power, of capacity to give all good things, and above them all life itself, and by being everywhere, being present in each, filling the earth, residing in the heavens, shed abroad upon supernatural powers, filling all things according to the deserts of each, Himself remaining full, being with all who are worthy, and yet not parted from the Holy Trinity. He ever "searches the deep things of God," ever "receives [λαμβάνει] from the Son," ever is being "sent," and yet not separated, and being glorified, and yet He has always had glory. (22)[30]

While this passage by itself would not have been decisive, yet in conjunction with the image of the three torches, it shows sufficiently clearly that St. Gregory understands the "receiving" of the Holy Spirit from the Son in John 16:15 to be a reference to an eternal reception. Indeed, Maspero translates λαμβάνει in this passage of Nyssa as "receives himself," on the grounds that the saint is speaking of the origin of the person of the Spirit.[31]

Another passage worth pondering in this same work concerns the relation of the Holy Spirit to the Son considered as the Father's power:

> Neither did the Universal God make the universe "through the Son," as needing any help, nor does the Only-begotten God work all things "by the Holy Spirit" as having a power that comes short of His design; but the fountain of power is the Father, and the power of the Father is the Son, and the spirit of that power

30 *PG*, 45:1328C–29A.

31 Maspero, "The Fire, the Kingdom and the Glory," 255.

> is the Holy Spirit; and Creation entirely, in all its visible and spiritual extent, is the finished work of that Divine power. (13)[32]

It does not seem to be forcing St. Gregory's words to say that if the Holy Spirit belongs to the Son insofar as the Son is considered as *power*, then he belongs to the Son insofar as the Son is a "cause" or principle of being. For an active power is "that by which something is able to come."

Yet another passage in this work shows how foreign to St. Gregory's thought is the suggestion that the economic relations between the three divine persons do not trace out in time their eternal relations. In commenting on St. Peter's words, "Him [Christ] did God anoint with the Holy Spirit," the bishop of Nyssa explains that this anointing denotes the co-eternity of the Son and the Spirit:

> For the Son is King, and His living, realized and personified Kingship is found in the Holy Spirit, Who anoints the Only-begotten, and so makes Him the Anointed, and the King of all things that exist. If, then, the Father is King, and Only-begotten is King, and the Holy Spirit is the Kingship, one and the same definition of Kingship must prevail throughout this Trinity, and the thought of "unction" conveys the hidden meaning that there is no interval of separation between the Son and the Holy Spirit. For as between the body's surface and the liquid of the oil nothing intervening can be detected, either in reason or in perception, so inseparable is the union of the Spirit with the Son. (16)[33]

That Gregory can pass directly from St. Peter's remark about the "anointing" of Jesus of Nazareth to an assertion of the co-eternity of the second and third persons, without even adverting to the fact that

32 *PG*, 45:1317A.
33 *PG*, 45:1322A.

he is so passing, shows that he took for granted that the relations of the eternal Trinity were to be discerned from those revealed in the economy.

Homily on the Lord's Prayer

Only a small fragment of this work remains; the whole of it may be quoted for our purposes:

> For the Son went out from the Father, as the Scripture says, and the Spirit proceeds out of God and from the Father. But just as to be without a principle, since it is of the Father alone, cannot belong to the Son or the Holy Spirit, so conversely, to be from a principle [τὸ ἐξ αἰτίας εἶναι], which is proper to the Son and the Spirit, can by nature not be considered as belonging to the Father. And since it is common to the Son and the Holy Spirit that they do not exist as unbegotten, lest any confusion arise on this matter, again we can find an incommunicable difference in their properties, so that what is common may be preserved and what is proper may not be confused. For the only-begotten Son is said by Scripture [to be] from the Father, and in this way the word defines what is proper to him. But the Holy Spirit is said [to be] from the Father [ἐκ τοῦ Πατρὸς λέγεται] and is also testified to be from the Son [ἐκ τοῦ Υἱοῦ εἶναι προσμαρτυρεῖται]. For, if anyone does not have the Spirit of Christ, it says, he is not his. Therefore the Spirit that is of God is also the Spirit of God. But the Son, who is of God is not and is not said to be the Son of the Spirit; the terms of the relationship cannot be reversed [οὐδὲ ἀναστρέφει ἡ σχετικὴ ἀκολουθία αὔτη].[34]

This text as it stands here is even clearer than the first one quoted from *Adversus Macedonianos*, in that it describes the Holy Spirit as being not

[34] *PG*, 46:1109A–C.

simply "of the Son." but "out of the Son." As with the former texts, there is not the slightest indication that the saint is referring to anything other than the hypostatic origination of the third person. There are, however, textual difficulties. Some manuscripts read not ἐκ τοῦ Υἱοῦ, but simply τοῦ Υἱοῦ. Bessarion bears witness that, in his day, the older codices had the former reading and the more modern ones had the latter.[35] According to A. Mai, the ἐκ is found in a manuscript of the seventh century.[36] Martin Jugie suggests that the change of verb from λέγεται to προσμαρτυρεῖται supports the reading ἐκ: since τοῦ Υἱοῦ, unlike ἐκ τοῦ Υἱοῦ, *is* said in Scripture, Gregory would not have needed to change the verb if he had used the former phrase.[37] On the other hand W. Jaeger maintains that it was the ἐκ that was the interpolation.[38] The conclusion of the penultimate sentence is particularly confusing: as it stands, it is a *non sequitur*, since one would expect not "of God" but "of the Son." This suggests that some corruption of the fragment occurred in the course of its transmission, by a scribe unfavorable to the "Latin" doctrine.

Nevertheless, despite these uncertainties, the intention of the saint to distinguish the Holy Spirit from the Son in virtue of the former's relation to both Father and Son is still clear. Also clear is that the only relation in question, as in the Letter to Ablabius, is that of "being from a principle."

Adversus Graecos de communibus notionibus

This work was written to rebut the charge of tritheism. The most important passage for our purposes is the following:

> The persons of the godhead are divided from each other neither by time nor by place nor by will nor by occupation nor by

35 Bessarion, Letter to Alexios Lascaris (*PG*, 161:437B).

36 Cited in Martin Jugie, *De Processione Spiritus Sancti* (Rome: Facultas Theologica Pontificii Athenaei Seminarii Romani, 1936), 160.

37 Jugie, *De Processione Spiritus Sancti*, 160.

38 Cited in Congar, *I Believe in the Holy Spirit*, 44n19.

> activity nor by any of the other affections which are seen among men; but only because He is the Father is He the Father and not the Son; only because He is the Son is He the Son and not the Father; and likewise the Holy Spirit, neither the Father nor the Son.[39]

St. Gregory here appears to be assigning the formal principle for the distinction of each divine person. The Father is distinct because he is Father, because he is in relation to the Son, and the Son is distinct only because he is Son, because he is in relation to the Father. The Holy Spirit is not mentioned as the reason for the distinct identity of the other two persons. The fact that by contrast they are both mentioned when the Holy Spirit is said to be distinct implies that just as Father and Son are distinct through their relation to each other, so the Holy Spirit is distinct in virtue of his relation to them both. Given the saint's assertion in both *Contra Eunomius* and the Letter to Ablabius that "causality" is the reason for distinction in God, this would imply that Father and Son are both the "cause" of the Holy Spirit.

Oratio catechetica magna

Like many of the other Fathers, St. Gregory of Nyssa saw a reference to the Trinity in the verse from the Psalms that reads, "by the word of the Lord the heavens were made, and by the breath [πνεῦμα] of his mouth all their host." More than his predecessors, however, he tried to understand what can be meant by referring to the Holy Spirit as "breath of the mouth." He attempts this particularly in the so-called *Great Catechism*, a work of apologetics directed to Jews and pagans.

---

[39] *PG*, 45:180C.

As then by the higher mystical ascent [ἀναλογικῶς] from matters that concern ourselves to that transcendent nature we gain a knowledge of the Word, by the same method we shall be led on to a conception of the Spirit, by observing in our own nature certain shadows and resemblances of His ineffable power. Now in us the spirit (or breath) [τὸ πνεῦμα], is the drawing of the air, a matter other than ourselves, inhaled and breathed out for the necessary sustainment of the body. This, on the occasion of uttering the word, becomes an utterance which expresses in itself the meaning of the word. And in the case of the Divine nature it has been deemed a point of our religion that there is a Spirit of God, just as it has been allowed that there is a Word of God, because of the inconsistency of the Word of God being deficient as compared with our word, if, while this word of ours is contemplated in connection with spirit, that other Word were believed to be quite unconnected with spirit [δίχα πνεύματος]. Not indeed that it is a thought proper to entertain of Deity, that after the manner of our breath something foreign from without flows into God, and in Him becomes the Spirit; but when we think of God's Word we do not deem the Word to be something unsubstantial, nor the result of instruction, nor an utterance of the voice, nor what after being uttered passes away, nor what is subject to any other condition such as those which are observed in our word, but to be essentially self-subsisting, with a faculty of will ever-working, all-powerful. The like doctrine have we received as to God's Spirit; we regard it as that which goes with the Word and manifests its energy [τὸ συμπαρομαρτοῦν τῷ Λόγῳ, καὶ φανεροῦν αὐτοῦ τὴν ἐνέργειαν], and not as a mere effluence of the breath; for by such a conception the grandeur of the Divine power would be reduced and humiliated, that is, if the Spirit that is in it were supposed to resemble ours. But we conceive of it as an essential power, regarded as self-centred in its own proper person, yet equally incapable of being separated

> from God in whom it is, or from the Word of God whom it accompanies, as from melting into nothingness; but as being, after the likeness of God's Word, existing as a hypostasis, able to will, self-moved, efficient, ever choosing the good, and for its every purpose having its power concurrent with its will. (2)[40]

The human word that he takes as the analogy for the divine Word is not, as in St. Augustine, that word in the mind that precedes every human language, but rather the spoken word itself.[41] Or perhaps we may say more precisely that he has in mind as the analogy for the divine Logos not simply the spoken word, but rather the meaningfulness of the spoken word, manifested by the human breath with which it makes only one thing. Does this analogy succeed in telling us anything about the procession of the Holy Spirit? It tells us, perhaps, that this procession is necessary for God's self-expression to be complete, as the breath is necessary for our self-expression. More than that we do not seem to find here. On the other hand, his statement that the Holy Spirit manifests not just the nature but the activity (ἐνέργεια) of the Word is significant: it is hard to see how the activity of the Word can be revealed by the eternal procession of the Spirit unless the procession of the Spirit is due to this activity.

Summary and Conclusion

St. Gregory of Nyssa teaches: that the Holy Spirit is through or by the Son; that when the Father does something through the Son, they work conjointly; that the relation of the Holy Spirit to the Son is different from that of creation to the Son because the Holy Spirit is unchangeable; that it is in (not into) the Son that the Holy Spirit shines forth;

40 *PG*, 45:17A–C.

41 St. Gregory Nazianzen in Oration 23, no. 11, speaks of the "mind, word and breath in us" as an image for the Trinity, but he does not develop the thought (*PG*, 35:1161D).

that the Son has "priority" over the Spirit only by "causality," not by nature; that he is eternally of Christ, as one torch is enkindled by another; that he is ever receiving from the Son; that he is through the power that is the Son; that he is distinct from the Son because he has a relation to both Father and Son (this in a context where the only relations in question are those of "being a principle" and "being from a principle"); that he is distinct from both the Father and the Son, just as they are distinct from each other by virtue of their mutual relation; and that he eternally manifests the Son's activity. I can hardly, therefore, agree with Siecienski when he writes that "it is doubtful that Gregory of Nyssa would have accepted the *filioque* [*sic*] as it was later understood in the West."[42] On the contrary, the assertion that the Holy Spirit proceeds from Father and Son "as from one principle" is the very thing that can harmonize the description of the Father as *αἰτία* with Gregory's constant suggestion of a dependence of the third person on the second, yet without jeopardizing the simplicity of the Holy Spirit.

---

42 Siecienski, *Filioque*, 44–45.

CHAPTER 10

SAINT AUGUSTINE

Introduction

IN A DISCOURSE that he pronounced before a general council of the North African Church in 393, St. Augustine observed that although wise men have exerted themselves to the utmost in explaining the personal union and distinction of the first two persons of the Holy Trinity, much less has been done in regard to the third:

> With respect to the Holy Spirit . . . there has not been as yet, on the part of learned and distinguished investigators of the Scriptures, a discussion of the subject full enough or careful enough to make it possible for us to obtain an intelligent conception of what also constitutes His special individuality [*proprium*]: in virtue of which special individuality it comes to

> be the case that we cannot call Him either the Son or the Father, but only the Holy Spirit.[1]

St. Augustine's own thought on the procession of the Holy Spirit is to be sought principally in his great work *De Trinitate*, of which he famously said: "Iuvenis inchoavi, senex edidi"—"I was young when I began it, and old when I published it."[2] Although it alludes occasionally to various heresies that had troubled the Church, it differs from the works that we have considered thus far in that it was written primarily not to combat heresy, but rather from a simple desire to understand the mystery, as far as possible. I shall summarize both his explicit teaching on the procession and those questions that he raises about the procession but does not fully answer.

The Holy Spirit Proceeds Eternally from the Father and the Son

There is no need to delay long on proving a fact so well-known. A passage in the fourth book will suffice, where St. Augustine is making a careful distinction between the eternal processions and the temporal missions of the divine persons:

> As, therefore, the Father begot, the Son is begotten; so the Father sent, the Son was sent. But in like manner as He who begot and He who was begotten, so both He who sent and He who was sent, are one, since the Father and the Son are one. So also the Holy Spirit is one with them, since these three are one. For as to

1 *PL*, 40:191. Many of the Migne volumes containing the works of St. Augustine lack the customary repartition of pages by the letters A–D. The discourse was later published as *De fide et Symbolo*, and the extract quoted comes in section 19 of this work as found in Augustine of Hippo, Selected Works, trans. Arthur Haddan, *NPNF*1 vol. 3. Translations from the *De Trinitate* are also from Haddan, except as stated.

2 St. Augustine, Epistle 174 (*ad Aurelium*), no. 1 (*PL*, 33:758). Bernard de Margerie concurs with Yves Congar in accepting I. Chevalier's conclusion that Augustine was familiar with the Trinitarian works of Athanasius, Basil, Nazianzen, and Epiphanius ("Vers une relecture du concile de Florence, grâce à la reconsidération de l'Ecriture et des pères grecs et latins," *Revue thomiste* 86 [1986]: 31–81, at 54n100).

> be born, in respect to the Son, means to be from the Father; so to be sent, in respect to the Son, means to be known to be from the Father. And as to be the gift of God in respect to the Holy Spirit, means to proceed from the Father; so to be sent, is to be known to proceed from the Father. Neither can we say that the Holy Spirit does not also proceed from the Son, for the same Spirit is not without reason said to be the Spirit both of the Father and of the Son. Nor do I see what else He intended to signify, when He breathed on the face of the disciples, and said, "Receive the Holy Ghost." For that bodily breathing, proceeding from the body with the feeling of bodily touching, was not the substance of the Holy Spirit, but a declaration by a fitting sign, that the Holy Spirit proceeds not only from the Father, but also from the Son [non tantum a Patre, sed a Filio procedere Spiritum sanctum]. (4.20.29)[3]

The parallelism between temporal missions and eternal relations that we have seen to be implied often in the other Fathers is here made fully explicit.

Was St. Augustine teaching this as merely a personal theory and not a matter of Catholic faith? This cannot be maintained, since he gives exactly the same account of the procession in his letter to the Arian bishop Maximinus, in which he was expressly intending to set forth the true faith, as against Arianism.[4]

The Holy Spirit Proceeds *Principaliter* from the Father

The Latin term *principaliter* first appears in the fifteenth and last book of the treatise. Augustine writes, according to Arthur Haddan's translation:

---

[3] *PL*, 42:908.

[4] St. Augustine, *Contra Maximinum haereticum Arianorum episcopum*, *PL*, 42:743–814, at 770.

> God the Father alone is He from whom the Word is born, and from whom [de quo] the Holy Spirit principally [*principaliter*] proceeds. And therefore I have added the word principally, because we find that the Holy Spirit proceeds from the Son also. But the Father gave Him this too, not as to one already existing, and not yet having it; but whatever He gave to the only-begotten Word, He gave by begetting Him. Therefore He so begot Him as that the common Gift should proceed from Him [de illo] also, and the Holy Spirit should be the Spirit of both. (15.17.29)[5]

The word "principally" is not a good translation of *principaliter* in this context: the English word suggests that the Holy Spirit proceeds "more" from the Father than from the Son. It would convey the saint's meaning more accurately if we were to render it "as from the principle without principle"; the same meaning that we have argued is expressed by the Cappadocian Fathers' use of the word αἰτία. But St. Augustine, as always, explains his own meaning so carefully that there is no need to press the point.

The Holy Spirit Proceeds from Father and Son as from a Single Principle

In the fifth book, Augustine considers whether the word *principium* can rightly be used of the Father in regard to the Holy Spirit: "If the begetter is a principle in relation to that which he begets, the Father is a principle in relation to the Son, because He begets Him; but whether the Father is also a principle in relation to the Holy Spirit, since it is said, He proceeds from the Father, is no small question" (5.14.15).[6] The hesitation is due, perhaps, to the fact that whereas Scripture says "in the beginning [principio] was

5 *PL*, 42:1081.

6 In this and the next quotation, Haddan translated *principium* as "beginning." I prefer to avoid this word to avoid giving the impression that the Holy Spirit began to exist. Cf. note 5 of chapter 7 (St. Gregory of Nazianzen).

the Word," a text that can be understood as referring to the relation of the Son to the Father, no equivalent passage is found that can be read as naming the Father as the *principium* of the Holy Spirit. However, he says, if the word can be correctly used in regard not only to "that which is born," but also in regard to "that which is given"—that is, in regard to the Holy Spirit—then we must speak of Father and Son as *one* principle:

> If, therefore, that also which is given has him for a principle by whom it is given, since He did not receive from elsewhere that which proceeds from him [quia non aliunde accepit illud quod ab ipso procedit];[7] it must be admitted that the Father and the Son are a principle of the Holy Spirit, not two principles; but as the Father and Son are one God, and one Creator, and one Lord relatively to the creature, so are they one principle relatively to the Holy Spirit [sic relative ad Spiritum Sanctum unum principium]. But the Father, the Son and the Holy Spirit are one principle in respect to the creature, as also one Creator and one God. (5.14.15)[8]

So speaks the great bishop of Hippo, praised for the soundness of his doctrine by the Second Council of Constantinople.[9]

The Holy Spirit Proceeds as Gift

In the previous quotation, the phrase "that which is given," *quod datur*, was used as a synonym for the Holy Spirit. St. Augustine has a particular

---

7 Haddan translated this phrase as "since it has received from no other source that which proceeds from him."

8 *PL*, 42:921. Haddan writes, "is one beginning," in the last sentence. The Latin has no verb.

9 I do not understand, therefore, how Jean-Miguel Garrigues can say: "Even if the *qui ex Patre Filioque procedit* is found in St. Augustine, he always recognized that the character of principle expressed by the Latin term *ex* belonged to the Father alone" (*L'Esprit Qui Dit "Père!": l'Esprit-Saint dans la vie Trinitaire et le problème du* Filioque, Croire et Savoir 2 [Paris: Téqui, 1982], 99; trans. mine). Likewise, Carl Krauthauser is wrong to suggest that Augustine sees a difference in kind between the Holy Spirit's procession from the Father and his procession from the Son ("The Council of Florence Revisited," *Eastern Christian Journal* 4, no. 1 [1997]: 141–54, at 144n9).

liking for this phrase, and for the equivalent term *donum*, even when, as in that quotation, he is speaking of the immanent Trinity. The Holy Spirit is not only a gift to rational creatures, but proceeds eternally as a gift. In this same book 5, the saint examines and justifies this use of language:

> But it is asked further, whether, as the Son by being born, has not only this, that He is the Son, but that He is absolutely; and so also the Holy Spirit, by being given, has not only this, that He is given, but that He is absolutely [omnino]—whether therefore He was, before He was given, but was not yet a *gift*; or whether, for the very reason that God was about to give Him, He was already a gift also before He was given. But if He does not proceed unless when He is given, and assuredly could not proceed before there was one to whom He might be given; how, in that case, was He [absolutely] in His very substance, if He is not unless because He is given? Just as the Son, by being born, not only has this, that He is a Son, which is said relatively, but His very substance absolutely, so that He is. Does the Holy Spirit proceed always, and proceed not in time, but from eternity, but because He so proceeded that He was capable of being given [procedebat ut esset donabile], was already a gift even before there was one to whom He might be given? For there is a difference in meaning between a gift and a donation [donatum]. For a gift may exist even before it is given; but it cannot be called a donation unless it has been given. (16)[10]

We must note that the sentence in this extract that begins "does the Holy Spirit proceed always . . ." is not raising a question about whether there is an eternal procession; the question bears on the latter part

[10] *PL*, 42:921. Haddan translates *donatum* as "a thing that has been given," which turns the last phrase of the extract into a tautology.

of the phrase, which gives a suggestion for why this can be called the procession of a *gift*. Since St. Augustine does not return again to this question, we may take it that he is satisfied with the answer that he gives here: the Holy Spirit proceeds as a gift, since he proceeds as one who is able to be given in time. It is important to note also that St. Augustine does not say that Holy Spirit is a gift from the Father to the Son: they are perfectly one in their relation to the Holy Spirit.

The Holy Spirit Pertains to the Affective Life of God

St. Augustine's Intuition

It has been said that St. Augustine was the first person to identify the procession of the Holy Spirit with the volitional or affective life in God.[11] He himself would have denied this. Already in the discourse later published as *De fide et Symbolo*, after noting that some people have wished to identify the Holy Spirit as "the communion of the Father and the Son, and (so to speak) their Godhead [*deitatem*], which the Greeks designate θεότης," he continues: "This Godhead, then, which they wish to be understood likewise as the love and charity subsisting between these two [persons], the one toward the other, they affirm to have received the name of the Holy Spirit" (9.19).[12] In the *De fide et Symbolo* itself he does not definitely align himself with this view.

Again, when he introduces the same motif into the *De Trinitate*, it is by way of a gloss on a gnomic saying of St. Hilary of Poitiers that

11 Mauxilio T.-L. Penido, "Gloses sur la procession d'amour dans la Trinite," *Ephemerides theologicae lovanienses* 14 (1937): 33–68, at 34.

12 *PL*, 40:191: "Hanc ergo deitatem, quam etiam dilectionem in se invicem amborum caritatemque volunt intelligi, Spiritum sanctum appellatum dicunt" (trans. mine). Congar suggests that one of those whom St. Augustine had in mind as proponents of this view was Marius Victorinus (*I Believe in the Holy Spirit*, vol. 3, Milestones in Catholic Theology [New York: Crossroad, 1997], 55n9). Victorinus in his *Hymn on the Trinity* (written around 370) had addressed the Holy Spirit as "the association of the Two," *complexio duorum* (*PL*, 8:1146B). Zeno of Verona, in his *Second Treatise on the Origin* (dated to 381), says of the Father and the Son: "The one exults in the other, with the fullness of the Holy Spirit shining forth in one original co-eternity" (*PL*, 11:392A; trans. mine). Emile Bailleux notes that Augustine does not adopt the expression "common deity" as a description of the Holy Spirit in his later writings ("L'Esprit du Père et du Fils chez saint Augustin," *Revue thomiste* 77 [1977]: 5–29, at 26).

"eternity is in the Father, form in the Image, use in the Gift [usus in munere]."[13] Having explained the first two members of this description, St. Augustine goes on:

> That unspeakable conjunction of the Father and His image is not without fruition, without love, without joy. Therefore that love, delight, felicity, or blessedness [dilectio, delectatio, felicitas vel beatitudo], if indeed it can be worthily expressed by any human word, is called by him, in short, Use; and is the Holy Spirit in the Trinity, not begotten, but the sweetness [suavitas] of the begetter and of the begotten. (6.10.11)[14]

This paragraph appears as a monument in the history of Trinitarian theology. For, whereas it is far from clear that St. Hilary was speaking of the immanent life of God in mentioning *usus* in connection with the Holy Spirit,[15] and whereas we have found only a faint suggestion in Athanasius and Ambrose that the third person proceeds by reason of the eternal joy or love, here we have a clear and unhesitating statement that such is indeed the characteristic mark of the procession.

This paragraph, appearing as it does in book 6, anticipates what will come only much later in the treatise, in the fifteenth book. Before that final book, the connection between the Holy Spirit and the affective or volitional life of God is treated only in passing. At the end of book 8, he notes that love has a necessarily threefold character, insofar as there is always "he that loves, and that which is loved, and love." But he does not

---

[13] *PL*, 42:931. St. Hilary apparently wrote *infinitas*, not *aeternitas*, in the first member of the phrase (*CCSL*, 62:38).

[14] *PL*, 42:932. We can recall that the Latin verb *utor*, unlike the English word "use," can be employed without any offense to refer to the relation between two persons: "Ioannes utitur Iacobo," for example, means "John is a friend (or acquaintance) of James."

[15] Thus E. Watson and L. Pullan take it to be a reference rather to the believer, translating "usus in munere" as "our enjoyment of Him in the gift" (St. Hilary of Poitiers, *De Trinitate*, *NPNF*2 vol. 9). Stephen McKenna translates the obscure Latin phrase with the equally obscure "the use in the Gift" (St. Hilary of Poitiers, *On the Trinity*, trans. Stephen McKenna, Fathers of the Church 25 [Washington, DC: Catholic University of America Press, 1954]).

proceed to identify these three terms with the three divine persons. At the start of book 9, he writes: "Our wish is to see whether the Holy Spirit is properly that love which is most excellent; which if He is not, either the Father is love, or the Son, or the Trinity itself; since we cannot withstand the most certain faith and weighty authority of Scripture, saying, God is love" (9.1.1). But even here he postpones the enquiry for another six books. The commentary above on the short phrase in St. Hilary appears, then, not as the conclusion of an argument, but as a sudden illumination, requiring further defense and explanation.

Proof from Scripture

St. Augustine's approach to the question of whether the Holy Spirit can be particularly identified with love in God is not a priori or philosophical; he will seek the answer from revelation. Although he begins by considering, as we shall see, various "trinities" within the human soul, of which love or volition is always the third member, he does not conclude on this basis that the Holy Spirit proceeds as or by way of love, but rather by the witness of Scripture. It is in the last book that he reveals the Scriptural texts on which he rests.

The first passage is from 1 John 4:

> Beloved, let us love one another; for love is of God, and he who loves is born of God and knows God. He who does not love does not know God; for God is love. . . . If we love one another, God abides in us and his love is perfected in us. By this we know that we abide in him and he in us, because he has given us of his own Spirit. (1 John 4:7–8, 12b–13)

From the assertion that love is of God ("dilectio ex Deo est"), he concludes that love can be identified in a particular way either with the Son or with the Holy Spirit, since these two divine persons, but not the Father, may be said to be *ex Deo* (*De Trinitate* 15.17.31).

From the two assertions in the second half of the passage from St. John—that if we love each other, God abides in us, and that if God has given us his Spirit, then he abides in us—he concludes that the Holy Spirit is love. For the Holy Spirit and love are said to produce the same effect: the divine indwelling. The saint uses a striking phrase of the Holy Spirit: "Ipse est igitur Deus dilectio"—"He is therefore himself God as love."[16]

Augustine's other scriptural proofs are based on the identification of the Holy Spirit as the Gift of God par excellence, along with the fact that love, *caritas*, is also this supreme gift, since it alone can avail for salvation, according to 1 Cor 13. For example, Christ speaks of the rivers of living water in John 7:38, and the evangelist identifies this with the Spirit in the following verse; but Christ calls the living water the gift of God when speaking to the woman of Samaria in John 4:10; therefore, the Holy Spirit is the Gift (15:33). Again, when Simon Magus seeks to buy the power to confer the Holy Spirit, St. Peter rebukes him for thinking to obtain the gift of God with money (Acts 8:19–20). Having quoted these and other passages, Augustine remarks that "there are many other testimonies of the Scriptures, which unanimously attest that the Holy Spirit is the gift of God" (15.19.35). He concludes: "If there be among the gifts of God none greater than love, and there is no greater gift of God than the Holy Spirit, what follows more naturally than that He is Himself love, who is called both God and of God?" (15.19.37).

It is not my purpose in this passage to assess the exegesis of St. Augustine as such or defend it against possible criticisms, but simply to show that it is indeed by Scripture that he seeks to prove that the Holy Spirit is properly called love in the Trinity, even though each of the persons and the whole Trinity may also be called love (15.17.28). In this

16 *PL*, 42:1082. Haddan translates this as "therefore He is the God who is love," which is accurate but not quite as forceful as the original.

way he finds solid support for the intuition arising from Hilary's obscure phrase *usus in munere*, and from other, unnamed predecessors, that the Holy Spirit in some way is the *dilectio*, *delectatio*, *felicitas*, and *beatitudo* of the first two divine persons.

The Holy Spirit Is Common Love

In commenting on St. Hilary's term *usus*, Augustine mentions terms that pertain in a general way to what I have called the affective life of God, but in the rest of the treatise he concentrates on the idea of love (*dilectio*, *caritas*, *amor*) rather than that of delight or joy, perhaps because love is the principle of the whole affective life. Thus, summarizing his investigations, he writes:

> I have shown nothing in this enigma [that is, the human soul considered as a mirror of the Trinity] respecting the Holy Spirit such as might appear to be like Him, except our own will, or love, or affection, which is a stronger will [voluntatem nostram, vel amorem, vel dilectionem quae valentior est voluntas]. (15.23.41)[17]

The Holy Spirit is sometimes described as "the mutual love of the Father and the Son," and the unnamed authors whom St. Augustine mentioned in the *De fide et Symbolo* already thought in this way when they spoke of Him as "dilectionem in se invicem amborum" ("the love of both for each other"). St. Augustine, however, uses the term *communis* ("common"), rather than the term *mutuus* ("mutual"), in speaking of the Holy Spirit as love.[18] In book 15, having recalled the various trinities in the soul, he asks:

---

17 *Voluntas* does not appear to refer to a distinct *faculty* here. "Willing" might therefore be a better translation. According to Bailleux, *voluntas* and *caritas* are used as synonyms ("L'Esprit," 15).

18 The point is of importance, since, if the formal principle of the procession was *reciprocal* love strictly as such, it would be difficult to maintain, with the Council of Florence, that the Holy Spirit proceeds from Father and Son "as from one principle." See Penido, "Gloses," 62–66. Bailleux does not seem to see this difficulty ("L'Esprit," 20).

> Do we, I say, in such manner also see the Trinity that is God; because there also, by the understanding, we behold both Him as it were speaking, and His Word, i.e. the Father and the Son; and then, proceeding thence, the love common to both, namely, the Holy Spirit [procedentem caritatem utrique communem, scilicet Spiritum sanctum]?" (15.6.10)

(This is phrased as a question not in order to put in doubt whether the Holy Spirit is rightly so characterized, but because he is reflecting on whether we can be said through created analogies to *see* that God is a Trinity, or just believe so.) While the description of the Holy Spirit as "the love common to both" could indeed suggest *mutual* love, it can also be understood in a more general sense, as the love by which Father and Son love not only each other but also themselves and the Holy Spirit and creatures.

Later in the same book there is a similar though more cautious description of the third person:

> The Holy Spirit, according to the Holy Scriptures, is neither of the Father alone nor of the Son alone, but of both [amborum]; and so intimates to us a common love, wherewith the Father and the Son reciprocally love one another [communem, qua invicem se diligunt Pater et Filius, nobis insinuat caritatem]. (15.17.27)[19]

I call this more cautious in that Augustine does not simply identify the Holy Spirit as the *caritas communis* here, but says that his procession from both "intimates" to us this common love. For, he has already warned us earlier in the same book against the error of so identifying the Holy Spirit with love that the Father and Son would love nothing by themselves, but only by the Holy Spirit (15.7.12). On the other

19 Haddan translates *communem* as "mutual," which I have altered here.

hand, it does seem to be the idea of mutuality that is uppermost in his mind here when he uses the word *communis*, since he speaks of the love by which Father and Son love *each other*.

A third passage in the same book again mentions the Holy Spirit in connection with the mutual love of the Father and the Son: "If the love by which the Father loves the Son, and the Son loves the Father, ineffably demonstrates the communion of both, what is more suitable than that He should be specially called love, who is the Spirit common to both [communis ambobus]" (15.19.37). St. Augustine does not say here that the Holy Spirit is the love of the Father and the Son; his thought is rather that because mutual love—more than mutual knowledge—necessarily implies "having something in common," the Holy Spirit, who is also common to Father and Son, has the name "love" appropriated to Him.

Near the end of the same book, Augustine refers to the Holy Spirit as "a kind of consubstantial communion [communio quaedam consubstantialis] of Father and Son" (15.27.50). He does not explain whether he is thinking here of the Holy Spirit simply as "that which the Father and Son have in common" or more precisely as the love they have in common; though, as he has said above that it is love that ineffably demonstrates the communion of Father and Son, love and the Holy Spirit are clearly associated in his thought at this point also. On the other hand we can note that neither here nor elsewhere does he adopt the suggestion aired in the *De fide et Symbolo* that the Holy Spirit might properly be characterized as the *deitas* common to Father and Son: such a suggestion is ruled out by his emphasis throughout the treatise that "Father," "Son," and "Holy Spirit" are relative terms, whereas deity and all the divine attributes are predicated of God absolutely, and not as denoting a relation.

Finally, we can also notice the question that he raises much earlier in the treatise of whether we are to call the Holy Spirit "that absolute love [summa caritas] which joins together Father and Son, and joins us also from beneath [coniungens . . . subiungens]" (7.6.6). He does not repudiate this use of language, but as we have seen, when he comes to consider the question more extensively in book 15, he prefers the use of words denoting "commonness" to the language of "joining," perhaps to avoid the idea that Father and Son are in any way passive in regard to the third person.

To sum up this section: the Holy Spirit is said in different places in the treatise to be the love common to Father and Son, to put us in mind (*insinuare*) of the love by which they love each other, and to be their consubstantial communion. At the same time, we are told that Father and Son, and the whole Trinity, can rightly be named "love," and that we must not suppose that the Father and Son are not loving from themselves but from the Holy Spirit. He does not quite explain how the first and last of these points are simultaneously true; there is still room for the more precise characterization of the procession that a later theology will bring, whereby the Holy Spirit will be said not simply to proceed *as* love, but rather to proceed *by reason* of love.

Images of the Trinity in the Soul

We have seen that, at the end of book 8, St. Augustine notes that all love involves three things: the lover, the beloved, and love itself. This is, however, not a dominant theme of the *De Trinitate*, even when the author is attempting to characterize the Holy Spirit. Perhaps he thought it suggested a dissymmetry between Father and Son that would make it difficult to show how they are "one principle" of the Holy Spirit. Far more time is spent on the consideration of trinities that exist within *one* human being. Of the various trinities he mentions, by which he seeks to lead the reader upward from more earthly to more sublime realities, he allows the name of "*image* of the Trinity" only to those that pertain to man's soul as spiritual, not to those that involve the senses. He seems to distinguish five such images: the mind, its knowledge of itself, and its love of itself (9.4.4); the mind, a thought within the mind, and the love of what is thought of (9.7.13); the memory of something, the actual thought of that same thing, and the love that leads the mind to go from remembrance to actual thought (10.8.13); the mind's own remembrance of itself, its actual thought of itself, and the love that leads it to go from remembrance to thought (14.7.10 through 14.8.11); the mind's remembrance of God, its thought of God, and its love of God (14.12.15). These five images may also be reduced to two, the second and third, insofar as the other three are examples of them. We are thus left with (1) the mind, a thought within the mind, and the love of what is thought of; and (2) the memory of something, the actual thought of that same thing, and the love that leads the mind to go from remembrance to actual thought.

This last image seems to be St. Augustine's preferred one, since he returns to it at the very end of his treatise, before concluding with a prayer:

> That light itself shows to you these three things in yourself, wherein you may recognize an image of the highest Trinity itself, which you cannot yet contemplate with steady eye. Itself shows to you that there is in you a true word, when it is born of your knowledge,[20] i.e. when we say what we know: although we neither utter nor think of any articulate word that is significant in any tongue of any nation, but our thought is formed by that which we know; and there is in the mind's eye of the thinker an image resembling that thought which the memory contained, will or love as a third combining these two as parent and offspring. (15.27.50)[21]

[20] What he here calls knowledge, *scientia*, is apparently the same as what he calls memory, *memoria*, in book 10.

[21] His preference for one "trinity" over another as an image for the Blessed Trinity is not, apparently, fixed. In 14.12.15, he seems to give the preference to the fifth of the five trinities I have distinguished.

There is one obvious difficulty with this analogy: love, or will, appears here as a reason for the "generation" of the thought or "word of the heart." This would suggest that the Trinitarian order should be Father, Holy Spirit, Son. St. Augustine is conscious of this difficulty (15.26.47), but simply notes that it is impossible to suppose that the Holy Spirit preceded the Son, as there is no time in God. This, however, still leaves the problem that the Holy Spirit could seem to be a reason for the generation of the Son, even though the two are eternally simultaneous. Later still he insists that in this psychological trinity, willing also *proceeds* from thinking, as well as giving rise to the thought, since no one wills that of which he is wholly ignorant (15.27.50). There is thus a certain incoherence at this point in the treatise, or at least an unresolved problem.

Given all this, one may wonder why the saint does not give preference to the other of his two main images, as Aquinas was to do, and speak of the mind, its knowledge of itself, and its love of itself as the most perfect image of the Trinity. The answer is perhaps that, in this image, the first term (the mind) has a superiority over the other two terms, being substantial while these are accidental. The Arian crisis is still a living memory.

Will (*Voluntas*) Is Not an Image of Thought (*Cogitatio*)

The last question that the saint raises concerning the Holy Spirit is why he is not called a Son. Like the authors who proceeded him, he acknowledges the extreme difficulty of the subject, which will be understood only by the mind that enjoys the direct vision of God:

> In that light there will be no place for inquiry: but here, by experience itself it has appeared to me so difficult—as beyond doubt it will likewise appear to them also who shall carefully and intelligently read what I have written—that although in the

> second book I promised that I would speak thereof in another place, yet as often as I have desired to illustrate it by the creaturely image of it which we ourselves are, so often, let my meaning be of what sort it might, did adequate utterance entirely fail me; nay, even in my very meaning [intellectu] I felt that I had attained to endeavour rather than accomplishment. (15.25.45)[22]

Yet, despite this humility, and unlike the Fathers who preceded him, St. Augustine does sketch an answer to the question of why the procession of the Holy Spirit is not generation, in a passage of which we have already considered one part:

> And let us grant that there is in the mind's eye of the thinker an image resembling that thought which the memory contained, will or love as a third combining these two as parent and offspring. And he who can, sees and discerns that this will proceeds indeed from thought (for no one wills that of which he is absolutely ignorant what or what sort it is), yet is not an image of the thought: and hence that there is insinuated in this intelligible thing a sort of difference between birth and procession, since to behold by thought is not the same as to desire or even to enjoy by will. (15.27.50)[23]

In other words, thinking of a thing has a resemblance to remembering it that willing or loving it does not possess, since the first two activities belong to the intellectual realm and the last to the affective realm. While St. Thomas Aquinas will not answer this question of why the

---

22 *PL*, 42:1092.

23 *PL*, 42:1097: "Sitque in acie cogitantis imago simillima cogitationis eius quam memoria continebat, ista duo scilicet velut parentem ac prolem tertia voluntate sive dilectione iungente. Quam quidem voluntatem de cogitatione procedere (nemo enim quod omnino quid vel quale sit nescit), non tamen esse cogitationis imaginem; et ideo quamdam in hac re intelligibili nativitatis et processionis insinuare distantiam, quoniam non hoc est cogitatione conspicere quod appetere, vel etiam perfrui voluntate, cernit discernitque qui potest." I have slightly changed Haddan's translation.

Holy Spirit is not a second Son in quite the same way, he will retain three principles from St. Augustine's treatment of the question: first that the distinction between the two Trinitarian processions can be grasped, however imperfectly, by the analogy of man's spiritual acts; secondly that spiritual acts can be distinguished according to whether they properly and according to their very notion consist in the forming of a likeness; and thirdly that this distinction enables us to distinguish generation and procession in God. The validity of St. Augustine's intuition that the uniqueness of the Holy Spirit is to be sought through the idea of love is thus confirmed by its fruitfulness in distinguishing his procession from the Son's generation.

CHAPTER 11

SAINT CYRIL OF ALEXANDRIA

Introduction

WHILE ST. CYRIL (†444) SPEAKS in many places of the relation of the Son to the Holy Spirit, he considers this question not so much for its own sake, but as part of his defense of the divinity either of the second person or of the third. Since he uses many of the same phrases and illustrations in his different works as he explains this relationship, it seems most useful to avoid repetitions and to treat his thought thematically, rather than to look at each work in turn.[1]

The Holy Spirit Is Eternally from the Son

St. Cyril says in many places, talking of the eternal origin of the Holy Spirit, that he is "from" or "from the substance of" the Son. These two

[1] Passages from the commentary on St. John's Gospel are from Cyril of Alexandria, *Commentary on St. John's Gospel*, books VI–XI, trans. H. Liddon (London: Walter Smith, 1885), which will be cited by the chapter and verse of the Gospel. Other translations are my own from Migne, unless otherwise stated.

expressions are used interchangeably. For example, in his commentary on the ninth anathema against Nestorius, he writes:

> Although the only-begotten Word of God was made man, yet he remained God, having all things in common with the Father except for paternity; and having as his own the Holy Spirit, who is from [ἐξ] himself and who is essentially in him [οὐσιωδῶς ἐμπεφυκὸς αὐτῷ], he worked the signs of divine power. Accordingly, after he was made man, he remained God, and thus performed miracles through the Spirit by his proper power.[2]

The sequence of thought shows that it is because the Holy Spirit is from the Son eternally that he is the proper power of the Son after the Incarnation.

Elsewhere the saint draws more of a contrast between the eternal and the economic relations of Son and Holy Spirit, yet still with the insistence that the Spirit is from the Son within the Trinity. In his commentary on the book of Joel, he is discussing the restoration of the grace of prophecy, which Adam had enjoyed before the fall:

> It was restored in Christ, who is the second Adam. How was it restored? Insofar as the Son is God, and from God according to nature (for he was born from God and the Father), the Spirit is proper to him, and in him and from him, just as the same Spirit is understood to be in God and the Father [ᾗ μὲν γὰρ ἐστι θεός, καὶ ἐκ θεοῦ κατὰ φύσιν ὁ ⊠ιὸς (γεγένηται γὰρ ἐκ θεοῦ καὶ Πατρός), ἴδιον αὐτοῦ τε, καὶ ἐν αὐτῷ, καὶ ἐξ αὐτοῦ τὸ Πνεῦμα ἐστι, καθάπερ ἀμέλει καὶ ἐπ᾿αὐτοῦ νοεῖται τοῦ θεοῦ καὶ Πατρός]. And insofar as he is man, like us, he is said to have the Spirit upon him. For it descended upon him in the likeness of a dove.[3]

---

2 *PG*, 76:308D–9A.

3 *PG*, 71:377D–80A.

In various places, Cyril uses the expression "from the substance" or "essence" of the Son. The following passage is taken from his *Thesaurus de Sancta et Consubstantiali Trinitate* and forms part of his explanation of proposition 33 of that work, "that the Holy Spirit is God by nature and of the essence of the Father and that he is given to creatures through the Son":

> Paul writes to some in this way: "But you are not in the flesh, but in the Spirit, if indeed the Spirit of God dwells in you. But if anyone does not have the Spirit of Christ, he is not his. But if Christ is in you, the body indeed is dead because of sin, but the Spirit is life because of justice." From here you can draw the right understanding of the Spirit, and learn that he subsists from the essence of the Savior [ἀπὸ τῆς τοῦ σωτῆρος ὑπάρξον οὐσίας], nor is he foreign to the one deity. For when he had said "the Spirit of God," he immediately adds "the Spirit of Christ" so that he might show that all things that are proper to the Father, naturally pass into the Son born from him. Again, he calls Christ the Spirit, saying, "but if Christ is in you," declaring that he is not foreign to the nature of the Word, but so united to him, although he has his own hypostasis, that he exists in the Son and the Son in him on account of the identity of essence.[4]

It might be asked whether there is any significance in the fact that Cyril employs the word ἀπό rather than ἐκ in this passage. Apparently there is none, since very soon afterward he uses the latter preposition to describe the Holy Spirit as subsisting from the substance of Christ, ἐκ τῆς οὐσίας ὑπάρξον.[5] Elsewhere he uses the preposition παρά, again with no apparent difference of meaning, speaking of "the Spirit who is

[4] *PG*, 75:568B–C.
[5] *PG*, 75:569C.

proper to him and flows forth from him by nature [τὸ ἴδιον αὐτοῦ καὶ παρ᾽αὐτοῦ κατὰ φύσιν προχεόμενον Πνεῦμα]."[6]

Naturally, St. Cyril also holds that the Holy Spirit is from the essence of the Father. He uses the expression, for example, in the commentary on the same proposition 33 that has been mentioned, shortly before using the expression already quoted, "subsisting from the essence" of Christ.[7] The fact that he can juxtapose these two expressions without further qualification indicates that he saw no difference between the way the Holy Spirit is from the essence of the Father and the way that he is from the essence of the Son.

The Holy Spirit May Be Equally Said to Be "of" and "through" the Son

St. Cyril uses certain verbs that express an eternal relation between the Son and the Holy Spirit with the preposition διά, and also with the preposition ἐκ. For the verb πρόειμι ("go forth"), this usage is found his commentary of St. John's gospel. Commenting on John 15:26–27, he writes:

> As the Spirit naturally belongs to the Son, being in Him and proceeding through Him, so also He belongs to the Father [Ὡς γὰρ ἐστιν ἴδιον Πνεῦμα τοῦ Υἱοῦ φυσικῶς, ἐν αὐτῷ τε ὑπάρχον, καὶ δι᾽ αὐτοῦ προϊόν, οὕτως καὶ τοῦ Πατρός]. But the qualities of Their Substance cannot be distinct, where the Spirit is common [κοινόν] to both.[8]

Commenting on 16:12–3, he writes: "The Holy Spirit is not in truth alien from the Substance of the Only-begotten, but proceeds naturally from it [πρόεισι δὲ φυσικῶς ἐξ αὐτῆς], having no separate existence from Him so far as identity of nature is concerned."[9]

6 *Commentary on St. John's Gospel*, 1:33 (*PG*, 73:212B).
7 *PG*, 75:569A.
8 *PG*, 74:417C.
9 *PG*, 74:444B.

Something similar is found in regard to the verb προχέω, literally "pour forth," and sometimes translated "flow forth" when the middle voice is used. In the *Thesaurus*, the following passage occurs in dialogue 2:

> You will think of the Father as the ultimate root, beyond which there is nothing at all, while you will say the Son to be him who proceeded and was born from that ultimate root, not indeed produced in time like created things, nor as putting forth the glory of his nature as less than the nature of the Father, but as co-eternal and equal to the Father in all things, except for this one thing that it is the Father who begot—for this pertains only to God and the Father. You will say that the holy Spirit is he who flows forth [προχεόμενον] naturally from the Father through the Son, and in the likeness of the breathing that comes from the mouth shows us his being.[10]

In *De adoratione in spiritu et veritate*, he is discussing, in the form of a dialogue, the initial formation of man. Having mentioned that the Holy Spirit was breathed into man at creation, his interlocutor asks whether, therefore, man's soul became the divine spirit. Cyril replies:

> How would it not be most absurd to think this? For then the soul, being immutable, would have remained as it was; but in fact the soul is mutable. But the Spirit is not mutable in any way; if it suffers from the weakness of mutability, this blemish would affect the nature of God itself, for he indeed is God, of both the Father and the Son, he who flows forth substantially from both, that is from the Father through the Son [ἐστι τοῦ Θεοῦ καὶ Πατρὸς καὶ μὴν τοῦ Υἱοῦ, τὸ οὐσιωδῶς ἐξ ἀμφοῖν, ἤγουν ἐκ Πατρὸς δι' Υἱοῦ προχεόμενον Πνεῦμα]. It would therefore be foolish to think that the Holy Spirit was changed into the soul.[11]

[10] *PG*, 75:721D–24A.
[11] *PG*, 68:148A.

These passages shows that ἐκ and διά are interchangeable in St. Cyril's mind when it comes to describing the relation between the Son and the Holy Spirit as God. So, although there is no passage extant where he uses the preposition ἐκ of the Son after the verb ἐκπορεύεσθαι, there seems no reason why he would have not done so, had occasion offered.[12]

The Holy Spirit Proceeds in the Son

Occasionally St. Cyril uses a slightly different manner of speaking and talks of the Holy Spirit as proceeding *in* the Son, a usage that we have already met in Gregory of Nyssa. This is found, for example, in his defense of proposition 34 of the *Thesaurus*. Having used the illustration of the Son as the right hand of the Father and the Holy Spirit as the finger of that hand, he says that the Spirit is "naturally and substantially proceeding in the Son from the Father [ἐν δὲ τῷ ⊠ιῷ φυσικῶς καὶ οὐσιωδῶς διῆκον παρὰ Πατρός]."[13] It is important to note that he does not say "into the Son." The Son is presented by this expression rather as the "place" where the procession occurs, not as the recipient of the Spirit.[14]

The Father and the Son Have the Same Relation to the Holy Spirit

We have already quoted above the passage in *De adoratione in spiritu et veritate* where the saint says that the Spirit is poured forth substantially from both. There it was quoted as showing the equivalence of ἐκ and διά. It is also a striking testimony to the fact that the Father and the Son have the same relation to the third person according to St. Cyril. "He indeed is God, of both the Father and the Son, he who flows

---

12 Bernard de Margerie also suggests that there is nothing in St. Cyril to suggest that he would use this verb only in relation to the Father as "principle without principle" ("Vers une relecture du concile de Florence, grâce à la reconsidération de l'Ecriture et des pères grecs et latins," *Revue thomiste* 86 [1986]: 31–81, at 40).

13 *PG*, 75:577A.

14 This is the same usage that was noted in St. Gregory of Nyssa (see the section on the *Contra Eunomium* in ch. 9).

forth substantially from both." Although in the passage as a whole he is discussing the infusion of the Spirit into Adam at creation, it is not possible to maintain that St. Cyril is saying only that this infusion is caused by Father and Son.[15] The context shows that the "substantial flow" from the Father and the Son is presented as the reason why the Holy Spirit is God: it is a reference to the immanent Trinity.

There are other passages where the saint explicitly identifies the activity of Father and Son in regard to the eternal existence of the Holy Spirit. In the *Commentary on St. John's Gospel*, regarding 16:15 we read:

> Since then, [Christ] says, it is seen to be natural to God the Father to reveal Himself in His own Spirit to those who are worthy of Him, and to accomplish through Him all His purposes, and since this kind of action belongs to Me also, for this cause I said, "He receiveth of Me and will show it unto you." And let no man be perplexed when he here hears the word "receiveth," but rather let him consider the following fact, and he will do well. The things of God are spoken of in language as though God were even as we are; but this is not really the case, for His ways are superhuman. We say then that the Spirit receives of the Father and the Son the things that are Theirs in the following way [λαμβάνειν τε οὕτως τὸ Πνεῦμα φαμεν, ἔκ τε τοῦ Πατρὸς καὶ τοῦ Υἱοῦ τὰ αὐτῶν]; not as though at one moment He were devoid of the knowledge and power inherent in Them, and at the next hardly acquires such knowledge and power when He is conceived of as receiving from Them. For the Spirit is wise and powerful, nay, rather, absolute Wisdom and Power, not by participation in anything else, but by His own Nature. But, rather, just as we should say that the fragrance of

15 Contrary to what André de Halleux claims in "Cyrille, Theodoret et le *Filioque*," *Revue d'histoire ecclésiastique* 74 (1979): 597–625, at 614.

> sweet-smelling herbs which assails our nostrils is distinct from the herbs so far as their conception in thought is concerned, but proceeds from the herbs in which it originates only by being a recipient of the faculty of giving scent in order to its display, and is not in fact distinct from them, because its existence is due to, and is wrapped up in, them [διὰ τὸ ἐξ αὐτῶν τε καὶ ἐν αὐτοῖς πεφυκέναι]; even such an idea, or rather one transcending this, must you imagine about the relation of God to the Holy Spirit. For He is, as it were, a sweet savour of His Substance, working plainly on the senses, conveying to the creature an effluence from God, and instilling in him through Itself participation in the Sovereign Substance of the Universe. For if the fragrance of sweet herbs imparts some of its power to garments with which it comes in contact, and in some sort transforms its surroundings into likeness with itself, surely the Holy Ghost has power, since He is by nature of God, to make those in whom He abides partakers in the Divine Nature through Himself. The Son then, being the Fruit and express Image of the Father's Person by nature, engrosses all that is His. And therefore He says, *All things whatsoever the Father hath are Mine: therefore said I unto you, that He taketh of Mine and shall declare it unto you*—the Spirit, that is, Who is through Him and in Him, by Whom He personally dwells in the Saints. For His Spirit is not distinct from Him, even though He may be conceived of as having a separate and independent existence: for the Spirit is Spirit, and not the Son.[16]

Here the Holy Spirit is said to come forth from the Father and the Son as the scent from an herb. Despite the reference in the second part of the passage to the sanctification of the creature, it is clear that the first

16 *PG*, 74:452C–53B.

part is a reference to the eternal procession: St. Cyril is discussing the way in which the Holy Spirit exists as "absolute wisdom and power" (αὐτόχρημα σοφία καὶ δύναμις). The fact that he passes so naturally to a discussion of the saving action of the Spirit is simply one more indication of something that we have already frequently encountered: the Fathers take for granted that the economic Trinity will correspond in its relations to the immanent Trinity.[17]

The Father and the Son Are One in the Procession of the Holy Spirit

This point may seem hardly distinct from the previous one, but what is important is that, for St. Cyril, the Father and the Son have in regard to the Holy Spirit an activity that is not only "specifically" the same, but numerically the same, in the sense in which St. Augustine spoke of Father and Son as *unum principium*, and the Council of Florence defined them to be μία ἀρχή. In the sixth dialogue of the *Thesaurus*, the following passage occurs:

> "Of whom shall we say that the Holy Spirit is proper [ἴδιον]? Only to God and the Father, or also to the Son; or to each separately and to both as one, from the Father through the Son, on account of the identity of the substance? [ἢ καὶ ἀναμέρος ἑκατέρου καὶ ἀμφοῖν ὡς ἕν, ἐκ Πατρὸς δι' Υἱοῦ διὰ τὴν ταυτότητα τῆς οὐσίας;]."
>
> "I should say the latter."
>
> "You are right my friend, and be glad for this keenness of mind. I say that this judgment of yours corresponds wonderfully to the Holy Scriptures. For God the Father is understood to subsist in himself, but the Son also subsists in a proper way [ἰδικῶς]; but although each is distinct in virtue of his person, there is certainly no place for separation. For the Son is not

[17] For the correspondence in St. Cyril between the immanent and economic Trinity, see George Berthold, "Cyril of Alexandria and the *Filioque*," *Studia Patristica* 19 (1989): 143–47.

separated from the Father as one angel from another, and as one man from another among us, where there is complete separation; nor is the principle of distinction such as to make them wholly separate, for otherwise they would be two gods. Rather, since the godhead is, and is understood to be, one and unique, we shall see the Son living and subsisting in the Father, and the Father, conversely, in the Son. For he is the impress of his substance.

"I agree."

"Therefore the Spirit is also of one nature, and flows forth [προχεῖται] from the Father as from a source. Yet he is not foreign to the Son. For the Son is begotten and has everything proper to the Father in himself. For since he is the fruit of the supreme deity, how could he be thought to lack any of the good things of the Father? Now the property of the deity is sanctification, of which the Spirit is capable. For he is holy by nature, and sanctifies the whole of creation."

"How will you prove this, and how can I clearly learn that the Holy Spirit is proper to the Son just as he certainly is to the Father?"

"I shall not look for any outside witness; I shall bring in Christ himself, saying, 'I still have many things to teach you, but you cannot bear them now. But when the Spirit of truth comes, he will teach you all things. . . .' Do these things not suffice as a proof for the wise, insofar as he calls the Paraclete his own, since he named him the 'Spirit of Truth,' and there is no other truth besides himself? But when he adds, 'he will receive of mine,' he clearly shows the substantial and natural relationship [τὴν οὐσιώδη καὶ φυσικὴν οἰκειότητα], insofar as his Spirit is one thing with him."[18]

---

[18] *PG*, 75:1009B–12C.

Note St. Cyril's allusion in the first paragraph to the Holy Spirit as not just proper both to Father and to Son, but proper to them both ὡς ἕν, "as one thing." It does not much matter whether we understand this last phrase as denoting the Father and the Son or as denoting the Holy Spirit. For, in the latter case, if the Holy Spirit is said to be proper to the Father and the Son precisely in his *oneness*, then they must have no duality in that by which they have him as proper. And since, as we have seen above, he is proper to them as flowing forth from them, we can conclude that, for St. Cyril, the Holy Spirit eternally comes forth as God from the Father and the Son as from one principle.

The Holy Spirit Proceeds from the Divine Substance

We have seen above certain references in St. Cyril to the third divine person proceeding "from the substance" of the Father or the Son. It is worth drawing attention to this point, since anti-filioquist writers have sometimes claimed that to speak of the divine substance as a principle of procession was a Latin deviation, undermining a properly personal conception of God.[19] Other passages speak of a procession simply "from the substance" without explicitly mentioning Father or Son. This, of course, reinforces what was said above of the Father and Son as one principle of the procession. The *Commentary on St. John's Gospel*, on 16:14, once more furnishes an important example:

> We must in no wise suppose that the Comforter, that is, the Spirit, is lacking in innate and inherent power in such a way that, if He did not receive assistance from without, His own power would

[19] In this connection, A. Edward Siecienski cites the twentieth-century Romanian theologian D. Staniloae (*The Filioque: History of a Doctrinal Controversy* [New York: Oxford University Press, 2010], 198). At the Council of Florence, Mark of Ephesus had affirmed that the phrase ἐκ τοῦ οὐσίας could not refer to the principle of procession on the grounds that substance did not generate or spirate (*AG*, 286). I have already argued that this is a simple confusion of the principle "who" and the principle "by which" (see the subsection "Can the One Principle from which the Holy Spirit Proceeds Be the Divine Essence" in ch. 1 ("The 1995 Statement on the *Filioque*").

> not be self-sufficient to fully accomplish the Divine designs. Anyone who merely imagined any such idea to be true about the Spirit would with good reason undergo the charge of the worst blasphemy of all. But it is because He is Consubstantial with the Son, and divinely proceeds through Him [πρόεισι θεοπρεπῶς δι' αὐτου], exercising universally His entire activity and power, that Christ says, "He shall receive of Me." For we believe that the Spirit has a self-supporting existence and is in truth that which He is, and with the qualities predicated of Him; though, being inherent in the Substance of God, He proceeds and issues from it [ἐνυπάρχον γε μὴν τῇ οὐσίᾳ τοῦ θεοῦ, προκύπτει τε καὶ πρόεισιν ἐξ αὐτῆς] and has innate in Himself all that that nature implies [πάντα τὰ αὐτῆς ἔχον ἐν ἑαυτῷ φυσικῶς].[20]

In this short passage he passes from speaking of the Holy Spirit proceeding through the Son to speaking of him proceeding from the divine substance. If he does not reach the technical refinement of saying that the Father and the Son are the principle "from whom" and the divine substance a principle "in virtue of which," there is no reason to think that he would dispute these phrases.

One other passage may be quoted, this time from his explanation of assertion 34 in the *Thesaurus*:

> The Spirit whom Moses affirms was breathed by God into man, Christ renews in us after the resurrection from the dead, breathing into the disciples and saying, "Receive the Holy Spirit." Thus re-made according to the original image, we are conformed in nature to the Creator by the participation of the Spirit. Therefore since the Holy Spirit, sent into us, makes us conformed to God and proceeds from [πρόεισι ἐκ] the Father and

---

20 *PG*, 74:449A–B.

> the Son, it is clear that he is of the divine essence, substantially in it and proceeding [προϊόν] from it.[21]

The Holy Spirit's ἐκπόρευσις from the Father Is Not Distinct from His "Coming Forth" or "Flowing Forth"

Faced with such and so many Cyrilline texts, one might think it impossible for anyone to deny that he would have supported the doctrine defined at the Council of Florence. One would, alas, underestimate the resources of anti-filioquism. A. Edward Siecienski avers: "[Nowhere] in his writings, does Cyril say that the Spirit *proceeds* (ἐκπορεύεται) from the Father and the Son. Rather he consistently maintains that the Spirit *progresses* or *flows forth* (προϊέναι [*sic*], προχεῖται) from the Son, which is something rather different."[22] In fact, of course, a difference in the words does not prove a difference in the things named by the words. Here and elsewhere Siecienski seems to overlook this obvious but all-important fact. Apparently relying on the same linguistic facts, Yves Congar claimed that, for St. Cyril, the Holy Spirit receives his "hypostatic existence" from the Father alone, but his "substantial existence" from the Father and the Son.[23]

In fact, however, no such distinction between deriving hypostatic existence and substantial existence is to be found in the Cyrilline passages that we have considered. The passages in which St. Cyril talks of the Holy Spirit "progressing" or "flowing forth" from the Son, or simply says that he is from the Son, speak of the Holy Spirit as a distinct divine person with the divine nature and divine attributes. There is then no distinct reality left in God that remains to come forth in a way that

21 *PG*, 75:585A.

22 Siecienski, *Filioque*, 49.

23 Yves Congar, *I Believe in the Holy Spirit*, vol. 3, Milestones in Catholic Theology (New York: Crossroad), 1997, 200. Unfortunately, Congar does not here quote or cite any texts in support of his claim. Likewise, Jean-Miguel Garrigues claims that there are "innumerable texts" in which Cyril distinguishes ἐκπόρευσις and προϊέναι or ὑπάρχειν (to exist), but those he quotes in support of this claim do not in fact draw any such distinction, or even use the word ἐκπόρευσις (*L'Esprit Qui Dit "Père!": l'Esprit-Saint dans la vie Trinitaire et le problème du* Filioque, Croire et Savoir 2 [Paris: Téqui, 1982], 82).

would be denoted by the supposedly distinctive term ἐκπόρευσις. At the most, one could say that St. Cyril is accustomed to reserve the *word* ἐκπόρευσις for the coming forth of the Holy Spirit from the Father, even though, as we have seen, he teaches that the third person comes forth from the first two "as one," ὡς ἕν.[24]

There is moreover one passage in St. Cyril that explicitly confirms that the term ἐκπόρευσις does not denote some reality distinct from the reality denoted by similar verbs that are used of the coming-forth of the Holy Spirit. It is found in Letter 55, *On the Holy Creed*. Having spoken at length about the article of the Creed that treats of the Son, he continues:

> After the thrice-blessed Fathers have brought to an end the statement about Christ, they mention the Holy Spirit. For they stated that they believe in him, just as they do in the Father and in the Son. For he is consubstantial with them and he is poured forth—that is, he proceeds [προχεῖται ἤγουν ἐκπορεύεται]—from the fountain of God the Father and is bestowed on creation through the Son. Wherefore Christ breathed upon the holy apostles, saying, "receive the Holy Spirit." Therefore God the Spirit is from God and not different from that substance that is the highest of all, but is from that substance and is in it and has it as its own. (40)[25]

Here he takes for granted the identification between the ἐκπόρευσις and the "pouring forth." Since he talks elsewhere of the Son pouring forth the Holy Spirit in contexts that clearly refer to the immanent Trinity,

24 I thus concur with Martin Jugie, who writes that St. Cyril "was wholly unaware of the difference of meaning which later Greeks invented, between the word ἐκπορεύεσθαι and synonymous words such as προέρχεσθαι, προϊέναι, προχεῖσθαι, πεφῆναι etc" (*De Processione Spiritus Sancti* [Rome: Facultas Theologica Pontificii Athenaei Seminarii Romani, 1936], 138–39). Bessarion states in his *Oratio Dogmatica de Unione* (*PG*, 161:543–614, at 578A) that Cyril uses the word πεφῆναι of the Son's eternal generation in his letter to Valerian. The text of Cyril's letter in *PG*, 77:272B, reads γεννηθείς, "begotten," with πεφηνώς, "appearing," given as an alternative reading in a note. The most recent English translation of the letter, number 50 in Cyril's collected letters, reads "begotten" (*Letters 1–50*, trans. John McEnerney [Washington, DC: Catholic University of America, 2007], 224).

25 *PG*, 77:316D–17A.

one can say that the coming forth of the Spirit that is ἐκπόρευσις is also from the Son, even if he gives it this name only when he is thinking of it as being from the Father. We shall see why this may be so at the end of our survey of the Fathers.[26]

The Holy Spirit Is Consubstantial with the Son

At the Council of Florence, Mark Eugenikos quoted the following passage from Cyril's commentary on St. Luke's Gospel:

> Just as the finger depends on the hand, since it is not foreign to it, and naturally exists in it, so the Holy Spirit by reason of consubstantiality is conjoined and united [συνήπται πρὸς ἕνωσιν] to the Son, even though he proceeds from the Father.[27]

The metropolitan of Ephesus claimed that this was equivalent to saying that the Holy Spirit did not proceed from the Son.[28] In reality, Cyril's intention is not to deny that the Son is a principle of the Holy Spirit, but rather to guard against the view that the scriptural statement of the Holy Spirit proceeding from the Father implies that the Spirit is not naturally united to the Son. From the other passages of the saint, it is clear that a union "by reason of consubstantiality" does not mean, as Mark assumed, "by reason of consubstantiality alone."

The Letter to Nestorius with the Twelve Anathemas

This letter, number 17 in his collected letters, does not contain distinctive statements beyond those which we have already considered. It is of particular importance, however, because it was accepted by two

---

26 See the section on "ἐκπορεύεσθαι and *procedere*" in chapter 17 ("Concluding Linguistic Remarks"). We may also note that St. Cyril does not reserve the verb ἐκπορεύεσθαι for speaking about the Holy Spirit. On at least one occasion he uses it of the eternal relation of the Son to the Father (see *A Patristic Greek Lexicon*, ed. G. W. H. Lampe [Oxford: Oxford University Press, 1969], s.v. ἐκπορευω, IIA).

27 *PG*, 72:704B.

28 *AG*, 382.

ecumenical councils, Ephesus and Chalcedon, as a statement of the Catholic faith. Most of it, of course, is devoted to an explanation of the unity of the incarnate Word. However, toward the end of the letter, he considers the relation of the Word to the Holy Spirit:

> If we think rightly, we do not say that the one Christ and Son, needing glory from another, received glory from the Holy Spirit; for neither greater than he nor above him is his Spirit, but because he used the Holy Spirit to show forth his divinity in his mighty works, therefore he is said to have been glorified by him just as if anyone of us should say concerning his inherent strength, for example, or his knowledge of anything, "they glorified me." For although the Spirit subsists in his own person, and so is considered as distinct, inasmuch as he is Spirit and not Son, yet he is not alien from him, for he is called the Spirit of Truth, and Christ is the Truth, and he flows forth from him [προχεῖται παρ᾽αὐτοῦ] just as from God the Father. When then the Spirit worked miracles through the hands of the holy apostles after the ascension of our Lord Jesus Christ into heaven, he glorified him. For it is believed that he works through his own Spirit, being God according to nature. Therefore he also said, "he will receive of mine and declare it to you." Yet this is not to be understood as if the Holy Spirit were wise and powerful by participation, for he is perfect in all respects and in need of nothing. But because he is the Spirit of the power and wisdom of the Father—that is, of the Son—therefore he himself is absolute wisdom and power.[29]

In the first part of this extract, we have the familiar doctrine that the Holy Spirit "flows forth" from both the Father and the Son. The second half, as Henry Barclay Swete remarks, shows that this is to be

[29] *The Decrees and Canons of the Seven Ecumenical Councils*, ed. Henry Percival, *NPNF*2, 14:204–205 (translation slightly altered; see the body of the text for the relevant discussion); *PG*, 77:117C–D.

understood of an essential derivation, not simply of a temporal mission.[30] For the Holy Spirit is said to be of the Son and to receive from the Son insofar as he, the Spirit, is absolute (αὐτόχρημα) wisdom and power; in other words, he receives his nature from the Son, though not, of course, so as to exclude his also receiving it from the Father. Henry Percival, on the other hand, translates the προχεῖται παρ᾽αὐτοῦ as "is sent by him,"[31] while Norman Tanner gives "was poured forth by the Son."[32] Both these translations are unsatisfactory, as seeming to limit the phrase to the temporal mission. This letter of St. Cyril's was read at the Council of Ephesus in June 431 and, in Swete's words, "was tacitly approved, no remark being elicited by the statement as to the Holy Ghost."[33]

To this extract from St. Cyril's letter corresponds the ninth anathema subjoined to the same letter:

> If anyone shall say that the one Lord Jesus Christ was glorified by the Spirit, as making use of an alien power that worked through him and as having received from him the power to master unclean spirits and to work divine wonders among people and does not rather say that it was his own proper Spirit through whom he worked the divine wonders, let him be anathema.[34]

The anathemas themselves were accompanied by the reading of St. Cyril's own explanations. In connection with the ninth anathema, the saint declared:

> Although the only-begotten Word of God became man, yet he remained God, having all things which the Father has beside

[30] Henry Barclay Swete, *On the History of the Doctrine of the Procession of the Holy Spirit: From the Apostolic Age to the Death of Charlemagne* (Cambridge: Deighton and Bell, 1876; repr., n.p.: Nabu, 2014), 142.

[31] *NPNF2*, 14:201–205.

[32] *Decrees of the Ecumenical Councils: From Nicaea I to Vatican II*, ed. Norman P. Tanner and Giuseppe Alberigo, vol. 1 (Washington, DC: Georgetown University Press, 1990), 57.

[33] Swete, *On the History of the Doctrine of the Procession of the Holy Spirit*, 144.

[34] Tanner and Alberigo, *Decrees of the Ecumenical Councils*, 1:60.

> paternity; and he worked divine signs, having as his own the holy Spirit, who is from himself [τὸ ἐξ αὐτοῦ], and substantially innate to him [οὐσιωδῶς ἐμφεκὸς αὐτῷ].[35]

The Third Ecumenical Council thus approved Cyril's ninth anathema under the understanding that the Son has the Holy Spirit coming from him in the divine substance, just as the Father does. The Council of Chalcedon in 451, in its first session, explicitly recognized the letter of Cyril to Nestorius, describing it and an earlier one as "canonical."[36]

Summary and Conclusion

St. Cyril's own words are so explicit that there is little need to draw any further conclusion from them. He teaches in many places and in many ways that the Holy Spirit is eternally from the Son as well as from the Father. Although he does not in any extant text use the particular phrase ἐκπορευέται ἐξ Υἱοῦ, his teaching is identical to that of the Catholic Church, that the Holy Spirit proceeds eternally from the Father and the Son as from one principle. Swete remarks on the happy harmony between East and West at this period:

> Some sixteen hundred miles further to the West S. Augustine had recently proclaimed in the Latin tongue the Procession of the Holy Ghost from the Father and the Son. S. Cyril, following the tradition of his own Church, and working under the guidance of the earlier Greek theologians, reached substantially the same result; and his teaching received at least the tacit consent of contemporary Eastern Catholics.[37]

35 *PG*, 76:308D–9A.
36 *NPNF2*, 14:201; Mansi, 6:935D–38A. See also appendix 2 of the present volume.
37 Swete, *On the History of the Doctrine of the Procession of the Holy Spirit*, 151.

Sergei Bulgakov, by contrast, is unable to find any coherent doctrine of the procession in St. Cyril. He acknowledges the existence of those texts in the saint's work that seem to support the *Filioque* and deprecates the attempts of those whom he calls "Orthodox polemicists" to show that such texts refer only to a temporal mission. At the same time he declares that the picture is confused by the fact of passages that speak of procession from the Father (without mentioning the Son). He concludes:

> In our opinion it is impossible to unite these texts into a harmonious whole and to extract a coherent theological theory from all of this. All that one can say with any definiteness is that the problem of the procession of the Holy Spirit as such did not exist for him.[38]

To this one can only reply that while it is no doubt true, as Bulgakov remarks, that St. Cyril's main concern in the passages that I have considered was to uphold the divinity of the Holy Spirit and to combat Nestorianism, there is nonetheless in these passages a perfectly coherent account of the procession of the third divine person; and it was accepted both by the Council of Ephesus and also, a thousand years later, by the Council of Florence.

[38] Sergei Bulgakov, *The Comforter*, trans. Boris Jakim (Grand Rapids, MI: Eerdmans, 2004), 83.

CHAPTER 12

ROOTS OF ANTI-FILIOQUISM IN THE PATRISTIC ERA

Opposition to the doctrine of the procession of the Holy Spirit from the Father and the Son did not spring fully formed from the brain of Photios of Constantinople in the ninth century. In the next section, we shall see how the Western formulation of this doctrine was used by monothelites in the seventh century as a charge against the pope and the Western bishops. In this section we shall briefly note the first stirrings of anti-filioquism in a doubtful Christology of the fifth century.[1]

Theodore of Mopsuestia

It is not immediately apparent why there should be a connection between opposition to the doctrine of the Holy Spirit's procession from

[1] I shall not consider the earlier controversy between Eusebius of Caesarea and Marcellus of Ancyra, for although the former argued against the latter's account of an eternal procession from the Father and the Son, he did so not in favor of a procession from the Father alone, but on the contrary, to deny a direct dependence of the Holy Spirit on the Father; see Henry Barclay Swete, *Doctrine of the Procession of the Procession of the Holy Spirit: From the Apostolic Age to the Death of Charlemagne* (Cambridge: Deighton and Bell, 1876; repr., n.p.: Nabu, 2014), 80–87.

the Son and what may be called Nestorian tendencies in Christology. Historically, however, such a connection seems to have existed.[2] It may be that in an Antiochene tradition associated with Theodore of Mopsuestia, Nestorius himself, and Theodoret of Cyr, an insistence that the Holy Spirit formed the perfect humanity of Christ and glorified him led to an uncertainty about the eternal dependence of the Holy Spirit on the Word.

Theodore of Mopsuestia was a contemporary of St. Augustine but was either silent about or in opposition to the notion of an eternal derivation of the Holy Spirit from the Son. In his commentary on John 15:26 he writes:

> The Spirit Himself bears witness, who proceeds from the Father. For if by the word "proceed" he had understood not a natural procession but some external mission, it would have been uncertain about which of the many spirits who are sent in mission he was speaking, concerning which the apostle Paul says: "Are they not all ministering spirits, who are sent in mission?" But here he notes something proper, from which he can be known to have alone proceeded from the Father.[3]

Although the word "alone" qualifies the Holy Spirit here and not the Father, it seems significant that there is no mention of the Son, as also guaranteeing the distinction of the Holy Spirit from the angels. This is particularly so when this commentary is put in conjunction with his commentary (from the same work) on Christ's breathing upon the apostles on the day of the resurrection and saying, "receive the Holy Spirit":

---

2 St. Thomas Aquinas noted this in part on the basis of his study of the *acta* of the Council of Ephesus (*Summa theologiae* I, ed. Institutum Studiorum Medievalium Ottavienses, 5 vols. [Ottawa: Studium Generalis Ordo Praedicatorum, 1941], q. 36, a. 2, ad 3).

3 *PG*, 66:780B (trans. mine).

> The word "receive" which He uses means "you shall receive." For if in breathing out he had given the Spirit, as some have very foolishly supposed, it would have been superfluous to say to them afterwards, especially in the time of the ascension into heaven, not to depart from Jerusalem but to await the promise of the Spirit.[4]

This exegesis, which was anathematized by the twelfth canon of the Second Council of Constantinople, would come naturally to one who denied the eternal derivation of the Holy Spirit from the Son, but not to anyone else.

The creed attributed to Theodore contains an explicit denial of such derivation:

> We believe in the Holy Spirit, who is from the substance of God, who is not a Son, who is God by substance, being of the substance of which is God the Father, from whom according to substance he is. "For we have not," he says, "received the spirit of the world but the Spirit who is from God," separating him from all creation and joining Him to God, from whom he is in a proper manner beyond that of all creation; we consider creation to be from God not according to substance but by a creative cause; and we neither consider him a Son, nor as taking his being from the Son [οὔτε διὰ Υἱοῦ τὴν ὕπαρξιν εἰληφός].[5]

The authenticity of this creed is disputed. It was denied at the Council of Chalcedon, and the *Clavis Patrum Graecorum* lists it among the spurious works of Theodore. It was, however, earlier presented as his at the Council of Ephesus, where it was apparently taken to be genuine

4 *PG*, 66:783A.
5 *PG*, 66:1016D–17A (trans. mine).

by St. Cyril. The editors of Migne's *Patrologia Graeca*, who consider it genuine on grounds both of content and of style, suggest that its authorship was denied at Chalcedon, on account of its unorthodox statements about the Incarnation, by those who revered the memory of the bishop of Mopsuetia.[6] Henry Barclay Swete considered it "probably a genuine work."[7] André de Halleux, however, considers it certainly inauthentic.[8] Nevertheless, it could hardly have been treated as authentic at Ephesus, just a year or two after the death of its supposed author, unless it came either from Theodore himself or from someone close to him.[9]

Theodoret

Theodoret (†before 466), bishop of Cyr, had been a pupil of Theodore of Mopsuestia, and Nestorius appealed to him for his support before the Council of Ephesus. In his polemic against St. Cyril of Alexandria, Theodoret was led into a denial of the derivation of the Holy Spirit from the Son. As we have seen, Cyril had taught in the ninth anathema received at Ephesus that Christ had worked miracles by the Holy Spirit as by the Spirit proper (ἴδιον) to himself. Theodoret in reply stated:

> We will confess that the Spirit is proper to the Son, receiving this as a religious expression, if [Cyril] means that he is of the same nature as him and proceeds from the Father. But if he means it in the sense of from [ἐκ] the Son, or having existence through the Son [δι' Υἱοῦ τὴν ὕπαρξιν ἔχον], we reject this as impious blasphemy.[10]

---

6 *PG*, 66:74B–C.

7 Swete, *History of the Doctrine of the Procession of the Holy Spirit*, 140.

8 André de Halleux, "Cyrille, Theodoret et Le *Filioque*, " *Revue d'histoire ecclésiastique* 74 (1979): 597–625, at 623.

9 There is a fine historical irony in the fact that the fathers of the Council of Ephesus passed their famous prohibition against making new creeds—the prohibition that was later to be alleged against the *Filioque*—after the reading of this "Creed of Theodore," containing as it did perhaps the first credal *denial* of this doctrine.

10 Quoted in St. Cyril, *Apologeticus contra Theodoretum* (*PG*, 76:432C–D; trans. mine).

St. Cyril in his reply chose not to go deeply into the question of the eternal relation of the Son and the Holy Spirit, remaining focused on his main goal to vindicate the simple identity of the eternal Word with the man Jesus.[11] Nevertheless, he writes as follows:

> The Spirit was and is his, just as the Father's. . . . The Holy Spirit proceeds from God and the Father, according to the word of the Savior, but he is not foreign to the Son, for he has all things with the Father. And he himself taught this, saying about the Holy Spirit: "All that the Father has are mine. Therefore I said that he will take what is mine and declare it to you."[12]

This is clearly not an acceptance of Theodoret's account of the procession, even though Mark of Ephesus at the Council of Florence claimed Cyril for himself on the ground that he had not been more explicit in this place in denying the doctrine of the bishop of Cyr.[13] Bessarion noted that the anti-unionist Greeks of his day relied especially on the argument that Theodoret's attack on St. Cyril's anathemas was known to the Council of Ephesus, and that they did not condemn Theodoret's opinion about the procession of the Holy Spirit.[14] To this the Greek cardinal replies that such an argument would return upon themselves, since Theodoret denied not only the ἐξ Υἱοῦ but also the δι' Υἱοῦ, which latter phrase they wish to maintain; and, further, all the writings of Theodoret against St. Cyril were condemned as a whole in subsequent councils.[15] We may add, as was mentioned in the section on St. Cyril, that the ninth anathema was approved at Ephesus with the saint's own

---

11 As Hubert Manoir also remarks; Hubert du Manoir, *Dogme et spiritualité chez Saint Cyrille d'Alexandrie* (Paris: Vrin, 1944), 225.

12 St. Cyril, *Apologeticus contra Theodoretum* (*PG*, 76:433B–C).

13 *AG*, 378–82.

14 See *ODDU* and *PG*, 161:614B.

15 *ODDU* and *PG*, 161:593B. The Second Council of Constantinople anathematized these writings in its thirteenth canon.

explanation that the Son has the Holy Spirit from him in the divine substance, just as the Father does.[16]

Theodoret maintained his teaching about the derivation of the Holy Spirit from the Father alone even after the reconciliation between the Antiochene patriarchate and the rest of the Church. Writing to his patriarch John, he explains that he accepts St. Cyril's "Formula of Union" (μία φύσις τοῦ θεοῦ λόγου σεσαρκωμένη; "one nature of the Word of God incarnate"), but understood as a repudiation of the twelve Cyrilline chapters canonized at Ephesus. In particular, he writes that "the Holy Spirit is not of the Son nor derives existence through the Son [οὐκ ἐξ Υἱοῦ ἤ δι' Υἱοῦ τὴν ὕπαρξιν ἔχον], but proceeds from the Father, and is proper to the Son as being of one substance."[17]

Martin Jugie suggested that Theodoret's intention in such passages was simply to resist a return of the Eunomian doctrine according to which the Holy Spirit was a creation of the Son.[18] He cites Theodoret's commentary on Romans 8:11:

> He [St. Paul] has taught us also in these words the one nature of the deity. For he has called the Holy Spirit both of God and of Christ; not that, as some detestable heretics say, he is created [δεδημιουργῆται] from God through the Son, but since He is of the same substance as the Father and the Son, and proceeds from the Father, according to the teaching of the gospel; and His grace is supplied to those who are worthy through Christ.[19]

---

16 A. Edward Siecienski is therefore incorrect to state that St. Cyril accepted Theodoret's criticism of the ninth anathema (Siecienski, *The Filioque: History of a Doctrinal Controversy* [New York: Oxford University Press, 2010], 49). St. Cyril's *Explicatio XII capitum* (Explanation of the Twelve Chapters) is later than his reply to Theodoret (Martin Jugie, *De Processione Spiritus Sancti* [Rome: Facultas Theologica Pontificii Athenaei Seminarii Romani, 1936], 142).

17 Theodoret of Mopsuestia, Letter 171 (*PG*, 83:1484C; trans. mine). According to Halleux, the authenticity of this letter is no longer disputed ("Cyrille, Theodoret et le *Filioque*," 604).

18 Martin Jugie, *Theologia Dogmatica Christianorum Orientalium ab Ecclesia Catholica Dissidentium*, vol. 2, *De Theologia Simplici, De Oeconomia, De Hagiologia* (Paris: Letouzey et Ané, 1933), 490–92.

19 *PG*, 82:132C (trans. Jugie in *Theologia Dogmatica*, 2:490).

Halleux also argued that Theodoret, in saying οὐκ ἐξ Υἱοῦ ἤ δι᾽ Υἱοῦ, wished only to make a double denial that the Holy Spirit was a creature.[20] Others have maintained that the first part of the phrase was intended to deny that the Holy Spirit was a son of the Son, the second part that he was a creature.[21] However, while resistance to Eunomianism may indeed have led Theodoret to deny the derivation of the Holy Spirit from the Son, his words at any rate go beyond such opposition. In making room for no sense in which the Holy Spirit could be said to have his existence from the Son, and in explaining the relation of the second and third person simply by reference to consubstantiality, the bishop of Cyr appears as a true precursor of Photios of Constantinople.

---

20 Halleux, "Cyrille, Theodoret et le *Filioque*," 623. Bernard de Margerie endorsed Halleux's conclusion ("Vers une relecture du concile de Florence, grâce à la reconsidération de l'Ecriture et des pères grecs et latins," *Revue thomiste* 86 [1986]: 31–81, at 81).

21 José Grégoire, "La relation éternelle de l'Esprit au Fils d'après les écrits de Jean de Damas," *Revue d'histoire ecclésiastique* 64 (1969): 713–55, at 740.

CHAPTER 13

SAINT LEO THE GREAT

THE GREAT FIFTH-CENTURY BISHOP OF ROME did not write extensively on the Holy Spirit. Only one passage relevant to our question is assigned to him with certainty. It comes in his Sermon 75, preached, appropriately enough, on Pentecost Sunday. Having mentioned the visible mission of the Paraclete in the upper room, Leo goes on to correct a possible misunderstanding:

> But although, dearly-beloved, the actual form of the thing done was exceeding wonderful, and undoubtedly in that exultant chorus of all human languages the Majesty of the Holy Spirit was present, yet no one must think that His Divine substance appeared in what was seen with bodily eyes. For His Nature, which is invisible and shared in common with the Father and the Son, showed the character of His gift and work by the outward sign that pleased Him, but kept His essential property

> within His own Godhead: because human sight can no more perceive the Holy Ghost than it can the Father or the Son. For in the Divine Trinity nothing is unlike or unequal, and all that can be thought concerning Its substance admits of no diversity either in power or glory or eternity. And while in the property of each Person the Father is one, the Son is another, and the Holy Ghost is another, yet the Godhead is not distinct and different; for whilst the Son is the Only begotten of the Father, and the Holy Spirit is the Spirit of the Father and the Son, He is not as creatures are, which are also of the Father and the Son, but as living and having power with Both, and eternally subsisting of That Which is the Father and the Son [siquidem cum et de Patre sit Filius unigenitus, et Spiritus Sanctus Patris Filiique sit spiritus, non sicut quaecumque creatura, quae et Patris et Filii est, sed sicut cum utroque vivens et potens, et sempiterne ex eo quod est Pater Filiusque subsistens]. (3)[1]

The slightly unusual phrase that is used at the end of this extract, "subsisting of That Which is the Father and the Son," indicates that the Father and Son are the principle of the Holy Spirit in the unity of their essence. As far as one can tell, however, St. Leo's reason for using this phrase was not to counter any view that they were two principles, but simply in order to mention the divine essence; for the point of the whole passage is that the personal properties in the Trinity do not imply more than one divine nature.

The Pope goes on to give a scriptural justification for the teaching on the procession of the Holy Spirit, which is the verse that we have

[1] Pope St. Leo the Great, Letters and Sermons, trans. C. Feltoe, *NPNF*2 vol. 12, pt. 1. I have slightly changed Feltoe's translation of the last sentence, from *PL*, 54:402A. He rendered the Latin as "for whilst the Son is the Only begotten of the Father, the Holy Spirit is the Spirit of the Father and the Son, not in the way that every creature is the creature of the Father and the Son, but as living and having power with Both, and eternally subsisting of That Which is the Father and the Son." This slightly obscures the point that Leo is making, that personal properties do not introduce a difference of substance in God. The point about the *Filioque*, however, is not affected.

already frequently encountered from St. John's Gospel: "All that the Father has is mine; therefore I said that he will take what is mine and declare it to you" (John 16:15). He explains: "Accordingly, there are not some things that are the Father's, and other the Son's, and other the Holy Spirit's: but all things whatsoever the Father has, the Son also has, and the Holy Spirit also has: nor was there ever a time when this communion did not exist, because with Them to have all things is to always exist" (3).

This, then, is the position of St. Leo, who was listed by the Second Council of Constantinople as among those doctors whom it followed in every way.[2] Is there any way to invalidate his testimony? A. Edward Siecienski offers only one possible argument: Leo accepted the Council of Chalcedon's reaffirmation of the Nicene-Constantinopolitan Creed in its original form, without the *Filioque*.[3] The weakness of this argument need hardly be pointed out: no one at the time was proposing the insertion of the *Filioque* into that Creed, so St. Leo's acceptance of the Creed has no bearing on our question. Sergei Bulgakov, for his part, makes no mention of St. Leo, or of Constantinople II's praise of his doctrine.

---

2 See record in *NPNF2* vol. 14, *The Decrees and Canons of the Seven Ecumenical Councils*, ed. Henry Percival.

3 A. Edward Siecienski, *The Filioque: History of a Doctrinal Controversy* (New York: Oxford University Press, 2010), 64.

CHAPTER 14

SAINT GREGORY THE GREAT

Introduction

LIKE HIS PREDECESSOR LEO, St. Gregory wrote no treatise on the Holy Spirit. Various places in his writings, however, speak of the procession. Curiously, while Henry Barclay Swete observes that "the writings of S. Gregory the Great give no uncertain sound"[1] on this subject, A. Edward Siecienski maintains that "Gregory's true views on the procession are difficult, if not impossible, to discern."[2] In this section we shall consider all the passages that either author mentions.

Procession from the Father

Siecienski begins by citing two passages from the *Moralia in Iob* where he claims St. Gregory mentions only a procession from the Father.

1 Henry Barclay Sweet, *On the History of the Doctrine of the Procession of the Holy Spirit: From the Apostolic Age to the Death of Charlemagne* (Cambridge: Deighton and Bell, 1876; repr., n.p.: Nabu, 2014), 157.

2 A. Edward Siecienski, *The Filioque: History of a Doctrinal Controversy* (New York: Oxford University Press, 2010), 70–71.

From the first he quotes simply a phrase: "The Holy Spirit proceeds from the Father [qui de Patre procedens]."[3] It will be more helpful to quote the entire sentence. The saint is commenting on Job 4:12: "There was a word spoken to me in private, and my ears by stealth as it were received the veins of its whisper." He writes: "For what is designated by the voice of a gentle breeze except the knowledge of the Holy Spirit who, proceeding from the Father and receiving from that which is of the Son [de eo quod est Filii accipiens], is poured sparingly into the knowledge of our weakness?" Clearly, St. Gregory has no intention to put in question the procession from the Son; he is simply using the traditional scriptural terminology to express it.

The other passage Siecienski quotes is "the Spirit which proceeds from the Father before all ages [idem Spiritus qui de Patre ante saecula procedit]."[4] He gives the reference as section 74 of book 24, but there is no such section in the *Moralia*: book 24 has only fifty-five sections. He also gives a reference to volume 79 of the *Patrologia Latina* (76:19), but the phrase he quotes is not to be found in this section of the *Moralia* either, which is not speaking about the procession of the Holy Spirit.

Procession from the Son

We may now consider passages where the saint apparently speaks of a procession from the Son. In the first book of the *Moralia*, expounding the allegorical meaning of Job 1:5, "Job sent and sanctified them," he writes:

> Rightly is he said to sanctify by sending, since, when he bestows the Holy Spirit who proceeds [procedit] from him upon the hearts of the disciples, he purifies any guilt that might be within them. (1.30)[5]

---

3 Siecienski, *Filioque*, 70. He cites it as coming from section 65 of book 5, which is correct, but he gives the *PL* reference as 75:419; the correct reference is 75:715A. In parenthetical citations of the *Moralia* that follow in main text, the second number denotes sections, not chapters.

4 Siecienski, *Filioque*, 70.

5 *PL*, 75:541B: "Bene autem mittendo sanctificare dicitur, quia dum sanctum Spiritum, qui a se procedit,

Procedere here is naturally taken to refer to the eternal procession, both because this had long been the standard meaning of the term and because the proceeding is distinguished from the bestowal of the Holy Spirit on the disciples.

Near the end of the second book, Gregory is discussing St. John the Baptist's reference to "the one on whom the Spirit abides" (John 1:33). He writes:

> The Spirit indeed comes upon all the faithful, but he remains upon the Mediator alone in a unique way, since he has never forsaken the humanity of him from whose divinity He proceeds. (2.90)[6]

He develops the thought a little further in the same book, writing:

> The Mediator of God and man, the man Christ Jesus, in all respects has him present both continually and perpetually, since the same Spirit comes forth from him substantially. Rightly therefore, although he remains in holy preachers, he is said to remain in the Mediator in a unique way, since he remains in them by grace for certain things, while in him He remains by substance for all things. (2.92)[7]

St. Gregory does not develop these observations, since his intention was not to write a detailed Trinitarian theology. Again, however, it would be implausible to see them as anything other than a reference to the eternal procession of the Holy Spirit from the Son. Although according to Catholic theology the Holy Spirit does dwell substantially in the just soul, and not just in virtue of his gifts, yet to speak

---

discipulorum cordibus tribuit, quidquid culpae inesse potuit emundavit." Translations are my own.

6 *PL*, 75:598B: "In cunctis namque fidelibus Spiritus venit, sed in solo Mediatore singulariter permanet, quia eius humanitatem nunquam deseruit, ex cuius divinitate procedit."

7 *PL*, 75:599A: "Mediator autem Dei et hominum homo Christus Iesus, in cunctis eum et semper et continue habet praesentem, quia et ex illo isdem Spiritus per substantiam profertur. Recte ergo et cum in sanctis praedicatoribus maneat, in Mediatore singulariter manere perhibetur, quia in istis per gratiam manet ad aliquid, in illo autem per substantiam manet ad cuncta."

without qualification of the Spirit "coming forth [from the Son] substantially," and not to refer to a *terminus ad quem* of this coming forth, would be a very unusual way of referring to a temporal mission.

The following passage from the *Moralia* is not so clear a reference to an eternal procession, but it is valuable as providing an interpretation for the phrase that puzzled St. Basil, "the mouth of the Lord." St. Gregory is commenting on Job 37:2, "Hear yet attentively the terror of his voice, and the sound that cometh out of his mouth":

> By the mouth of God, the only-begotten Son may be denoted: just as He is called God's arm, since the Father works all things through him, . . . so also he is called his mouth. Hence it is that the prophet says, "the mouth of the Lord has spoken these things." He speaks all things to us through him; so it is as if, by the word "mouth," he had explicitly said, "Word," rather as we are accustomed to say "tongue" when we mean "words," such as when we say the Greek or Latin tongue, meaning Latin or Greek words. Therefore not without reason do we understand him to be the mouth of the Lord. This is why the bride in the Song of Songs says, "Let him kiss me with the kiss of his mouth." It is as if she were to say, "Let him touch me with the gentle presence of the only-begotten Son, my Redeemer." So also to denote the same Spirit, it is elsewhere written, "suddenly there came a sound from heaven, as of a mighty wind coming." Therefore the sound proceeds from the mouth of the Lord when the Spirit consubstantial with him, coming to us through the Son, breaks through the deafness of our insensibility. (27.34)[8]

[8] *PL*, 76:418D–19B: "Potest autem per os Dei, unigenitus designari Filius, qui sicut brachium eius dicitur, quia per eum cuncta Pater operatur . . . ita etiam os dicitur. Hinc est enim quod Propheta ait: Os enim Domini locutum est haec. Per quem nobis omnia loquitur, ac si oris nomine patenter diceretur verbum, sicut nos quoque pro verbis linguam dicere solemus, ut cum Graecam vel Latinam linguam dicimus, Latina vel Graeca verba monstramus. Os ergo Domini non immerito ipsum accipimus. Unde et ei sponsa in Canticis canticorum dicit: Osculetur me osculo oris sui. Ac si dicat: Tangat me dulcedine praesentiae unigeniti Filii redemptoris mei. Per sonum vero oris potest eiusdem Domini sanctus Spiritus designari. Unde et alias in eiusdem Spiritus

On the other hand, a clear reference to the eternal procession may be found in book 30, where St. Gregory is expounding John 16:25, "I will show you plainly of the Father":

> Indeed, he declares that he shows plainly concerning the Father, since in manifesting the appearance of his majesty, he shows both how he comes forth equal to the one who begets him, and how the Spirit of each proceeds co-eternal to each. For we shall then clearly see how the one who exists by coming forth is not later in time to the one from whom he comes forth, and how the one who is produced by procession is not preceded by those who bring him forth. We shall then clearly see both how the One by distinction is Three, and how the Three are indivisibly One. (30:17)[9]

One could not wish for a clearer statement of the *Filioque*. Having premised that he is speaking of the eternal procession, St. Gregory identifies the Father and the Son as the *proferentes*, "those who bring forth."[10]

Procession and Mission

The twenty-sixth homily in St. Gregory's *Homiliae in Evangelia* is of interest for its affirmation that the temporal missions mentioned in the

significatione scriptum est: Factus est repente de caelo sonus tamquam advenientis spiritus vehementis. Sonus igitur de ore Domini procedit, cum consubstantialis ei Spiritus ad nos per Filium veniens surditatem nostrae insensibilitatis rumpit."

9 *PL*, 76:533D–534A: "Palam quippe de Patre annuntiare se asserit, quia per patefactam tunc majestatis suae speciem, et quomodo ipsi gignenti non impar oriatur, et quomodo utrorumque Spiritus utrique coaeternus procedat ostendit. Aperte namque tunc videbimus quomodo hoc quod oriendo est ei de quo oritur subsequens non est, quomodo is qui per processionem producitur a proferentibus non praeitur. Aperte tunc videbimus quomodo et unum divisibiliter tria sint, et indivisibiliter tria unum." It is pleasant to note the similarity between this and the passage quoted from Gregory's successor Pius XII in note 6 of the introduction to the present volume.

10 Siecienski gives a reference to this same passage of the *Moralia*, 30.17, citing the correct column in the *PL*, yet quotes it simply as, "The Spirit of the Father and the Son who issues from both . . . proceeds ever from the Father." Wherever he has taken his version of this text from, it cannot be *PL*. The edition of the text in *CCSL* vol. 143B has the same text verbatim as does *PL*.

Gospels show forth the eternal Trinitarian relations. Commenting on the words "as the Father sent me, so do I send you," he writes:

> That is, "when I send you among the stumbling blocks of persecutors, I love you with the same charity with which the Father loves me, whom he caused to come to endure sufferings." Yet, the sending can also be understood in regard to the nature of the divinity. For the Son is said to be sent by the Father by the very fact that he is generated by the Father. For the same Son declares that he sends the Holy Spirit, who although he is co-equal to the Father and the Son, yet was not made incarnate, saying, "when the Paraclete comes, whom I will send you from the Father." For if to be sent were to be understood only as to be made incarnate, then the Holy Spirit would certainly not be said to be sent, since he was by no means made incarnate. But his mission is the very procession by which he proceeds from the Father and the Son. Therefore, just as the Spirit is said to be sent inasmuch as he proceeds, so also the Son may not unfitly be said to be sent inasmuch as he is begotten.[11]

It is unusual simply to identify, as Gregory does here, the procession with the mission, rather than to say that the one is the precondition for the other. However, the parallel that is established between the procession of the Holy Spirit and the generation of the Son leaves no doubt that he is speaking of an eternal procession from the Father and the Son.

---

11 *PL*, 76:1198BC: "Id est, ea vos charitate diligo cum inter scandalum persecutorum mitto, qua me charitate Pater diligit, quem venire ad tolerandas passiones fecit. Quamvis mitti etiam iuxta naturam divinitatis possit intelligi. Eo enim ipso a Patre Filius mitti dicitur, quo a Patre generatur. Nam sanctum quoque Spiritum, qui cum sit coaequalis Patri et Filio, non tamen incarnatus est, idem se mittere Filius perhibet, dicens: Cum venerit Paraclitus, quem ego mittam vobis a Patre. Si enim mitti solummodo incarnari deberet intelligi, sanctus procul dubio Spiritus nullo modo diceretur mitti, qui nequaquam incarnatus est. Sed eius missio ipsa processio est qua de Patre procedit et Filio. Sicut itaque Spiritus mitti dicitur quia procedit, ita et Filius non incongrue mitti dicitur quia generatur."

St. Gregory in Greek

Although St. Gregory's doctrine is sufficiently shown by the texts already quoted, one other passage is of some historical importance. It comes in the second book of the *Dialogues*, chapter 38. His interlocutor, the deacon Peter, has asked the Pope why greater miracles are sometimes worked in answer to prayers made to martyrs in places where their bodies are not. He answers that "weak minds" might doubt whether they hear our prayers in the absence of their relics, and so such people need greater signs to convince them that they do. He shows that it is a sign of a weak faith to require the bodily presence of the one to whom one is praying, strengthening the argument with some words of Christ:

> The Truth himself, to increase the faith of the disciples, said, "if I do not go, the Comforter will not come to you." Since it is certain that the Paraclete Spirit always proceeds from the Father and from the Son, why does the Son say that he will withdraw so that that he may come, when he never withdraws from the Son? It is because the disciples, seeing the Lord in the flesh, longed always to see him with their bodily eyes, and so it is rightly said to them, "unless I go, the Comforter will not come." It is as if he said plainly, "if I do not take away my body, I will not show who the love of the Spirit is; and if you do not cease to see me bodily, you will never learn to love me spiritually."[12]

[12] *PL*, 66: 204B: "Ipsa quoque Veritas, ut fidem discipulorum augeret, dixit: "Si non abiero, Paracletus non veniet ad vos." Cum enim constet quia Paracletus Spiritus a Patre semper procedat et Filio, cur se Filius recessurum dicit ut ille veniat quia a Filio numquam recedit? Sed quia discipuli in carne Dominum cernentes, corporeis hunc oculis semper videre sitiebant, recte eis dicitur, "Nisi abiero, Paracletus non veniet"; ac si aperte diceretur, Si corpus non subtraho, quis sit amor Spiritus non ostendo: et nisi me desieritis corporaliter cernere, numquam me discetis spiritaliter amare." For "quis sit amor Spiritus non ostendo" here, another reading of *quis* is *quid*, yielding "what" rather than "who." This book of the *Dialogues*, dealing as it does with the life of St. Benedict, is not included in *PL* among St. Gregory's own works, but is placed in the volume containing the Rule of St. Benedict.

The word "always," *semper*, in the second sentence shows that this is a reference to the eternal procession. However, there exists a Greek translation of the *Dialogues* that was produced by one of St. Gregory's successors in the see of Rome, Pope Zacharias (741–752). In the version of this translation that has come down to us, the phrase "a Patre semper procedat et Filio" is rendered as Ἐκ τοῦ Πατρὸς προέρχεται, καὶ ἐν τῷ Υἱῷ διαμένει ("he proceeds from the Father and abides in the Son").[13] There are apparently three possible explanations for the discrepancy: St. Gregory originally wrote what the Greek text presents him as saying and a later Latin scribe, unfamiliar with the expression, altered it; or Pope Zacharias, in writing the Greek text that we have, changed Gregory's expression to one more familiar to Greek ears; or a later hand altered Zacharias's Greek version. The first possibility seems unlikely: the phrase "proceeds from the Father and abides in the Son" was apparently not in use among Western theologians as a reference to the Holy Spirit's eternal existence. Again, even if Gregory had adopted it from an Eastern source, perhaps as a result of his sojourn in Constantinople, there would have been no need for a later scribe to alter it, as it contains nothing offensive to Latin ears. That leaves the second and third possibilities. The earliest known reference to the problem is found in the ninth-century Roman author called John the Deacon. In his *Life of St. Gregory* he says that Pope Zacharias himself made a faithful translation of the controverted passage, but that "the crafty perversity of Greeks" (*astuta Graecorum perversitas*), removed the reference to the Son.[14] Martin Jugie, however, believed that the translation is from Pope Zacharias himself, who would have understood the danger, in particular during the ascendancy of the iconoclasts in Byzantium, of introducing a description of the procession unfamiliar to Greek ears.

13 The Greek text is placed next to the Latin text in *PL*.

14 Quoted by the editor in *PL*, 66:204–5D. The editor of the volume of *PL* containing the other books of the *Dialogues* mentions his personal opinion that the change was made by Photios himself, who praised the *Dialogues* and Zacharias's translation of them (*PL*, 77:145–46).

A manuscript containing the Greek translation but written, according to Jugie, "in a Latin and Roman hand-writing" is dated to 800.[15] In any case, enough has been quoted to show that St. Gregory the Great, to whom has been attributed both the final determination of the Order of Mass in the West and of the Liturgy of the Pre-sanctified in the East, held and taught the *Filioque.*

---

15 Martin Jugie, *De Processione Spiritus Sancti* (Rome: Facultas Theologica Pontificii Athenaei Seminarii Romani, 1936), 224–27.

CHAPTER 15

SAINT MAXIMUS

Introduction

St. Maximus the Confessor (†662) is an author of particular interest, as the first known witness to difficulties experienced or alleged by some Greek speakers in connection with the Latin phrase *procedit a Filio* or *ex Filio* used of the Holy Spirit. His significance is further revealed by the fact that at the Council of Florence in 1439, the chief spokesman for the anti-unionist position among the Greek bishops, Mark Eugenikos, declared that he would not accept as authentic any Latin patristic text about the procession of the Holy Spirit unless it agreed with the doctrine of Maximus.[1]

As a native of Constantinople who was for a long time resident within Latin-speaking North Africa, St. Maximus was also well placed

1 *SYR*, 394. See also Joseph Gill, *The Council of Florence* (Cambridge: Cambridge University Press, 1959), 231–35. For the supposed incompatibility between Maximus's account of the procession and that defined by the Council of Florence, see the editorial comments of Emmanuel Ponsoye in St. Maximus the Confessor, *Opuscules théologiques et polémiques* (Cerf: Paris, 1998), 76–86.

to understand the question. Although he did not write a treatise on the procession, three of his writings contain relevant, though brief, passages.

Question 63 to Thalassius

The work called *Quaestiones ad Thalassium de Scriptura* (Thalassius's Questions on Scripture) contains replies to a miscellaneous collection of questions bearing especially on the interpretation of Scripture. In question 63, St. Maximus is commenting on Zechariah's vision of the golden lampstand (Zech 4:2–3) and arguing that the seven lamps are the gifts and operations of the Holy Spirit that Christ gives to his Church. The saint explains eloquently how Christ assumed what was ours in order to give us what was his:

> For me the Word was made man, for me he worked all salvation through the things that were mine, to me in turn, on account of whom he was made man, he gave the things that were his own; and receiving for my sake, he brought about a manifestation of what was his. And in his love for man, reckoning the grace as mine, he ascribes to me the natural power of his own virtues. This is why he is now said to receive the one who is by nature present to him eternally and ineffably. For the holy Spirit, as he is naturally of God and the Father by essence, so also is he naturally of the Son by essence [Τὸ γὰρ Πνεῦμα τὸ ἅγιον, . . . οὕτως καὶ τοῦ Υἱοῦ φύσει κατ'οὐσίαν ἐστὶν], as the one who proceeds ineffably from the Father substantially through the begotten Son [ὡς ἐκ τοῦ Πατρὸς οὐσιωδῶς δι' Υἱοῦ γεννηθέντος ἀφράστως ἐκπορευόμενον]; and to the candle-stand, that is, to the Church, he gives his workings and breathings, like lamps.[2]

[2] St. Maximus, *Questions à Thalassios*, tome 3, *Questions 56 à 65*, trans. Françoise Vinel (Cerf: Paris, 2015), 162–64 (trans. mine from the French). It is worth noting that this is apparently the first extant occurrence of the phrase δι' Υἱοῦ ἐκπορευόμενον. Since we are already in the seventh century, one can see that it is rather misleading to claim that this is *the* typical formulation of the Greek Fathers.

Despite the reference to the illumination of the Church at the end of this passage, the saint is clearly talking also about an eternal relation of the Son to the Holy Spirit. A. Edward Siecienski's hesitation on this point is hard to understand.[3] St. Maximus could hardly be more emphatic: it is as the one who proceeds *substantially* through the Son that the Holy Spirit belongs by *nature* to the Son's *essence*. Siecienski glosses this passage by saying, "the Spirit, intimately aware of the Father's begetting of the Son, comes forth from the begetter through the begotten as the Spirit eternally manifesting their common nature."[4] This is apparently an attempt to exclude the Son from being a principle of the Holy Spirit. But so tortuous an explanation of the Greek preposition διά is hardly required by Maximus's own words. Jean-Miguel Garrigues, on the other hand, states without further explanation that Maximus's use of the aorist participle γεννηθέντος, rather than the perfect, implies that the Son is "involved" in the procession only insofar as he is engendered; in other words that "through the Son" means "from the Father of the Son."[5] I cannot see any good reason for this claim; the aorist simply characterizes the Son as begotten and does not indicate a relation between this "begottenness" and the procession.[6] The precise meaning of δι' Υἱοῦ ἐκπορευόμενον, however, is not clear from this passage alone.[7]

Quaestiones et dubia 34

In the miscellaneous series called *Quaestiones et dubia*, number 34 is this: "Why cannot we say 'the Father of the Spirit' or 'Christ of the

3 A. Edward Siecienski, *The Filioque: History of a Doctrinal Controversy* (New York: Oxford University Press, 2010), 77.

4 Siecienski, *Filioque*, 78.

5 Jean-Miguel Garrigues, "A la suite de la clarification romaine: Le *Filioque* affranchi du 'Filioquisme,'" *Irenikon* 69 (1996): 189–212, at 211.

6 In any case, the two tenses are not clearly distinct by this period: "The aorist was used increasingly for the perfect, as well as vice versa, to such an extent that eventually in the fourth century A.D. the perfect as a distinct tense is altogether eclipsed. . . . In Byzantine texts [the perfect] is no longer distinguishable from the aorist in meaning" (Nigel Turner, *Grammar of New Testament Greek*, vol. 3, *Syntax* [Edinburgh: T. & T. Clark, 1963], 68).

7 I shall consider the grammar of the phrase more closely in connection with St. John Damascene. See the subsection "The Position of José Grégoire" (under "The Holy Spirit Proceeds δι' Υἱοῦ") in ch. 16 (St. John Damascene).

Spirit,' in the way that concerning the Father and the Son we say indifferently either 'The Spirit of God' or 'the Spirit of Christ'?" St. Maximus's answer is terse:

> As the Mind is the author [αἴτιος] of the Word, so also of the Spirit, though with the Word as the intermediary [διὰ μέσου δὲ τοῦ λόγου]. And just as we do not say that the word is of the voice, so we cannot say that the Son is of the Spirit.[8]

George Berthold remarks of this passage that "it is clear that we are speaking here not of economic processions or missions *ad extra* but of the inner trinitarian life."[9] However, as with the previous passage, Siecienski wishes to see the διά here as devoid of any "causal" significance, arguing that Maximus and "many of the Greek fathers" speak of a progression or procession "through the Son" simply in order to express the truth that the Father in spirating remains Father of the Son (the same interpretation that was given by Gregory of Cyprus in the thirteenth century).[10] It is not too much to say that this does violence to the text. The διά is directly related grammatically to the αἴτιος; as such it suggests an involvement of the Son in the "causal" activity.

Letter to Marinus (*Opusculum* 10)

This letter, if authentic, was written by St. Maximus after the Roman synod of 649 that anathematized monothelitism. A synodal letter had been written by the pope (either Martin I or Theodore) that was attacked by monothelites in Constantinople.[11] In response, Maximus

---

8 St. Maximus, *Quaestiones et dubia*, ed. J. H. Declerck, in *CCSG*, 10:151 (trans. Siecienski).

9 George Berthold, "Maximus the Confessor and the *Filioque*," *Studia Patristica* 18, no. 1 (1985): 113–17, at 114.

10 Siecienski, *Filioque*, 78.

11 The 1995 document by the Pontifical Council for Promoting Christian Unity, discussed in the introduction to the present volume and included as appendix 4, tactfully refers to these monothelites simply as "Byzantines."

defends the orthodoxy of the pope's synodal letter in a letter to Marinus, a priest of Cyprus.

One of the objections raised against the synodal letter was that it had spoken of the Holy Spirit proceeding not only from the Father but also from (κἀκ) the Son. Defending this language of the pope and his theologians, St. Maximus writes:

> They brought forth testimonies in agreement from the Latin fathers; also testimonies from Cyril of Alexandria, in the commentary which he produced on the evangelist St. John. From these they showed that they do not make the Son the cause [αἰτίαν] of the Spirit; for they know that the Father is the one cause of the Son and the Spirit; of the former, according to generation, and of the latter, according to procession. But they wrote in this way to show that he goes forth [προϊέναι] through him, and thus to show the conjunction of substance [τὸ συναφὲς τῆς οὐσίας] and its invariableness.[12]

The interpretation of these words depends on the exact sense given to the term αἰτία. We have already seen that, when used of God the Father by the Cappadocian Fathers, it must mean not simply principle, but first principle, or "principle without principle." It is therefore reasonable to understand it in the same sense here, particularly since, as we have seen, St. Maximus's words in question 34 suggest that the Son is involved in the Father's "causing" of the Holy Spirit.

Emmanuel Ponsoye is therefore reading into this passage something that is not there when he writes:

---

[12] *PG*, 91:136AB. A French translation of the *opusculum* by Ponsoye may be found in *Opuscules théologiques et polémiques*, 181–84. This translation, however, fails to include the key phrase "he goes forth [προϊέναι] through him." This appears to be simply an oversight, since the editor discusses it in his introduction at some length (80–84).

> If the pope had considered the Son a cause of the procession of the Holy Spirit (whether the Son was a second cause, or whether he was with the Father a unique cause), Maximus would not have considered his position acceptable.[13]

Ponsoye further argues that for Maximus the only acceptable meaning of the Latin *Filioque* is what is mentioned in the end of the extract, "the conjunction of substance and its invariableness." But in fact St. Maximus says that the Latins use the term in order to denote the going-forth through the Son, and *thus* (ταυτῇ) to show the connection and identity of substance. The going-forth is therefore the reason for the identity of substance; the two are not the same idea. Moreover, the reference to the Latin doctors and to St. Cyril shows that Maximus wishes to uphold the doctrine that they upheld; and we have already seen that they considered the Son an active principle of the Holy Spirit in his eternal existence.

Siecienski wishes to see in this letter a confirmation of his own theory that ἐκπόρευσις refers to the hypostatic origin of the Holy Spirit and that προϊέναι refers to the Holy Spirit's "comprehension of the Father's unique relationship to the Son."[14] But he offers no good reason for thinking that St. Maximus is using the verb προϊέναι in a way so unrelated to its actual meaning.

Does St. Maximus, even while not objecting to the doctrine of the "Latins," nonetheless object to the Latin phrase *ex Filio procedere*, or at any rate to the translation of this phrase as ἐξ Υἱοῦ ἐκπορεύεσθαι? The answer to this depends on the translation one gives of a passage that follows in this same letter. In Greek it is:

> Μεθερμηνεύειν δὲ τὰ οἰκεῖα, τοῦ τὰς ὑποκλοπὰς χάριν διαφυγεῖν τῶν ὑποπιπτόντων, κατὰ τὴν ὑμετέραν κέλευσιν παρεκάλεσα τοὺς Ῥωμαίους· πλὴν ἔθους κεκρατηκότος οὕτω ποιεῖν καὶ στέλλειν

---

13 St. Maximus, *Opuscules théologiques et polémiques*, 82. English translations from Ponsoye's French edition are my own.

14 Siecienski, *Filioque*, 84. Comprehension appears to mean simply "knowledge."

οὐκ οἶδα τυχὸν εἰ πεισθεῖεν. Ἄλλως τε καὶ τὸ μὴ οὕτως δύνασθαι διακριβοῦν ἐν ἄλλῃ λέξει τε καὶ φωνῇ τὸν ἑαυτῶν νοῦν ὥσπερ ἐν τῇ ἰδίᾳ καὶ θρεψαμένῃ καθάπερ οὖν καὶ ἡμεῖς ἐν τῇ καθ'ἡμᾶς τὸν ἡμέτερον. Γενήσεται δὲ πάντως αὐτοῖς πείρᾳ τὴν ἐπήρειαν μαθοῦσι καὶ ἡ περὶ τούτων φροντίς.[15]

Ponsoye's French rendering of this translates to:

> At your request, I have asked the Romans, in order to avoid obscurities and insinuations [sous-entendus], to translate what they mean by that. Apart from their constant habit of doing and writing it, I don't know if they have complied. Furthermore, there is the difficulty of not being able to express oneself with exactitude in another language as one can in one's maternal tongue, as we can express our affairs in our language. In any case, what will happen is that they will learn the harm that they are doing, and the concerns about this subject. [16]

Secienski translates (not including the last sentence):

> At your request, I asked the Romans to translate what is unique to them in order to avoid such obscurities. But since the practice of writing and sending letters has already been observed, I do not know if they will comply. Especially they might not be able to express their thought with the same exactness in another language as they might in their mother tongue, just as we could not do.[17]

---

15 *PG*, 91:136C.

16 St. Maximus, *Opuscules théologiques et polémiques*, 183: "A votre demande, j'ai prié les Romains, pour éviter obscurités et sous-entendus, qu'ils nous traduisent ce qu'ils entendent par là. En dehors de leur habitude constante de le faire et d'écrire, je ne sais si pour autant ils ont obtempéré. En outre, il y a le fait de ne pouvoir exprimer avec exactitude dans une autre langue sa pensée, comme dans sa langue maternelle; comme nous dans la nôtre nos affaires. Ce qui arrivera en tout cas, c'est qu'ils apprendront par expérience le tort qu'ils font, et l'inquiétude à ce sujet."

17 Siecienski, *Filioque*, 83. The "letters" are presumably synodal letters.

Both these vernacular versions imply that St. Maximus considers the Latin phrase *procedere ex Filio* to be at fault, an "obscurity" that needs to be translated into Greek; yet at the same time they suggest that the Latins could not express themselves so precisely in Greek! This suggests that something is awry both with Ponsoye's version and with Siecienski's.[18] The Greek word ὑποκλοπή—in the first sentence of the extract in the accusative plural, ὑποκλοπάς, translated by these authors as "obscurities"—is apparently a rare one, appearing neither in Henry Liddell and Robert Scott's *Greek–English Lexicon* nor in G. W. H. Lampe's *Patristic Lexicon*.[19] However, the cognate adjective ὑποκλοπός does appear in both lexicons, though with the sense of "guileful," not of "obscure" or "misunderstood." Is then the saint accusing the pope and his theologians of guile? Hardly: he will in due time suffer with the Roman pontiff at the hands of the monothelites who have control of Byzantium. Ὑποκλοπάς here governs the genitive ὑποπιπτόντων. The meanings given for this in Liddell and Scott are "fall down, cringe, get under, befall, enter the mind"; Lampe gives the additional meanings of "lapse, prostrate oneself." Ponsoye seems to be translating it as *sous-entendus* ("insinuations," "[false] implications"), and Siecienski omits it. The correct sense of the term here seems to be "lapsed"; this allows us to give a satisfactory interpretation of the phrase τὰς ὑποκλοπὰς . . . τῶν ὑποπιπτόντων, which will then be translated as "the deceits of those who have lapsed."

St. Maximus is thus warning that the phrase *procedere ex Filio* leaves the Latins open to the tricks or guile of those who have lapsed from the faith, meaning the monothelites.[20] Doubtless he has in mind that the heretics will accuse the Latins of reviving Eunomianism. That the guile

18 Garrigues similarly translates this sentence: "I have asked the Romans to translate what is proper to them [the *Filioque*], in order to avoid the obscurities that could result from it" (*L'Esprit Qui Dit "Père!": l'Esprit-Saint dans la vie Trinitaire et le problème du* Filioque, Croire et Savoir 2 [Paris: Téqui, 1982], 82).

19 *A Greek–English Lexicon: With a Revised Supplement*, ed. Henry G. Liddell and Robert Scott, 9th ed. (Oxford: Clarendon, 1996); *A Patristic Greek Lexicon*, ed. G. W. H. Lampe (Oxford: Oxford University Press, 1969).

20 F. Combefis, the Dominican editor of the relevant volume of Migne's *Patrologia Graeca*, sees that the phrase refers to the heretics in Constantinople and not to the Latins, and he renders it picturesquely as "ad cavendas sic ex cuniculis obrepentium fraudes dolosque," literally "to beware of the harm and deceits of those thus creeping out of their holes," meaning the monothelites.

belongs to the accusers of the Latins is also indicated by the proceeding sentence, in which (as Ponsoye agrees) Maximus says that the Latins have been accused without reason, whereas their accusers, the monothelites, are justly accused and have neither defended nor rejected the teaching which they surreptitiously introduced.

Again, if St. Maximus is not saying that the Latins express themselves obscurely in Latin and could not express themselves so clearly in Greek, what is he saying? He apparently means that although he has asked them whether they could find another phrase to explain (μεθερμηνεύειν) the words *ex Filio procedere*, he acknowledges that this may be unlikely, both because the phrase is so well established and because it is not always possible to express exactly the same idea in another form of words. The phrase ἐν ἄλλῃ λέξει τε καὶ φωνῇ does not necessarily indicate a translation to another language, as both Ponsoye and Siecienski assume. Likewise, ἐν τῇ ἰδίᾳ καὶ θρεψαμένῃ [λέξει] does not necessarily mean "in their mother tongue" (that is, in Latin); literally, it means, "in the characteristic and accustomed" speech—that is, using the theological idiom with which they are familiar.

In other words, while the saint may be saying that ἐκπορεύεσθαι ἐκ τοῦ Υἱοῦ leaves more room for captious interpretations than *ex Filio procedere*, he may be saying that each of them is equally liable to such interpretation. In any case, there is nothing to suggest that Maximus rejects either the Latin or the Greek phrase in itself, even though he foresees that some will use them to forge accusations of heresy against the Romans.

Finally, the last sentence of this extract is badly rendered by Ponsoye. As already mentioned, the "harm" is being done by the heretics and not, as Ponsoye's rendering says, by the pope and the Latin bishops. A better translation would be: "They [the Latins] will certainly give thought to these things also when they experience their [the heretics'] insults."[21]

21 Migne has: "Prorsus vero rem et ipsi curabant [sic], qui experimento, quod inde est damnum iniuriamque, didicerint"—"they themselves also were certainly giving thought to it when they will have learned what harm and injuries/insults arise from it." *Curabant* is presumably a typographical error for *curabunt*, "they will give thought to."

The Authenticity of the Letter to Marinus

The authenticity of this letter has long been a subject of dispute.[22] Ponsoye notes that the passage concerning the *Filioque* is not found in all manuscripts, and that a critical edition of the text is still lacking.[23] He also cites V. Karayiannis as arguing against its authenticity on the grounds that the subject of the *Filioque* had not yet become a point of dispute between Greek and Latin theologians, and that if St. Maximus had interested himself in the question, it would be surprising that he should treat it in so cursory a way and in just one work.[24] These arguments are weak. To the first, one may simply reply that it begs the question. Some theologian had to be the first to allude to the discrepancy between Latins and Greeks, so why not St. Maximus, a Greek theologian living in Latin territory? To the second argument, Ponsoye replies that Maximus did not write extensively either on Trinitarian theology in general or on the procession of the Holy Spirit in particular, and so one need not be surprised that he did not speak more extensively of the *Filioque*. He adds that it was in the lifetime of St. Maximus, at the Fourth Council of Toledo in 633, that the words *et Filio* appear to have been recited as part of the Creed for the first time.[25]

Siecienski mentions as other possible objections to the authenticity of the letter the fact that it is first mentioned by Anastasius Bibliothecarius in 874 and the fact that Maximus speaks in another letter to Marinus of a letter that was falsely attributed to himself, which may or may not have been this letter.[26] The former of these two facts, however, is not particularly significant, given the briefness of the letter, and the latter is inconclusive. Again, Siecienski cites P. Sherwood and A. Alexakis to the effect that "stylistic and other internal

22 It is accepted as authentic in *CPG*, 3:436.

23 St. Maximus, *Opuscules théologiques et polémiques*, 77.

24 St. Maximus, *Opuscules théologiques et polémiques*, 78.

25 St. Maximus, *Opuscules théologiques et polémiques*, 79. The Sixth Council of Toledo, in 638, used the word *Filioque* itself.

26 St. Maximus, *Opuscules théologiques et polémiques*, 79.

evidence excludes [*sic*] the possibility of a ninth-century fabrication."[27] Ponsoye notes that while there has been a certain historical tendency for Latins and pro-unionist Greeks to cast doubt on the letter, and for anti-unionist Greeks to accept it, nevertheless, the general consensus has been in its favor: the pro-unionists John Bekkos, Manuel Kalekas, and Joseph of Methone all accepted it.[28] In more modern times, Martin Jugie stated that there was no strong reason to doubt its authenticity.[29] In this section I have argued that, in any case, it gives no more support to anti-filioquism than do St. Maximus's other writings.

27 Siecienski, *Filioque,* 79.

28 St. Maximus, *Opuscules théologiques et polémiques*, 77.

29 Martin Jugie, *De Processione Spiritus Sancti* (Rome: Facultas Theologica Pontificii Athenaei Seminarii Romani, 1936), 186n1.

CHAPTER 16

SAINT JOHN DAMASCENE

Introduction

WITH ST. JOHN OF DAMASCENE, who died in 747, our survey of the patristic evidence will come to an end. Although he sought only to synthesize the teaching of those who had preceded him, some of his remarks about our question are not found in the authors considered hitherto. Damascene's Trinitarian teaching is to be found mostly in his *De fide orthodoxa*, though some other works are also relevant, particularly his short treatise *De Sancta Trinitate*.[1]

The Word Possesses the Holy Spirit

In *De Sancta Trinitate*, using language reminiscent of St. Gregory Nazianzen's Oration 41, Damascene writes: "Neither was the Son ever

[1] Parenthetical references are to *De fide orthodoxa*, quoted from John Damascene, *On the Orthodox Faith*, trans. S. Salmond, *NPNF2* vol. 9, pt. 2. Translations from other works are my own. *De Sancta Trinitate* is in large part a reproduction of an earlier work by an unknown author, formerly identified with Cyril of Alexandria (Yves Congar, *I Believe in the Holy Spirit*, vol. 3, Milestones in Catholic Theology [New York: Crossroad, 1997], 36).

lacking to the Father, nor was the Holy Spirit ever lacking [ἐνέλιπέ] to the Son."[2] In *De fide orthodoxa*, he develops this thought in a way reminiscent of Gregory of Nyssa's *Oratio catechetica magna*:

> The Word must also possess [ἔχειν] Spirit. For in fact even our word is not destitute [ἄμοιρος] of spirit; but in our case the spirit is something different from our essence. For there is an attraction and movement of the air which is drawn in and poured forth that the body may be sustained. And it is this which in the moment of utterance becomes the articulate word, revealing [φανεροῦσα[3]] in itself the force [δύναμιν] of the word. But in the case of the divine nature, which is simple and uncompound, we must confess in all piety that there exists a Spirit of God, for the Word is not more imperfect than our own word. (1.7)[4]

José Grégoire notes that the triad νοῦς–λόγος–πνεῦμα is Damascene's favored analogy for the triune God.[5] Yet, as in the case of St. Gregory of Nyssa, one can wonder what explanatory value the second half of this image has. If the divine Breath is "uncompound" and not of a different essence from the Breather, what still remains of the original idea of "breath" able to give us some analogue of the Holy Spirit or of his procession? The answer could be that the description of the Holy Spirit as "breath" connotes an eternal revelatory relation to the Word: as the human breath in speaking is the bearer of meaning, so the Holy Spirit in proceeding reveals the "force of the Word."[6] Elsewhere, he calls the

2 *PG*, 95:13A.

3 An alternative reading is φέρουσα, "bearing."

4 *PG*, 94:804.

5 José Grégoire, "La relation éternelle de l'Esprit au Fils d'après les écrits de Jean de Damas," *Revue d'histoire ecclésiastique* 64 (1969): 713–55, at 726. All translations of Grégoire's French in this work will be my own.

6 In his psychology, Damascene distinguishes the immanent word or concept (λόγος ἐνδιάθετος) from the spoken word (λόγος προφορικός). The former is the analogue for the divine Word insofar as it is of the same nature as the mind, while the latter is the analogue insofar as it is accompanied by breath (Grégoire, "La relation éternelle," 727, 749n1).

Holy Spirit the "image of the Son" (a phrase familiar in the East at least since Gregory Thaumaturgos[7]): "The Son is the Father's image, and the Spirit the Son's, through which Christ dwelling in man makes him after His own image" (1.13). Insofar as an image is what it is because of the original, but not the other way round, the term "image," like the phrase "revealing [or bearing] the power," implies some kind of dependence of the Holy Spirit on the Son; but it leaves the nature of the dependence undetermined.

The Holy Spirit Proceeds δι' Υἱοῦ

Damascene affirms the procession δι' Υἱοῦ in several places.[8] For example:

> The Holy Spirit is the power of the Father revealing the hidden mysteries of His Divinity, proceeding from the Father through the Son [ἐκ Πατρὸς δι' Υἱοῦ ἐκπορευομένη] in a manner known to Himself, but different from that of generation. (1.12)[9]

As was noted in connection with St. Maximus, the question arises of how to understand the διά.

The Position of José Grégoire

Grégoire states that Damascene uses the phrase δι' Υἱοῦ without giving the slightest explanation of it.[10] He first considers and rejects the suggestion of N. Bogorodsky that it be translated as "at the same time as"; to have a temporal meaning, διά must be followed by a temporal

---

7 See Thaumaturgos's *Confession of Faith* as quoted in A. Edward Siecienski, *The Filioque: History of a Doctrinal Controversy* (New York: Oxford University Press, 2010), 36.

8 In addition to the passages quoted from *De fide orthodoxa* in this section and in the section "The Holy Spirit Rests in the Son" below, examples may be found in *Dialogus contra Manichaeos* (*PG*, 94:1512B) and *De hymno Trisagio* (*PG*, 95:60C).

9 *PG*, 94:849A.

10 Grégoire, "La relation éternelle," 751.

substantive, which is not the case here. Moreover its temporal meaning is "during," not "at the same time as," and "during the Son" is meaningless.

Next, a passage in his *Dialogus contra Manichaeos* shows that the procession δι᾽ Υἱοῦ refers to the eternal divine relations, and not simply to the economy. Damascene writes: "I do not say that having previously not been Father, he later became Father, for he always was such, having his own Word from himself, and through his Word having his Spirit proceeding from himself [διὰ τοῦ Λόγου . . . ἐκπορευόμενον]."[11]

Next Grégoire asks whether the preposition διά could express the Son as the secondary or instrumental cause of the Holy Spirit.[12] He denies this for two reasons. In the first place, he claims, Damascene lacks the concept of an instrumental cause. Having surveyed all three hundred passages in the works certainly or probably attributed to the saint where the terms αἰτία, ἀρχή, αἴτιον, ἄναρχος, μοναρχία, πηγή, or ἀναίτιος occur, whether in speaking of the Trinity or not, he concludes that the notion of two superimposed causalities that would each be the total cause of the same effect is foreign to Damascene's thought.[13]

Secondly, Grégoire examines the grammar of the phrase ἐκπορεύεται/ἐκπορευόμενον διὰ τοῦ Υἱοῦ. In principle, the verb could be in either the middle or the passive voice;[14] the Holy Spirit "brings himself out" or "is brought out." Grégoire argues that a passive sense is unlikely because of Damascene's use elsewhere of the phrase διὰ τοῦ Υἱοῦ προϊόν as active.[15] He concludes that ἐκπορεύεται is therefore a middle. But, in that case, διά cannot have an instrumental sense, for when it has this sense, it has it in relation to the grammatical subject of the sentence, and we cannot suppose that the Son is an "instrument" of the Holy Spirit. Rather, the structure of the sentence and the root meaning of

11 *PG*, 94:1512B.

12 The phrase "instrumental cause" is of course doubly inaccurate in this context, but his meaning is clear enough.

13 Grégoire, "La relation éternelle," 722–23.

14 Grégoire, "La relation éternelle," 752 (with note 1). The verb is used classically only as a middle, but the aorist passive participle ἐκπορευθέν is found already in the fourth-century author Didymus of Alexandria (*PG*, 39:448C).

15 In *De hymno Trisagio* (*PG*, 95:60C).

the verbs ἐκπορεύεσθαι and προϊέναι mean that we should understand διά, "through," in a local and not a causal sense.[16]

Of course, Grégoire does not think that Damascene really supposed local movement or space to be found in the Godhead. He notes, however, that spatial metaphors are frequent in Greek patristic descriptions of the Trinity, and in particular that Damascene (and Pseudo-Cyril, from whom he frequently drew), often use the spatial metaphor of "compenetration." By using the expression "through the Son," therefore, Damascene would be expressing the Holy Spirit's procession from the Father as the reason for his indwelling in the Son: "The δι' Υἱοῦ is the dynamic expression . . . of the perichoresis; the compenetration and remaining of the hypostases in each other being the eternal 'result' of the procession through the Son."[17]

If Grégoire is correct in seeing ἐκπορεύεται as a middle rather than a passive, then he seems also to be correct in stating that the διά introduces a spatial metaphor and denying that it directly names the Son as the co-principle of the procession. However, he seems incorrect in seeing the δι' Υἱοῦ as simply referring to the procession of the Holy Spirit from the Father considered as "resulting in" the Holy Spirit's indwelling in the Son. If this were the only reason for Damascene's use of the phrase, then he could also have spoken of the Son as being begotten διὰ Πνεύματος, since the Son's generation also "results in" his indwelling in the Spirit; but in fact this latter phrase is never found. There must be some other consideration that led Damascene to use the former spatial metaphor and not the latter.

The Sun, the Sunbeam, and the Radiance

Damascene expresses the relation of the second and third divine persons in the following way, which may be taken as his own commentary on the phrase δι' Υἱοῦ:

---

16 I.e., the διά is necessarily being used like the word "by" in the sentence "the water comes out by the pipe," not like the word "by" in the sentence "the man moves the ball by [means of] the pipe."

17 Grégoire, "La relation éternelle," 753.

> We do not speak of the Father as derived from anyone, but we speak of Him as the Father of the Son. And we do not speak of the Son as Cause or Father, but we speak of Him both as from the Father, and as the Son of the Father. And we speak likewise of the Holy Spirit as from the Father [ἐκ τοῦ Πατρός], and call Him the Spirit of the Father. And we do not speak of the Spirit as from the Son: but We call Him the Spirit of the Son. *For if anyone has not the Spirit of Christ, he is none of His,* says the divine apostle. And we confess that He is manifested and imparted to us through the Son [δι' Υἱοῦ πεφανερῶσθαι καὶ μεταδίδοσθαι]. *For He breathed upon His Disciples, says he, and said, Receive the Holy Spirit.* It is just the same as in the case of the sun from [ἐκ] which come both the ray and the radiance (for the sun itself is the source of both the ray and the radiance), and it is through the ray that the radiance is imparted to us, and it is the radiance itself by which we are lightened and in which we participate. Further we do not speak of the Son of the Spirit, or of the Son as derived from the Spirit. (1.8)[18]

Is this passage referring simply to the temporal mission of the Holy Spirit, sent from the Son? Its position within *De fide orthodoxa* seems to exclude this. It is found within what was later called (apparently by analogy with Peter Lombard's *Sentences*) "book 1," where the saint is treating of God in himself and not directly of creation. The reference to our illumination by the Holy Spirit therefore seems to be intended as an aid to understanding the eternal relation between the Son and the Spirit, not to be his only description of their relation. It is in eternity that they are related as ray and radiance; Damascene presents the "radiance" as existing independently of us, so that we may participate in it.[19]

Theodoros Alexopoulos sees in this passage a "manifestation" of the

---

[18] *PG*, 94:832A–33A.

[19] Grégoire writes that "Damascene is unacquainted with the intransigent [*farouche*] separation of economy and theology that characterizes later Byzantine thought" ("La relation éternelle," 724).

Holy Spirit through the Son that would be distinct from his hypostatic procession from the Father alone.[20] But the saint would have been obliged to present this distinction explicitly if he had wished his readers to perceive it. He is clearly talking at the start of the passage about the origins of the divine hypostases, and likewise in the last sentence quoted. It is not plausible that so careful and didactic a writer should not have made his intention clear if he was to speak in the middle of this passage about an eternal coming forth of the Holy Spirit that was somehow not his hypostatic coming forth.

While allowing for the inadequacy of any material image to express a spiritual reality, we can notice that the sunbeam is a real principle of the illumination caused by the sun. I do not think it forcing the evidence, therefore, to conclude that in speaking of the Holy Spirit proceeding δι' Υἱοῦ, Damascene had in mind that the Holy Spirit received from the Son. Even if, as Grégoire affirms, the explicit category of secondary causality is absent from Damascene's philosophy, it is a category that anyone who has used a tool possesses implicitly and practically; and that is enough for it to have been shaping Damascene's thought and its expression. In other words, if he introduces the spatial metaphor of the Holy Spirit proceeding through the Son, it is because, in the procession of the Holy Spirit, the Son is second in regard to the Father, as that which one goes through is second in regard to that from which one starts. And since, when one excludes the literal, spatial meaning, "being second" in this context can only mean being a principle of the procession in dependence on the Father, the δι' Υἱοῦ does ultimately imply that the Son is co-principle with the Father, even though, as Grégoire points out in his grammatical analysis of the phrase, it does not say this directly.[21]

Grégoire objects to attributing an active role to the Son in the

20 See Theodoros Alexopoulos, "The Eternal Manifestation of the Spirit 'Through the Son' (διὰ τοῦ Υἱοῦ) according to Nikephoros Blemmydes and Gregory of Cyprus," in *Ecumenical Perspectives on the* Filioque *for the 21st Century*, ed. Myk Habets (London: Bloomsbury Academic, 2014), 71.

21 Hence the bull of union of the Council of Florence does not say simply that the expression "through the Son" is equivalent to "from the Son," but that the former expression leads to the latter, "ad hanc intelligentiam tendit." See appendix 1 for the full text.

spiration of the Holy Spirit on the basis of the metaphor of the sunbeam; one might equally deny such a role, he argues, given Damascene's use of the image of Eve coming directly from the side of Adam as an illustration of the ἐκπόρευσις.[22] There is a difference, however. In the former case, Damascene is directly intending to say something about the *relations* of the divine persons, whereas in the latter case, he is intending to assert that each divine person has a distinct hypostatic property, τρόπος ὑπάρξεως.

Siecienski, for his part interprets the δι' Υἱοῦ to mean that "there is an eternal relationship between the Father and the Son (since 'the Father could not be so called without a Son') that demands that one uphold the Son as a condition of the Spirit's coming forth from the Father."[23] But, again, had Damascene wished his words to be understood in this way, it would have been incumbent on him to explain his meaning, or to have explained himself with a different image. The sunbeam, after all, is not a mere condition *sine qua non* of the illumination. When we say that the sun causes the brightness by its ray, we do not mean that the sun, which would not exist without having a ray, causes radiance without it.

The Holy Spirit Rests in the Son

A noteworthy aspect of Damascene's account of the divine persons is that the Holy Spirit is said to rest (ἀναπαύεσθαι) in the Son.[24] This phrase occurs in chapters 7, 8, and 13 of the first book of *De fide orthodoxa*,

22 Grégoire, "La relation éternelle," 746. Damascene uses this illustration, borrowed from Nazianzen, in *De fide orthodoxa* (*PG*, 94:816C–17A).

23 Siecienski, *Filioque,* 91.

24 Yves Congar states that "this idea of resting in the Son is to be found among other Greek Fathers" (*Diversity and Communion*, North American ed. [Mystic, CT: Twenty-Third Publications, 1985], 102). However, the passages that he quotes, from St. Athanasius (*PG*, 26:565B) and from Didymus (*PG*, 39:425A) use the terms πρόσεστι ("he is near") and μένει ("he remains"). Grégoire notes that two of Damascene's uses of it are taken from Pseudo-Cyril. He sees the origins of the phrase in Alexandrine commentaries on Isaiah 11:2 ("The Spirit of the Lord will rest upon him"), where the Septuagint uses the verb ἐπαναπαύσεται and Codex Sinaiticus has ἀναπαύεσθαι ("La relation éternelle," 729n2).

and always in conjunction with the Spirit's being said also to proceed from the Father. For example:

> We must contemplate [the Holy Spirit] as an essential power, existing in His own proper and peculiar subsistence, proceeding from the Father and resting in the Word, and shewing forth the Word, neither capable of disjunction from God in Whom He exists, and the Word Whose companion He is, nor poured forth to vanish into nothingness, but like the Word existing as a person. (1.7)[25]

How are we to understand this "resting"? Damascene himself does not explain it. The editor of Migne's *Patrologia Graeca* here (1.7) takes it to be a simple statement that the divine persons are not separated from one another, and compares it to St. Cyril of Alexandria's use of the verb μένειν, "to remain," in the same context. Yet the phrase "rest in" arguably suggests something more, connoting as it does satisfaction or delight. Insofar as spiritual rest means a delight in a good securely possessed, it is common to all three divine persons. If it is appropriated to the Holy Spirit, this is perhaps in part because the Holy Spirit "completes" the Trinity, and one rests at the completion of an activity and in part because of the "resting" of the dove upon the head of Christ at his baptism; and in part it may suggest the association of the Holy Spirit with the "affective life" of God, since the notion of rest is closely connected to that of satisfaction.

What does Damascene mean when he says of the Holy Spirit not only that he rests, but that he rests in the Son? Is it possible to conceive it as if the Son were akin to a final cause of the procession—as if the Father spirated the Holy Spirit in order that he might bestow Him

[25] I have changed Salmond's translation here, in that he refers to the Holy Spirit as "it," and also translates the last phrase as "being in subsistence with the likeness of the Word" (καθ'ὁμοιότητα τοῦ Λόγου καθ'ὑπόστασιν οὖσαν).

upon the Son? Such an interpretation has no basis in the saint's own sources. It therefore seems better to understand Damascene's phrase as another way of expressing what is elsewhere expressed by the term δι' Υἱοῦ: both Father and Son are intrinsic to the ἐκπόρευσις, and the Father alone is principle without principle. The Father is thought of as the starting point for the procession and the Son as the end point, although only in the sense that the Son is from the Father and not conversely. This is why the Holy Spirit is said to rest on the Son and not on the Father.

"We Do Not Say ἐκ τοῦ Υἱοῦ"

St. John Damascene's most famous remark about the *Filioque* is perhaps his verbal denial of the doctrine.[26] We have already seen one such passage in discussing the sense of the δι' Υἱοῦ. A similar expression is found later in *De fide orthodoxa*:

> But the Holy Spirit is not the Son of the Father, but the Spirit of the Father as proceeding from the Father. For there is no impulse without Spirit. And we speak also of the Spirit of the Son, not as though proceeding from Him, but as proceeding through Him from the Father [δι' αὐτοῦ ἐκ τοῦ Πατρὸς ἐκπορευόμενον]. For the Father alone is cause [αἴτιος]. (1.12)[27]

Is this verbal denial of the doctrine also a real denial? The question has long been discussed.[28] We can note, first, that the verbal denial of the doctrine is followed in each case by what sounds like an affirmation of

---

[26] By some strange oversight, or special providence, this was not included in the anti-unionist arguments at the Council of Florence, to judge from the Greek *acta*. Bessarion confirms this in his Letter to Alexios Lascaris (*PG*, 161:423D). On the other hand, Mark of Ephesus made use of it in his *Encyclical to all Orthodox Christians* (*OAU*, 451).

[27] (*PG*, 94:849B).

[28] St. Thomas Aquinas, having said that on this question Damascene had followed "the error of the Nestorians," adds that some people say that Damascene in these words is neither affirming nor denying the *Filioque* (*Summa theologiae* I, ed. Institutum Studiorum Medievalium Ottavienses, 5 vols. [Ottawa: Studium Generalis Ordo Praedicatorum, 1941], q. 36, a. 2, ad 3).

the dependence of the Holy Spirit on the Son. In the first extract, discussed above, this consisted in the statement that the Holy Spirit is "of the Son" (τοῦ Υἱοῦ) and the example of the sun, the ray, and the radiance; even though this image is used to illustrate the gift of the Holy Spirit to the believer, the fact that it is used in the context of a description of the eternal Trinity strongly suggests that it applies there also.[29] In this second extract, the verbal denial is followed by the assertion of the διά. We have already argued that the image of the ray, which is given as an explanation of the διά, in fact implies the *Filioque*. Does this mean, then, that when Damascene says, "we do not say 'from the Son,'" he is merely affirming nothing more than that, as a matter of fact, this phrase is not used by the Greeks? It does not seem so: he seems at least to be affirming that it is more suitable to reserve the preposition ἐκ for the Father. For he not only mentions the Greek custom, but also gives a reason for it: "the Father alone is cause."[30]

Since we have argued above that Damascene has in mind an active role for the Son in the procession, it would follow that here he intends simply to affirm that the Father alone is principle without principle, and hence that he is not really denying the *Filioque*.[31] According to Grégoire, St. John has no polemical intent in his Trinitarian writings except against Arians and Manichees.[32] At the same time, he apparently lacks the concept of the Father and Son as a single principle of the procession, as well as St. Augustine's explanation of what it means for the

---

29 As Alexopoulos concedes ("Eternal Manifestation," 71).

30 Martin Jugie believes that "we" here means "we moderns," and that John is distinguishing the fixed terminology of his day from the more fluid use of earliest times (*De Processione Spiritus Sancti* [Rome: Facultas Theologica Pontificii Athenaei Seminarii Romani, 1936], 186–87). In this case, he would also be giving a reason for the "modern" term. Damascene's terminology of "proceeding through the Son" was used by the patriarch Tarasius of Constantinople at Nicaea II in 787, forty years after Damascene's death, in the creed that he sent to the other Eastern patriarchs (Mansi, 12:1122D).

31 In *Dialogus contra Manichaeos*, Damascene says that though the term ἀρχή is used in many ways, it is properly said to be that which does not itself have an ἀρχή (*PG*, 94:1509B). It is reasonable to suppose that he understood the word αἰτία in a similar way, especially given its use by the Cappadocians and by St. Anastasius of Antioch. See the section on St. Gregory of Nazianzen's Oration 34 in ch. 7, the section on St. Gregory of Nyssa's *Contra Eunomium* in ch. 9, and the section on ἐκπορεύεσθαι and *procedere* in ch. 17 ("Concluding Linguistic Remarks"). This passage from *Dialogus contra Manichaeos* puts further in doubt Grégoire's claim that the saint has no explicit concept of "super-imposed causality."

32 Grégoire, "La relation éternelle," 755.

Holy Spirit to proceed *principaliter* from the Father. For this reason, Damascene is not able to produce a fully satisfactory synthesis of his thought, a sign of which fact is the absence of any explanation in his work of the "rest" of the Holy Spirit in the Son. One may say that while the deeper tendency of his thought is in favor of the *Filioque*, a habit of language has grown up that obstructs the expression of the doctrine.

The Difference between Generation and Procession

Damascene shows himself the disciple of St. Athanasius and the Cappadocian Fathers in professing himself unable to define the distinction between generation and procession. He writes frankly: "We have learned that there is a difference between generation and procession, but the nature of that difference we in no wise understand" (1.8). There is nonetheless a certain, though undeveloped, idea in Damascene that what characterizes the Holy Spirit is something to do with the volitional or affective life in God. We have already seen the use he makes of the idea of "resting" in describing the procession of the third divine person, and also that resting, in its spiritual sense, denotes a stable joy. Again, in *De Sancta Trinitate*, he writes, "he is called Spirit, because he inclines and blows [νεύειν καὶ πνεῖν], wherever he wills."[33] Freedom, or free will, is thus in effect appropriated to the Holy Spirit. This could have led Damascene to ask whether the distinction between generation and procession is that the former occurs by way of intellect and the latter by way of will; but here as elsewhere he appears unaware of St. Augustine's theology. In fact, when he speaks explicitly of will in connection with the Trinity, it is the Son and not the Holy Spirit whom he mentions, writing that "the Father has no reason, wisdom, power, will, save the Son Who is the only power of the Father" (1.12).

Elsewhere he characterizes the third divine person in these terms:

33 *PG*, 95:16C.

> The Holy Spirit is God, being between the unbegotten and the begotten, and united to the Father through the Son. We speak of the Spirit of God, the Spirit of Christ, the mind of Christ, the Spirit of the Lord, the very Lord, the Spirit of adoption, of truth, of liberty, of wisdom (for He is the creator of all these things)." (1.13)

These are all traditional phrases: Nazianzen had spoken of the Holy Spirit as between the unbegotten and the begotten in his Fifth Theological Oration, while St. Cyril of Alexandria had called him "the mind of the Son."[34] We may note that to be "between" the Father and the Son, while it is not explained by either Nazianzen or Damascene, implies that a relation to both the Father and the Son is intrinsic to the person of the Holy Spirit. Yet, taken as a whole, this list of terms does not give a new insight into the difference between procession and generation. As the patristic period reaches its close, one is struck less by the difference between a Western *ex Filio* and an Eastern δι' Υἱοῦ than by the failure of St. Augustine's association of spiration with love to be more generally affirmed.[35]

34 Cyril does this, e.g., in the *Thesaurus de Sancta et Consubstantiali Trinitate* (*PG*, 75:584B).

35 For this reason I am surprised by Jean-Miguel Garrigues's claim that the weakness of Latin pneumatology is the failure to recognize the "unfathomable difference" (*insondable antinomie*) between generation and procession (*L'Esprit Qui Dit "Père!": l'Esprit-Saint dans la vie Trinitaire et le problème du* Filioque, Croire et Savoir 2 [Paris: Téqui, 1982], 71). With regard to the bishop of Hippo, B. Altaner wrote: "No Greek theologian or hierarchy [*sic*] from the fifth to the ninth centuries had even the most modest claim to an adequate acquaintance with the writings and theology of the great Augustine.... The life and work of Augustine constituted for the Greek Church a scroll sealed with seven seals" (trans. Aidan Nichols in "The Reception of St. Augustine and his Work in the Byzantine-Slav Tradition," *Angelicum* 64 [1987]: 437–52, at 443).

CHAPTER 17

CONCLUDING LINGUISTIC REMARKS

FOR EACH OF THE FATHERS EXAMINED HERE, I have explained why I consider that he would have accepted the definition of the Council of Florence that the Son has from the Father that he is with the Father one principle of the eternal spiration of the Holy Spirit, while at that same time acknowledging that this teaching is more evident in some of the Fathers, and in others more a conclusion that may be legitimately deduced from their writings taken as a whole. I therefore do not think it necessary to summarize their views again here. However, some concluding linguistic remarks on some points of Greek and Latin usage may be useful.

Bessarion

Why did no Greek Father in his extant writing use the precise phrase ἐκπορεύεται ἐκ τοῦ Υἱοῦ? Few people can have considered this question so earnestly as Bessarion of Nicaea. He answers it in a treatise on the procession of the Holy Spirit written to a certain Alexios Lascaris some years after the Council of Florence and intended to justify its definitions. It is the testimony of a Greek bishop who had made himself proficient in Latin, and who had come to be convinced through his study of the Fathers of East and West that there is no difference of doctrine between them.

Bessarion begins by noting that, as no human word can express what God is in himself, we must always in using words of God accept the truth they express and reject the limitations that they connote. In regard to the procession of the Holy Spirit, two truths must be maintained. First, that the Father and the Son spirate the Holy Spirit *aequaliter et simpliciter*: they are equal in spirating, and they do so as a single and simple principle. Secondly, in spirating, as in all other things, the Son has a "relation and order" to the Father. He goes on:

> If therefore one word were sufficient to express at the same time both their complete identity of power and the supreme order of one to the other, we should certainly use that one in preference to all others. But in fact, it is not only impossible to find any such word—and so of necessity we express the first idea by one word and the second by another—but also, from the very fact that each word signifies only one of the aforementioned ideas, each signifies that idea imperfectly.[1]

When something is said to be done by two persons, the prepositions *ex* and ἐκ signify equality when placed before each person; but they do not signify an order between the two persons. On the other hand, the words *per* and διά placed before the second person signify the order

1 *PG*, 161:443B: "Si igitur unum nomen esset sufficiens, et summam potentiae eorum identitatem, et summum ad invicem ordinem simul significare, illo profecto omnibus aliis postpositis utendum esset. Nunc verum non solum impossibile est unum tale reperire nomen: et necesssario uno nomine alterum horum, altero vero alterum exprimendum est, verum etiam haec diversa nomina ad hoc quod utrumque per se unum tantum praedicatum significatorum praedictorum significant, etiam imperfecte illud significant" (trans. mine).

but not the equality. Therefore, when the Fathers and doctors of East or West wished to speak of the equality of the Father and the Son in the spiration, they used the former prepositions; when they wished to speak of the order, they used the latter. "Yet," Bessarion says, "there are some saints who emphasized [*maioris fecerunt*] the order, such as the majority of the Eastern ones; and there are some who emphasised the equality or identity, as many of the Western ones."[2] He adds that, in the Greek language, the preposition ἐκ signifies the "principal cause" (αἰτία προκαταρκτική), which is why the Greek Fathers rarely used it to refer to the Son's creation of the world. Indeed, the Eastern doctors have been so keen that no one should believe in a first principle other than God the Father that they tend to avoid using the simple word αἰτία of the Son or of the Holy Spirit even in regard to creatures, "even though the Son and the Holy Spirit are universally believed by the faithful to be the cause of the world."[3] This corresponds exactly to St. Basil's words in the treatise *De Spiritu Sancto*: "The expression 'through whom' contains a confession of an antecedent cause [προκαταρκτικῆς αἰτίας], and is not adopted in objection to the efficient cause [οὐκ ἐπι κατηγορίᾳ τοῦ ποιητικοῦ αἰτίου παραλαμβάνεται]" (21).[4] At the same time, one may note that, considered precisely in regard to the spiration itself, neither the Father nor the Son is more principal than the other, since they are both one principle; this is why a phrase such as ἐκ τοῦ Υἱοῦ is sometimes found among the Greek Fathers, as we have seen, even though not accompanied by the word ἐκπορεύεται.

ἐκπορεύεσθαι and *Procedere*

Bessarion's words help to clarify the need for a variety of prepositions to express the Holy Spirit's relation to the Son, and they give a reason

2 *PG*, 161:444A. One may notice how nuanced this statement is.

3 *PG*, 161:444B. At Florence, the Latins had explained that they tended to avoid the expression *per Filium*, so as not to imply that the Son was a mere "channel" of the Holy Spirit, or an instrument of the Father (*AG*, 413).

4 Basil, *On the Holy Spirit*, in Selected Works, trans. Blomfield Jackson, *NPNF*2 vol. 8 (cited by section).

why ἐκ was not more frequently used by the Greek Fathers in reference to the Son. One may add that there is another reason why the precise phrase ἐκπορεύεται ἐκ τοῦ Υἱοῦ should not be found, whereas the Latin phrase *procedit ex Filio* is found. The Greek phrase with its double ἐκ—preposition and verbal prefix—would emphasize the idea of the Son as source or origin more than does the Latin phrase, where the verbal prefix does not express the idea of coming out of, but rather of going forward from. The distinction is no doubt fine, but it is real. This is shown by the fact that the Greek Fathers used the expression ἐκ τοῦ Υἱοῦ with other verbs that did not have the verbal prefix ἐκ, in particular the phrase ἐκ τοῦ Υἱοῦ προεῖσι.[5] Ἐκπορεύεται ἐκ τοῦ Υἱοῦ, by emphasizing so strongly the role of the Son as source, could thus have risked obscuring the role of the Father as "principle without principle" in a way that is not true of the phrase *procedit ex Filio*.

It is often said that the Latin language, in comparison with Greek, is poor in terms that express a relation of origin, and that this is why the same verb, *procedere*, is found in the Vulgate to translate both ἐξιέναι and ἐκπορεύεσθαι in John 8:32 and 15:26, understood as referring to the hypostatic origin of the Son and the Holy Spirit respectively.[6] In fact there are quite a number of Latin verbs that may be used to express the relation of origin of one divine person to another, and that are found in the translations of Greek texts: *procedere*, *exire*, *egredior*, *emanare*, *scaturire*, *oriri*, *elucescere*, *proficisci*, *prodire*, *progredi*. However, ἐκπορεύεσθαι does appear to contain a nuance of meaning not found in any Latin verb: going out *and then* going forward. The simple verb

5 Also worthy of note is the phrase ἐξ αὐτοῦ δεικνὺς αὐτο ὑπάρχειν, "showing him [the Holy Spirit] to exist from him [the Son]," used by St. Anastasius I of Antioch († 598/9) in his exposition of John 20:22. The Greek text is quoted in Martin Jugie, *De Processione Spiritus Sancti* (Rome: Facultas Theologica Pontificii Athenaei Seminarii Romani, 1936), 177. Anastasius nevertheless reserves the word αἴτιος for the Father, further proof that the term means not just "active principle," but "principle without principle." The Greek *acta* of the Council of Florence show that St. Anastasius was one of the authors whom the Eastern bishops consulted in their private discussions, even though he was apparently not quoted in the public sessions (*AG*, 428). See also *ODCC*, "Anastasius I," 58.

6 Aidan Nichols, *Rome and the Eastern Churches: A Study in Schism* (Edinburgh: T. & T. Clark, 1992), 225.

πορεύεσθαι by itself has the sense of "to march," whereas the Latin verbs listed all suggest *either* the going out or the going forward, but not so much both together. This is why it was more natural in Greek to reserve the phrase ἐκπορεύεται ἐκ for God the Father, insofar as the Holy Spirit may be imagined as coming out of the Father and going forward through the Son, though of course only in the sense that the Son has it from the Father that he is a principle of the Holy Spirit and not vice versa. Strictly speaking, however, since the Father and the Son are one principle of the Holy Ghost and have numerically the same relation toward him, any verbal phrase that names the coming forth of the Holy Spirit simply as such must be applicable either to the Father or to the Son. Hence if by the term ἐκπόρευσις one seeks to name precisely what is distinctive about the emanation of the Holy Spirit, as opposed to what it has in common with the emanation of the Son, one may not refuse to say ἐκπορεύεται ἐκ τοῦ Υἱοῦ.[7] The Council of Florence, having regard to the strict use of words, was therefore justified in using, in the Greek version of the bull of union, the phrases "ἐξ ἀμφοτέρων . . . ἐκπορεύεται" and "ἐκ τοῦ Υἱοῦ ἐκπορεύεται."[8] If, however, one seeks to express by the term ἐκπόρευσις both what is proper to the emanation of the Holy Spirit and also a note that it has in common with the emanation of the Son—namely, the dependence on the Father as the principle without principle—then one would not say this.[9]

---

7 This appears to be what St. Thomas Aquinas had in mind when he wrote in his *Commentary on St. John's Gospel*: "Some Greeks say that one should not say that the Holy Spirit proceeds from the Son, since the preposition 'from' with them designates the principle without principle, which is the Father alone. But this does not follow, since the Son is with the Father one principle of the Holy Spirit" [Dicunt tamen aliqui Graecorum, quod non est dicendum Spiritum sanctum procedere a Filio, quia haec praepositio *a* vel *ab* apud eos designat principium non de principio, quod convenit soli Patri. Sed hoc non cogit: quia Filius cum Patre est unum principium Spiritus sancti]" (*Super Ioan* 15, lec. 5; trans. mine).

8 The Pastoral Instruction issued after the Second Vatican Council by the Latin Catholic hierarchy in Greece ("On the Adoption of the [Original] Form of the Nicene-Constantinopolitan Creed in the Latin Liturgy in the Greek language") is therefore at odds with the Florentine definition signed by the Greeks when it claims that it is impossible to use the phrase ἐκπορεύεται καὶ ἐκ τοῦ Υἱοῦ (quoted in Jean-Miguel Garrigues, *L'Esprit Qui Dit "Père!": l'Esprit-Saint dans la vie Trinitaire et le problème du* Filioque, Croire et Savoir 2 [Paris: Téqui, 1982], 121). Yves Congar held that the Council of Florence's decision to use the phrase is "difficult to understand" (*I Believe in the Holy Spirit*, vol. 3, Milestones in Catholic Theology [New York: Crossroad, 1997], 187).

9 Hence I do not think Jugie is necessarily correct when he writes that in the Florentine definition, the term

ἐκ and παρά

Finally, it is well known that the clause about the procession of the Holy Spirit from the Son did not form part of the creed said to have been promulgated by the First Council of Constantinople, but rather was added later in the West. It is less well known that the expression used of the relation of the Holy Spirit to the Father by this creed is not exactly that which is contained in the New Testament. In John 15:26, Christ speaks of the Holy Spirit as the one who "ἐκπορεύεται παρὰ τοῦ Πατρός"; the Creed uses the expression "ἐκ τοῦ Πατρός ἐκπορευόμενον." The preposition παρά does not have precisely the same range of meanings as the preposition ἐκ. They can both be translated as "from," but παρά will rarely if ever be translated as "out of," as ἐκ may be; that is, παρά does not convey the sense as coming from *within* something. With the genitive, it will often rather have the sense of "coming from the place where something is," or "coming from alongside a thing."[10] If the word ἐκ, therefore, used of the origin of the Holy Spirit, especially when coupled with the word ἐκπορεύεται, has the tendency to move the mind toward the Father, as "first" origin, rather than the Son, the word παρά does not have this tendency. And if the phrase ἐκπορεύεται ἐκ τοῦ Πατρὸς καὶ τοῦ Υἱοῦ could require explanation, lest it appear to imply two "principles without principle," the phrase ἐκπορεύεται παρὰ τοῦ Πατρὸς καὶ τοῦ Υἱοῦ has less danger in this regard; in fact, insofar as παρά can mean "coming from the place where," it could even be seen as connoting the divine essence as the principle by which the Father and the Son spirate, the divine essence being seen by a legitimate metaphor as the "place" of the divine persons.

ἐκπορεύεσθαι has lost its special sense and become equivalent to *procedere* (*De Processione Spiritus Sancti*, 15); one could say, on the contrary, that it was being used in the most "formal" way possible.

10 William Watson Goodwin and John H. Betts, *A Greek Grammar* (London: Bristol Classical Press, 1997), 259. In this sense, παρά is naturally rendered by *a*/*ab*/*abs* in Latin, as is done in the Vulgate version of John 15:26, while ἐκ is most naturally rendered by *ex*.

Martin Jugie remarked that the preposition παρά, unlike ἐκ, does not strictly indicate origin, but rather a relation between persons conceived of as already existing.[11] He suggests that it is for this reason that Constantinople I made the change of preposition, that it might make clear that it was speaking of the eternal emanation, not of a temporal mission, of the Holy Spirit.[12] Nevertheless, one can wonder what would have happened had the fathers of that Council retained the preposition that the Holy Spirit himself had inspired St. John to employ. Perhaps the later Western addition would have occasioned less trouble.

---

11 Jugie, *De Processione Spiritus Sancti*, 71–72. This is not necessarily true of *a/ab/abs*, however. Jugie notes here that παρά is common after verbs meaning to receive, learn, know, ask, seek, come or set out from someone, come or set out by someone's command, or be sent by someone.

12 Jugie also holds that John 15:26 referred primarily and directly to the sending of the Holy Spirit, and only secondarily to his eternal procession (*De Processione Spiritus Sancti*, 71–72). The *Vetus Latina*, attested by Marius Victorinus, had *adveniet* ("he will come") and not *procedit* in this verse, which is clearly a reference to a temporal mission (199). Congar, however, writes that the Council fathers "replaced παρά with ἐκ, assuming that the two prepositions were equivalent" (*I Believe in the Holy Spirit*, 34). André de Halleux takes the same view as Jugie, but adds that the use of a present participle, rather than an aorist participle as is used of the Son's relation to the Father (γεννηθέντα), carries some economic connotation ('Pour un accord oecuménique sur la procession de l'Esprit Saint et l'addition du *Filioque* au symbole," *Irenikon* 15 [1978]: 451–69, at 466–68).

Part II

The Theory of Ecumenical Councils

CHAPTER 18

THE IDEA OF AN ECUMENICAL COUNCIL

Introduction

NOW THAT THE PATRISTIC WITNESS to the procession of the Holy Spirit has been considered, our other principal task is to consider the ecumenicity of the Council of Florence. The direct consideration of that Council will occupy the final part of the present work. Before that, however, I shall discuss the nature and authority of ecumenical councils in general: this is the object of the second main section of this book.

In keeping with the "ecumenical" aim of this work, I shall base my search for a theory of councils on the history of the seven great councils that are accepted in common by Catholics and Orthodox, and on what was said about them by the Fathers of the Church.[1] I shall first quote patristic testimonies to establish that there is a certain kind

[1] Yves Congar advocated such an approach: "We have histories of the councils, but few studies of the notion of a council by means of history" ("Bulletin d'ecclésiologie: conciles et papauté," *Revue des sciences philosophiques et théologiques* 60 [1976]: 281–308, at 281.

of council of the Church that has a power to declare the contents of divine revelation in an infallible and therefore irreformable way, and then show how this council came to be distinguished with the name "ecumenical." I shall then argue, secondly, that the history of the early councils, along with the patristic testimonies, shows that ecumenicity consists in (1) the presence of bishops who are sufficient to represent the whole Church and (2) papal headship. I shall also suggest two alternative accounts of how the idea of "sufficient representation" may be understood. Thirdly I shall consider two alternative accounts of the authority of ecumenical councils: the later Byzantine theory of the pentarchy acting in accord with the Roman emperor, and the modern theory or ideal of "reception."

Irreformable Conciliar Teaching

St. Paul described the Church as "the pillar and bulwark of the truth," στῦλος καὶ ἑδραίωμα τῆς ἀληθείας (1 Tim 3:15). In the *Adversus haereses* of St. Irenaeus, we find the conviction that those in authority within the Church have collectively the power to expound divine revelation in such a way that the truth will always be preserved:

> It is incumbent to obey the presbyters who are in the Church—those who, as I have shown, possess the succession from the apostles; those who, together with the succession of the episcopate, have received the certain gift of truth [charisma veritatis certum] according to the good pleasure of the Father. . . . For these also preserve this faith of ours in one God who created all things; and they increase that love for the Son of God, who accomplished such marvellous dispensations for our sake; and they expound the Scriptures to us without danger [Scripturas sine periculo nobis exponunt]. (4.26)[2]

---

[2] *PG*, 7a:1053C–56B.

As soon as the age of the great councils begins, we find the conviction that this sure charism of the truth possessed by the successors of the apostles can be exercised by them when gathered together in council. In his *De synodis*, written around 359–360, St. Athanasius contrasts the Council of Nicaea with the numerous other assemblies of bishops held in the decades following it.[3] To the former he gives the title of "ecumenical" (οἰκουμενικὴν σύνοδον), a word that apparently implies in his mind the reliability of its teaching. The fathers of that council, speaking of the eternal existence of the Son, wrote not "it seems good," as they did when establishing the date of Easter, but "the Catholic Church believes," to show that what they wrote was nothing other than the teaching of the apostles (5). The fathers of Nicaea pronounced judgment "once for all" (9). He uses the synonymous expression "general council," καθολικὴ σύνοδος, to refer to the meeting of Ariminum in 359, but only insofar as it was a council in prospect (2), or insofar as the Western bishops, from whom the Eastern ones had already been physically separated, remained for a while firm in professing the Nicene faith (11). In the second section of a synodal letter to the bishops of Africa, written in 369 or 370, he again contrasts the Nicene Council with later assemblies:

> This was why an ecumenical synod has been held at Nicæa, 318 bishops assembling to discuss the faith on account of the Arian heresy, namely, in order that local [κατὰ μέρος] synods should no more be held on the subject of the Faith, but that, even if held, they should not hold good [μὴ κρατῶσι].[4]

He writes in the same section that the Nicene synod is to later ones as the whole to the part, which is why it prevails over them. They also differ

[3] Athanasius, *De synodis* (*PG*, 26:681–794), in Selected Works and Letters, trans. Archibald Robertson, *NPNF2* vol. 4. Parenthetical citations in main text are to section numbers in the work.

[4] Athanasius's *Epistola ad Afros Episcopos* (*PG*, 26:1052B), in *NPNF2* vol. 4.

in regard to their cause. The Nicene council was called for a legitimate reason (αἴτιον εὔλογον), whereas the later ones were arranged by force, out of hatred and greed. He also refers here to the widespread consent that the former synod received: "Indians have acknowledged it, and all Christians of other barbarous nations." Given his original statement that the universal synod was held so that local ones might not be needed, this last quotation cannot be taken as showing that St. Athanasius held that the consent of the various nations was needed for the validity of the Nicene Creed; this universal consent is rather a sign that God was with the 318 Fathers. He expresses his conviction of the irreformability of that creed in a memorable phrase: "The word of the Lord which came through the ecumenical Synod at Nicæa, abides forever."

The same note is struck in the west by St. Ambrose when writing to Emperor Valentinian to refuse his command to debate the divinity of Christ with an Arian bishop, with laymen acting as arbiters. In reference to Arianism, Ambrose writes: "This was decreed at the synod of Ariminum, and with good reason do I abhor that Council; following as I do the doctrine of the Nicene Council, from which neither death nor the sword can ever separate me."[5] These are the words not of one who simply agrees with the doctrine of Nicaea, but of one who is convinced that the council itself had an irrefragable authority.

Early in the fifth century, Socrates Scholasticos bears witness to the same conviction. Having mentioned the taunt of Sabinus, an Arian, that the fathers of Nicaea were ignorant men, he says: "Even if those who were at the synod were unlettered, yet as being illuminated by God and the grace of the Holy Spirit, they were utterly unable to err from the truth [οὐδαμῶς ἀστοχῆσαι τῆς ἀληθείας ἐδύναντο]."[6]

St. Augustine, writing to the Arian bishop Maximinus, says that the *homoousion* was set forth at Nicaea "by the authority of truth and the

5 Ambrose, Letter 21, no. 14, in Letters and Hymns, in *NPNF*2 vol. 10. See also Ambrose's *De Spiritu Sancto*.
6 *PG*, 67:88B.

truth of authority." This balanced, lapidary phrase suggests, though it does not explicitly state, that the inerrant divine revelation has an infallible council as an adequate organ of definition.[7]

A passage in another letter from St. Augustine to Januarius, apparently a catechumen or neophyte, is also of interest:

> As to those other things which we hold on the authority, not of Scripture, but of tradition [illa . . . quae non scripta sed tradita custodimus], and which are observed throughout the whole world, it may be understood that they are held as approved and instituted either by the apostles themselves, or by plenary [plenariis] Councils, whose authority in the Church is most useful [saluberrima].[8]

The translation "most useful" is arguably too weak, since it can be lawful to neglect something even when that thing would be very useful. A better translation might be "undoubtedly pertains to our salvation." However, St. Augustine does not directly address here the question of the *doctrinal* authority of councils; Januarius has asked him about the customs to be observed within the Church, and his mention of councils is connected with a list of liturgical observances. Again, the expression "plenary councils" does not correspond exactly to what would later be called ecumenical councils; in his work *On baptism against the Donatists* he states that many plenary councils have already been held.[9] Joseph Wilhelm remarks in this connection that "the terms *concilia plenaria, universalia,* or *generalia* are, or used to be, applied indiscriminately to all synods not confined to a single province."[10] St. Augustine therefore does not here address the question of the qualitative difference between a council that

7 *PL*, 42:772.

8 Augustine, Letter 54, ch.1, no. 1, in Selected Works, trans. J. Pilkington and J. Cunningham, *NPNF*1 vol. 1.

9 *PL*, 43:129.

10 Joseph Wilhelm, "Councils, General," in *Catholic Encyclopedia* (New York: Encyclopedia Press, 1913), 424.

is, in the modern sense, general or ecumenical and lesser assemblies that nonetheless unite bishops from several provinces.[11]

St. Leo the Great is particularly clear on the power of certain councils to make an irrevocable definition of faith. Writing to Theodoret of Cyr after the Council of Chalcedon, he says:

> Our help is in the name of the Lord, who has made heaven and earth: who has suffered us to sustain no harm in the person of our brethren, but has corroborated by the irrevocable assent of the whole brotherhood [universae fraternitatis irretractabili firmavit consensu] what He had already laid down through our ministry.[12]

Somewhat later, writing to his namesake, the Roman emperor, Leo asserts the impossibility of reopening the doctrinal question that Chalcedon has resolved:

> To seek what has been laid bare, to reconsider what has been completed, and to demolish what has been defined [quae patefacta sunt quaerere, quae perfecta sunt retractare, et quae definita sunt convellere], what else is it but to return no thanks for things gained and to indulge the unholy longings of deadly lust on the food of the forbidden tree? And hence by deigning to show a more careful regard for the peace of the universal Church, you manifestly recognize what is the design of the heretics' mighty intrigues—that a more careful discussion should take place between the disciples of Eutyches and Dioscoros and the emissary of the Apostolic See, as if nothing had already been

[11] Congar notes that the Greek term οἰκουμενική was sometimes rendered in Latin as *universalis*, sometimes as *generalis*; sometimes it was transliterated as *(o)ecumenicus* ("1274–1974. Structures ecclésiales et conciles dans les relations entre Orient et Occident," *Revue des sciences philosophiques et théologiques* 58 [1974]: 355–90, at 378).

[12] Leo the Great, Letter 120, no. 1, in Letters and Sermons, trans. C. Feltoe, *NPNF2* vol. 12, pt. 1 (*PL*, 54:1047A).

> defined [definitum], and that what with the glad approval of the Catholic priests of the whole world was determined at the holy Synod of Chalcedon should be rendered invalid [infirmum].... Hence, if there are any who disagree with these heaven-inspired decisions [his quae coelitus sunt constituta], let them be left to their own opinions and depart from the unity of the Church with that perverse sect which they have chosen.[13]

Leo's successors in the see of Rome maintained the same doctrine with equal force. Pope Simplicius I, warning Acacius of Constantinople in 476 against the wish for a new Christological council, explains that Nicaea, Ephesus, and Chalcedon have made doctrine sufficiently clear. Acacius is to let others know that it is not permissible that those who have been once condemned by the judgments of the priests of the Lord from the whole world should be later acquitted.[14]

The so-called "Gelasian Decrees," considered to be a compilation of papal documents from the years 380–519, speak in a similar tone:

> Although no one can lay any other foundation beside that which had been laid, which is Christ Jesus, yet the holy Roman Church, after the writings of the old and new Testaments, which we duly receive, does not forbid these writings unto upbuilding: the holy Nicene Synod, [the holy Constantinopolitan Synod, in which the heretic Macedonius received fitting condemnation], the holy Ephesian Synod, the holy Chacledonian Synod.[15]

Pope Gregory I likewise places the ecumenical councils in the second place after Sacred Scripture, in a letter to the other patriarchs: "I confess that I receive and revere, as the four books of the Gospel,

---

[13] Leo the Great, Letter 162, nos. 1–2 (*NPNF*2 vol. 12, pt. 1; *PL*, 54:1144A–C).

[14] DH no. 343.

[15] DH no. 352. The editors of DH note that the reference to the Council of Constantinople is subsequent to 519.

so also the four Councils." (His contemporary, St. Isidore of Seville, uses the same comparison, and also compares them to the four rivers of paradise.)[16] Having added that he accepts the Second Council of Constantinople with equal veneration, Gregory continues:

> All persons whom the aforesaid venerable councils repudiate I repudiate; those whom they venerate I embrace; since, given that they have been constituted by universal consent [universali sunt consensu constituta], he overthrows not them but himself, whosoever presumes either to loose those whom they bind, or to bind those whom they loose.[17]

Slightly earlier, Gregory's predecessor Vigilius, from the church of St. Euphemia in Chalcedon, whither he had taken sanctuary against Emperor Justinian, not only spoke in his profession of faith about the four councils but also affirmed that the creed of Nicaea had been drawn up by the 318 fathers through the revelation of the Holy Spirit: *Sancto Spiritu . . . revelante.*[18]

Vigilius's namesake, the bishop of Thapse in North Africa in the late fifth century, had already affirmed that later councils may never contradict earlier ones. Speaking of anyone who would accuse Chalcedon of having contradicted Nicaea, he says:

> [Such a one is] ignorant of the rule and custom of universal councils, whereby later councils establish new decrees, as may be required by the emergence of new heretics, yet in such a way that the decrees promulgated by earlier councils against the old heretics remain in force.[19]

16 *PL*, 82:243B.

17 Gregory the Great, Letter 25, in *The Book of Pastoral Rule and Selected Letters*, trans. James Barmby, *NPNF2* vol. 12, pt. 2; DH no. 472.

18 DH no. 412.

19 Vigilius of Thapse, *Against Eutyches* 5.62: "Nescientem regulam et consuetudinem conciliorum catholicorum,

From Fulgentius Ferrandus, a deacon of the church in Carthage from the first half of the sixth century, we have a similar testimony, this time with an explicit assertion of the importance of the first see: "Universal councils, in particular those which have received the consent of the Roman Church, are the next highest authority after the canonical books."[20] Fearing that the proposal to condemn the "Three Chapters" at the assembly that would become Constantinople II would mean the rescinding of the Council of Chalcedon, Ferrandus lays particular stress upon the irreformability of conciliar definitions: "Whatever has once been laid down by the judgment of the assembly of the holy Fathers, must forever enjoy perpetual inviolability."[21]

The councils themselves in their acts of judgment show their conviction of their own infallibility. St. Athanasius's remark has already been quoted, that the fathers of Nicaea in drawing up the Creed made use not of the expression "it seems good," but of the absolute expression "the Catholic Church believes." The fathers of Ephesus, in their letter to Pope Celestine, show a similar consciousness of representing the Church when they contrast their own assembly with that held concurrently by John of Antioch. They ask:

> What kind of a synod could thirty men hold, some of whom were marked with the stamp of heresy, and some without sees and ejected? Or what strength could [John's synod] have in opposition to a synod from the whole world?[22]

In his own letter to the Council, Pope Celestine had appealed to Christ's words: "Where two or three are gathered in my name, there

sic nova posterioribus conciliis, prout necessitas emergentium haereticorum exegerit, sancire decreta; ut tamen invicta maneant quae dudum antiquioribus conciliis contra veteres haereticos fuerant promulgata" (*PL*, 62:135D).

20 Fulgentius Ferrandus, Letter to Pelagius and Anatolius: "Universa concilia, praecipue illa quibus Ecclesiae Romanae consensus accessit, secundae auctoritatis locum post canonicos libros tenent" (*PL*, 67:926A).

21 Fulgentius Ferrandus, Letter to Pelagius and Anatolius: "Quidquid semel statuitur in consilio et congregatione sanctorum Patrum, perpetuam debet obtinere iugiter firmitatem" (*PL*, 67:922B).

22 *The Decrees and Canons of the Seven Ecumenical Councils*, ed. Henry Percival, *NPNF2*, 14:239.

am I in the midst of them." He goes on to base the authority of councils also on the example set by the apostles themselves:

> If the Holy Spirit is not absent from so small a number how much more may we believe He is present when so great a multitude of saints is assembled! Every council is holy on account of the veneration which is due to it; for in every such council the reverence which should be paid to that most famous council of the Apostles of which we read is to be had regard to.[23]

The Council of Chalcedon, having expounded the doctrine of the Incarnation, decrees that "no one is permitted to produce, or even to write down or compose, another creed or to think or teach otherwise."[24] At Constantinople II, the fathers explicitly invoked the promise of Christ that the gates of hell should not prevail against the Church as a guarantee of the accuracy of their synodal sentence.[25] The Third Council of Constantinople repeats the prohibition of Chalcedon against writing or thinking anything other than what it has defined, and also describes itself as setting its seal to the creed in a manner inspired by God, Θεοπνεύστως ἐσφράγισε.[26] The Second Council of Nicaea again invokes the promises of Christ as a guarantee of the truth of its teaching and declares that it is defining the true doctrine of sacred images "with all accuracy and harmony [ὁρίζομεν σὺν ἀκριβείᾳ πάσῃ καὶ ἐμμελείᾳ]."[27]

These patristic and conciliar quotations show the conviction that existed in the first millennium that the decrees of a certain kind of council are, to borrow a phrase from the First Vatican Council's definition of the infallibility of the Roman pontiff, "irreformable of

23 Mansi, 4:1283C–D.

24 *Decrees of the Ecumenical Councils: From Nicaea I to Vatican II*, ed. Norman P. Tanner and Giuseppe Alberigo, vol. 1 (Washington, DC: Georgetown University Press, 1990), 87.

25 *NPNF2*, 14:311.

26 Tanner and Alberigo, *Decrees of the Ecumenical Councils*, 1:125.

27 Tanner and Alberigo, *Decrees of the Ecumenical Councils*, 1:135.

themselves, and not by the consent of the Church."[28] I am therefore unsure why the late Francis Sullivan, S.J., wrote that "there is no evidence that the bishops who took part in the councils of the first millennium were explicitly aware of the infallibility of their decisions";[29] while they may never have formulated the very proposition "ecumenical councils are infallible," their language shows that such was nevertheless their firm and conscious belief.

The Phrase "Ecumenical Council"

The word οἰκουμένη means "the inhabited world," and within the Roman Empire could be used as a synonym for that empire. The phrase σύνοδος οἰκουμενική was not in origin a religious one. According to Henry Chadwick, in fact, the phrase is first found to refer to international meetings of actors![30] The fathers of the Council of Nicaea, though doubtless conscious of composing a synod importantly different from any that had gone before, insofar as all the greatest sees were represented and the emperor himself was, in a sense, presiding, did not give to their gathering the name "ecumenical council." They described it, rather, as "sacred" and "great."[31] Eusebius of Caesarea is the first author known to have applied the phrase σύνοδος οἰκουμενική to Nicaea, in his *De vita Constantini*, written before 340.[32] We have seen that St. Athanasius employs the phrase also, already with the clear implication that such a gathering enjoys an irrefragability that a non-universal council would lack. The Constantinopolitan synod of 382 described the gathering of the previous year with the same phrase, even

28 DH no. 3075.

29 Francis Sullivan, *Creative Fidelity: Weighing and Interpreting Documents of the Magisterium* (Eugene, OR: Wipf and Stock, 2003), 45. Sullivan holds, following H. Sieben, that the first author explicitly to attribute infallibility to ecumenical councils was the ninth-century Arab bishop Theodore Abu Qurra (85).

30 Henry Chadwick, *East and West: The Making of a Rift in the Church, from Apostolic Times until the Council of Florence* (Oxford: Oxford University Press, 2005), 73.

31 Tanner and Alberigo, *Decrees of the Ecumenical Councils*, 1:16; 1:7.

32 *PG*, 20:1060B.

though the West had not been represented there.[33] They were perhaps using the phrase here to mean, "a synod going beyond the border of a civil diocese."[34] The Council of Ephesus begins its synodal letter about the Antiochene bishops with the phrase "this holy and ecumenical synod, gathered together in Ephesus," and later describes itself as "the orthodox and ecumenical synod."[35] In Norman Tanner's view, "it is doubtful whether the word was being used in a technical sense" even as late as Ephesus.[36] By "a technical sense" he apparently means designating not simply a group of bishops gathered from a great part of the inhabited world, or at least of the Roman Empire, but rather such a group of bishops considered as possessing by virtue of their universality a supreme doctrinal and legislative authority. Nevertheless, the use of the term by St. Athanasius already shows the consciousness that a council that represents the Church possesses the prerogatives promised to the Church by Christ.[37]

Tanner holds that the Council of Chalcedon was a decisive moment for the "explicitation" of the idea of such a council. After describing itself as "the sacred and great and ecumenical council," he remarks, it went on to repeat and endorse the decrees of Nicaea, Ephesus, Constantinople I, and no others. "*Ecumenical* thus became a technical term, and the canon of ecumenical councils was established."[38] Yet Ephesus also endorsed the

33 Tanner and Alberigo, *Decrees of the Ecumenical Councils*, 1:29.

34 This is the view of Peter L'Huillier in *The Church of the Ancient Councils: The Disciplinary Work of the First Four Ecumenical Councils* (Crestwood, NY: St. Vladimir's Seminary Press, 1996), 86n20. The reforms of Diocletian had divided the empire into fourteen civil dioceses (P. Fourneret, "Diocèse," in *DTC*, 4:1362–63).

35 Tanner and Alberigo, *Decrees of the Ecumenical Councils*, 1:62, 64.

36 Norman P. Tanner, *The Councils of the Church: A Short History* (New York: Crossroad, 2001), 14.

37 According to *Lumen Gentium*, the Dogmatic Constitution on the Church, issued by the Second Vatican Council: "The infallibility promised to the Church is also present in the body of bishops when, together with Peter's successor, they exercise the supreme teaching office" (§25; *Vatican Council II*, vol. 1, *The Conciliar and Post-Conciliar Documents*, ed. Austin Flannery, O.P., new rev. ed. [Dublin: Dominican Publications; New York: Costello, 1975]); and according to the *Catechism of the Catholic Church*, this is true "above all in an Ecumenical Council" (*CCC* §891). These doctrines, if they are part of the deposit of revelation, must on Catholic principles have been so from the beginning, and therefore also have been held, in varying degrees of explicitness, by the universal episcopate itself in each generation. It would follow from this that, in speaking of a council as universal, worldwide, or ecumenical, the bishops themselves as a body always understood that such a council was able to act with the infallibility promised to the Church.

38 Tanner, *The Councils of the Church*, 15.

decrees of Nicaea in its synodal letter, as did the Synod of Constantinople in 382.[39] On the other hand, Chalcedon's decree was certainly an important stage in the fixing of the canon of the recognized councils. The status of Constantinople I had been somewhat unclear, as it was not mentioned by Ephesus and as its canons had not been approved by Rome. From this point, the idea takes root that these four councils all in some relevant sense possessed the same authority—an idea helped, no doubt, by the analogy with the four Gospels.[40] This very fact itself would naturally lead to further reflection about what the "relevant sense" was, or in other words, about the criteria of ecumenicity. The "canon" or list of the councils was reinforced by the next three assemblies, Constantinople II, Constantinople III, and Nicaea II, which repeated the existing list and extended it by adding themselves.[41]

39 Tanner and Alberigo, *Decrees of the Ecumenical Councils*, 1:64.

40 Nevertheless, Pope Felix III, who died in 492, still speaks of Nicaea, Ephesus, and Chalcedon without mentioning Constantinople (Leo Davis, *The First Seven Ecumenical Councils (325–787): Their History and Theology* [Collegeville, MN: Liturgical, 1990], 130).

41 Tanner and Alberigo, *Decrees of the Ecumenical Councils*, 1:108–13, 124–27, 133–35.

CHAPTER 19

THE ESSENCE OF ECUMENICITY

Introduction

WE HAVE SEEN THAT already in the patristic period a certain kind of council, called from an early date "ecumenical," was considered to have the power to teach irreformably. Our next task is to consider more precisely how the criteria of ecumenicity were understood during the time of the first seven councils. One author has observed: "Councils were convened before there was any ecclesiological teaching about Councils [*sic*]. The two sources from which such teaching can best be gleaned are the manner in which councils were conducted, and what the participating pope and bishops had to say about them."[1] My approach will follow this suggestion, with the addition that I shall also include other witnesses who lived at a time when the canon of ecumenical councils was still undisputed between New and Old Rome.

[1] Lorenz Jaeger, *The Ecumenical Council, the Church and Christendom* (London: Geoffrey Chapman, 1961), xii.

Since the word "ecumenical" means, in practice, "universal," the first question that arises is what universality is necessary for such a council; to use the terminology of John de Turrecremata (1388–1468), the Dominican who founded the systematic discipline of ecclesiology, what its *ratio universalitatis* is.[2] The second question, which will emerge from the first, concerns the role of the Roman pontiff. I shall not delay over criteria necessary for the validity of any legal act, such as the requirements that the judges must understand the meaning of the words that they use, or that they must not act under grave fear.

Many neo-Scholastic writers distinguished three forms of ecumenicity: in convocation, in deliberation, and in judgment.[3] Thus, a council may be convoked as ecumenical but not pronounce judgment as such. In what follows, I shall be principally interested in the criteria for an ecumenical judgment or sentence, since this is the kind of ecumenicity most obviously bound up with infallibility.

Universality

Only implicit or indirect definitions of ecumenical councils are found in the first millennium.[4] In considering what universality is necessary for a council to be ecumenical, it therefore seems helpful to approach the question by induction. That is, I shall look at the individual instances of the councils that came to receive this name in order to seek for the general principle which they realized.

The First Seven Ecumenical Councils

For each of the first seven councils, we may consider the numbers of bishops who promulgated the doctrinal decrees and their repartition according to the principal ecclesiastical divisions of the time. This

2 John de Turrecremata, *Summa de Ecclesia* 3.3 (Venice, 1561).

3 E.g., Joannes de Groot, *Summa Apologetica de Ecclesia Catholica ad Mentem S. Thomae Aquinatis*, vol. 2 (Regensburg: G. J. Manz, 1890), 2; Christian Pesch, *Praelectiones Dogmaticae*, vol. 1 (Fribourg: Herder, 1903), 276.

4 Vittorio Peri, "Le pape et le concile oecuménique," *Irenikon* 56 (1983): 163–93, at 166.

will involve considering the distinction of bishops into Eastern and Western and the representation of the various patriarchates or other principal areas in the Church. One complication is that the Western "patriarchate" did not correspond perfectly to the western empire (or former empire), since the province of Illyricum, while belonging originally to the western patriarchate—a claim that was never renounced by the popes of this period—was largely peopled by Greek speakers, and jurisdiction over it was sometimes claimed by both the emperors and patriarchs in Constantinople.[5] In speaking of "Western bishops" in what follows, I understand those who were not part of an Eastern patriarchate, or of an extra-patriarchal church such as that of Cyprus.

The letters of convocation are not extant for the Council of Nicaea.[6] The great nineteenth-century historian of the councils, Karl Josef von Hefele, wrote that all the world's bishops without distinction appear to have been invited to it.[7] He cites Eusebius of Caesarea's *De vita Constantini* in support of this claim.[8] But while Eusebius does indeed state that "[Constantine] convoked a general council, and invited the speedy attendance of bishops from all quarters" (3.6), the passage is a highly rhetorical one. Immediately afterwards, Eusebius writes that "the most distinguished of God's ministers from all the churches that abounded in Europe, Lybia, and Asia were here assembled" (3.7), even though it is generally accepted that the West was represented by only a small number of bishops and two papal legates.[9] Eusebius states that more than two hundred and fifty bishops were present in total (3.8), while St. Athanasius, a participant, speaks on several

5 Adrian Fortescue, *The Orthodox Eastern Church* (London: Catholic Truth Society, 1920), 44. Fortescue adds that the question of jurisdiction "was never agreed upon till the great schism" (45). I sometimes place the phrase "patriarchate" in quotation-marks when speaking of the West, since the popes themselves did not generally speak of themselves as patriarchs.

6 Charles-Joseph Hefele, *Histoire des conciles d'après les documents originaux*, trans. and ed. Henri Leclercq et al., 19 vols. (Paris: Letouzey et Ané, 1907–1938), 1/1:403.

7 Hefele, *Histoire*, 1/2:25.

8 Eusebius of Caesarea, *De vita Constantini* (*PG*, 20), in Selected Works, trans. Ernest Richardson, *NPNF*2 vol. 1.

9 Leo Davis lists the western bishops as Caecilia of Carthage, Domnus of Pannonia, Nicasius of Gaul, Mark of Calabria, and Ossius of Cordoba (*The First Seven Ecumenical Councils (325–787): Their History and Theology* [Collegeville, MN: Liturgical, 1990], 58).

occasion of approximately three hundred bishops, and on one occasion of precisely 318, the famous number that was accepted by later writers.[10] Some modern scholars have argued from the extant lists that there could have been as few as 220, but such guesses have little weight against the explicit testimony of eyewitnesses.[11] Leo Davis notes that "the major sees of the Eastern Empire were well represented," mentioning Alexandria, Antioch, Ancyra, Jerusalem, Palestinian Caesarea, and Nicomedia, among others, with two bishops coming from beyond the empire, from Persia and "Scythia."[12] Only two bishops refused to sign the creed that the council promulgated, while another three refused to sign the anathemas.[13]

The First Council of Constantinople was in origin an Eastern synod.[14] As with Nicaea, the letters of convocation are not extant. One hundred and fifty bishops took part in it, not including the thirty-six "Macedonian" or "Pneumatomachian" bishops who attended the early sessions and then left.[15] All four of the areas that would soon become recognized as the four Eastern patriarchates were represented by the metropolitans of Constantinople, Antioch, Jerusalem, and eventually Alexandria, and unanimity was attained by all the bishops who remained.[16] A simple comparison with the number of bishops present at Nicaea, together with the fact that only five Western bishops had attended that earlier council, shows that only a small part of the universal episcopate was present at Constantinople. When this latter

---

10 Hefele, *Histoire*, 1/2:409. It is difficult to judge what proportion of the universal episcopate was present at Nicaea, as reliable estimates of the total number of Catholic bishops in the world during the early centuries are scarce. Pierre-Thomas Camelot notes that in the fifth century, there were between five and six hundred bishops in the province of Africa alone; this figure, however, includes Donatists as well as Catholics ("Les conciles oecuméniques des IVème et Vème siècles," in *Le concile et les conciles: contributions à l'histoire de la vie conciliaire de l'Église*, ed. Bernard Botte, Yves Congar, et al. [Paris: Chevetogne, 1960], 53).

11 Davis, *First Seven Ecumenical Councils*, 57.

12 Davis, *First Seven Ecumenical Councils*, 58. Sozomen mentions the presence of what he calls the "apostolic sees" of Rome, Alexandria, Antioch, and Jerusalem (*Historia Ecclesiastica*; *PG*, 67:912B).

13 Davis, *First Seven Ecumenical Councils*, 63.

14 Davis, *First Seven Ecumenical Councils*, 63.

15 Davis, *First Seven Ecumenical Councils*, 63. Norman Tanner refers to the 150 bishops as "eastern Orthodox"! (*Decrees of the Ecumenical Councils: From Nicaea I to Vatican II*, ed. Norman Tanner and Giuseppe Alberigo, 2 vols. [Washington, DC: Georgetown University Press, 1990], 1:21).

16 This is stated by Sozomen in his *Historia Ecclesiastica* 7.9 (trans. A. Zenos, *NPNF*2 vol. 2).

council was accepted in the West is a matter of debate. The disciplinary canons, as opposed to the doctrinal decrees, were not accepted by the popes of that time; in particular, the canon that accorded second place among the Church's sees to Constantinople was not officially accepted until 1439, at the Council of Florence.[17] According to Photios, writing in the ninth century, the decrees of the Council were confirmed by Pope Damasus, who died in 384. This must therefore refer only to the doctrinal portion of its decrees.[18] Pope Hormisdas, who died in 523, recognized its authority, while we have already seen that Gregory I includes it in the list of the four great councils.[19] It would seem, however, that if it is to be ranked as an ecumenical council, it must indeed have been confirmed, at least as to its doctrinal decrees, by a pope, such as Damasus, who reigned contemporaneously with at least some of the bishops who promulgated those decrees. For, as we shall argue below, papal headship is a part of the notion of an ecumenical council, and it is hard to see how such headship can be exercized over bishops who are no longer governing the Church.

Ephesus is the first of the councils for which the letters of convocation are extant. Emperor Theodosius II summoned not all the bishops, but rather the metropolitans, instructing them to bring with them the most eminent among their suffragans.[20] In fact, the Western bishops largely failed to attend, leaving themselves to be represented by the legates of the bishop of Rome.[21] Several things explain this: the troubled state of the Western empire; the fact that the controversy to be resolved was principally an Eastern one; the related fact that the emperor in Constantinople and not the one in Ravenna was the moving force behind the Council; and the shortness of the time between

---

17 DH no. 1308. On the other hand, the creed of the First Council of Constantinople was recognized at Chalcedon (Tanner and Alberigo, *Decrees of the Ecumenical Councils*, 1:22).

18 Cited in *The Decrees and Canons of the Seven Ecumenical Councils*, ed. Henry Percival, *NPNF*2, 14:186.

19 Davis, *First Seven Ecumenical Councils*, 130.

20 Hefele, *Histoire*, 1/1:25. Here and elsewhere I understand the term "metropolitan" in its customary Western sense of a bishop with jurisdiction over other bishops who also enjoy jurisdiction.

21 Hefele, *Histoire*, 1/1:291n3.

convocation and the first session. The Western presence consisted simply in the three papal legates and a deacon who represented the bishop of Carthage. Of the Eastern metropolitans, some, like John of Antioch, followed the letter of Theodosius's decree, while others, such as the bishop of Ephesus itself, convoked all their suffragans.[22] One hundred and ninety-seven bishops signed the Ephesian decree, as opposed to the forty-three who signed the creed composed by John of Antioch, which condemned the council.[23] Of the leading sees in the Church, Rome, Alexandria, Ephesus, Thessalonika, and Jerusalem supported the Council, while Constantinople (in the person of Nestorius himself) and Antioch opposed it. The reconciliation of John and his followers was achieved initially not by their acceptance of the anathemas of St. Cyril approved at Ephesus, but by their subscription to a more restrained statement of faith, the so-called "Formula of Union."[24] However, the Council of Chalcedon, in its first session, approved the original anathemas, describing them as "canonical."[25]

The next four ecumenical councils were also largely Eastern affairs. According to a letter written from the Council of Chalcedon to Pope Leo I, five hundred bishops attended that gathering, while a letter written by the Pope himself places the figure at six hundred.[26] Apart from the five papal legates and two African bishops (who appear, however, to have come primarily as fugitives from the Vandals, rather than in answer to Emperor Marcian's summons), all the rest were Eastern.[27] The patriarchs of Antioch, Jerusalem, and Constantinople personally subscribed to the Council's statement of faith, as did their bishops; the patriarch of Alexandria, Dioscoros, was deposed and the bishops of his patriarchate were permitted to abstain from signing in the consequent absence of any ecclesiastical superior.[28]

22 Hefele, *Histoire*, 1/1:291n3.
23 Davis, *First Seven Ecumenical Councils*, 155–56.
24 Tanner and Alberigo, *Decrees of the Ecumenical Councils*, 1:69.
25 Percival, *Decrees and Canons of the Seven Ecumenical Councils*, 14:248.
26 Tanner and Alberigo, *Decrees of the Ecumenical Councils*, 1:75.
27 Hefele, *Histoire*, 2/2:669.
28 Davis, *First Seven Ecumenical Councils*, 184.

The Second Council of Constantinople, in 553, opened with 151 bishops in attendance, some of whom represented absent colleagues. The patriarchs of Alexandria, Antioch, and Constantinople were personally present, while Jerusalem was represented by proxy. Eight African bishops were present for the last sessions.[29] All the bishops present, numbering 160, signed the final decrees. Pope Vigilius, despite having had his name stricken from the diptychs during the seventh session by order of Emperor Justinian, finally confirmed the decree of the council after a delay of some eight months.[30] Davis notes that "in the West, opposition to the Council was strong and widespread," particularly in North Africa, Illyricum, and Italy; the metropolitan of Aquileia led northern Italy and Dalmatia into a formal schism that lasted until the end of the century.[31]

The Third Council of Constantinople (680–681) had not originally been intended by Emperor Constantine IV to be ecumenical, but it nevertheless described itself as such in its opening session, perhaps because of the unexpected arrival of delegates from Alexandria and Jerusalem.[32] Only 43 bishops or representatives of bishops were present at the opening of the Council, but 174 signed at the end.[33] The patriarch of Constantinople was present, as was Macarios, patriarch of Antioch; the latter was deposed and replaced in the course of the council.[34] The Pope sent as legates three Italian bishops and four other clergy,[35] and three bishops of Illyricum were present who described themselves as representing the Pope.[36] In his letter to the Pope, the emperor reports that all who were present agreed in the same faith, apart from one—a reference to Macarios.[37]

---

29 Hefele, *Histoire*, 3/1:68. Davis writes that "in all 151 to 168 bishops attended, including six to nine from Africa" (*First Seven Ecumenical Councils*, 241).
30 Tanner and Alberigo, *Decrees of the Ecumenical Councils*, 1:105.
31 Davis, *First Seven Ecumenical Councils*, 248–49.
32 Hefele, *Histoire*, 3/1:485.
33 Hefele, *Histoire*, 3/1:485.
34 Davis, *First Seven Ecumenical Councils*, 279–81.
35 Davis, *First Seven Ecumenical Councils*, 279.
36 Hefele, *Histoire*, 3/1:486.
37 Mansi, 11:721D.

According to Davis, between 258 and 335 bishops were present at the opening of the Second Council of Nicaea in 787.[38] All those present accepted the decree issued in favor of images at the fourth session.[39] Hefele states that 308 bishops and bishops' representatives signed the record of the *acta*.[40] The patriarch of Constantinople was present, but Alexandria, Antioch, and Jerusalem were not formally represented, since Islamic occupation had prevented the letters of convocation from reaching these cities. Two monks were accepted as representing these patriarchates, even though they had not formally been appointed to do so.[41] The Pope was represented by two legates. Also present were eight Sicilians and six Calabrians:[42] these belonged, therefore, to that part of the Roman "patriarchate" that the iconoclast Emperor Leo III had claimed to place under the jurisdiction of Constantinople some fifty years before.[43]

The Synod of Serdica

The "inductive" attempt to discover the criteria for universality will be helped by considering a council that was called in order to be ecumenical but has not generally been treated as such, the Council of Serdica.[44]

The Council of Serdica, modern Sofia in Bulgaria, was held in 342 or 343, at the wish of Pope Julius I of Rome and Emperor Constans. Davis writes: "The council opened with about ninety western bishops headed by Ossius of Cordoba and about eighty easterners, including

---

38 Davis, *First Seven Ecumenical Councils*, 308. The ancient authorities vary.

39 G. Fritz, "Nicée, Deuxième Concile de," in *DTC*, 11/2:417–41, at col. 424.

40 Hefele, *Histoire*, 3/2:760; Tanner and Alberigo, *Decrees of the Ecumenical Councils*, 1:131.

41 Hefele, *Histoire*, 3/2:759. Hefele notes that some have spoken of the monks' letter as a "fraud," but points out that they made no attempt to claim a direct commission from the stranded patriarchs, and that the facts of the case would have been understood by all present.

42 Davis, *First Seven Ecumenical Councils*, 308.

43 Davis, *First Seven Ecumenical Councils*, 300. The Second Council of Nicaea is also of interest in that it sketches a description of a true ecumenical council, as part of its condemnation of the pseudo-synod of Hieria. See the section "The Theory of the Pentarchy" in ch. 20 ("The Later Byzantine Theory of Ecumenical Councils").

44 It might be suggested that a consideration of "Ephesus II," the *latrocinium*, would also be useful here. Pope St. Nicholas I, writing to Emperor Michael III, used it as a sign that the Roman pontiff's judgment outweighed the combined view of the four eastern patriarchs (Carlo Passaglia, *De conciliis oecumenicis: theses Caroli Passaglia de conciliis deque habitu quo ad Romanos pontifices referuntur*, ed. Heribert Schauf [Rome: Herder, 1961], 62). However, the violence exercised on the bishops at Ephesus in 449 would have rendered its acts canonically null, whoever had agreed to them.

the principal sees—Antioch, Ephesus, Caesarea in Palestine, Caesarea in Cappadocia, and Heraclea, metropolitan see of the region around Constantinople."[45] Alexandria was also represented in the person of Athanasius himself. The Eastern bishops withdrew *en masse* in protest at Athanasius's presence and held their own gathering at Philippopolis. The Western bishops continued to deliberate at Serdica, issuing an explanation of the Nicene Creed and a series of canons, including one that declared the universal appellate jurisdiction of the bishop of Rome; these canons were approved by the Pope.[46]

Hefele holds that the Council of Serdica ceased to be ecumenical from the time of the withdrawal of the Eastern bishops. While acknowledging that the withdrawal of bishops cannot of itself cause such a change—otherwise it would always be possible for a party that feared defeat to nullify a council by leaving—he argues that the number of Western bishops that remained was so small that it could have been ecumenical only if they represented a large number of absent ones.[47] In fact, when the Serdican decrees were circulated, although they were signed by approximately two hundred more bishops, of whom eighty-four were from Egypt, and one each from Cyprus and Palestine, none of the others were from the rest of the Orient or Africa.[48] The meeting at Serdica has not been generally placed in lists of ecumenical councils, neither those composed by later councils themselves nor those drawn up by individual theologians. For example, it is not included in the so-called "Roman Edition" of the ecumenical councils drawn up by scholars working under the patronage of Paul V between 1608 and 1612.[49] St. Robert Bellarmine, who was himself one of these scholars,

---

45 Davis, *First Seven Ecumenical Councils*, 84.

46 Davis, *First Seven Ecumenical Councils*, 85–87.

47 Hefele, *Histoire*,1/2:820.

48 Hefele, *Histoire*,1/2:820.

49 Norman Tanner, *The Councils of the Church: A Short History* (New York: Crossroad, 2001), 7. This edition is apparently the source of what became the standard Catholic list of the councils (Yves Congar, "Structures ecclésiales et conciles dans les relations entre Orient et Occident," *Revue des sciences philosophiques et theologiques* 58 [1974]: 355–90, at 379).

lists it among the councils that are "partly approved and partly rejected" in his treatise *De conciliis*.[50] In the seventeenth century, the claim by the theologian Natalis (Noel) Alexander that Serdica should be reckoned as ecumenical was reproved by the Roman censors.[51]

Conclusions about Universality

What conclusions may be drawn from these facts about the universality needed if a conciliar decree is to be "ecumenical"? First we find that there is always an attempt to secure some representation of the major jurisdictional divisions of the Church (what would at least from the middle of the fifth century be recognized as the patriarchates), and that in the case of councils recognized as ecumenical, the majority of such divisions have in fact been represented and supported the decree.[52] Next we may note some negative conclusions. First, it is not necessary that a majority of bishops, or even of metropolitans, should actually attend the council and there pronounce in favor of its decrees. It is not certain that either kind of majority would have been reached by any of the first seven councils, owing to the paucity of Western representation. Certainly no such majority could have been enjoyed by Ephesus, when one adds the party of John of Antioch to the absent western bishops.

Next, several of these councils show that it is not necessary that all the existing major patriarchs should be in agreement for an ecumenical judgment to be passed: Dioscoros of Alexandria was deposed by Chalcedon, and Macarios of Antioch was deposed by Constantinople III.

Again, the desired universality is apparently not obtained by the simple fact of all bishops, or a great majority, being originally

---

50 St. Robert Bellarmine, *De conciliis* 1.7, in *Omnia Opera* vol. 2 (Paris: Vives, 1870). It is partly rejected because the meeting of the Eastern bishops, taken as part of the council, was rejected because of its unsatisfactory creed.

51 Hefele, *Histoire*, 1/2:823.

52 For this reason Constantinople I was apparently not ecumenical in its decrees but received its status later, by what may perhaps be called a *sanatio in radice* from the Roman pontiff. For the use of the term *sanatio* to refer to the subsequent confirmation of a council lacking due presidency, see Louis Billot, *Tractatus de Ecclesia Christi sive Continuatio Theologiae de Verbo Incarnato*, vol. 1 (Prati: Giachetti, 1909), 702.

summoned, or by the fact that a majority of those present vote in favor of its decrees. Otherwise, the decrees of the Council of Serdica would rank as ecumenical, something that has not been generally held either in East or in West.

There appear to be two possible explanations of how a council has the universality necessary to rank as ecumenical in its judgment. The first is that a clear majority of the Church's bishops judge in favor of a given doctrine, either in person or by representation: this representation can itself exist either in virtue of a formal mandate or at least from the council fathers' knowledge of the mind of their colleagues. Thus, the bishops at Ephesus in 430 apparently spoke for the West as well as for themselves, while the bishops of Serdica did not speak for the whole of the West (since the African bishops did not sign the decrees), nor for the East, and in that way lacked a clear majority.

On this view, in order to know whether or not bishops at a given council were sufficient to represent the Church, it might be necessary to look at what follows the council and whether those colleagues agree to what was done there. This would not mean that the work of an ecumenical council needs to be confirmed or "received" by local churches if it is to be valid, but that such confirmation might be a sign by which the historian, even abstracting from authoritative statements by the Church, could judge of the ecumenicity of a given council. On this view, the bishops present at a council might know themselves to be speaking for a majority of the universal episcopate, and thus be able to describe themselves as forming an ecumenical council, and speak with the authority proper to such a gathering, without waiting for the reception of their decrees. In the case of a council such as Serdica that does not express the judgment of majority of the episcopate, it would still possible for the pope to confirm its decrees, but he would then, on this hypothesis, not be confirming the judgment of an *ecumenical* council.[53]

53 Bellarmine held that the papal confirmation of a local synod was an infallible act (*De conciliis* 2.5, where he claims that the opposite sentence, though supported by some theologians, is proximate to heresy).

Another possible view, consistent with the facts of history, of the universality needed for ecumenicity is that the pope, simply by convoking or consenting to the convocation of a council that will represent the major parts of the Church, by that very fact gives to the council a share in his own universal office of teaching.[54] In this case, whatever the pope in union with some portion of such a council decrees, even if these bishops do not represent a majority of the episcopate, will be a universal, ecumenical decree, and in the case of a doctrinal definition, irreformable.[55] These two views correspond to the twofold explanation that Turrecremata gave of the *ratio universalitatis*: it can exist either in virtue of those who are convoked, insofar as bishops come from the whole world, or in virtue of the one who convokes, meaning the pope as *totius ecclesiae princeps et rector*.[56]

The historical study of the early councils does not allow us to decide between these two theories. Hence it does not resolve the question of whether a decree supported by only a slight majority, or even by only a minority of the bishops, could nevertheless be promulgated by the pope as the act of an ecumenical council. In other words, it does not show us whether the universality needed may be achieved simply by the fact that the Roman pontiff has called upon the bishops to exercise their "collegial" power.[57] However, to take the most stringent view of the evidence, it does show us that when a council has been convoked from most of the larger Christian provinces and no bishop who wished to attend has been excluded, then, if a large majority of the bishops present, representing a

---

54 According to *Lumen Gentium* §22, the Second Vatican Council's Dogmatic Constitution on the Church, the "college of bishops," defined as all consecrated bishops in hierarchical communion with the Roman Pontiff, has a supreme power over the Church (DH no. 4146). Hence Umberto Betti argues that by convoking a council, the pope does not create the collegial power, but makes it possible for it to be validly exercised ("Relations entre le pape et les autres membres du collège épiscopal," in *L'Eglise de Vatican II*, ed. Guilherme Barauna and Yves Congar, vol. 3, Unam Sanctam 51c [Paris: Cerf, 1966], 791–803, at 798).

55 If we were to take this view, we should have to conclude that if the Council of Serdica was not ecumenical, this was because, as a result of the departure of the Eastern delegates, the Pope effectively revoked its mandate to represent the whole Church.

56 Turrecremata, *Summa de Ecclesia* 3.3. Turrecremata argues here that, in the latter sense, many universal councils have been held at which only bishops from Italy were present.

57 Likewise, it does not determine the question of whether a majority of what I have called "the main jurisdictional divisions" of the Church must support the decree.

large majority of the worldwide episcopate and a majority of the main jurisdictional divisions of the Church and including the Roman pontiff, declare that a certain doctrine is divinely revealed, then it may be promulgated in an ecumenical—that is, irreformable—manner.

Moral Unanimity?

In modern times, some authors have put forward a very strong version of the first of the two accounts of universality, arguing that not only must the decrees represent a majority of the episcopate, but that a "moral unanimity" of bishops is required.[58] Bellarmine, in the sixteenth century, had already raised the question of how many bishops were necessary for an ecumenical council, noting that this was a matter of debate among Catholics and not simply between Catholics and heretics. He stated that it was necessary that the holding of the council should be made known to all the larger Christian provinces, and that no bishop who wished to attend must be excluded;[59] yet in order that a conciliar decree should be binding, a simple majority was necessary.[60] More recently, however, some authors have required a similar universality in *judgment* as Bellarmine required in convocation, if a council is to represent the Church.[61] Thus, shortly after the promulgation of papal infallibility by the First Vatican Council, St. John Henry Newman writes in a private letter: "Till better advised, nothing shall make me say that the mere majority in a council, as opposed to moral unanimity, in itself creates an obligation to receive its dogmatic decrees."[62] Yves

---

58 Such authors do not always explain whether they have in mind a moral unanimity of those bishops present, or of the worldwide episcopate, but generally they seem to have in mind the former insofar as it guarantees the latter.

59 Bellarmine, *De conciliis* 1.17.

60 Bellarmine, *De conciliis* 2.11: "Est autem verum decretum concilii, quod fit a maiore parte."

61 The idea of an ecumenical council as representing the Church was used by Pope Martin V in the bull *Inter Cunctas* of 1418; those suspected of adhering to the positions of John Wycliffe or Jan Hus were to be asked, among other things, whether they accepted that "every general council . . . represents the universal Church" (DH no. 331). Pope Paul VI, in a letter of 1964 to Cardinal Tisserant, uses the same expression about the Council of Trent and the two councils of the Vatican (*AAS* 56 [1964]: 747).

62 Quoted in Luis M. Bermejo, *Infallibility on Trial: Church, Conciliarity and Communion* (Westminster, MD: Christian Classics, 1992), 96.

Congar writes in 1960: "Ecumenicity is not a question of quantity; rather, it seems to be connected, in the mind of the councils themselves, to the *unanimity* of witnesses who are gathered there, however many they are."[63] Joseph Ratzinger, writing as a private theologian in 1988, states that "even ecumenical councils can only decide on matters of faith and morals in *moral unanimity*."[64] Luis Bermejo, who strongly supports the same thesis, claims that "a very broad unanimity has already emerged on this point."[65]

The history of the early councils, however, as we have seen, does not establish this thesis. A significant number of bishops left Constantinople I, refused to attend Ephesus, and failed to sign at Chalcedon. Nor can it be demonstrated by the official texts of the Catholic Church concerning councils.[66] It is also contrary to the teaching of the earlier Catholic *auctores probati*. Joseph Wilhelm, for example, holds that a pope would be free either to promulgate or not to promulgate, as a conciliar act, a decision reached by a simple majority.[67] According to Christian Pesch (1835–1925), that there is not a need for unanimity is proved by the definition of papal infallibility at Vatican I, where fifty-five bishops absented themselves rather than vote in favor of the doctrine. He adds that the lack of such a requirement was in any case "clear from the unanimous teaching of earlier theologians, who reckoned that a definition would be valid, even if only a minority of bishops agreed with the supreme pontiff."[68] Joannes de Groot affirms that it is

63 Yves Congar, "Conclusion," in *Le concile et les conciles: contributions à l'histoire de la vie conciliaire de l'Église*, ed. Bernard Botte, Yves Congar, et al. (Paris: Chevetogne, 1960), 318.

64 Quoted in Bermejo, *Infallibility on Trial*, 96.

65 Bermejo also cites Karl Rahner in support of the same view (*Infallibility on Trial*, 96).

66 The question of the proportion of the episcopate that must consent to a conciliar resolution is not raised by *Lumen Gentium* or by the Latin or Eastern Code of Canon Law.

67 Joseph Wilhelm, "Councils, General," in *Catholic Encyclopedia* (New York: Encyclopedia Press, 1913), 423–35. Pope Pius IX had also stated during the Vatican I that definitions could be made by majority and not by unanimity (Yves Congar, "Bulletin d'ecclésiologie: conciles et papauté," *Revue des sciences philosophiques et théologiques* 60 [1976]: 281–308, at 287).

68 Pesch, *Praelectiones Dogmaticae*, 1:279. The celebrated Dominican theologian Melchor Cano had already taught this in the sixteenth century (*De Locis Theologicis* 5.5, ed. Juan Belda Plans [Madrid: Biblioteca de Autores Cristianos, 2006], 192: "errare poterit maior pars concilii"). Pesch also cites Bellarimne in support of his thesis, but in fact the latter notes cautiously that "it has perhaps never happened that the pope has

by a "wise economy" and not by a legal necessity (*iuris non est*) that decrees are generally made only when there is a large majority and "an almost unanimous consent" in their favor.[69] Jacques Forget, writing in the monumental *Dictionnaire de théologie catholique* states that "the thesis of moral unanimity rests on no solid basis," pointing out that it would in practice give the minority more rights than the majority.[70]

Moral unanimity may be in practice necessary for a council to achieve its ultimate aim, yet this does not mean that it is necessary for its decrees to be binding and irreformable. The idea that such unanimity is absolutely necessary has perhaps arisen not only from a confusion between the criteria for ecumenical convocation and those for ecumenical judgment, but also from a tendency to see the bishops as witnesses for the Church, rather than as judges and teachers.[71] For, as long as competent witnesses give conflicting testimonies, then a matter appears to remain uncertain, even if there is a majority on one side. A bench of judges, on the other hand, is easily understood to issue a definitive verdict even when it is only a majority verdict. Therefore, if we understand that the bishops in council are primarily members of a legal assembly that has received some definite guarantees from the Holy Spirit, then the supposed need for unanimity, even "moral," disappears.

Papal Headship

"The council does not represent the teaching Church till the visible head of the Church has given his approval, for, unapproved, it is but a headless, soulless, impersonal body, unable to give its decisions the binding force of laws for the whole Church."[72] We must now complete the definition of an ecumenical council by considering witnesses from

---

supported the minority in a council, when the judgments have been given without violence and deceit" (*De conciliis* 1.18).

69 Groot, *Summa Apologetica*, 2:14.

70 Jacques Forget, "Conciles," in *DTC*, 3:647–76, at cols. 668–69.

71 See the section on Yves Congar in ch. 21 ("Do Ecumenical Councils Need to be 'Received'?").

72 Wilhelm, "Councils, General," 430.

the patristic period and a little beyond to the role of the papacy. We shall see an impressive consensus in East and West to the belief that, by the divine constitution of the Church, papal confirmation is both necessary and sufficient to ensure the truth of the doctrinal decrees of a universal council of the Church, or in other words, that papal headship is the "formal principle" of such a council.

Authors have distinguished three properties within the concept of headship: the right to convoke councils as magisterial bodies; the right to preside over them, either in person or by delegates; and the right to confirm their decisions, antecedently, concomitantly, or subsequently.[73] In what follows, I shall be directly concerned with witnesses who attest that the pope's consent is a necessary condition for an ecumenical council to be teaching irreformably, although this attestation may be either explicit or else implicit in a more general statement about the papal headship of such councils. In this section I shall be concerned with the pope's position in relation to other members of the hierarchy; later, I shall consider his role in relation to the Roman emperor.[74]

St. Athanasius, in his *Apologia contra Arianos*, includes a letter written by Pope Julius I (r. 337–352) to the party of Eusebius of Nicomedia. The Pope notes that some of Eusebius's ambassadors had requested that he, the Pope, call a council to examine Athanasius, a request from which Eusebius himself had later resiled. In his letter, Julius taxes Eusebius with this inconsistency:

> Supposing that [Eusebius's messengers] had not desired a Council, but that I had been the person to propose it, in discouragement of those who had written to me, and for the sake of our brethren who complain that they have suffered

73 See, e.g., Groot, *Summa Apologetica*, 6.

74 See the section "The Role of the Emperor" in ch. 20 ("The Later Byzantine Theory of Ecumenical Councils").

> injustice; even in that case the proposal [ἡ προτροπή] would have been reasonable and just, for it is agreeable to ecclesiastical practice, and well pleasing to God [ἐστι γὰρ ἐκκλησιαστικὴ καὶ θεῷ ἀρέσκουσα]. (22)[75]

Despite the tactful word προτροπή, which Julius uses in writing to his fellow bishop, it is clear that he is asserting a right to convoke bishops from outside his own "patriarchate," and that he considers Eusebius at fault for not heeding the summons.[76] The (Anglican) translator's phrase "agreeable to ecclesiastical practice" perhaps somewhat weakens the force of the Pope's expression. Julius simply says that such an exhortation to meet would have been "ecclesiastical"; that is, it is how the Church functions.

Socrates Scholasticos, writing in Constantinople, refers to the same letter in his *Historia Ecclesiastica*, describing what it says about the council held by the Eusebians without the Pope:

> Julius first replied to the bishops who had written to him from Antioch, complaining of the acrimonious feeling they had evinced in their letter, and charging them with a violation of the canons [παρὰ κανόνας ποιοῦντας], because they had not requested his attendance at the council, seeing that the ecclesiastical law required that the churches should pass no decisions contrary to the views of the bishop of Rome [τοῦ ἐκκλησιαστικοῦ κανόνος κελεύοντος, μὴ δεῖν παρὰ γνώμην τοῦ ἐπισκόπου Ῥώμης κανονίζειν τὰς ἐκκλησίας]: he then censured them with great severity for clandestinely attempting to pervert the faith. (2.17)[77]

---

75 Athanasius, *Apologia contra Arianos* (*PG*, 25:285B; Selected Works and Letters, trans. Archibald Robertson, *NPNF*2 vol. 4).

76 The verb προτρέπω means "to urge, exhort, persuade."

77 Socrates, *Church History*, trans. A. Zenos, in *NPNF*2 vol. 2; *PG*, 67:219A.

This testimony to papal headship over councils slightly differs from that of St. Athanasius as far as explicit statements are concerned, in that Socrates mentions Julius's reference not to the papal right of convocation, but rather to the right of consent to conciliar decrees. Earlier in the same book, Socrates makes the same assertion on his own authority:

> There were present at this Synod ninety bishops from various cities. Maximus, however, bishop of Jerusalem, who had succeeded Macarius, did not attend, recollecting that he had been deceived and induced to subscribe the deposition of Athanasius. Neither was Julius, bishop of the great Rome, there, nor had he sent a substitute, although an ecclesiastical canon commands [κανόνος ἐκκλησιαστικοῦ κελεύοντος] that the churches shall not make any ordinances against the opinion [παρὰ τὴν γνώμην … κανονίζειν] of the bishop of Rome. (2.8)[78]

As the context indicates, in speaking of "setting in order" or "canonizing" the churches, Socrates is not denying the right of "patriarchal" churches to govern themselves according to their own canons, but is referring to matters that transcend the boundaries of any one part of the Church.[79] A dispute between Antiochene bishops and the patriarch of Alexandria, being of this kind, could not be settled against the judgment of the first see.

Socrates's contemporary Sozomen—originally from Palestine but also writing in Constantinople—describes the same events in his own *Historia Ecclesiastica*:

---

78 Socrates, *Church History* (*PG*, 67:196B).

79 Bellarmine mentions the claim of the group of Protestant historians known as the "Centuriators of Magdeburg" that κανονίζειν means "to dedicate" and that Pope Julius was complaining that he had not been invited to the consecration of a new church in Antioch! While it is true that such a consecration occurred at the time of the synod, yet, as Bellarmine points out, the letter as a whole (for example, no. 17, quoted in the text) makes it clear that this was not the Pope's objection (*De conciliis* 1.12).

> [Julius] replied at the same time to the letter of the bishops who were convened at Antioch, for just then he happened to have received their epistle, and accused them of having clandestinely introduced innovations contrary to the dogmas of the Nicene council, and of having violated the laws of the Church [παρὰ τοὺς νόμους τῆς Ἐκκλησίας], by neglecting to invite him to join their Synod; for he alleged that there is a sacerdotal canon [Εἶναι γὰρ νόμον ἱερατικόν] which declares that whatever is enacted contrary to the judgment [τὰ παρὰ γνώμην πράττομενα) of the bishop of Rome is null [ἄκυρα]. (3.10)[80]

The (Anglican) translator's use of the word "alleged" in the last sentence could make it appear that Sozomen denied or doubted the existence of the law which Julius invoked. Yet, while the statement that there is such a law is contained in reported speech (as is shown by the use of the infinitive, εἶναι, rather than the indicative), there is nothing in the context to show that Sozomen wishes to disavow Pope Julius's statement. On the contrary, he shows no disapproval of the Pope's letter, and strong disapproval of those to whom it is written. The mid-twentieth-century author Heribert Schauf points out the strongly legal nature of Sozomen's language in the phrases παρὰ τοὺς νόμους, νόμον ἱερατικόν, ἄκυρα, τὰ πράττομενα.[81] Neither he nor Socrates speaks of the reference to Rome as a mere praiseworthy custom; for both it is a legal necessity.[82]

---

80 Sozomen, *Historia Ecclesiastica* (*PG*, 67:1057A–B).

81 Schauf, in Passaglia, *De conciliis oecumenicis*, 53. To Schauf, incidentally, is attributed the coining of the phrase "the Roman School" to refer to the theological movement initiated by the Jesuits teaching in the eternal city during the middle decades of nineteenth century (C. Michael Shea, "*Ressourcement* in the Age of Migne: The Jesuit Theologians of the *Collegio Romano* and the Shape of Modern Catholic Thought," *Nova et Vetera* 15, no. 2 [2017]: 579–613, at 580).

82 It is curious that an allusion to closely connected events is found in the surviving books of the *History* written by the fourth-century pagan author Ammianus Marcellinus. Though Ammianus was not writing an ecclesiastical history and had an imperfect knowledge of Christianity, he was aware of the place of the bishop of Rome in the Christian system. Having mentioned a deposition of Athanasius, whom he correctly identifies as bishop of Alexandria, Ammianus writes that the emperor sought to have the deposition confirmed by Pope Liberius: "For although Constantius, who was always hostile to Athanasius, knew that the matter had been carried out, yet he strove with eager desire to have it ratified also by the higher power also of the bishop of the eternal city [Id enim ille Athanasio semper infestus, licet sciret impletum, tamen auctoritate quoque potiore aeternae urbis episcopi

In the following century, an important witness to the need for papal consent to an ecumenical council comes from the Antiochene patriarchate. After the Council of Ephesus, Bishops Eutherius and Helladius, followers of John of Antioch who were shocked that he should have come to terms with St. Cyril in 433, wrote to Pope Sixtus III to ask him to withhold his consent from that Council, celebrated during the reign of his predecessor three years before:

> Frequently, whenever heretical tares of this kind arose from Alexandria, your apostolic see has always sufficed to refute the lie and to check the impiety, and to correct whatever was needful and to defend the whole world for the glory of Christ. . . . We beseech you, prostrate before the feet of your piety, that you would stretch out a saving hand and prevent the shipwreck of the world and order that an enquiry be made into all these things [that were done at Ephesus].[83]

Toward the end of the same century, Pope Gelasius, warning the bishops of Dardania against the schism of Acacius, and insisting at length that what has once been ratified by synodal authority cannot again be brought into question, makes this point clearly:

> Every true Christian will be aware that no see must be more true to the decisions of a synod, approved by the assent of the universal Church than the first see, which confirms every synod with its own authority and protects every synod with its continual oversight. It does this, of course, in virtue of the ruling power, received through the voice of our Lord, which the

firmari desiderio nitebatur ardenti]" (*History: Books XIV–XIX*, trans. J. Rolfe [London: W. Heinemann, 1935], 161–62).

83 *PL*, 50:595B–C, 601A: "Saepius iam, ex Alexandria huiusmodi haereticis zizaniis insurgentibus suffecit vestra apostolica sedes per universum tempus illud ad mendacium convinciendum, impietatemque reprimendam, et corrigenda quae necessarium fuit, muniendumque orbem terrarum ad gloriam Christi. . . . Rogamus vero, et sanctis tuae religiositatis provolvimur pedibus, ut manum porrigas salutarem, et auferas mundi naufragium, omniumque horum inquisitionem iubeas fieri."

> blessed apostle Peter has always held and holds, with the Church following in harmony.[84]

This nuanced statement summarises the nature (universality under papal headship) and the principal property (irreformability) of an ecumenical decree. In the same letter, Gelasius affirms that the first see may stand alone against a synod that it disapproves. Having mentioned the protection granted by his predecessors to St. Athanasius and St. John Chrysostom when these prelates had been condemned by Eastern synods, he recalls the events of the second synod of Ephesus in 449:

> When Flavian of holy memory had been condemned by an assembly of bishops, this apostolic see absolved him, because it alone did not consent to what had been done. Indeed, it condemned with its authority the one who had been received there, Dioscoros, the bishop of the second see, and by refusing its consent it nullified that wicked synod.[85]

We have already seen that the decisions of Ephesus II, being extorted by threats and violence, would have been null even without this rejection by the first see. However, Gelasius's predecessor, Leo I, affirms that the lack of papal consent invalidates what would otherwise be valid conciliar decisions. Addressing Empress Pulcheria about canon 28 of the Council of Chalcedon, which sought to make Constantinople the second see in the Church, Leo writes:

---

84 Mansi, 8:51D: "Nullus iam veraciter Christianus ignoret uniuscuiusque synodi constitutum, quod universalis ecclesiae probavit assensus, non aliquam magis exequi sedem prae ceteris oportere, quam primam, quae et unamquamque synodum sua auctoritate confirmat, et continua moderatione custodit, pro suo scilicet principatu, quem beatus Petrus apostolus domini voce perceptum, ecclesia nihilo minus subsequente et tenuit semper, et retinet."

85 Mansi, 8:55A: "Sanctae memoriae Flavianum pontificum congregatione damnatum . . . quoniam sola sedes apostolica non consensit, absolvit, potius qui illic receptus fuerat, Dioscorum secundae sedis praesulem sua auctoritae damnavit, et impiam synodum non consentiendo submovit."

> With your piety and faith uniting yourself to us, we invalidate the agreements of the bishops that are contrary to the rules of the holy canons established at Nicaea, and by the authority of the blessed apostle Peter, we wholly nullify them by a general decree. . . . Even if many more than those [318 of Nicaea] should decide something other than what they had decreed, it should be held in no honor.[86]

The papal legate Lucentius, during the first session of the Council of Chalcedon, spoke of Dioscoros of Alexandria's usurpation of authority at the "Robber Synod" two years before: "He ventured to hold an arbitrating council without the apostolic see."[87] The legate's words do not refer to usurping a power to convoke the synod, since Leo had ratified its convocation. They refer to Dioscoros's having managed the synod and promulgated its decrees without regard to the papal legates.

As we have seen above in chapter 18 of the present volume, Fulgentius Ferrandus, deacon of Carthage, speaks in the first part of the sixth century of the inviolability of ecumenical councils. He also explicitly associates this property with the consent of the Roman pontiff. Speaking of Chalcedon, he writes: "Whatever that synod defined, when it had the apostolic see before it in the person of the legates and giving its consent, received thereby a strength not to be overcome."[88]

The Italian statesman Cassiodorus, writing in the middle of the same century, refers briefly to the papal headship in his *Historia tripartita*. Speaking of the same events as Socrates and Sozomen mentioned above, he notes that Pope Julius was not invited to the Antiochene council, "even though the ecclesiastical rule certainly

86 *PL*, 54:1000B–C: "Consensiones vero episcoporum, sanctorum canonum apud Nicaeam conditorum regulis repugnantes, unita nobiscum vestrae fidei pietate in irritum mittimus, et per auctoritatem beati Petri Apostoli, generali prorsus definitione cassamus. . . . Etiam si multo plures aliud, quam illi statuere, decernant, in nulla reverentia sit habendum."

87 Mansi, 6:581B: "Σύνδον ἐτόλμησε ποιῆσαι ἐπιτροπῆς δίχα τοῦ ἀποστολικοῦ θρονοῦ."

88 Fulgentius Ferrandus, Letter to Pelagius and Anatolius: "Ante se habens in legatis suis apostolicam sedem, qua consentiente, quidquid illa definivit synodus, accepit robur invictum" (*PL*, 67:925D).

commands that councils should not be held except by the decision of the Roman pontiff." (4.9)[89]

Pope Pelagius II, at the end of the sixth century, had to confront the pretensions of John IV of Constantinople, who was using the title of "Oecumenical Patriarch" and had called the Eastern bishops together in council. The Pope's letter to the bishops states first that "the authority of convoking a general synod has been given by a unique privilege to the apostolic see of Blessed Peter," and he adds that "no synod has ever been known to be valid that did not rely on the apostolic authority."[90] He affirms that this right is included in Christ's words to St. Peter, entrusting him with the keys of the Kingdom, and adds that "we are instructed, finally, by many apostolic, canonical and ecclesiastical rules that, without the agreement of the Roman Pontiff, councils must not be held."[91] He also reminds the bishops that the papal archives contain many letters that both the current patriarch and his predecessors have sent to Rome, signed by their own hand, in which they anathematize themselves in advance if they should ever violate the privileges of the Roman Church.

St. Maximus the Confessor in the seventh century, disputing about monothelitism with Theodosios, bishop of Caesarea in Bithynia, speaks of the Lateran synod held under Martin I in 649, which he calls "the apostolic synod," as the rule of faith that both the emperor and the patriarch must accept before he can be in communion with them.[92] Although this synod is not traditionally numbered among the ecumenical councils, we may argue *a fortiori* that if the pope can bind

---

89 Cassiodorus, *Historia tripartita*: "Cum utique regula ecclesiastica iubeat non oportere praeter sententiam Romani pontificis concilia celebrari" (*PL*, 69:960D).

90 *Magnum Bullarium Romanum, ab Leone Magno usque ad S.D.P. Clementem X* (Lyon: P. Borde and J. and P. Arnaud, 1692), 23: "Generalem Synodum convocandi auctoritas Apostolicae Sedi B. Petri singulari privilegio sit tradita et nulla umquam Synodus rata legatur, quae Apostolicae auctoritate non fuerit fulta."

91 *Magnum Bullarium Romanum*, 23: "Multis denuo Apostolicis, Canonicis atque Ecclesiasticis instruimur regulis, non debere absque Sententia Romani Pontificis concilia celebrari."

92 In *Vita et acta Maximi* (*PG*, 90:153B–C). Congar states that St. Maximus held the Lateran synod to be ecumenical, but the word is not found in the references that the French Dominican gives in support of this claim ("Structures ecclésiales et conciles," 372–74).

the consciences of Catholics by confirming a local synod, he must do so still more by confirming an ecumenical one. While St. Maximus says that this submission to Rome is required by the "canon," he does not make it a matter of what today would be called simple ecclesiastical law: in the letter he wrote at Rome after the Lateran synod, he affirms that the Roman Church enjoys indefectibility in the faith as a result of Christ's own promise.[93] At the same synod, Stephen, bishop of Dora in Palestine, reports that St. Sophronios, the recently deceased patriarch of Jerusalem, charged him to go to the apostolic see as quickly as possible and not to cease to ask for help until the new dogmas had been completely overthrown by the divine apostolic wisdom, ἐξ ἀποστολικῆς θεοσοφίας.[94]

St. Stephen the Younger, the monk of Constantinople who was martyred by the iconoclasts in 764, bears witness to the doctrine of papal headship over councils in words that recall those of St. Athanasius. His *vita* written by a deacon of Hagia Sophia some forty years after his death records that he spoke to the iconoclasts about their synod of 754 in these terms:

> How can you call your council ecumenical, which has not been approved by the bishop of Rome, when it is laid down by law that ecclesiastical affairs may not be decided without the bishop of Rome [καίπερ κανόνος προκειμένου, μὴ δεῖν ἐκκλησιαστικὰ δίχα τοῦ Πάπα Ῥώμης κανονίζεσαι]?[95]

Nicephoros, who was born shortly after the iconoclast synod and became patriarch of Constantinople in 806, writes in these terms of Nicaea II:

93 *PG*, 91:138–40.
94 Mansi, 10:896C.
95 *PG*, 100:1144B.

> This synod possesses the highest authority. . . . In fact it was held in the most legitimate and regular fashion conceivable, because, according to the divine rules established from the beginning [ἀρχῆθεν τετυπωμένους θείους θεσμούς], it was directed and presided over by that glorious portion of the Western Church, I mean by the Church of Ancient Rome. Without [the Romans], no dogma discussed in the Church, even if sanctioned in a preliminary fashion by canonical decrees and ecclesiastical usages, can be considered to be approved [τὴν δοκιμασίαν οὐ σχοίη], or abrogated [δέξαιτο . . . τὴν περαίωσιν].[96]

Writing about the orthodoxy of this same Nicephoros, which had come into question, St. Theodore the Studite (759–826) explains that if a council can be held at which the five patriarchs are represented, the Roman patriarch will possess power over it (ᾧ καὶ τὸ κράτος ἀναφέρεται τῆς οἰκουμενικῆς συνόδου).[97]

Theodore Abu Qurrah, the Chalcedonian bishop of Haran (ca. 740–820), is the author of the earliest known treatise on councils. He writes with an explicitness that Bellarmine himself would not surpass that the approbation by the pope is by divine law the means to distinguish a true from a false council: "The Holy Spirit would not have allowed an error in any matter to issue from the council of St. Peter, that is, the bishop of Rome."[98] Or again:

---

[96] *PG*, 100:597A–B. Migne translates the last Greek phrase into Latin as *deducetur in praxim*, "put into practice." Περαίωσις means "a crossing over" in classical Greek; in the fifth century after Christ it is found with the sense "expiry" (*A Greek-English Lexicon: With a Revised Supplement*, ed. Robert Scott and Henry G. Liddell, 9th ed. [Oxford: Clarendon, 1996]).

[97] *PG*, 99:1420A.

[98] Theodore Abu Qurrah, "On the Councils," in *Theodore Abu Qurrah*, trans. J. Lamoreaux, Library of the Christian East 1 (Provo, UT: Brigham Young University Press, 2005), 78. Congar says of Theodore's work: "One might suppose it to be a treatise of apologetics composed between Vatican I and Vatican II, with its very strong affirmation of the magisterial authority of the bishop of Rome" ("Bulletin d'ecclésiologie," 284).

> Through the grace of the Holy Spirit, our sole goal is to build ourselves on the foundation of St. Peter, he who directed the six [*sic*] holy councils. These councils were gathered by command of the bishop of Rome, the city of the world. Whoever sits on that city's throne is authorized by Christ, to have compassion on the people of the Church, by summoning the ecumenical council, and to strengthen them.[99]

Likewise, a ninth-century Slavonic commentary on the twenty-eighth canon of Chalcedon, perhaps written by St. Methodios (ca.790–847), states that "without [the pope's] participation, manifested by the sending of some of his subordinates, every ecumenical council is non-existent, and it is he who renders legal what has been decided in council."[100]

Pope Nicholas I sums up the witness of tradition when writing to Emperor Michael III in Byzantium in the middle of the ninth century:

> If you think over the days of old with the wisdom that God has given to you, and call to mind the first rulers of your realms, you will certainly discover with what veneration your predecessors honored the see of blessed Peter, and with what charitable love they always welcomed its decrees. Finally, in universal councils, what is confirmed, what is thoroughly accepted, except for what the see of blessed Peter has approved, as you yourself know? And on the other hand, that which this see alone has rejected, remains rejected until now by virtue of this alone.[101]

---

99 Theodore Abu Qurrah, "On the death of Christ," in *Theodore Abu Qurrah*, 128.

100 Quoted by Robert Fastiggi in "The Petrine Ministry and the Indefectibility of the Church," in *Called to Holiness and Communion: Vatican II on the Church*, ed. Steven C. Boguslawski and Robert L. Fastiggi (Scranton, PA: University of Scranton Press, 2009), 180.

101 Pope Nicholas, Letter to Emperor Michael III: "Si dies antiquos secundum datam vobis divinitus sapientiam cogitatis, priscosque sedium vestrarum praesules ad memoriam ducitis, quanta veneratione sedem beati Petri praedecessores vestri celebraverint, quantoque caritatis amore decreta ipsius semper amplexi sunt, profecto reperietis: denique in universalibus synodis quid ratum, vel quid prorsus acceptum, nisi quod sedes beati Petri probavit (ut ipsi scitis) habetur: sicut e contrario quod ipsa sola reprobavit, hoc solummodo consistat hactenus reprobatum" (quoted by Schauf in Passaglia, *De conciliis oecumenicis*, 150).

Finally, an anonymous Byzantine *vita* of St. John Chrysostom written in the tenth century presents the saint as saying to his Alexandrian accusers at the "Synod of the Oak" in Constantinople in 403: "You have no right to hold a synod against us without the pope of Rome."[102] Venance Grumel, a French Assumptionist priest from the first half of the twentieth century and sometime secretary of the *Revue des études byzantines*, remarks that this text, composed some five hundred years after the events, while not evidence for Chrysostom's own beliefs, is still an important testimony to the view still prevailing in New Rome at the end of the first millennium, that only Old Rome could supervise affairs transcending patriarchal boundaries.

Alternative Views

The Church historian Hermann Sieben, basing himself on a similar historical study of the first seven councils, listed eight criteria that an ecumenical council must fulfill:

> An Ecumenical Council is an assembly of the Church that is (1) convened by the emperor, (2) supported [getragene] by the consensus of the whole Church, or, more precisely, by the consensus of the five patriarchs, (3) with the pope in particular co-operating, (4) in which a question concerning the whole Church, especially a question concerning the faith, (5) is treated under the existing law, (6) above all, with a free discussion, (7) whose conclusion is consistent with the content of preceding councils, and (8) which was received [rezipiert] by the whole Church.[103]

---

[102] Quoted in Venance Grumel, "Quelques témoignages byzantins sur la primauté romaine," *Echos d'Orient* 30 (1931): 422–30, at 429: " Οὔτε ὑμᾶς δίχα τοῦ Πάπας τοῦ Ῥώμης σύνοδον κρατῆσαι καθ'ἡμῶν." Summarizing this and other texts, Grumel comments: "In the century after Photios as well as in that before him, . . . the sentiment of the Roman primacy as something real and efficacious was a part of the religious psychology of the Byzantines" (430–31).

[103] Hermann Josef Sieben, *Studien zum Ökumenischen Konzil: Definitionen und Begriffe, Tagebücher und Augustinus-Rezeption* (Paderborn: Ferdinand Schöningh, 2010), 106.

Sieben argues that these are criteria *sine quibus non*, all of which must be fulfilled in order that one may speak of an ecumenical council. Only four, he says, are proper to an *ecumenical* council: imperial convocation, the agreement of the five patriarchs, the cooperation of the pope, and the need that the matter be relevant to the whole Church. The other four criteria belong to any Church council.[104]

Sieben's approach is sociological rather than theological. He gives criteria for ecumenical councils that were frequently mentioned by people of the time, at least by the end of the period under discussion. Yet he does not reach the essence of ecumenicity. For example, if we apply his criteria literally, number (7) would mean that there could be no valid first council, and therefore no valid succeeding ones.[105] Again, he does not sufficiently distinguish the *de facto* from the *de iure*. The emperor was doubtless involved in the convocation of the councils; but does it therefore follow that the Church of the first millennium understood imperial convocation to be of the *essence* of ecumenicity? Nevertheless, Sieben's list indicates three areas that must be examined, within the limits allowed by the present work: the role of the emperor, the theory of the pentarchy, and the appeal to "reception." The first two of these themes can be considered together as constituting what may be called the later "Byzantine theory" of ecumenicity.

---

104 Sieben, *Studien zum Ökumenischen Konzil*, 106.

105 Still more obviously, since there is no longer a Roman emperor, it would follow that an ecumenical council in the sense understood in the first millennium is no longer possible, and that at least the two Vatican councils have been ecumenical only in an equivocal sense.

CHAPTER 20

THE LATER BYZANTINE THEORY

Introduction

IN THE PREVIOUS CHAPTER, I sketched an account, with two possible variations, of ecumenicity, flowing from the recognition of the binding authority of the seven councils from First Council of Nicaea to the Second Council of Nicaea, and from the testimonies of the saints of the same period. It may be called the "papal" account of ecumenicity, insofar as it sees the pope as the "form of the whole council."[1] This was also the view of ecumenicity widely held among Latin theologians in later centuries, including at the time of the Council of Florence.[2] In

[1] The phrase is from D. Palmieri, *Tractatus de Romano Pontifice*, quoted in Bernard de Margerie, "L'analogie dans l'oecuménicité des conciles: Notion clef pour l'avenir de l'oecuménisme," *Revue thomiste* 84, no. 3 (1984): 425–46, at 438n51.

[2] For example, it was held by St. Thomas Aquinas in *De potentia Dei*, q. 10, a. 4, ad 13: "Just as a later synod has the power to interpret a creed composed by an earlier one, and putting forward some things to explain it, as is clear from what has been said, so also the Roman pontiff can do this by his authority, by whose authority alone a synod can be gathered, and from whom the judgment of the synod is confirmed; and to him appeal can be made by a synod [Sicut autem posterior synodus potestatem habet interpretandi symbolum a priore synodo conditum, ac ponendi aliqua ad eius explanationem, ut ex praedictis patet; ita etiam Romanus pontifex hoc

the Byzantine world, however, a different theory or ideal of ecumenicity had grown up after the separation from Rome. It may be described as the "imperio-pentarchic" theory, insofar as it affirmed that an ecumenical council relied on the "five patriarchs" acting under the governance of the Roman (Byzantine) emperor. In this chapter, I shall summarize and partly criticize this rival view of ecumenicity, again using the authorities and history of these early centuries.

The Role of the Emperor

In the later Byzantine period, there was a tendency to attribute the dominant role rather to the Roman emperor. George Kedrenos, a Byzantine historian from the twelfth century, wrote that councils "were named ecumenical, because bishops of the whole Roman empire were invited by imperial orders."[3] The generally accepted view in the later Byzantine period was that the emperor had the right of summoning general councils.[4] Norman Tanner has recently claimed, in effect, that the emperor was the head of the early councils:

> [The eastern emperors] summoned, presided over, either in person or through their officials, and subsequently promulgated the decrees of all the first seven ecumenical councils.... According to present Roman Catholic canon law, the pope (the bishop of Rome), alone has the right to convene, preside over (in person or through deputies), and to approve the decrees of an ecumenical council. But this must be seen as a regulation that

---

sua auctoritate potest, cuius auctoritate sola synodus congregari potest, et a quo sententia synodi confirmatur, et ad ipsum a synodo appellatur]" (trans. mine).

3 John Meyendorff, "Was There an Encounter between East and West at the Council of Florence?," in *Christian Unity: The Council of Ferrara-Florence, 1438/39–1989*, ed. Giuseppe Alberigo, Bibliotheca Ephemeridum Theologicarum Lovaniensium 97: International Symposium on the Unity of the Christians 550 years after the Council of Ferrara-Florence, Florence, Italy, 1989 (Leuven: Leuven University Press, 1991).

4 Martin Jugie, *Theologia Dogmatica Christianorum Orientalium ab Ecclesia Catholica Dissidentium*, 5 vols. (Paris: Letouzey et Ané, 1926–1935), 4:499. Jugie relates here that Macarius Ancyranus, in his early fifteenth-century work *Against the Error of the Latins*, went so far as to claim that even a local synod in Italy must be convoked by the emperor and not by the pope (*Theologia Dogmatica*, 4:499).

> could be changed or modified, since it was not observed during the first half of the church's history.[5]

The evidence of the first millennium shows that this summary of the facts is simplistic and ignores several well-established distinctions. In accordance with the definition of headship already mentioned, I shall consider in turn the convocation, presidence, and confirmation of councils.[6]

Emperor and Pope: Convocation of Ecumenical Councils

It is certain that the Roman emperors were of great importance in summoning the ecumenical councils of the first millennium. Joseph Wilhelm summarizes the facts thus:

> The convocation, in the loose sense of invitation to meet, of the first eight general synods, was regularly issued by the Christian emperors. . . . Nor is it possible in every case to prove that they acted at the formal instigation of the pope; it even seems that the emperors more than once followed none but their own initiative for convening the council and fixing its place of meeting.[7]

We can consider each of the first seven councils in turn. As already noted, according to Eusebius of Caesarea, Constantine himself issued the writs of convocation, now lost, for Nicaea I. The conciliar fathers, in their letter to the Egyptians, declare accordingly that they were assembled by "the grace

5 Norman P. Tanner, *The Councils of the Church: A Short History* (New York: Crossroad, 2001), 19–20. The statement of canon law draws on *Codex Iuris Canonici Auctoritate Ioannis Pauli PP. II Promulgatus* (Vatican City: Libreria Editrice Vaticana, 1983), cans. 337–41 and 749.

6 It may be asked why I bother to consider the rival claims of the pope and emperor, given that they were united at the Council of Florence. The answer is that if it could be shown that the pope was not, after all, the formal principle of ecumenicity for the early councils, then it would be necessary to determine what this principle was, and to assess Florence in the light of that.

7 Joseph Wilhelm, "Councils, General," in *Catholic Encyclopedia* (New York: Encyclopedia Press, 1913), 423–35, at 428.

of God and the most pious emperor Constantine,"[8] making no mention of Pope Sylvester I. Socrates Scholasticos has preserved a letter from the emperor to the Church of Alexandria in which Constantine simply says: "By divine admonition [ὑπομνήσει τοῦ θεοῦ], I assembled most of the bishops at the city of Nicaea."[9] Rufinus (ca. 345–410), in his continuation of Eusebius's *Historia Ecclesiae*, adds that the emperor took this step by the advice of the clergy—*ex sententia sacerdotum*.[10] Unfortunately he does not state whether the Pope was one of the *sacerdotes* consulted, though it is highly unlikely that the first see could have been neglected in so important a matter. The Third Council of Constantinople in 680–681 explicitly stated that the emperor and the pope by their joint authority had convened (συνέλεγον) the synod of Nicaea.[11] This testimony is important, emanating as it does from a city whose bishops had become rivals to those of Rome, and from a council where Greeks greatly preponderated.[12] The *Liber Pontificalis*, dated to the sixth century, though based on earlier redactions, likewise states that the consent of Pope Sylvester brought about this Council.[13]

Although it does not concern an ecumenical council, we may note the attitude of Emperor Valentinian I (r. 364–375), as recorded by Sozomen. The latter states that when Valentinian was asked by some Thracian bishops for permission to hold a council, the emperor replied: "I am but one of the laity, and have therefore no right to interfere in these transaction; let the priests, to whom such matters appertain,

---

8 *Decrees of the Ecumenical Councils: From Nicaea I to Vatican II*, ed. Norman Tanner and Giuseppe Alberigo, 2 vols. (Washington, DC: Georgetown University Press, 1990]), 1:16: "Τῆς τοῦ θεοῦ χάριτος καὶ τοῦ θεοφιλεστάτου βασιλέως Κονσταντίνου συναγηγόντας ἡμᾶς."

9 *PG*, 67:85A.

10 Charles-Joseph Hefele, *Histoire des conciles d'après les documents originaux*, trans. and ed. Henri Leclercq et al., 19 vols. (Paris: Letouzey et Ané, 1907–1938), 1/2:12.

11 Mansi, 11:661A.

12 As Hefele points out (*Histoire*, 1/1:14). Leo Davis dismisses the testimony as "legendary," but without argument (*The First Seven Ecumenical Councils (325–787): Their History and Theology* [Collegeville, MN: Liturgical, 1990], 56).

13 Jacques Forget, "Conciles," in *DTC*, 3:647–76, at col. 649, quoting from the *Liber Pontificalis*: "Huius (Sylvestri) temporibus factum est concilium cum eius consensu." Davis is therefore in error when he claims that the role of Pope Silvester is not mentioned before the seventh century.

assemble wherever they please."[14] Such was not the usual attitude of the emperors, however, with regard to ecumenical gatherings.

The First Council of Constantinople was called by the emperor Theodosius I.[15] He assembled the bishops from the eastern part of the empire to condemn the Pneumatomachian heresy in 381; the Western bishops were apparently not invited, as their provinces were less affected by the error. However, the letter sent the following year from the same Eastern bishops, meeting once more in Constantinople, to Pope Damasus and to other Western bishops indicates the cooperation between pope and emperor needed for the summoning of universal synods. The Eastern bishops note that Damasus had convoked a synod in Rome and invited them to it by means of a letter from the Western emperor, and they send their apologies for their inability to attend at such short notice.[16] They also state that their present synod of 382 results from Damasus's letter of the previous year to Theodosius.[17] This suggests an awareness that the Roman pontiff must be involved in the convocation of a council that covers more than one patriarchate, even though there is no extant proof that this had happened in the case of the synod of 381.[18]

The Council of Ephesus was convoked by Emperor Theodosius II. The emperor justifies his action in the very letter of convocation:

> As the true religion depends upon a right manner of life, so society depends upon both. Therefore, since God has given us the reins of the empire and has willed that we should be the link between the piety of our subjects and the correctness of

14 Sozomen, *Historia Ecclesiastica* 6.7.

15 Davis, *First Seven Ecumenical Councils*, 119.

16 Tanner and Alberigo, *Decrees of the Ecumenical Councils*, 1:26.

17 Tanner and Alberigo, *Decrees of the Ecumenical Councils*, 1:27.

18 It is, however, impossible to be certain about the details of the convocation of the council of 381, since, as J. Bois remarks, "the historical information about this synod is very limited" ("Constantinople, 1er concile de," in *DTC*, 3:1227–31, at col. 1227).

> their life, we guard and maintain inviolate the harmony between these two things, acting as mediator between the providence of God and mankind.[19]

He adds in the same letter: "We will not tolerate the voluntary absence of anyone."[20] Pope Celestine I gave his consent to this council before it began, in a letter of May 15, 431, to the emperor.[21] The synodal fathers, though presided over by legates of Pope Celestine I, describe the synod as "gathered together [συγκροτηθεῖσα] at the behest of the most pious princes [Theodosius II and Valentinian III]."[22] The Pope himself, though insisting that the council repeat his own condemnation of Nestorianism, does not claim to have convoked the synod, and in a letter to the emperor speaks of it as the council "which you ordered" (*quam esse iussistis*).[23]

After the "Robber Synod" of 449, Pope Leo I asked the same Emperor Theodosius to convoke a new council to condemn monophysitism, but the emperor did not do so. Theodosius died the following year, being succeeded by Pulcheria and Marcian. The latter wrote to Pope Leo and declared his intention of summoning a council. He expresses his hope that the Pope will be able to come but asks him to send a representative if he cannot, so that the bishops may assemble at a place to be chosen by him (Marcian).[24] The empress, in her letter to Pope Leo, states that the bishops will make their doctrinal decree on the Pope's authority (*te auctore*; σοῦ αὐθεντοῦντος).[25] The emperor did not receive the Pope's reply disparaging the idea of another great synod in the East until he had already convoked it, whereupon Leo accepted the *fait accompli*.[26]

---

19 Mansi, 4:1111E–14A: "Ut vera quidem religio per vitam inculpate actam, ipsa vero respublica constans ex utrisque florescat. Cum itaque Deus imperii habenas nobis tradiderit, iisque qui imperio nostro parent, pietatis et vitae recte instituendae vinculum nos esse voluerit, harum inter se societatem indivulsam conservamus, Dei providentiae hominumque sequestres."

20 Mansi, 4:1115A: "Nullum aequo animo abesse sinemus."

21 Hefele, *Histoire*, 1/1:16.

22 Tanner and Alberigo, *Decrees of the Ecumenical Councils*, 1:62.

23 Mansi, 4:1291B.

24 *PL*, 54:904C.

25 *PL*, 54:907A–8A.

26 Tanner and Alberigo, *Decrees of the Ecumenical Councils*, 1:75.

The Council of Chalcedon, then, describes itself as "assembled by the grace of God and by the decree [θέσπισμα] of the most religious and Christ-loving emperors, Valentinian and Marcian."[27] Pope Leo, in a letter written to the bishops after the council, described it as having been brought about "both by the command of the Christian princes and by the command of the apostolic see."[28] Likewise, the bishops of the Balkan province of Moesia remark in a letter to Emperor Leo I (r. 457–474) that the assembly at Chalcedon had taken place "at the bidding of Leo the Roman pontiff [per iussionem Leonis romani pontificis]."[29]

The story of the authorization of the Second Council of Constantinople is somewhat complex. Tanner writes: "The emperor Justinian and Pope Vigilius decided to summon this council after the latter withdrew his 'Judgment' condemning the 'Three Chapters' of Theodore of Mopsuetia, Theodoret and Ibas."[30] Then, when the emperor had issued a decree on his own authority condemning the "three chapters" once more, Vigilius withdrew his consent to the Council and excommunicated those who took part in it. The council assembled notwithstanding and also condemned what the emperor had condemned. Justinian, speaking to the fathers, told them, "We have called you to our royal city," and speaking to them of Vigilius, says, "we have likewise bidden him [mandavimus illi], by our judges and by some of yourselves, to come to join himself to all of you."[31]

The Third Council of Constantinople was summoned by Emperor Constantine IV after consultation with Rome.[32] Having received a request from Constantinople to send a delegation, Pope Agatho presided over a Roman synod that condemned monothelitism. The papal delegates arrived in the imperial city with the profession of faith in

---

27 Tanner and Alberigo, *Decrees of the Ecumenical Councils*, 1:83. This formula was used at the beginning of each session except for the fifteenth (Forget, "Conciles," col. 649).

28 *PL*, 54:1029B: "Generale concilium, et ex praecepto Christianorum principum et ex praecepto apostolicae sedis, placuit congregari."

29 Mansi, 7:546C.

30 Mansi, 7:546C.

31 Mansi, 9:182A.

32 Tanner and Alberigo, *Decrees of the Ecumenical Councils*, 1:123.

September 680, and on the tenth day of the month, the emperor issued an edict to the patriarch of Constantinople ordering him to summon the bishops. The council fathers described Constantine IV as a new David, who had given himself no rest "until through this holy assembly of ours, brought together by God, he had found the perfect proclamation of the right belief."[33] They also wrote to Pope Agatho declaring that they had vanquished heresy by means of the letter that he had sent to them.[34] Shortly afterward, Pope Leo II, writing to the emperor, speaks of it as the "holy and great and universal sixth council which your Clemency carefully convoked by the will of God."[35]

The convocation of a council against the iconoclasts, the future Nicaea II, was announced by the Empress Regent Irene to Pope Hadrian I in a letter of August 29, 784.[36] She writes in the name of herself and of her son Constantine VI, addressing the Pope as *Sanctissimum Caput* ("Most holy head"):

> Those to whom the imperial dignity or the dignity of the sovereign priesthood have been conferred by our Lord Jesus Christ are bound to take thought and counsel about that which is pleasing to him, and to govern according to his will the peoples that he has entrusted to them. . . . This is why, obedient to the inspirations of a pure heart and of true piety, in harmony with all our subjects and with the learned priests in this place, we have reflected at length upon the situation and after mature deliberation, we have decided to bring about an ecumenical council [decrevimus, ut fieret universale consilium].[37]

---

33 Tanner and Alberigo, *Decrees of the Ecumenical Councils*, 1:126.

34 Hefele, *Histoire*, 1/1:21.

35 Mansi, 11:730D: "Sancta igitur universalis et magna sexta synodus quam nutu Dei vestra clementia sedule convocavit."

36 Tanner and Alberigo, *Decrees of the Ecumenical Councils*, 1:131.

37 Forget, "Conciles," 647; Mansi, 12:984E–985B.

In the same letter, the empress and her son ask the Pope to come himself or at least to send legates.[38] As always in the case of the Eastern synods, he did not attend in person.[39] The council fathers described themselves as "assembled by the grace of God and by order of our pious and Christ-loving emperor and empress."[40] They condemned the iconoclast synod of Hieria in 754, attended by 338 bishops,[41] mentioning that it lacked the cooperation of "the Pope of the Romans,"[42] though they do not refer specifically to the question of its convocation. In a letter written several years later to Charlemagne, the Pope remarks that Nicaea II took place "according to our ordinance."[43]

What does the historical evidence imply about the right to convoke general councils? The Roman emperor apparently considered it his proper task to summon at least the chief bishops of his empire when religious differences threatened the tranquillity of his realm, or when the spread of heresy threatened to bring the divine displeasure upon it. He does not speak as if he had simply a ministerial office entrusted to him by the Roman pontiff.[44] On the other hand, with the exception of Justinian's treatment of Vigilius, we do not find him commanding the pope to come to a council, but rather requesting him to do so, or to send legates. Again, the emperor apparently considered that he could command bishops to use their authority to judge in religious matters, but as we shall see more clearly when we consider the presidence of councils, he realized that he himself was not the source of that

---

38 Tanner and Alberigo, *Decrees of the Ecumenical Councils*, 1:131.

39 St. Robert Bellarmine argues that the popes acted thus both because it is not fitting that the head should follow the members, and so that the Roman pontiff should not have to sit beneath the Roman emperor, who was accustomed to sit in the place of honor in bishops' councils just as in the senate (*De conciliis* 1.19, in *Omnia Opera* vol. 2 [Paris: Vives, 1870]).

40 Tanner and Alberigo, *Decrees of the Ecumenical Councils*, 1:131.

41 Davis, *First Seven Ecumenical Councils*, 302. No papal legate or patriarch had attended this council.

42 Mansi, 13:208E–9A: " Οὐκ ἔσχε συνεργὸν τὸν τῶν Ῥωμαίων πάπαν." See section "Papal Headship" in ch. 19 ("The Essence of Ecumenicity").

43 Forget, "Conciles," 650: "Et sic synodum istam secundum nostram ordinationem fecerunt."

44 Forget, "Conciles," 649. We may contrast this with the frankly instrumental account of the emperor's activity given by John of Montenero at the Council of Florence. According to him, in convoking the early councils, the emperors had acted as the secular arm (*brachium seculare*) at the consent and command of the pope (*consentiente et mandante papa*; *AG*, 245).

authority. His convocation was therefore material rather than formal;[45] that is, he brought the bishops together so that they might teach the true faith, but did not invest them either as individuals or as a body with magisterial rights.[46]

The popes themselves during the early councils neither contest the imperial right of convocation nor teach it. They adapt themselves to circumstances, understanding that various things made it almost inevitable that the emperors would act as having the right to summon councils, at least of Eastern bishops: Roman law forbade any large assembly to take place without imperial permission; the costs of the council would have to be defrayed by public expense; until the acquisition of the papal states, the pope was *de facto* an imperial subject. All these things made it reasonable that the pope at this period should request, rather than command, the emperor to summon a council. We have also seen that they assert their own authority nonetheless, and in regard to convocation as well as to definition: they speak of councils sometimes as deriving from themselves, sometimes from the emperor, according as the doctrinal authority or the material assemblage of the bishops is uppermost in their minds.

As for the council fathers themselves, meeting as they often did in the imperial presence, with the emperor himself seated in first place, it is unsurprising that they repeatedly describe themselves as assembled by his authority. Yet, in such formulas as "gathered by the grace of God and the command of the emperor," we may well see a reference to the distinction of "formal" and "material" convocation mentioned above. A phrase such as the "grace of God" indicates the power that enabled them to

[45] Joannes de Groot, *Summa Apologetica de Ecclesia Catholica ad Mentem S. Thomae Aquinatis*, 2 vols. (Regensburg: G. J. Manz, 1890), 10; Forget, "Conciles," 651. When Yves Congar criticizes this distinction for being a "theoretical distinction without a real basis in facts," he seems to forget that it is not meant to describe the clear understanding of all who were involved in the early councils, but to show how the historical facts are coherent with Catholic theology ("Quelle idée s'est-on faite du concile entre Nicée I et Nicée II?," *Revue des sciences philosophiques et théologiques* 63 [1979]: 429–34, at 430).

[46] This is also seen by the fact, mentioned by St. Maximus the Confessor in his reply to Theodosius, that emperors did not convoke local councils (*PG*, 90:148A).

make binding judgments in Christ's name—a power that, as they knew, could only belong to their assemblies by the authority of the Roman pontiff, as being, in the words of Empress Irene, *Sanctissimum Caput.*

Emperor and Pope: Presidence of Ecumenical Councils

Who presided over the first seven general councils? Authors have distinguished three forms of presidence: of authority, of honour, and of protection.[47] Presidence of authority is the right to govern the assembly precisely qua ecumenical council, a body that can define doctrine and establish canons. It is thus the presidence in the formal sense, without which a mere assembly of bishops, no matter how large and how prestigious the sees represented, lacks the distinctive ecumenical character. Presidence of honor means to sit in the most honored place and to receive tokens of honor from all present. Presidence of protection means ensuring that the assembly has the tranquillity and material means necessary for it to bring its business to a good end.

The general principle observed during the councils of the first millennium was that the pope, through his legates, presided in the first sense and that the emperor, either in person or through his delegate, presided in the second and third senses. In practice the lines could sometimes be blurred, for example, with papal and imperial delegates both calling upon bishops to pronounce their verdicts.[48]

Having premised this much, we may once more run briefly through the early councils. Of Nicaea I, Tanner writes:

> It is impossible to be certain who presided over the sessions. What can be stated with confidence is that in the extant lists

---

47 See, for example, J. Forget, "Conciles," 653; Carlo Passaglia, *De conciliis oecumenicis: theses Caroli Passaglia de conciliis deque habitu quo ad Romanos pontifices referuntur*, ed. Heribert Schauf (Rome: Herder, 1961), 23; Leclercq in Hefele, *Histoire*, 1/1:41n3.

48 This is perhaps because the question had not been settled of whether an emperor could require the bishops to come, if not to the decision that he favored, at least to some decision or other about a disputed doctrinal question.

> of the bishops who were present, which may well be original, Ossius of Cordova, and the two presbyters who represented the apostolic see, Vitus and Vincentius, are listed before the other names. Nevertheless it is more likely that it was Eustathius of Antioch or Alexander of Alexandria who presided over the sessions.[49]

Tanner gives no reason for the last statement in this extract. Probably he mentions Eustathius because Theodoret attributes to him the opening discourse in honor of the emperor.[50] Yet Theodoret elsewhere says of Ossius of Cordoba, "what council did he not lead [Ποίας γὰρ οὐχ ἡγήσατο συνόδου]?"[51] The task of addressing the emperor could naturally be given to any fluent speaker, provided he was of sufficient eminence, without implying anything about the presidence. Tanner perhaps mentions Alexander of Alexandria because the synodal letter to the church of that province refers to him as a leader (κύριος) in the things that were done; but again, this is a vague term, and it is significant also that it lacks a definite article.[52] Karl Josef von Hefele after a long discussion concludes that Ossius and the two papal legates presided, noting that their names are not preceded by the name of any ecclesiastical province they represented, and hence that they took their places as presidents and not as representatives of a particular church.[53] Leo Davis states without argument that Ossius sat "as imperial counselor and not as papal legate."[54] Presumably it would have been possible for him to occupy both roles. If one accepts Hefele's reasoning, one may say that, through his legates, the Pope presided over the Council in the sense of the presidence of authority. And, of

49 Tanner and Alberigo, *Decrees of the Ecumenical Councils*, 1:2.
50 *PG*, 82:917D.
51 Quoted in Hefele, *Histoire*, 1/1:55.
52 Tanner and Alberigo, *Decrees of the Ecumenical Councils*, 1:18.
53 Hefele, *Histoire*, 1/1:57.
54 Davis, *First Seven Ecumenical Councils*, 58.

Ossius, one may say that if he was not a papal legate, then it is reasonable to suppose, by analogy with the later councils and with the clear distinction drawn by the fathers of Chalcedon, that his presidence was "for the sake of decorum."[55]

Since Constantinople I was not ecumenical in its sessions, in that it apparently did not include representatives from the west, the question of its presidence does not arise here.

In regard to the Council of Ephesus, it is well known that St. Cyril of Alexandria, who opened the council, was acting in virtue of a commission from Pope Celestine I. Throughout the *acta*, Cyril is frequently referred to as the Pope's representative (διέπων τὸν τόπον) and is placed at the head of the list of members of the Council.[56] When the other papal legates arrived, after the first session of the Council, they confirmed Cyril's action. One of them, the presbyter Philip, read a strong declaration of papal primacy, in which it was stated that St. Peter was "prince and head of the apostles," that "the most holy and blessed pope Celestine is his successor and holds his place," and that they themselves were supplying Celestine's place in the synod.[57] Theodosius II had sent Candidian, the captain of the guard, to preserve order in the city and at the synod, but expressly stipulated that he was not to meddle with the doctrinal discussions, since "it is not lawful for anyone who is not enrolled among the holy bishops to interfere with ecclesiastical questions."[58] Nestorius himself provides us with an unconscious testimony of the authority of the pope over an ecumenical council in his bitter complaint: "Who was judge? Cyril. Who was accuser? Cyril. Who was bishop of Rome? Cyril."[59]

---

55 See quote at note 63, just below.

56 Hefele, *Histoire*, 1/1:49–50. In asking that the emperor remit his judgment against Cyril and Memnon, the synodal fathers ask that their synod be not made "headless" (ἀκέφαλον; Mansi, 4:1461D).

57 Quoted in Davis, *First Seven Ecumenical Councils*, 157.

58 Mansi, 4:1120A: "Ἀθέμιτον γάρ, τὸν μὴ τοῦ καταλόγου τῶν ἁγιωτάτων ἐπισκόπων τυγχάνοντα τοῖς ἐκκλησιαστικοῖς σκέμμασιν ἐπιμίγνυσθαι."

59 Davis, *First Seven Ecumenical Councils*, 156.

Pope Leo I, writing to the fathers of Chalcedon before their discussions, said of his legates:

> In these brethren who have been deputed by the Apostolic See, that is Paschasinus and Lucentius, bishops, and Boniface and Basil, presbyters, let your brotherhood reckon that I am presiding at the Synod [me synodo vestra fraternitas aestimet praesidere].[60]

Writing afterward to the bishops of Gaul, Leo spoke of the legates as "my brothers, who in my place presided over the Eastern council."[61] Tanner remarks that "by [the papal legates'] side were the imperial commissars and those serving on the Senate, whose responsibility was simply to keep order in the council's deliberation."[62] The bishops themselves were well aware of the distinction between the role of the pope and that of the emperor. They say in their letter to the Leo: "You certainly had precedence, as the head over the members, by means of [the legates] who took your place in your kindness; however, the faithful emperors presided very fittingly for the sake of decorum."[63] The pope, as the head of the body, is thus seen as a vital principle of the council, the emperor as an external protection and ornament.

Since Constantinople II was not attended by the pope or his legates, despite the efforts of the emperor Justinian, it was presided in their absence by the archbishop of Constantinople, Eutychius.[64] In its seventh session, instructed by the emperor, the council went so far as to strike Pope Vigilius's name from the diptychs, though adding:

60 Pope Leo I, Letter 93, no. 1 (*PG*, 54:937B).

61 *PL*, 54:988B: "Fratres mei, qui vice mea orientali synodo praesederunt."

62 Tanner and Alberigo, *Decrees of the Ecumenical Councils*, 1:75.

63 Mansi, 6:147C: "Tu quidem, sicut membris caput, praeeras in his qui tuum tenebunt ordinem benevolentiam praeferens. Imperatores vero fideles ad ornandum decentissime praesidebant." *Tenebunt* is presumably a mistake for *tenebant*.

64 Hefele, *Histoire*, 1:1:45.

"Let us preserve unity to the Apostolic See of the most holy Church of ancient Rome."[65]

Emperor Constantine IV was personally present at Constantinople III; Tanner writes that "there were 18 sessions, at the first eleven of which the emperor presided."[66] Hefele remarks, however, that the *acta* make a clear distinction between the emperor (and his retinue) and the council properly speaking, since after naming the former group, they go on to name the bishops with the introductory phrase "the holy and ecumenical Council also being assembled [συνελθούσης δὲ καὶ τῆς ἁγίας καὶ οἰκουμενικῆς συνόδου]."[67] While the papal legates signed the decrees of the Council first, the emperor signed them last, after the bishops. Again, whereas the bishops in general sign with the words "defining I subscribe [definiens subscripsi]," the emperor ratified their signatures with the words "we have read and approved [legimus et consensimus]."[68] All this tends to show that the presidence of the emperor was not exercised over the bishops insofar as they were a magisterial assembly, but under some other aspect, for example, insofar as they were citizens of his empire.

Of Nicaea II, Tanner writes: "The papal legates presided over the council and were the first to sign the acts; but in reality it was Patriarch Tarasius [of Constantinople] who presided";[69] by this is meant that Tarasius effectively directed the discussions. Empress Irene and her son, Constantine VI, had the presidency of honor at the final session.[70] Having had the decree of the council read to them and having been assured that it represented the mind of the whole synod, they signed the decree that had already been signed by the bishops.[71] As noted above, Pope Hadrian I, writing to Charlemagne, said that the bishops

---

65 *The Decrees and Canons of the Seven Ecumenical Councils*, ed. Henry Percival, *NPNF2*, 14:304.
66 Tanner and Alberigo, *Decrees of the Ecumenical Councils*, 1:123.
67 Hefele, *Histoire*, 1/1:44.
68 Mansi, 11:639C–55A. The legates of the pope or of other sees signed with the single word *subscripsi*.
69 Tanner and Alberigo, *Decrees of the Ecumenical Councils*, 1:131.
70 Hefele, *Histoire*, 1/1:44.
71 Mansi, 13:414–15.

of this council, in restoring the sacred images, "acted according to our ordinance [secundum ordinationem nostram fecerunt]."

In summary: the evidence of the first seven councils suggests that the presidence of the Roman pontiff, either personal or delegated, and understood strictly speaking—as presidence over the council as a teaching and governing body—is necessary for a council to be ecumenical in its deliberation. Only in the case of Constantinople II do we find a council regarding itself and regarded by posterity as ecumenical that claimed to issue decrees for the universal Church while lacking such presidence. But Constantinople II would not have attained that rank either in the eyes of the Church of that time or of posterity without the confirmation that it later received from the pope. Moreover, the distinction between the doctrinal presidence of the pope and the simply extrinsic presidence or guardianship exercised by the emperor or his delegates was well understood during this time, both by the bishops and by the imperial power itself.

Emperor and Pope: Confirmation of Ecumenical Councils

Who, if anyone, confirmed the decrees of the first seven councils? We have seen that Tanner speaks of the Roman emperors as "promulgating" the decrees of these councils, and argues on this basis that the requirement of modern canon law that conciliar decrees need the approval of the Roman pontiff is subject to revision. But there is here an important ambiguity, as was seen with regard both to convocation and to presidence. A doctrinal decree qua doctrinal is promulgated by a magisterial organ, declaring that a certain truth is contained in or required by divine revelation or natural law. When the emperors promulgated or "confirmed" the decrees of a council, it was in another sense: not as guaranteeing their doctrinal correctness in virtue of a supposed imperial right to define saving truth, but as causing them to become laws of the empire, or as decreeing banishment for those subject to the

Church's authority who resisted them.[72] Many patristic witnesses insist that imperial authority does not extend to defining matters of faith or to giving laws to the Church, whether in connection with a council or not. In his *Historia Arianorum*, St. Athanasius writes in connection the attempts to impose that heresy by Constantius II (r. 337–361):

> When did a judgment of the Church receive its validity from an Emperor [πότε κρίσις Ἐκκλησίας παρὰ Βασιλέως ἔσχε τὸ κῦρος]? Or rather when was his decree ever recognised by the Church? There have been many Councils held heretofore; and many judgments passed by the Church; but the Fathers never sought the consent of the Emperor thereto, nor did the Emperor busy himself with the affairs of the Church. (52)[73]

Evidently the bishop of Alexandria is not urging that an orthodox emperor have no concern for the welfare of the Church, but rather upholding the exclusive right of the episcopate to define doctrine. In the same work, he quotes with approval the words of Ossius of Cordoba to the same emperor Constantius: "Intrude not yourself into ecclesiastical matters, neither give commands unto us concerning them; but learn them from us. God has put into your hands the kingdom; to us He has entrusted the affairs of His Church" (44).

St. Ambrose writes in similar vein to the emperor Valentinian, who had wished that the bishop of Milan and Arian bishops should appear before an imperial consistory so that judgment might be made between them concerning the Nicene doctrine:

---

72 For the promulgation of imperial edicts approving the councils, see Tanner and Alberigo, *Decrees of the Ecumenical Councils*, 1:4 (Nicaea I), 1:23 (Constantinople I), 1:38 (Ephesus), 1:76 (Chalcedon), and 1:123 (Constantinople III). Tanner says that it is not known whether the decrees of Nicaea II became the subject of an imperial edict (1:132), but we have already seen that the empress-regent and her son signed its decrees. Constantinople II was under the effective control of the emperor Justinian, who approved its decrees at the seventh session (Hefele, *Histoire*, 1/1:60).

73 Athanasius, *Historia Arianorum* (*PG*, 25:756C).

> When did you hear, O merciful emperor, that lay folk judged bishops in a question of faith? . . . Who is there who would deny that, in a question of faith—I repeat, in a question of faith—bishops are accustomed to judge Christian emperors, and not emperors bishops?[74]

It is because the emperor did not constitute an ecumenical council as a magisterial body that his consent to a conciliar definition, however desirable, was not a condition of its truth. Thus, St. Maximus the Confessor, when told by Theodosius of Caesarea that he should renounce the Lateran synod held under Pope Martin I in 649 because it was not called at the command of the emperor, replied that imperial commands do not validate (κυροῦσιν) synods.[75]

Pope St. Leo II, writing to Constantine IV in 682, summarizes the duties of the emperor in regard to synodal decrees. Having spoken of the definition of faith made by Constantinople III, the Pope continues:

> It is truly worthy, and very acceptable to God, that the truth of the apostolic preaching, which makes the imperial power beautiful and preserves the clemency of rulers, should increase in the whole world through the edict of your noble piety. . . . Therefore by the conciliar judgment and the authority of the imperial edict, as if by a two-edged sword of the spirit, this new, wicked error has been pierced through, along with the heresies of old times.[76]

---

74 St. Ambrose, Letter 32: "Quando audisti, clementissime imperator, in causa fidei de episcopo iudicasse? . . . Quis est qui abnuat in causa fidei, in causa, inquam, fidei, episcopos solere de imperatoribus Christianis non imperatores de episcopis iudicare?" (*PL*, 16:1046A; the reference is sometimes wrongly given as *PL*, 16:1004).

75 *PG*, 90:145C.

76 Mansi, 11:730B: "Hoc vere dignum Deoque gratissimum existit, quod apostolicae praedicationis veritas, quae imperialem exornat potentiam, et principalem clementiam servat, per augustissimae pietatis edictum in toto orbe terrarum percrebuit. . . . Synodali igitur sententia et imperialis edicti censura, tamquam ancipiti spiritus gladio, cum priscis haeresibus etiam novae pravitatis error expunctus est."

The imperial "promulgation" of conciliar decrees, in other words, was not a magisterial act, but the means by which the true faith already defined at a council might take firm root within the empire.

The following century, Pope Gregory II reminds the iconoclast emperor Leo III that the emperor is not competent to determine doctrine:

> Constantine the great, Theodosius the great, Valentinian the great, and Constantine the father of Justinian, who was present at the sixth synod: they were emperors who governed piously; and gathering synods with the bishops in a common understanding and decree, and seeking out the truth of dogmas, they made the churches strong and beautiful. . . . Listen, O emperor, to our lowliness: desist, and follow the holy Church, as you found her and received her; dogmas are not a matter for emperors but for bishops; for it is we who have the mind of Christ.[77]

St. John Damascene, also writing in defense of the holy images, is equally blunt: "It is not for kings to give laws to the Church [οὐ βασιλέων ἐστι νομοθετεῖν Ἐκκλησίᾳ]."[78]

Finally, St. Theodore the Studite († 826), receiving like Ambrose of Milan a command from the emperor to debate with heretics in the imperial presence so that judgment might be given, refuses in terms that the Italian saint could have used more than four centuries earlier: "The question is not of things of the world and of flesh, the power to judge which belongs to the emperor and to the secular judge; it is one

[77] Mansi, 12:976D–E, 977B: "Constantinus magnus, Theodosius magnus, Valentinianus magnus, et Constantinus Iustiniani pater, qui sextae synodo interfuit: imperatores isti religiose imperarunt, et cum pontificibus uno consilio ac sententia synodos congregantes, atque veritatem dogmatum perquirentes, sanctas ecclesias constituerunt et ornarunt. . . . Audi humilitatem nostram, imperator: cessa, et sanctam Ecclesiam sequere, prout invenisti atque accepisti: non sunt imperatorum dogmata, sed pontificum; quoniam Christi sensum nos habemus."

[78] *PG*, 94:1295C.

of divine and heavenly dogmas."[79] The role of an emperor at a synod, Theodore adds, is not to judge, but rather to provide help, giving his seal of approval (συνεπισφραγίζειν) to the decrees and reconciling those who have been at enmity.

Were the first seven councils confirmed by the pope? Authors have distinguished three kinds of confirmation: anterior, concomitant, and subsequent.[80] The Second Vatican Council, in its dogmatic constitution *Lumen Gentium*, states that "a council is never ecumenical unless it is confirmed or at least accepted as such by the successor of Peter" (§22).[81] The qualifying clause "or at least accepted" apparently alludes to two old controversies: the first is whether a council at which the pope is represented by his legates requires subsequent confirmation by the pope, in addition to the consent which his legates gave to their decrees; the other is, if such a confirmation is unnecessary, whether it was nevertheless given by the pope to the oriental councils of the first millennium. Many authors, including John de Turrecremata, Thomas Cajetan, Melchior Cano, Giovanni Perrone, and Ignaz von Döllinger, have argued that such a confirmation is theologically necessary. St. Robert Bellarmine and Carlo Passaglia denied it. Hefele attempted to show that, whether or not such confirmation was necessary *de iure*, it had always in fact been given; Henri Leclercq, his translator, annotator, and continuer argued against this thesis.[82]

We may briefly look at the strongest arguments that have been put forward in favour of subsequent confirmation. With regard to Nicaea I, a Roman synod held in 485 under Felix III sent a letter to the monks and clergy of the East excommunicating Acacius, patriarch of Constantinople. The synodal letter states that "the 318 holy fathers gathered at Nicaea sent to Rome for the confirmation and authorization

---

79 *PG*, 99:1417B.

80 See, e.g., Leclercq in Hefele, *Histoire*, 1/1:58 n2.

81 DH no. 4146: "Concilium Oecumenicum numquam datur, quod a Successore Petri non sit ut tale confirmatum vel saltem receptum."

82 Hefele, *Histoire*, 1/1:58–68, with Leclercq's comments in the notes.

of the affairs [confirmationem rerum atque auctoritatem]."[83] Leclercq accepts the statement that a letter was sent from the Nicene fathers to Rome, but holds that it requested the confirmation of sentences passed in Nicaea against individuals and not of the actual doctrinal decrees of the council.[84] Yet the synodal letter itself does not explain the meaning of the phrase "confirmationem rerum atque auctoritatem," nor does it refer explicitly to individuals condemned at Nicaea. Henry Chadwick therefore described the synodal letter of 485 as referring to "the decisions of the Council of Nicaea," without any limitation.[85]

Since Constantinople I is not reckoned as ecumenical except in virtue of the later acceptance of it by the Roman Church, the question of the need for an additional confirmation to be given to the decree of an existing ecumenical council does not arise in its regard.

For the Council of Ephesus, some have claimed to see a subsequent confirmation in some words of Pope Sixtus III to Cyril of Alexandria. Concerning the bishops of the party of John of Antioch, the Pope writes that they are to be pardoned if they return to a right way of thinking and "if they reject that which the holy council rejected, with our approval [nobis confirmantibus]."[86] Since Sixtus did not come to the throne until after the close of the Council, it is argued that in the last two words of the quotation he is referring to a subsequent confirmation of the Ephesian decrees. Leclercq supposed that the Pope was referring by the word *nobis* to the Holy See, and to its action at the time of the Council.[87] It seems better to say that Sixtus is indeed referring to his own approval of the Council, but that the brief phrase *nobis confirmantibus* by itself, attached to a sentence treating of a different subject,

---

83 Mansi, 7:1140D–E: "Trecenti decem et octo sancti patres apud Nicaeam congregati confirmationem rerum atque auctoritatem sanctae Romanae ecclesiae detulerunt." Davis gives the date of the synod as 484 (*First Seven Ecumenical Councils*, 203).

84 Hefele, *Histoire*, 1/1:61n2. The same view was taken by Forget in "Conciles," 657.

85 Henry Chadwick, *East and West: The Making of a Rift in the Church, from Apostolic Times until the Council of Florence* (Oxford: Oxford University Press, 2005), 51.

86 Mansi, 5:375A.

87 Hefele, *Histoire*, 1/1:63n2.

can hardly be taken as a legal ratification, or as proof that he had given such a ratification previously.

For the Council of Chalcedon, Hefele quotes the end of the letter of the synod to Pope Leo I, which declares: "We have recognized that you have complete power over what we have done, to ensure our unity and to confirm and approve what we have done."[88] Leclercq shows convincingly that the request here is for a confirmation not of the doctrinal decree, which had been drawn up under the supervision of the papal legates and in harmony with Leo's own well-known *Tome*, but of the controversial canon 28, refused by the papal legates, which claimed precedence for Constantinople over the other Eastern sees. Later, it is true, Emperor Marcian asked Leo for a confirmation of the doctrinal decree itself. However, as Leclercq also shows, what was sought on this occasion was not a legal act without which the conciliar decree would have been considered invalid by the emperor, but so to speak a political act that would disconcert the remaining supporters of Eutyches.[89] Thus, Leo begins his reply to the emperor's request by noting that there could be no real ground for doubting that he did approve of the doctrine defined at Chalcedon; he adds that he is nonetheless writing the present letter in order that none of the Eutychians might claim to be ignorant of his approval. In this way, all would know that he was of one mind with the synod, not only through his legates, but also through his personal approval (*approbationem*).[90]

Constantinople II, as we have seen, met without papal authorization. Pope Vigilius's final consent to it was thus not something given in addition to an approval by legates. In his letter of December 553 to Patriarch Eutyches, he effectively gave this consent by anathematizing the "Three Chapters," though without mentioning the Council as

88 Mansi, 6:156A: "Πᾶσαν ὑμῖν τῶν πεπραγμένων τὴν δύναμιν ἐγνωρίσαμεν εἰς σύστασιν ἡμέτεραν καὶ τῶν παρ᾽ἡμῶν πεπραγμένων βεβαίωσιν τε καὶ συγκατάθεσιν."

89 Hefele, *Histoire*, 1/1:65n4.

90 *PL*, 54:1030A.

such, and speaking instead rather euphemistically of "bishops who are staying in this royal city."[91]

The evidence for a subsequent confirmation of a regularly constituted ecumenical council is perhaps strongest for the sixth such gathering, Constantinople III. The synodal fathers write to the pope to ask for such an act on his part: "We have clearly preached with you the splendid light of the orthodox faith, and we ask you, Holy Father, that you would once more confirm it by your noble reply."[92] In his reply to Constantine IV, Pope Leo II writes: "Through our ministry, this apostolic see admits without hesitation or difficulty the definitions of the Council, and by the authority of blessed Peter it confirms [confirmat] them as being firmly and divinely placed upon the solid rock which is Christ."[93] Leclercq acknowledges that it is difficult here not to speak of a subsequent confirmation; but he argues that it is not presented as a juridical necessity, and that what follows this passage indicates that, for Leo, the Council "independently of [the confirmation] and anterior to it, possesses all its value from God himself."[94] In fact, in the following passage, after having listed the previous five councils, the Pope writes: "We receive the holy sixth council with equal veneration and with the same judgment, and we decree that it is worthy to be reckoned along with those councils, as assembled by one and the same grace of God."[95] There may seem to be a certain tension here between the word "veneration" and the word "decree," the former suggesting, as Leclercq says, a reality that requires no ratification by the pope, and the latter suggesting just such a ratification. This tension is resolved if we allow

---

91 Mansi, 9:413A–20A.

92 Mansi, 11:687B: "Orthodoxae autem fidei splendiam lucem vobiscum clare praedicavimus: quam ut iterum per honorabilia vestra rescripta confirmetis vestram oramus paternam sancitatem." The Greek word for "confirm" here is ἐπισφραγίσαι, literally, "put a seal on."

93 Mansi, 11:730E.

94 Hefele, *Histoire*, 1/1:67n5. This of course is not to be confused with the so-called conciliarist theory, according to which a council did not require papal headship, having a power directly from God.

95 Mansi, 11:731A: "Sanctum sextum concilium, ut eorum pedissequum et ea interpretans pari veneratione atque censura suscipimus, et hoc cum eis digne connumerari, tamquam una et aequali Dei gratia congegatum decernimus."

that the pope has the power to declare a "dogmatic fact," in this case that a certain gathering of bishops was an ecumenical council, without thereby claiming to create that fact.

Finally, when Patriarch Tarasius, at the end of Nicaea II, wrote to Pope Hadrian I to inform him that the Pope's letter on sacred images had been unanimously acclaimed by the bishops, he did not request a special act of confirmation.[96] Hadrian did not directly reply, as he was still waiting for a response from the emperor to his requirement that the papal patrimony that had been confiscated by Emperor Leo III be returned.[97] In speaking to Charlemagne about the council, he uses the phrase "suscepimus synodum" ("we accepted/received the council"), and a little further on, the verb *recipio*.[98] There is, however, no evidence that the Pope meant this phrase in the sense of a legal ratification: his concern is rather to ensure that the king of the Franks knows that the doctrine of Nicaea II is the doctrine taught by the Catholic Church.

To sum up: while the popes, either spontaneously or at the request of others, did sometimes speak of confirmation or approval of a council that had already been held in the presence of their own legates, there is no clear evidence that either the popes themselves or others regarded such subsequent confirmation as a legal ratification necessary for such a council to have binding force in its doctrinal decrees.[99] The nearest suggestion of such a ratification is found in regard to Constantinople III, but even here neither the language of the Council nor that of the Pope strictly implies it. Moreover, the attitudes of Leo I toward Chalcedon and of Hadrian I toward Nicaea II indicate that they did not consider such a ratification necessary.

Nevertheless, it is abundantly clear from the foregoing historical survey that papal consent was an element of the first seven councils.

---

96 Mansi, 13:458C–62D.
97 Tanner and Alberigo, *Decrees of the Ecumenical Councils*, 1:132.
98 Mansi, 13:808C.
99 Forget, "Conciles," 663.

Either the popes confirmed councils that until that point lacked either validity (Constantinople II) or ecumenicity (Constantinople I), or else instruct their legates in advance so that their consent is juridically speaking the consent of the Roman pontiff (the other five councils). It matters little whether, in accordance with the usage already mentioned, we call this latter kind of consent "subsequent confirmation," or whether with *Lumen Gentium* we call it "acceptance." Moreover, it appears that such confirmation or acceptance was also generally regarded as *necessary* in order that a council should be truly ecumenical, and therefore binding in its judgments. In the case of the five councils where papal headship was exercised by way of presidence during the sessions themselves, the need for such acceptance is included in the very notion of such presidence, since a body cannot act validly without its head. In the case of Constantinople II, the persistence with which Emperor Justinian strove to gain Vigilius's acceptance of the anathemas sufficiently indicates the belief in the necessity of the Roman pontiff's consent to an ecumenical council. Finally, for Constantinople I, although the synodal fathers refer to their gathering as an ecumenical council, it does not seem that they are using the phrase in the later, technical sense. In any case, they were well aware of being in agreement with Pope Damasus and the other Western bishops in regard to faith in the Trinity.

The Roman Emperor's Role: Summary of the Evidence

This survey of the conduct of the first seven councils, along with the patristic citations from East and West, shows a consensus that the authority of the Roman emperor in regard to an ecumenical council was something extrinsic to the council strictly considered. He brought the bishops together insofar as they were a material assemblage and protected them during their deliberations but did not invest them with the right to deliberate or to judge. He promulgated their decrees but did not himself define doctrine; or if on occasion he attempted to do so, he was resisted. However necessary imperial authority was in practice at the time of the early councils, it was therefore not an essential criterion of ecumenicity. To adapt some words of Bellarmine that we shall see below, the imperial action belonged to the *well*-being of an ecumenical council, not to its being.

The Theory of the Pentarchy

In addition to the prominence given to the role of the Roman emperor, the later Byzantine account of ecumenicity relied on the famous "theory of the pentarchy." The term "pentarchy" refers to the five great sees that, from the time of the Council of Chalcedon, came to be preeminent in the Church.[100] The "pentarchic theory" was expressed in the following century in the legislation of Justinian I.[101] In the preface to *Novella ad religionem pertinentes*, the emperor defines heretics as:

> All those who are not members of the holy Catholic and apostolic church of God, in which all the holy patriarchs of the whole world, of elder Rome and of this royal city and of Alexandria and of Theopolis and of Jerusalem, and all the holy bishops who are constituted subject to them, preach the apostolic faith and tradition.[102]

The Eastern Orthodox theologian John Meyendorff speaks of "a certain 'sacralization' of the number 'five'" that began from this time.[103]

At this early period, there is no tension between the pentarchy and Roman primacy. [104] Both ideas are found in the same writers, though without an explicit account of the relation between the two. Thus,

100 Hilaire Marot, "Note sur la Pentarchie," *Irenikon* 32 (1959): 436–42, at 437.

101 Francis Dvornik, *Byzantium and the Roman Primacy* (New York: Fordham University Press, 1966), 95–96.

102 *PL*, 72:1009C–D: "Omnes qui non sunt membrum sanctae dei catholicae et apostolicae ecclesiae, in qua omnes concorditer sanctissimi [episcopi et] totius orbis terrarum patriarchae, et Hesperiae Romae et huius regiae civitatis et Alexandriae et Theopoleos et Hierosolymorum, et omnes qui sub eis constituti sunt sanctissimi episcopi apostolicam praedicant fidem atque traditionem." Theopolis is a later name for Antioch.

103 Meyendorff, "Was There an Encounter?," 155.

104 Dvornik, *Byzantium and the Roman Primacy*, 103–104.

while Justinian in his legislation consecrates the idea of the five great sees, he also addresses Pope John II (533–535) as "head of all the holy churches [caput . . . omnium sanctarum ecclesiarum]."[105] The emperor adds that he has made sure that all the Eastern clergy are united with and subject to Rome.[106] Again, according to St. Maximus the Confessor († 662), the apostolic see has primacy "from the incarnate Word of God Himself, and also from all the holy synods";[107] yet at the same time he can declare a monothelite synod invalid, since its encyclical letter was not published "by the consent of the patriarchs."[108]

The condemnation of the iconoclast synod of Hieria by Nicaea II mentions the pentarchy, but in the context of Roman primacy. The bishop of Neocaesarea asks:

> How, therefore, can a council pretend to be ecumenical that the leaders of the other churches neither received nor admitted unanimously; who, on the contrary, condemned it with anathema? A council that did not have as cooperator [συνεργόν] the Pope of the Roman Church then reigning, or, alternatively, his ecclesiastical collaborators, either by means of personal representatives or through an encyclical letter, as is statutory for councils [καθὼς νόμος ἐστι ταῖς συνόδοις]? A council that did not have the agreement of the Patriarchs of the East, of Alexandria, Antioch, and the Holy City, or of the fellow ministers and high priests who are with them?"[109]

We may note here that only the agreement of the Roman Church is declared to be *statutory* for an ecumenical council. The other sees are

105 Mansi, 8:795E.

106 Mansi, 8:795D: "Omnes sacerdotes universi orientalis tractus et subiicere et unire sedi vestrae sanctitatis properavimus."

107 St. Maximus the Confessor, Letter to the Noble Peter (Mansi, 10:692C).

108 St. Maximus the Confessor, *Disputatio cum Pyrrho* (*PG*, 91:352D). This does not necessarily mean simply the Eastern patriarchs, since elsewhere he calls the pope a patriarch (e.g., *PG*, 91:463C).

109 Mansi, 13:208E–9A.

mentioned for greater rhetorical effect, as a way of emphasising the illegitimacy of the pseudo-synod. He could not, in fact, have believed that the formal consent of all five sees was absolutely necessary; he cannot, for example, have been ignorant that Alexandria had refused its consent at the Council of Chalcedon.[110] Moreover, it had not even been possible to notify those Eastern patriarchs under Islamic dominion of the convocation of Nicaea II.[111] A letter sent to the Council from some monks and clergy of the occupied patriarchates affirmed that the absence of the patriarchs was principally compensated for, as at Constantinople III, by the fact that "the most holy and apostolic Roman pope agreed to the council and was present at it through his delegates."[112] The letter was accepted without demur.[113]

St. Theodore the Studite († 826), whom Yves Congar calls "the theorist of the pentarchy,"[114] defends Nicaea II on the grounds that it was received by the five patriarchs, whereas the iconoclast synod was condemned by four.[115]

> Who are [the Apostles'] successors? He who occupies the throne of Rome and is the first; the one who sits upon the throne of Constantinople and is the second; after them, those of Alexandria, Antioch, and Jerusalem. That is the five-headed body of the Church [τὸ πεντακόρυφον σῶμα τῆς Ἐκκλησίας]. It is to them that all decision belongs in divine dogmas.[116]

---

110 The same must be said of St. John Damascene, when, condemning the same pseudo-synod for lacking the consent of four of the patriarchs, he writes, "if even one [patriarch] is absent or does not submit himself to the synod, it is no synod but a perverse assembly" (*Adversus Constantinum Cabalinum* [*PG*, 95:332D]).

111 G. Fritz, "Nicée, Deuxième Concile de," in *DTC*, 11/1:417–41, at col. 418. See the subsection "The First Seven Ecumenical Councils" under "Universality" in ch. 19.

112 Mansi, 12:1133E: "Nullum ex hoc sanctae adhaesit synodo praeiudicium . . . praecipue cum sanctissimus et apostolicus papa romanus concordaverit et in ea inventus sit per apocrisarios suos."

113 Fritz, "Nicée, Deuxième Concile de," 422. This fact shows how erroneous Richard R. Gaillardetz's claim is that Nicaea II defined that the actual consent of the five patriarchs was necessary for ecumenicity (Richard R. Gaillardetz, *Teaching with Authority: A Theology of the Magisterium in the Church*, Theology and Life Series 41 [Collegeville, MN: Liturgical, 1997]).

114 Yves Congar, "1274–1974: Structures ecclésiales et conciles dans les relations entre Orient et Occident," *Revue des sciences philosophiques et theologiques* 58 (1974): 355–90, at 372–74.

115 *PG*, 99:1305B.

116 St. Theodore the Studite, Letter to Leo the Sacellarius (*PG*, 99:1417C).

Yet Theodore was also one of the most prominent defenders of Roman primacy. Writing to Pope Paschal I for help against the iconoclasts, he addresses him as "apostolic head [ἀποστολικὴ κάρα], shepherd of the sheep of Christ set up by God, door-keeper of the kingdom of heaven."[117]

St. Nicephoros of Constantinople, writing in 817 in defense of Nicaea II, after stressing the need for Roman confirmation of any conciliar decree,[118] adds that "it is the ancient law of the Church that whatever uncertainties or controversies arise in the Church of God, they are resolved and defined by the ecumenical synods, with the assent and approbation of the bishops who hold the apostolic sees."[119] With all these writers, then, the pentarchy remains clearly monarchic.

The pentarchic idea was particularly prominent at what the Catholic Church recognizes as the Fourth Council of Constantinople, in 869–870. For example, Elias, speaking on behalf of the patriarch of Jerusalem, declared that "the Holy Spirit established the patriarchal authorities [patriarchalia capita] in the world, so that scandals that might break out in the Church of God would be driven out by them."[120] Anastasius Bibliothecarius (ca. 810–879), papal aide and archivist, made the idea known in the West: in the preface to the Latin translation of the acts of the council, he mentions the famous metaphor of the five great sees as the five senses of the body, with Rome as the first and therefore representing the sense of sight.[121] We also see, however, at this Council, the beginning of a deviation from the Catholic understanding of the pentarchy in the speech of the patrician Baanes:

> God has set his Church upon the five patriarchates and confined it within the four Gospels, so that they would never wholly fail, for they are the heads of the Church. For indeed this is the meaning

---

[117] *PG*, 99:1153C.

[118] See the section "Papal Headship" in ch. 19.

[119] *PG*, 100:597C; also quoted in Dvornik, *Byzantium and the Roman Primacy*, 102. However, contrary to what Dvornik says here, Nicephoros does not state that there are *four* great Eastern sees.

[120] Mansi, 16:35A.

[121] Mansi, 16:7D.

> of what was said, "and the gates of hell will not prevail against it." When two have fallen, they run to the three; when three have fallen they run to the two; and should four ever fall, let the one which remains in Christ our God, the Head of all, call back the rest of the body of the Church.[122]

Here the Catholic, monarchic understanding of the pentarchy, has begun to give way to an oligarchic understanding, with no one see having a fixed primacy. Likewise, the pentarchy is presented as being in effect an institution of divine law.[123]

Later Developments of the Pentarchic Idea in the East

The Catholic understanding of the pentarchy became further obscured in the East in the course of the tenth and eleventh centuries.[124] By the middle of the eleventh century, Peter, bishop of Antioch, explicitly puts the five sees on the same level, and hence denies the universal jurisdiction of the pope.[125] By the twelfth and thirteenth centuries, the idea of the Pentarchy had become "an anti-papal weapon."[126] The earlier monarchic pentarchy either becomes a pure oligarchy, or even, with an anti-Latin polemicist such as Nicetas Seides in the twelfth century, has Constantinople at its head and Rome in third place.[127] At the start of the thirteenth century, John X Camateros, patriarch of Constantinople (r. 1198–1206), writes to Innocent III that just as none of the five senses of the body commands any of the others, so do none of the five great churches command another.[128] Though it may be acknowledged that the pentarchy is not apostolic, it has come to be considered as virtually pertaining to divine

122 Mansi, 16:140E–41A.
123 Martin Jugie, "Constantinople IV," in *DTC*, 3:1273–307, at col. 1294.
124 Jugie, *Theologia Dogmatica*, 4:453.
125 Martin Jugie, *Le schisme Byzantin: aperçu historique et doctrinal* (Paris: Lethielleux, 1941), 222, 232.
126 Dvornik, *Byzantium and the Roman Primacy*, 119.
127 Jugie, *Theologia Dogmatica*, 4:453–54.
128 Quoted in Jugie, *Theologia Dogmatica*, 4:456–57. Innocent himself took a somewhat different view. Writing to Camateros, the Pope avers that the pentarchy had been foreshadowed in the book of the Apocalypse by the four living creatures that surround the throne (*PL*, 215:959D).

law, having been sanctioned by ecumenical councils, and being therefore immutable.[129] The oligarchic nature of the pentarchy is assumed by many Greek authors of the fourteenth and fifteenth centuries. Thus Neilos Kabasilas (ca. 1298–1373), in his *De dissidio Ecclesiarum*, writes: "Although there are five Catholic churches, one of them [Rome] contradicts the rest [Πέντε τῶν καθολικῶν Ἐκκλησίων οὐσῶν, ἡ μία ταῖς λοιπαῖς ἀντιλέγει]."[130]

Yet, despite the popularity of this oligarchic view among later writers, no one who upholds the first seven ecumenical councils can coherently maintain that the consent of the five great churches was a necessary criterion for ecumenicity. To take but one example, the Church of Alexandria, as already mentioned, refused its consent to the Council of Chalcedon. It is true that an orthodox line of patriarchs was eventually established at Alexandria to uphold Chalcedon, but another line of patriarchs denying the council claimed (and claims) to be patriarchs of the same see. One could of course insist that the former of these lines was the legitimate one, because it upheld the ecumenical councils; but in order to avoid arguing in a circle, one is obliged to find a criterion for determining what the ecumenical councils are that does not appeal to the unanimous consent of the pentarchy.

In other words, for those who uphold the early councils, the pentarchic theory cannot logically be an alternative explanation for their ecumenicity, in opposition to the papal theory. The consent of the patriarchs has never been a necessary condition for ecumenicity, though it can be a striking sign of it. Bellarmine remarks that the pentarchy belongs to the well-being and not to the being of the Church.[131]

Nevertheless, inadequate as it was as an account of ecumenicity, the pentarchic ideal exercised a powerful influence over the imagination of the Byzantine world. After the failure of the Second Council of Lyon,

129 Jugie, *Theologia Dogmatica*, 4:450.
130 *PG*, 149:696B.
131 Bellarmine, *De conciliis* 2.17.

Barlaam, a south-Italian Byzantine monk, advised the pope that "the Byzantine church will accept union only if there is open discussion in an ecumenical council at which all five patriarchs or their vicars are represented"[132] (despite the "schism" of the pope, his presence was widely deemed in Constantinople to be necessary for the constitution of such a council).[133]

Meyendorff summarizes the late mediaeval Greek opinion about ecumenicity:

> These interconnected two elements—the theoretical legitimacy of the Byzantine emperor over the West and a lingering respect for the pentarchy, of which the Roman bishop was a leading member—made it into a requirement that a properly ecumenical council include the bishop of Rome (in spite of the schism), and the four Eastern patriarchs (although three of them were now heading churches which were barely in existence at all).[134]

In the final part of the present work we shall see how the Greeks at the time of the Council of Florence made the representation of the five great sees a proof of the ecumenicity of that assembly.[135]

---

132 Quoted in Deno Geanakoplos, "A New Reading of the Acta, Especially Syropoulos," in *Christian Unity: The Council of Ferrara-Florence, 1438/39–1989*, ed. Giuseppe Alberigo, Bibliotheca Ephemeridum Theologicarum Lovaniensium 97: International Symposium on the Unity of the Christians 550 years after the Council of Ferrara-Florence, Florence, Italy, 1989 (Leuven: Leuven University Press, 1991), 325–51, at 351.

133 Jugie remarks that, between Lyon II and Florence, the primacy of the pope was not officially attacked in the Byzantine church, but rather his orthodoxy ("Primautée dans les Églises separées d'Oriente," in *DTC*, 13/1:344–91, at col. 373).

134 Meyendorff, "Was There an Encounter?," 156.

135 As is well known, the Florentine bull of union, *Laetentur Caeli*, incorporates the pentarchic idea, but in its original, monarchic form. The Dominican provincial John de Montenero, speaking to the fathers of the Council in June 1439 after the public debates had finished, criticized the "aristocratic" version of the pentarchy, remarking that he had never read in the Scriptures or the councils that the Church was founded on three or five patriarchs (*AL*, 246).

CHAPTER 21

DO ECUMENICAL COUNCILS NEED TO BE "RECEIVED"?

Introduction

SO FAR, I HAVE SET FORTH CRITERIA for ecumenicity, based on the seven councils commonly accepted by both the Catholic Church and the Orthodox Church and brought forward patristic testimonies for the belief that councils fulfilling these criteria enjoy infallibility of themselves. I must now examine the view that, on the contrary, even councils fulfilling these criteria require some further process of *reception* before they can be judged infallible.

It is evident that, as Yves Congar liked to say, "reception is something real."[1] Especially in the days before modern transport and modern means of communication, it would take a considerable time for the decisions of an ecumenical council to be made known to all whom they concerned.

[1] Yves Congar, "La 'réception' comme réalité ecclésiologique," *Revue des sciences philosophiques et théologiques* 56 (1972): 369–403.

When these decisions were of questions that had been warmly discussed in a given region, it would often take time for those who had maintained the position contrary to the conciliar doctrines either to come to a wholehearted acceptance of them, or else to separate themselves openly from the Church that taught them. Such great turmoil and confusion might thus follow a council that its doctrine would need to be repeated a generation or two later, as the First Council of Nicaea's teaching was confirmed by First Council of Constantinople; and it might thus appear to men at the time, especially to the more superficial observers, as if it were the later council that enjoyed the greater authority, because it had the greater success. Or again, a pope might have a reason for not expressly declaring a council ecumenical, while nevertheless showing by his behavior that he considered it binding, as Hadrian II in regard to the Second Council of Nicaea; it might be only much later that one of his successors judged it opportune to assert the ecumenical status of the council—thus it was only in a letter from the pope to Peter of Antioch in 1053 that Rome explicitly declared Nicaea II ecumenical. These considerations show that the historian can rightly speak of "the reception of ecumenical councils." But history and theology are distinct disciplines; our question is whether, once an ecumenical council has defined a point of doctrine, some *further* authority is needed to render this decree binding for all time.

John Calvin on Conciliar Authority

Those bodies that separated themselves from the Catholic Church in the course of the first millennium naturally denied the binding character of the ecumenical councils that condemned their teaching. Yet we do not find, on the part of these early heretics, an explicit rejection of the principle that ecumenical councils have sufficient authority of themselves. Rather, they alleged some irregularity in the assemblies that condemned them, which deprived these assemblies of ecumenicity. With the Protestant Reformers, by contrast, and as a necessary consequence of the elevation of the Christian's private judgment above any authority exercised by men on earth, we do find an explicit denial of the infallibility of any ecclesial assembly, howsoever constituted. John Calvin, their most systematic thinker, expressed himself as follows:

> Whenever a decree of any council is brought forward, I should like men first of all diligently to ponder at what time it was held, on what issue and with what intention, what sort of men were present; then to examine by the standard of Scripture what it dealt with—and to do this in such a way that the definition of the council may have its weight and be like a provisional judgment, yet not hinder the examination which I have mentioned. . . . No names of councils, pastors, bishops (which can either be falsely pretended or truly used) can prevent our being taught by the evidence of words and things to test all spirits of all men by the standard of God's Word in order to determine whether or not they are from God.[2]

Testing Nicaea II by the standard of "God's Word," Calvin rejects it for "perverting and mangling the whole of Scripture."[3] That other apostle of Geneva, St. Francis de Sales, replies with characteristic common sense:

> The Councils, after the fullest consultation, when the test has been made by the touchstone of the Word of God, decide and define some article. If after all this another test has to be tried before their determination is received, will not another also be wanted? Who will not want to apply his test, and whenever will the matter be settled?[4]

---

2 John Calvin, *Institutes of the Christian Religion* 4.9, ed. John T. McNeill (Philadelphia: Westminster, 1960), 8, 12.

3 Calvin, *Institutes of the Christian Religion* 4.9.

4 Francis de Sales, *The Catholic Controversy* 2.4.3, trans. Henry Mackey (London: Burns & Oates, 1909).

The Oxford Movement and the Authority of Councils

The members of the Oxford Movement in the nineteenth-century Anglican Church, sought a *via media* between Protestantism and Popery. They wished to defend the binding authority of at least the first six councils without being obliged to admit either the plenary authority of the pope or the Calvinist right of private judgment. They were constrained by the twenty-first of the "Thirty-nine Articles" to which Anglican clergy were obliged to subscribe, which had been composed during the Council of Trent. This article stated:

> General Councils may not be gathered together without the commandment and will of Princes. And when they be gathered together, (forasmuch as they be an assembly of men, whereof all be not governed with the Spirit and Word of God,) they may err, and sometimes have erred, even in things pertaining unto God.

Edward Pusey, in his 1839 *Letter to Richard, Lord Bishop of Oxford*, explained his position in these terms: "We believe that (although Councils, which have been termed 'General,' or which Rome has claimed to be so, have erred,) no real Oecumenical Council ever did; i.e. no Council really representing the Universal Church."[5] Pusey sought to distinguish his position from the Roman one by affirming that the bishops assembled in council act as witnesses and not as judges, and that their task is not to select from competing opinions that one they believe to be correct, but to give witness to the universal belief of the Church.[6] He claimed to distinguish his position from the Protestant one by affirming that just as the Church as a whole is not a judge but a witness to faith, so the same is true also of the individual believer.

---

5 Edward Pusey, *A Letter to Richard, Lord Bishop of Oxford, on the Tendency to Romanism Imputed to Doctrines Held of Old, as Now, in the English Church* [1840] (n.p.: General Books, 2010), 44.

6 Pusey, *Letter to Richard*, 38–40.

Although Pusey does not explicitly say so, it is clear that the sign of whether the bishops have done their task correctly, and therefore of whether the council was not merely general but ecumenical, will be the universal consent of the Church to their decisions. Naturally, so learned a man was not under the impression that there had been from the early councils no dissenters among the baptized, but he argues that just as one does not take into account "monsters" when seeking to know the nature of the human body, so one does not need to take into account "a few heretics" when seeking to know the nature of the Christian faith. On this principle he vindicates the first six councils, while holding that Nicaea II was invalidated by its rejection by the Council of Frankfurt. He further adds that since Christ's promise was made to the Church as one, it is not possible at present to hold any general council, since the Church is no longer one.[7]

John Henry Newman, in his Anglican days, commented on the same article in *Tract 90*, the last of the series of "Tracts for the Times."[8] He attempted the same distinction as Pusey between general and ecumenical councils: "While Councils are a thing of earth, their infallibility is of course not guaranteed; when they are a thing of heaven, their deliberations are overruled, and their decrees authoritative." An ecumenical council, he explains, is a general council that is gathered in the name of Christ. Having reached this crucial point, he refuses to go further:

> What those conditions are, which fulfil the notion of a gathering "in the Name of CHRIST," ... it is not necessary here to determine. Some have included among these conditions, the subsequent reception of its decrees by the universal Church; others, a ratification by the Pope.

---

7 Pusey, *Letter to Richard*, 42–44.

8 John Henry Newman, *Tract 90* [1841] (n.p.: Ulan Press, 2012).

The only criterion that Newman asserts here is that "in points necessary to salvation, a Council should prove its decrees by Scripture." John Calvin would have been content with this, despite the Oxford Movement's wish to avoid Protestantism.

Those Anglican theologians who continued the tradition of Pusey and Newman in a more systematic fashion hardly got beyond their masters, and in some cases withdrew from the positions that these had maintained. The author of one standard manual writes as follows:

> The question remains, How is it to be known whether a Council is truly "General," and representative of the mind of the whole Church? To this it is believed that no answer can be returned at the moment [i.e. at the time of the council itself]. However large may be the number of the bishops present no guarantee is thereby afforded that they faithfully represent the mind of the universal Church. That which alone can show this is the after-reception of the decisions of the Council by the different parts of the Church. When the decisions win their way to universal acceptance, there we have the needful guarantee that the Council has faithfully reflected the mind of the universal Church, and we may well be content to believe that the Council has not erred.[9]

Yet, in the last resort, just as for Calvin, it is the individual believer who will judge the judgment of any council: "While he will rightly and naturally give the greatest weight to the judgement thus expressed, feeling that it is far more probable that he should be mistaken than that the whole Church should be wrong, yet in the last resort he himself must be judge."[10]

---

9 Edgar C. S. Gibson, *The Thirty-Nine Articles of the Church of England*, 3rd ed. (London: Methuen, 1902), 536.

10 Gibson, *Thirty-Nine Articles*, 525.

The Beginnings of the "Theory of Reception" in the Orthodox Church

Martin Jugie, writing in the first half of the twentieth century, was able to state that the common teaching of what he referred to as the "Greco-Russian Church" was that the body of bishops, at least when gathered in council, are the proper subject of active infallibility. This means that anything defined by an ecumenical council may be known to be certainly true—from the moment it is defined by the council itself. This is the thesis found in classic statements of belief, such as the "Confessions" of Peter Mogilas and of Dositheus.[11] It is also found in standard theological manuals still in use in the twentieth century, for example, that of Macarius Bulgakov.[12]

Nevertheless, Martin Jugie added, a contrary thesis was daily gaining ground according to which the whole body of the Church is the subject of active infallibility, with the bishops simply the legates of the body. This position was set forth by the Orthodox theologian Theophylact Gorski in a treatise of 1818. Gorski affirms here that "in councils, doctors and delegates of the Church are assembled, to whom the power of knowing and judging about the public interpretation of doctrine has been entrusted by the whole communion of believers."[13]

Similar ideas were being put forward in France later in the same century by the Russian exile Alexei Khomiakov.[14] Having mentioned certain Arianizing councils from the fourth century, he writes:

---

[11] Peter Moghila, *La Confession Orthodoxe de Pierre Moghila*, trans. A. Malvy and M. Viller, *Orientalia Christiana* 10, no. 39 (Rome: Pontificium Institutum Orientalium Studiorum, 1927), 50. Moghila († 1647) was metropolitan of Kiev, and his Confession was accepted by the patriarchs and the synod of Jerusalem in 1672. Dositheus was patriarch of Jerusalem from 1669 to 1702, and his Confession (to be found in *Conciliorum Collectio Regia Maxima*, ed. Jean Hardouin, vol. 11 [Paris, 1714]) was also accepted by the synod of 1672. It states that the bishop preserves the faithful from heresy (241D), and even more strikingly, that Christ "does not illuminate the Church herself immediately [οὐκ ἀμέσως] by the teaching of the Holy Spirit but through the holy fathers and through those set over the Catholic Church" (245B).

[12] Martin Jugie, *Theologia Dogmatica Christianorum Orientalium ab Ecclesia Catholica Dissidentium*, 5 vols. (Paris: Letouzey et Ané, 1926–1935), 4:485.

[13] Jugie, *Theologia Dogmatica*, 4:487.

[14] Alexei Khomiakov, *L'Eglise Latine et le Protestantisme au point de vue de l'Eglise d'Orient* (Lausanne: Benda, 1872). He rejects the theory of papal confirmation, holding that Liberius confirmed the Council of Ariminum.

> How does it come about that these councils have been rejected, even though they show no obvious difference from the ecumenical councils? It is because their decisions have not been recognized as the voice of the Church by "the whole ecclesiastical people," this people in which, for questions of faith, there is no difference between the learned and the ignorant, between the ecclesiastic and the lay man.[15]

Congar summarizes Khomiakov's position in two propositions: truth, not a council, has binding authority; the organ of truth is the Christian sense of the community of believers.[16]

The latter thesis was also intimated in the encyclical letter that the Orthodox patriarchs of Constantinople, Alexandria, Antioch, and Jerusalem published in 1848 in response to the letter *In Suprema Petri Apostoli Sede* of Pope Pius IX. Asserting the impossibility that Western errors should have entered also into the East, the patriarchs write:

> Neither Patriarchs nor Councils could then have introduced novelties amongst us, because the protector of religion is the very body of the Church, even the people themselves [διότι ὁ ὑπερασπιστὴς τῆς θρησκείας ἐστιν αὐτὸ τὸ σῶμα τῆς ἐκκλησίας, ἤτοι αὐτὸς ὁ λαός], who desire their religious worship to be ever unchanged and of the same kind as that of their fathers, . . . as, after the Schism, many of the Popes and Latinizing Patriarchs made attempts that came to nothing even in the Western Church.[17]

The implication is that an ecumenical council, even when duly constituted, has no guarantee of infallibility; it is the body of the Church as a whole that will prevent heresy from prevailing. The reference to

15 Khomiakov, *L'Eglise Latine et le Protestantisme*, 62.

16 Congar, "La 'réception,'" 377.

17 Patriarchs of the Eastern Churches, "Encyclical of the Eastern Patriarchs, 1848: A Reply to the Epistle of Pope Pius IX, 'to the Easterns,'" no. 17, Orthodox Christian Information Center, orthodoxinfo.com/ecumenism/encyc_1848.aspx.

Latinizing patriarchs living after the schism suggests that the encyclical envisages in particular the Councils of Lyon II and of Florence. The four patriarchs do not develop their theory in detail; it remains obscure, for example, whether the "body" of the Church is to be understood here as the laity or as all the baptized.

The Theory of Reception among Later Orthodox Theologians

These ideas exerted a great influence on subsequent Orthodox (especially Slavic) theology.[18] In the early twentieth century, Sergei Bulgakov, without denying the traditional teaching that an ecumenical council was the highest authority in the Church, wrote that such a council "acquires the authority of infallibility [only] as a consequence of its agreement with the self-consciousness of the Church."[19] In other words, "dogmas possess force in that degree in which they are received by the Church."[20] Unfortunately, "it is impossible to indicate where and when the acceptance is accomplished."[21]

According to John Meyendorff, Khomiakov "was eventually recognized very widely—especially his teaching about *sobonorst*—as an authentic voice of the Orthodox tradition."[22] He summarizes Khomiakov's position as the view that "in Orthodoxy, the responsible guardian of the true faith is not any visible head or institutions, but the 'people of God,' i.e. the whole church, including clergy and laity."[23] He explains (somewhat obscurely) that on this view, truth is made available

---

18 Francis Sullivan states that the Khomiakovian thesis introduced a division into Orthodox thought that has remained ever since (*Magisterium: Teaching Authority in the Catholic Church* [New York: Paulist, 1983], 88). Congar notes that Orthodox theologians opposed to the "slavophile" thesis often hold that the content of a council's doctrinal decrees, and not their reception, ensures the council's authenticity ("La 'réception,'" 377–78). In practice this apparently comes to the same thing: who is to judge of the content of the decrees if not the members of the Church? He lists Orthodox theologians opposed to Khomiakov in his "Conclusion" in *Le concile et les conciles: contributions à l'histoire de la vie conciliaire de l'Église*, ed. Bernard Botte, Yves Congar, et al. (Paris: Chevetogne, 1960), 288.

19 Sergei Bulgakov, "Is Orthodoxy Infallible?" (1926), *Eastern Christian Journal* 7, no. 1 (2000): 73–86, at 84.

20 Bulgakov, "Is Orthodoxy Infallible?," 86.

21 Bulgakov, "Is Orthodoxy Infallible?," 86.

22 John Meyendorff, *Rome, Constantinople, Moscow: Historical and Theological Studies* (Crestwood, NY: St. Vladimir's Seminary Press, 1996), 186. *Sobonorst* is a word of Russian origin meaning "communion" or "gathered unity." It is often translated as "conciliarity."

23 Meyendorff, *Rome, Constantinople, Moscow*, 186.

not by infallible institutions, but by "an experience always available in the communion of the Church—this communion being understood, of course, both as faithfulness to tradition and openness to the *consensus fidelium* today."[24]

Although Meyendorff accords a privileged role to the ecumenical council, such a council is, as it was for Pusey, a witness rather than a judge:

> There does not exist . . . any visible criterion of Truth, apart from the *consensus* of the Church, the normal organ of which is the ecumenical council. But this council, as we have seen, is not an authority *ex sese* outside and above the local churches; it is merely the expression and witness of their accord.[25]

While at times he wishes to maintain the tradition of the infallibility of ecumenical councils, Meyendorff nevertheless explains it in a way that makes it in practice dependent upon the council's reception:

> It would be wrong to see an opposition between this idea of "reception" and that of the infallibility of the councils, as is sometimes done. An ecumenical council truly representative of Christ will certainly be inspired by the Holy Spirit and will therefore be infallible. However it belongs to the Spirit and to the Church guided by him to judge whether a gathering which declares itself or is declared to be ecumenical is actually so or not. The Council is not an organ external to the body of the Church. The Church's infallibility is ultimately always the infallibility of

24 John Meyendorff, "What Is an Ecumenical Council?," *St. Vladimir's Theological Quarterly* 17 (1973): 259–73, at 270.

25 John Meyendorff, *Orthodox Church: Its Past and Its Role in the World Today*, trans. J. Chapin, 3rd rev. ed. (Crestwood, NY: St. Vladimir's Seminary Press, 1981), 194. The expression *ex sese*—"of itself"—is perhaps borrowed from the definition of papal infallibility made at the First Vatican Council.

> the Spirit of Truth alone, who resides in the whole organism of the Church.[26]

Elsewhere he has, with more logical consistency, suggested abandoning the idea of "the infallibility of ecumenical councils," stating that the idea prevents the assembling of such a council, since we are conscious that we cannot act infallibly.[27]

Metropoitan John Zizioulas also accepts the theory of reception: "No decision of a council is authoritative in itself unless it is *received* by the communities."[28] The consequence is that no council can be known to be a true council except with hindsight: "A true council becomes such only *a posteriori*; it is not an institution but an *event* in which the entire community participates and which shows whether or not its bishop has acted according to his *charisma veritatis*."[29]

Damaskinos Papandreou, writing about the Council of Florence, endorses the same principles. During the process of reception of conciliar decisions, he informs us, "the ecclesial body has the right and the duty to determine whether they express the spiritual experience of this body in an authentic manner." He adds that this was the common practice during the time of the first seven councils.[30]

Nicolai Afanasiev, while also subscribing to the same theory, frankly admits its difficulty.[31] How is one to know whether a doctrine has been received or not? He answers that the question is insoluble if one begins from what he calls a "universal ecclesiology," meaning by considering

---

[26] Meyendorff, *Orthodox Church*, 26.

[27] Meyendorff, "What Is an Ecumenical Council?," 270.

[28] John Zizioulas, *Being as Communion: Studies in Personhood and the Church*, Contemporary Greek Theologians 4 (Crestwood, NY: St. Vladimir's Seminary Press, 1985), 241.

[29] Zizioulas, *Being as Communion*, 242.

[30] Damaskinos Papandreou, "Via Synodica," in *Christian Unity: The Council of Ferrara-Florence, 1438/39–1989*, ed. Giuseppe Alberigo, Bibliotheca Ephemeridum Theologicarum Lovaniensium 97: International Symposium on the Unity of the Christians 550 years after the Council of Ferrara-Florence, Florence, Italy, 1989 (Leuven: Leuven University Press, 1991), 353–73, at 386. It is interesting to speculate what St. Leo the Great would have said to a man asserting his right not to assent to the *Tome* until he had investigated whether it corresponded to his spiritual experience.

[31] Nicolai Afanasiev, "Le concile dans a théologie orthodoxe russe," *Irenikon* 35 (1962): 316–39.

the Church in its universality. Reception should rather be understood in the perspective of a "Eucharistic ecclesiology," starting from the local church. It simply means one local church receiving the decisions of another.[32]

Bishop Hilarion of Voloklamsk has more recently developed the theory of reception in an even more radical way, denying a common Orthodox thesis:

> *The Ecumenical Council should not be regarded as the highest authority in the Church.* During the three centuries which preceded the first Ecumenical Council (325) the Church did not have Ecumenical Councils. Furthermore, since the seventh Ecumenical Council (787) the Orthodox Church has existed without Ecumenical Councils.[33]

Bishop Hilarion affirms that "the decisions of Ecumenical Councils were not binding to the Churches until approved by their own local Councils" and that "the reception of an Ecumenical Council presupposed not only the official promulgation of its teaching by Church authorities but also its acceptance by theologians, monks, and lay persons."[34] Apparently, for this author, the full reception of a council does not refer to its acceptance only by the members of the Orthodox churches, for he remarks that the Council of Chalcedon has still not been completely received.[35] It is true that he at times gives the impression that an ecumenical council has its authority *ex sese*, for he writes, "all members of the Universal Church of Christ must accept the essence of the dogma of the ecumenical Councils," though adding that "alternative understandings" of the "verbal formulae" of a council are

---

32 Afanasiev, "Le concile," 338.

33 Hilarion Alfeyev (archbishop of Voloklamsk/Podolsk), "The Reception of the Ecumenical Councils in the Early Church," *St. Vladimir's Theological Quarterly* 47 (2003): 413–30, at 413 (italics original).

34 Alfeyev, "Reception of the Ecumenical Councils," 414, 416.

35 Alfeyev, "Reception of the Ecumenical Councils," 421.

legitimate.[36] Yet at other times he apparently denies that any council can by itself have such a claim on the assent of the faithful: while acknowledging that the Council of Florence "had all the characteristic traits of an Ecumenical Council, and was the most representative, as far as its attendance is concerned, in the entire history of Christianity," he describes its later rejection by local churches without appearing to see anything illegitimate in this rejection.[37] Elsewhere he has written that "no outward attribute, as the history of the Church can attest, can guarantee the unimpeded realization of conciliarity."[38]

Critique of the Theory of Reception

It is not difficult to see that, as Jugie remarks, the theory of reception obliterates the distinction between the "Church teaching" and the "Church taught."[39] If the judgment of the universal episcopate is insufficient by itself to determine Christian truth without the consent of the faithful, then the bishops no longer enjoy, as St. Irenaeus supposed, the *charisma veritatis*. It also destroys the visibility of the Church, making it impossible for a Christian living at any given time to know what the Church teaches and what he ought to believe. Why, for example, should a Christian living in the year 650 have eschewed Nestorianism? The supporters of the theory of reception would perhaps reply that the decisions of the Council of Ephesus, at least as explained in the formula of union agreed between Cyril of Alexandria and John of Antioch, and as further explained in the Councils of Chalcedon and Constantinople II, had been received throughout the Church. Yet—contrary to Pusey's rhetoric about there being no need to pay attention to a few heretics—a large Nestorian body existed outside the confines of the Roman empire,

36 Alfeyev, "Reception of the Ecumenical Councils," 423.

37 Alfeyev, "Reception of the Ecumenical Councils," 421–23.

38 Hilarion Alfeyev, *Orthodox Christianity*, trans. Basil Bush, vol. 1 (Yonkers, NY: St. Vladimir's Seminary Press, 2011), 433–34.

39 Jugie, *Theologia Dogmatica*, 4:489.

sending missionaries and establishing a hierarchy as far east as China itself.[40] Why did their rejection of Ephesus and subsequent councils carry no weight? Someone might answer: because they were outside the Church, having rejected the true faith. But how could one ascertain that they had rejected the true faith? The supporters of the theory of reception could answer only that the proof that the Nestorians had rejected the true faith was that they had not accepted Ephesus and later councils. In other words, the argument is perfectly circular: in order to determine whether a council has been sufficiently received, and therefore is a true council, one must apply a test that supposes that one already knows independently which the true councils are. And if one does not know which the true councils are independently of their reception, it will never be possible to find out, unless perhaps all the baptized were ever to agree to the decrees of a council.

When Afanasiev, on the other hand, explains that "reception" simply means one local Church accepting the decisions of another, he at least describes something that is empirically recognizable; but it does not give us what we need, which is a criterion to decide whether a given council has taught the truth. The church of Rome and the church of Alexandria recognized each other's decisions at Ephesus, while the church of Antioch did not; Afanasiev's account of reception gives us no means to draw any theological conclusion from these historical facts. Perhaps he intends us to understand that all local churches must receive a decision before it can be known to be certainly true, but in that case, with the possible exception of Nicaea I, there is no council

---

[40] John Henry Newman had already urged this point to those whom he left behind in the Oxford Movement: "Driven by the Roman power over the boundaries of the Empire, it [the Nestorian Church] placed itself, as early as the fifth century, under the protection of Persia, and laid the foundations of a schismatical communion, the most wonderful that the world has seen. It propagated itself, both among Christians and pagans, from Cyprus to China; it was the Christianity of Bactrians, Huns, Medes, and Indians, of the coast of Malabar and Ceylon on the south, and of Tartary on the north. This ecclesiastical dominion lasted for eight centuries and more, into the depth of the middle ages—beyond the Pontificate of Innocent III" (*Certain Difficulties Felt by Anglicans in Catholic Teaching* [London: Longman and Green, 1908], 345–46). See also M. Costelloe, "Nestorian Church," in *New Catholic Encyclopedia* (Washington, DC: Catholic University of America Press, 1967), 343–47.

that can be relied upon. Bishop Hilarion indeed seems to accept this conclusion, in that for him Chalcedon has not yet been fully received. But it is hardly necessary to say how far this position is from the tradition of the Orthodox Church. Nor is it necessary to say how far the theory of reception is from the confidence with which the ecumenical councils themselves have defined their doctrines and anathematised their opponents.[41]

Finally, it is sometimes suggested that "reception" is merely an external criterion of ecumenicity, that an ecumenical council has binding authority of itself but the assent of the faithful is the means to discern that a given council was in fact ecumenical.[42] Evidently this position logically collapses into the former one; no council will in practice be binding unless it has already been received.[43]

Yves Congar

In his earlier writing, Congar frankly acknowledged that the first seven councils in no way supposed that their teaching needed to be received for it to be authoritative.[44] Later, though, he sought to find a greater place for the concept of reception. Congar defines reception as "the process by which an ecclesial body makes its own a determination that it had not given to itself, recognizing that the measure that was promulgated is a rule that belongs to its own life."[45] It is not, he says, the same as simple obedience, since the ecclesial body that "receives" a teaching must give "its own contribution of agreement [un apport

---

41 Not without reason does Bernard de Margerie speak of the "slavophile thesis" as a "myth"—an idea that derives its power from an appeal to the imagination and not to the reason ("L'analogie dans l'oecumenicité des conciles: notion clef pour l'avenir de l'oecuménisme," *Revue thomiste* 84 [1984]: 425–46, at 442n67).

42 For the thought of C. Androutsos, see Jugie, *Theologia Dogmatica*, 4:513, and Frank Gavin, *Some Aspects of Contemporary Greek Orthodox Thought*, 2nd ed. (London: Morehouse, 1936), 257. The same idea seems to be implied by George Bebis in "Tradition in the Orthodox Church," in *A Companion to the Greek Orthodox Church*, ed. Fotios Litsas (New York: Greek Orthodox Diocese of North and South America, 1984).

43 See below, under the section "Other Catholic Authors," for the discussion of this theory in connection with the writing of Francis Sullivan.

44 Yves Congar, "Conclusion," in Botte, Congar et al., *Le concile et les conciles*, 289.

45 Congar, "La 'réception,'" 370.

propre de consentement] and possibly of judgment," showing proof of its own spiritual vitality. At the same time, he maintains that "reception does not confer legitimacy upon a conciliar decision or on an authentic decree; these possess their legitimacy and their obligatory force from the authorities that enact them."[46]

What happens if an authentic conciliar decree is not "received"? Congar argues that, in this case, the teaching is shown not to be false, but rather inopportune: "It awakens no vital energies [aucune force de vie], and therefore does not contribute to edification."[47] This remark, while perhaps naïve (has any conciliar definition ever been received by everyone?) seems in itself doctrinally unobjectionable. We may say the same of his summarizing statement:

> Reception does not create the right to make a decision, since the authority possesses this right, but it declares that the Church recognises her good in the decision that has been made, and thus reception brings this decision to its fulfilment as far as its efficacy is concerned [elle achève celle-ci dans la ligne de son efficacité].[48]

More problematic are some remarks that he quotes, with apparent approval, from Paul Hinschius, a German scholar in the late nineteenth century:

> Reception is not an act that creates validity. . . . It only declares that the decisions were valid from the beginning; non-reception, on the other hand, does not interfere with perfect (juridical) validity, but rather it notes that the decisions suffered from nullity

46 Congar, "La 'réception,'" 396–97: "La réception ne confère pas leur légitimité à une décision conciliaire ou à un décret authentique: ceux-ci tiennent leur légitimité et leur valeur d'obligation des autorités qui les ont portés."

47 Congar, "La 'réception,'" 399.

48 Congar, "La 'réception,'" 403.

> since their formation [elle constate bien plutôt que les décisions ont ete frappé de nullité dès leur formation].[49]

This apparently means that a council can be juridically valid and yet still produce decrees that are somehow "null," and that the sign that this has occurred will be that the decrees are not received by those to whom they were directed. It seems that Congar wishes here to accept that a true council does indeed have its authority *ex sese* and yet to make of reception the decisive empirical criterion by which a council may be known to be true.[50] In practice it seems impossible to distinguish this view from the frankly Protestant view that each believer must test the decrees of a council against the touchstone of God's Word before submitting himself to them.

Congar's view, in other words, like the views of the Orthodox writers already discussed, appears to reverse the proper order of infallibility in teaching and infallibility in believing, as if the existence of infallible teaching can be known only through the infallible assent of the faithful. He writes, obscurely:

> The unanimity that the councils seek . . . does not express the numerical total, more or less perfect, of individual voices, but the totality as such of the Church's memory. This is the meaning of the expression "ego consensi et subscripsi": I have entered into the consensus that which has come to light [qui s'est dégagé] and by which has been manifested what the Church believes.[51]

This is reminiscent of Pusey's and Meyendorff's claim that the bishops in council are not judges but witnesses; it seems that, for Congar, their

49 Congar, "La 'réception,'" 398–99.

50 Congar writes both that reception is the true criterion for ecumenicity, and that the councils were conscious of being valid of themselves and not by the consent of the Church ("Structures ecclésiales et conciles dans les relations entre Orient et Occident," *Revue des sciences philosophiques et theologiques* 58 [1974]: 355–90, at 375–376).

51 Congar, "La 'réception,'" 395–96.

task is to discern what the Church as a whole believes and to consent to this infallible "memory."

Yet logically speaking, infallibility in teaching is the basis of infallibility in believing: it is because the Church is able to teach infallibly (in councils and in other ways) that the faithful are able to believe infallibly. The bishop's task, therefore, is not simply to discern and consent to what has always been believed, for he would not thereby differ from a historian of dogma who possesses the virtue of faith; his proper task is to *teach*. Likewise, the word *consensi* does not exactly mean "I have entered into the consensus," but "I agree that this is the true doctrine"; the bishop who writes it is consenting not to a consensus but to a proposition, which he is at the same time teaching. As Heribert Schauf explains:

> Bishops are not, at least not primarily, to be regarded as representing their particular churches, which they would make present by testifying as to their faith; the bishops *themselves* united in a college are directly teachers of the faith, and not delegates or vicars of particular churches or of the whole Church.[52]

Likewise, Avery Dulles writes that "at ecumenical councils the bishop-members are present not simply as consultors but as true pastors and judges of the faith."[53]

Later still Congar wrote that, while papal approval of a council is a necessary condition for ecumenicity, "the best criterion is ultimately reception by the Church." He adds that "one cannot ignore the fact

---

52 Heribert Schauf in Carlo Passaglia, *De conciliis oecumenicis: theses Caroli Passaglia de conciliis deque habitu quo ad Romanos pontifices referuntur*, ed. Schauf (Rome: Herder, 1961), 48.

53 Avery Dulles, *Magisterium: Teacher and Guardian of the Faith* (Naples, FL: Ave Maria University Press, 2007), 50. St. Robert Bellarmine likewise insists that the bishops in council are *iudices* who carry out a *iudicium*, not simply an *inquisitio* (*De conciliis* 1.18, in *Omnia Opera* vol. 2 [Paris: Vives, 1870]). The same insistence is found in: Melchior Cano, *De Locis Theologicis* 5.5, ed. Juan Belda Plans (Madrid: Biblioteca de Autores Cristianos, 2006), 193; Joannes de Groot, *Summa Apologetica de Ecclesia Catholica ad Mentem S. Thomae Aquinatis*, 2 vols. (Regensburg: G. J. Manz, 1890), 1:13; Christian Pesch, *Praelectiones Dogmaticae*, vol. 1 (Fribourg: Herder, 1903), 285; Louis Billot, *Tractatus de Ecclesia Christi sive Continuatio Theologiae de Verbo Incarnato*, vol. 1 (Rome: Giachetti, 1909), 702; Joseph Wilhelm, "Councils, General," in *Catholic Encyclopedia* (New York: Encyclopedia Press, 1913), 423–35, at 432; Jacques Forget, "Conciles," in *DTC*, 3:647–76, at col. 665.

that one part of the church has frequently refused to accept a particular council"; yet he does not conclude explicitly that such councils were not ecumenical.[54] He seems, in the end, to have been unable to find an account of ecumenicity that would satisfy either himself or the demands of coherence.

Other Catholic Authors

More recently, other authors writing as Catholic theologians have also sought a convergence with the modern Orthodox theory of reception. Luis Bermejo, S.J., and Richard Gaillardetz frankly embrace the theory. The former insists that "this absolute necessity of universal reception as the foundation of conciliar ecumenicity is largely accepted today in the theological community by both Catholic and non-Catholic authors."[55] Speaking of the Council of Florence, he writes that its "rejection by the East killed its ecumenicity."[56] Although he wishes to attribute some kind of "binding force" to a conciliar decree even considered simply in itself, yet without such a "universal reception" we can have no certainty that a conciliar teaching was opportune or even true.[57]

For his part, speaking of the early councils, Gaillardetz writes:

> The ecumenicity that was ultimately conferred on these councils was derived not from some juridical feature of the councils themselves but from both the weighty doctrinal problems addressed by the councils and the fact that the solutions these councils provided were ultimately accepted and *received* by the whole Church.[58]

---

54 Yves Congar, *Diversity and Communion*, North American edition (Mystic, CT: Twenty-Third Publications, 1985), 93.

55 Luis M. Bermejo, S.J., *Infallibility on Trial: Church, Conciliarity and Communion* (Westminster, MD: Christian Classics, 1992), 75.

56 Bermejo, *Infallibility on Trial*, 79.

57 Bermejo, *Infallibility on Trial*, 360–62.

58 Richard Gaillardetz, *Teaching with Authority: A Theology of the Magisterium in the Church*, Theology and Life Series 41 (Collegeville, MN: Liturgical, 1997), 195.

He maintains that the principal task of an ecumenical council was to enunciate the ancient faith of the Church, and that "it fell . . . to the local Churches to determine whether a council had preserved this agreement with antiquity."[59]

Francis Sullivan offers a slightly more subtle theory. He acknowledges that an ecumenical council has the power to teach infallibly but argues that it may in practice be difficult to know whether the conditions for infallible teaching have been fulfilled. In such cases, he claims, we must look to the "reception of the defined dogma in the faith-consciousness of the Church." On this view, "subsequent reception does not confer infallibility on the act of the magisterium, but it provides infallible confirmation of the fact that an infallible definition has taken place."[60] Like the ideas of Bermejo and Gaillardetz, Sullivan's have already been criticized in relation to Orthodox authors, and we may add that Sullivan's theory would lead to chaos and would in practice make the Church's teaching authority impotent. If it can be difficult, as he claims, to know whether the conditions for ecumenicity have been realized, would it not be far more difficult to know the state of the "faith-consciousness" of more than a billion human beings? Again, how many, or what percentage, of them would have to entertain doubts about a conciliar anathema for us to infer that it had not been taught infallibly? And what of the obvious fact that the overwhelming majority of Catholics have never studied even the more doctrinally central parts of conciliar teaching, let alone, for example, the anathemas of Constantinople II against the anti-Cyrilline writings of Theodoret of Cyr, or the letter said to have been written by Ibas the Persian? While it is Catholic doctrine that there exists an "infallibility in believing," which means that no doctrine professed as divinely revealed by the whole body of the faithful can be false (see §12 of the Second Vatican

59 Gaillardetz, *Teaching with Authority*, 197.
60 Sullivan, *Magisterium*, 111.

Council's Dogmatic Constitution on the Church, *Lumen Gentium*), it cannot be necessary for a member of the Catholic faithful to enquire from all his fellow members which conciliar definitions they believed in order to find out which ones he must believe. For, they would not know which they should believe until they had in turn found out which he believed! Sullivan's suggestion is both wildly impracticable and logically incoherent.

Confirmation by Local Councils

Since we have seen both Catholic and Orthodox writers arguing, in a rather abstract way, for the right of local councils to assess the authority of ecumenical ones, it may be of interest to consider two historical cases of "confirmation" by local councils of synods that had already received the consent of the Roman pontiff. This will help us to see the meaning of confirmation and its difference from the modern "theory of reception." The first example relates to the Roman synod of 649, which had been held under Pope Martin I, against the monothelites. After the synod, the Pope wrote about it to Amandus of Utrecht, in view of a synod of bishops in France that had been called to consider the same question:

> The wicked writings of the heretics have been examined and exposed and with the apostolic sword and by the definitions of the Fathers, we have condemned them with one mouth and one spirit. . . .Wherefore we have judged it good to send to you the records of the synodal acts with this present letter together with our own encyclical. From the account that they give, you will be able to acquaint yourselves with all things in detail, and along with us, as sons of light, to extinguish their darkness. For this reason, brother, may you be zealous to make these things known to everyone, so that along with us they may execrate this abominable heresy, . . . and so that in a synodal gathering of all

> our brothers, the fellow bishops of that region, they may put together writings in accordance with the encyclical that we have sent, and send them to us with your signatures, confirming and giving their consent to the things that have been ordained by us for the orthodox faith and for destroying the cunning of the heretics that has recently arisen.[61]

Evidently, in asking the bishops to "confirm" the synodal judgment, Martin did not mean that it required such ratification in order to be binding: his language leaves no room for doubt about whether monothelitism is to be considered an error. Rather, because the synodal judgment is binding, the bishops must confirm it—that is, exercise their own magisterium in publicly rejecting it. As the nineteenth-century ecclesiologist Carlo Passaglia explained, such a local confirmation is not juridically free, but necessary—the performing of a duty and not the exercising of a right to choose between alternatives.[62] The local confirmation, the same author explains, is not done in order to give legal strength to the decree, but "so that the agreement of [those who bear] the Catholic name may shine out more notably, and by that very fact the authority of ecumenical councils may be the more striking."[63]

The second example is taken from the acts of Pope Leo II (r. 682–683). Addressing the Spanish bishops and speaking to them of the work of the Third Council of Constantinople, Leo writes in these ringing terms:

61 Mansi, 10:1186B–D: "Haereticorum scelerosa scripta examinata, atque denudata sunt, et apostolico mucrone, patrumque definitionibus, uno ore unoque spiritu condemnavimus. . . . Unde praevidimus volumina gestorum synodalium in praesenti vobis dirigere, una cum encyclica nostra. Ex quorum serie omnia subtiliter potestis addiscere et tenebras illorum nobiscum, ut filii lucis, extinguere. Idcirco studeat fraternitas tua omnibus eadem innotescere, ut tam abominandam haeresim nobiscum execrentur . . . atque synodali conventione omnium fratrum et coepiscoporum nostrorum partium illarum effecta, secundum tenorem encyclicae a nobis directae scripta una cum subscriptionibus vestris nobismet destinanda concelebrent, confirmantes atque consentientes eis quae pro orthodoxa fide et destrucione haereticorum vesaniae nuper exortae a nobis statuta sunt."

62 Passaglia, *De conciliis oecumenicis*, 28.

63 Passaglia, *De conciliis oecumenicis*, 28: "Ut consenio catholici nominis illustrius splenderet quo splendore ipsa conciliorum oecumenicorum auctoritas vehementius percelleret."

> We exhort your whole body, then, dedicated as it is to the divine service in the truth of the faith, to show great care and take pains, and to be girded with like energy out of the love and the fear of God, for the advance of the Christian religion, and for the purity of the apostolic preaching that this may be published and made known to all the prelates, priests and peoples of your province, and that the signatures of all the venerable bishops, together with yours, may be joined to the definition of the holy council, and indeed, that each bishop of the churches of Christ may hasten to write his name in the book of life, so that in the harmony of the one, evangelical, and apostolic faith, he may agree with us and with the holy, universal synod through the confession implied by his signature, as if present in spirit.[64]

Here again it is evident that the local synod is not considered by the Pope as morally or juridically free to assent to the universal synod or not to assent. Nor are the signatures of the Spanish bishops needed to make Constantinople III binding. The signatures will serve, rather, as a proof that these bishops have the faith that has already been irreformably declared in that council, and give to that council, so to say, an additional *éclat* in the minds of the Spanish faithful.

The contrary theory had been, in fact, expressly reprobated in the previous century by Pope Pelagius I. When dissatisfaction arose in the West with the decrees of Constantinople II and certain people desired to subject them to scrutiny by local synods, Pelagius informed the Patrician Valerian of the impossibility of such scrutiny:

---

64 *PL*, 96:415A–B: "Hortamur proinde vestram divinis ministeriis mancipatam in fidei veritate concordiam, ut summam sedulitatem atque operam praebeatis, paribusque laboribus accingamini pro amore atque timore Dei, Christianaeque religionis profectu, et apostolicae praedicationis puritate, ut per universos vestrae provinciae, praesules, sacerdotes et plebes, per religiosum vestrum studium innotescat, ac salubriter divulgetur, et ab omnnibus reverendis episcopis una vobiscum subscriptiones in eadem definitione venerandi concilii subnectantur, ac sit profecto in libro vitae properans unusquisque Christi ecclesiarum antistes nomen ascribere, ut in unius evangelicae atque apostolicae fidei consonantia nobiscum et cum universali sancta synodo per suae subscriptionis confessionem tamquam praesens spiritu conveniat."

> It has never been permitted, and never will be, to convoke a particular council to stand in judgment over a general council. But any time doubt is raised among some in regard to a universal council, then in order to obtain an explanation on a matter they do not understand, those who desire the salvation of their soul come to the apostolic see to obtain a clarification.[65]

Conclusion

In summary, we may say that the "theory of reception" is, in its various forms, either incoherent or unworkable, that it would in practice destroy the infallibility of the Church, and that it is not supported by the theory or practice of the age of the great councils. Laboring as it does under these disadvantages, one may wonder how it has come find such favor, especially among theologians of the Slavic Orthodox tradition. Jugie is characteristically frank. Speaking of the 1848 Letter of the Four Patriarchs, he writes:

> They were brought to this astonishing doctrine for polemical reasons, namely as a way to explain why the Greek Church rejected the Council of Florence, and did not abide by the union that had been agreed there and signed by so many prelates.[66]

To this council I now turn.

---

65 DH no. 447.

66 Jugie, *Theologia Dogmatica*, 4:488.

Part III

The Ecumenical Council of Ferrara-Florence

Part III

CHAPTER 22

THE AUTHORITY OF THE COUNCIL OF FERRARA-FLORENCE

Introduction

IN THE SECOND PART OF THIS WORK, we saw that the ecumenical nature and binding authority of a council cannot depend on a subsequent process of "reception" by the faithful, since one cannot identify who the faithful are without independently identifying the Church's definitive acts of teaching. If, as the Fathers held, there are such things as ecumenical councils endowed with power to teach infallibly, it must be possible to discern which councils are ecumenical by considering historical facts available to everyone. From the history of the seven councils accepted by Catholics and Orthodox, and taking the most stringent view of the facts, we can say that a decree is ecumenical that is promulgated by a council convoked from most of the larger provinces of the Church, from which no Catholic bishop who wished to attend had been excluded, and where a large majority of the bishops present, representing a large majority of the worldwide episcopate and a majority of the main jurisdictional divisions of the Church and including the Roman pontiff, consented to the promulgation of the decree.[1]

In this third and final part, we shall see the ecumenical character of the Council of Florence, and thus the infallibility of its definitive teachings on matters of faith. Indeed, we shall see not only that it met the criteria for ecumenicity drawn from the first seven councils but also, more generally, how it met any criteria that were offered at the time by Greek or Latin theologians. Hence, unless one wished to say that the criteria for ecumenicity were simply unknown to the Church in the fifteenth century—which in turn would imply that the Church of Christ was not a trustworthy guardian of saving truth—one must acknowledge that this Council was indeed ecumenical, and its doctrinal decrees irreformable.

The Intention of Holding an Ecumenical Council

From the beginning of the negotiations between the Greeks and the Latins that led up to the assembly at Ferrara in 1438, both sides made clear their desire for a council that would be truly ecumenical, and therefore binding, after the manner of the seven councils of the first millennium accepted by all. John VIII, already reigning as co-emperor with his father Manuel II and writing to Pope Martin V as early as 1422, was explicit:

> We say that it is necessary for all the holy patriarchs and all the bishops of our provinces to be present.... When the sacred council shall have gathered according to the ancient manner and custom of the seven holy general councils of past times, and the truth shall have been sought for without strife, then let whatever

1 See the subsection "Conclusions about Universality," under the section "Universality" in ch. 19 ("The Essence of Ecumenicity").

> shall be revealed in this holy council by the inspiration of the Holy Spirit be accepted by each side and let the furthest parts of the earth follow. In this way let there be a union of the churches that is firm and unbreakable.[2]

Patriarch Joseph II of Constantinople was equally clear. Writing to the Council of Basel in 1433, he says:

> We are writing to your Reverences, with the desire that an ecumenical council be held with all the necessary persons present, according to the ancient manner and custom; that this council should be canonical, free, inviolate, in all ways following the model of the ancient ecumenical councils; and that everything that by God's help may be unanimously and harmoniously agreed in such a council should be considered as trustworthy, without any doubt or contradiction or dispute.[3]

The Armenian Catholicos, Constantine V, showed that he also looked forward to the holding of a council that would enjoy an indefeasible authority. In an encyclical letter to Armenians in Caffa (modern-day Feodosia, in Crimea), written in July 1438 after the opening of the Council but before the arrival of his delegation, he declares: "Whatever the Holy Spirit will show to the holy synod, we shall be ready to obey."[4]

Finally, in the letters of convocation sent to the various provinces of

---

2 *ODM*, 1:4: "Dicimus esse necessitatem, omnes sanctissimos patriarchas et omnes episcopos provinciarum nostrarum interesse. . . . Conveniente sacro concilio secundum antiquum sanctorum universalium conciliorum septem praeteritorum ordinem et constitutum, et veritate sine contentione quaesita, quidquid revelatum fuerit inspirante spiritu sancto in hoc sancto concilio, utrique parti placitum sit et subsequatur etiam omnis terminus mundi. Itaque fiat universalis unio et infragalis et firma ecclesiarum." Please note: in citations from *ODM*, the first number refers to the document (rather than a volume), and the second to the page.

3 *ODM*, 3:6–7: "Vestris reverentiis scribimus, querentes fieri concilium ycumenicum sub presentia omnium personarum necessario debentium adesse secundum antiquum ordinem et consuetudinem, et tale concilium fieri canonicum, liberum, inviolatum et simpliciter secundum formas antiquorum ycumenicorum conciliorum; et illud omne, quod deo dante in tali concilio unanimiter et concorditer conclusum fuerit, hoc firmum haberi indubitanter et sine contradictione et lite quacumque."

4 *ODM*, 31:35: "Quicquid spiritus sanctus illustraverit sanctum synodum, prompti sumus ei obedire."

the Church, Pope Eugenius IV explicitly describes the council to which he bids the bishops assemble at Ferrara as *ycumenicum*.[5] Writing to the Fathers gathered at Basel, he uses what is in this context the equivalent term, *generale*.[6]

An Ecumenical Council Was Convoked and Gave Judgment

Which bishops had to be invited or summoned to the council for this intention of holding an *ecumenical* council to be fulfilled? We may consider the question either in itself or from the point of the view of the participants at Florence. If we consider the question in itself, then the answer that St. Robert Bellarmine gave 150 years later—that "the holding of the council should be made known to all the larger [maioribus] Christian provinces, and that no bishop who wished to attend must be excluded"—seems satisfactory, corresponding as it does to the practice of the early councils, even though the word *maioribus* leaves some room for interpretation.[7]

Let us now try to put ourselves into the mentality of the potential participants of a fifteenth-century council. For the Greeks of that time, as we have seen, adequate convocation would be achieved by reuniting the five patriarchs, with whatever bishops each might choose to bring. For the Latins of the same period, the answer is not so clear, since the word "ecumenical" was not used in quite the same way as it has been since the time of Bellarmine, where it refers to an assembly representing all those bishops who are clearly in communion with the pope. Thus Fantinus Vallaresso, the Latin archbishop of Crete, wrote an apologia in 1442 for the Council "at the request of "many Greeks and Latins." He makes a

5 See *EP*, I:101–105, for Eugenius's letters to the Archbishop of Canterbury, the Duke of Savoy, the German princes, the universities of France, Spain, Germany, Brabant, Poland, Italy, England, and Scotland, the Duke of Austria, and the bishops of Italy. (For *EP*, which is vol. 1 in the *CFDS* collection, the first number is for part 1 of 3, rather than a separate volume, and hence marked by Roman numeral.)

6 *EP*, I:112.

7 By "Christian" here he apparently means "Catholic," since in the same place he declares that the presence of the Eastern patriarchs is now unnecessary, "since they are heretics, or at least schismatics."

distinction between councils that are "ecumenical and universal" and those that are "general." The former are composed from "each Church"—which in the context clearly means Latin and Greek. The latter represent the whole Church through the Roman Church—by which he must have in mind, for example, the first four Lateran Councils.[8] He reckons the Council of Florence as the ninth ecumenical council in the history of the Church, while noting that the Greeks consider it the eighth.[9] However, given that Fantinus states that even those that are simply "general" nevertheless represent the whole Church, and hence can presumably teach with infallibility, both kinds of council would now be called ecumenical.[10] So, while it was perhaps necessary for both Latins and Greeks to be invited to what Latins of the fifteenth century would call an ecumenical council, it does not follow that the Latins thought it was necessary for both sides to be invited for the council to be one that post-Bellarmine usage would call ecumenical.

From a pragmatic point of view, it was of course necessary that the Greek bishops be invited to a council whose principal aim was to heal the breach between Greek and Latin Christendom. But was it necessary for the Greek bishops to be convoked in order that the council should be one that would represent the whole Church, and hence be one that would be "ecumenical" in post- Bellarminian terminology? The answer must depend on whether, or in what sense, the Greek churches were at that time in schism from the Catholic Church. For a schismatic bishop is by definition not a Catholic bishop and therefore does not have to be summoned to an ecumenical council.

---

8 Fantinus Vallaresso, *Libellus de Ordine Generalium Conciliorum et Unione Florentina*: "Universalem ecclesiam representantia per Romanam eclesiam canonice congregata" (*CFDS* vol. 2/2, ed. Emmanuel Candal). It will be seen that his terminology is not consistent, since here he uses the word *universalis* for the second kind of council. Elsewhere, also, he uses "general" and "ecumenical" as synonyms! However, his thought is consistent, even if his language is not.

9 This was the common enumeration, before Bellarmine's edition of the councils. The Greeks did not recognize Constantinople IV.

10 The same is true of the distinction that Turrecremata makes in the *Summa de Ecclesia* between councils that are *universale* and those that are *universale et plenum*, the latter kind including delegates from outside the Latin Church (see Bernard de Margerie, "L'analogie dans l'oecumenicité des conciles: notion clef pour l'avenir de l'oecuménisme," *Revue thomiste* 84 [1984]: 425–46, at 428).

The question might seem superfluous, were it not that many recent authors have suggested that even today one should not strictly speak of a schism between the Catholic and the Orthodox Church. Louis Bouyer, for example, wrote that these two bodies "remain one Church, by fact and by right, despite contrary appearances," arguing in particular from the "fruits of holiness" that appear in both communions.[11]

It is true that it is difficult to say precisely when the rift began that certainly existed at the time of the Council of Florence. Martin Jugie remarked that the schism had taken place "virtually" in many hearts and minds before the time of Cerularius.[12] Joan Hussey, speaking of the events of 1054, observes that "the Humbert–Cerularius quarrel made virtually no impact at the time on Byzantine society and gets hardly a mention in contemporary writings."[13] For Jugie, these events were rather a failed attempt at reunion than the start of a definitive schism. In 1089 Emperor Alexis Komnenos ordered that the pope's name be restored to the diptychs. The patriarchal synod, being unable to find an official condemnation of the Roman Church in its archives, agreed "by economy" to restore it.[14] It is unknown how long the pope's name remained there, though the hostility shown in Constantinople toward the archbishop of Milan in 1113 suggests that it may already have been removed.[15]

Hussey, again, maintains that, although antagonism and polemic had built up in the ecclesiastical and political field during the twelfth century,

---

11 Louis Bouyer, *The Church of God, Body of Christ and Temple of the Spirit* (Chicago: Franciscan Herald, 1982), 512.

12 Martin Jugie, "Schisme Byzantin," in *DTC*, 14/1:1312–468, at col. 1358. Michael Cerularius was patriarch of Constantinople at the time of the mutual excommunications in 1054.

13 Joan Hussey, *The Orthodox Church in the Byzantine Empire*, Oxford History of the Christian Church (Oxford: Oxford University Press, 2010), 136. Already in 1959, Yves Congar could describe it as a "rather generally accepted thesis" that the events of 1054 were not the start of the schism (Yves Congar, *After Nine Hundred Years: The Background of the Schism between the Eastern and Western Churches* [New York: Fordham University Press, 1959], 1).

14 Martin Jugie, *Le schisme Byzantin: aperçu historique et doctrinal* (Paris: Lethielleux, 1941), 230, 247.

15 Jugie, "Schisme Byzantin," 1370. For Francis Dvornik, "the first signs of schism" are visible with the installation of a Latin patriarch in Antioch in 1100 (*Byzantium and the Roman Primacy* [New York: Fordham University Press, 1966], 143).

"Greeks and Latins were not yet in schism, [and] they did not normally regard each other as heretics," and holds that the sack of Constantinople in 1204 was when the real schism occurred.[16] Yet this is more a sociological than a properly theological perspective; at any rate, it does not correspond to the judgments of the contemporary Roman Pontiffs. Thus, Pope Pascal II writing to the Byzantine emperor in 1112 speaks of the need "to restore the unity of the Catholic Church," adding that "many years ago now the prelates of the royal city, with their clergy, heedlessly withdrew from the obedience and charity of the Roman church."[17] The English pope, Adrian IV, writing to the archbishop of Thessalonika in 1155, speaks of a *schisma*.[18] Innocent III, writing to the patriarch of Constantinople before the end of the twelfth century, declares that the Greek people "have fashioned for themselves another Church—if indeed that can be called a church which is other than the only one—and they have withdrawn from the unity of the apostolic see."[19]

Yves Congar observes that the authors of the time are inconsistent in their speech, sometimes speaking as if the Church existed in both West and East, sometimes calling each other heretics.[20] For example, Theodore Balsamon, the noted canon lawyer, wrote to the patriarch of Alexandria in the late twelfth century: "No Latin should be communicated unless he first declares that he will abstain from the doctrines and customs that separate us and that he will be subject to the canons of the Church in union with the orthodox."[21] Yet Balsamon was much criti-

---

16 Hussey, *The Orthodox Church*, 136, 182–83.

17 Pope Pascal II, Letter to the Byzantine Emperor: "Ex multis iam annorum curriculis adeo civitatis regiae praesules cum clero suo praeter omnem audientiam a Romanae ecclesiae charitate et oboedientia subtraxerunt" (quoted in Yves Congar, "Quatre siècles de désunion et d'affrontement," *Istina* 13 [1968]: 131–52, at 134n18).

18 Quoted in Congar, "Quatre siècles," 136n28.

19 *PL*, 214:328B: "[Graecorum populus] . . . aliam sibi confinxit Ecclesiam, si tamen quae praeter unam est, Ecclesia sit dicenda, et ab apostolica sedis unitate recessit."

20 Yves Congar, "1274–1974: Structures ecclésiales et conciles dans les relations entre Orient et Occident," *Revue des sciences philosophiques et theologiques* 58 (1974): 355–90, at 355–56. On the question of the *Filioque*, Jugie holds that there were three main camps among Byzantine theologians between Lyon II and Florence: strict Photians, Latinophrones, and dissident Photians. The last group admitted some kind of eternal mediation of the Son in regard to the Holy Spirit, but did not make him an active principle of the procession (*De Processione Spiritus Sancti* [Rome: Facultas Theologica Pontificii Athenaei Seminarii Romani, 1936], 319).

21 Quoted in Aidan Nichols, *Rome and the Eastern Churches: A Study in Schism* (Edinburgh: T. & T. Clark, 1992), 243.

cized in Constantinople and by other canonists for his "fierce rigidity" on this question.[22] One may perhaps say that the events of 1204 made the division that the popes had lamented for a century plain to all, such that people on both sides henceforth generally speak of "schism."[23] After the failure of the Second Council of Lyon in 1274, the popes refer freely to the Greeks as non-Catholics.[24]

By the time of the Council of Ferrara-Florence, the schism was surely undeniable. For the patriarch of Constantinople and the bishops in his company it meant, for example, that neither were they nominated by the pope nor did they inform him of their nomination or election; that they did not commemorate him in the Divine Liturgy; that they did not celebrate the Liturgy in churches that owned the Roman obedience, nor did they permit priests and bishops who owned the Roman obedience to celebrate the Mass or Divine Liturgy in their own cathedrals.[25]

True, the division was not yet so great as it would become. Mark of Ephesus himself, later the most determined opponent of papal authority, addressed Pope Eugenius at the start of the council in these terms: "So then, most holy Father, receive your sons who come to you from the remote parts of the East; embrace those, who have long been separated from you but who now fly to your arms."[26] When the most outspoken of the Greek bishops could speak to the pope of Rome in such terms, it does not seem too sanguine to suggest that reconciliation was a real possibility. Yet, from the Catholic point of view, the Eastern bishops did not, at

22 Hussey, *The Orthodox Church*, 182.

23 E.g., Humbert of Romans speaks thus in the document he prepared for the Second Council of Lyon in 1274, as does Michael VIII, in an address while at Lyon II (respectively: Joseph Gill, *Byzantium and the Papacy, 1198–1400* [New Brunswick, NJ: Rutgers University Press, 1979], 124; Hussey, *The Orthodox Church*, 232). A letter from Patriarch Manuel II to the pope in 1251 speaks of a διάστασις ("separation") rather than a σχῖσμα (Hussey, *The Orthodox Church*, 217).

24 For example, John XXII, in 1325, does so in refusing a request for a marriage dispensation, and Gregory XI, in 1375, distinguishing between the Greek *catholici* and the Greek *schismatici* who were intermingled on Crete, and forbidding *communicatio in sacris* with the latter (Gill, *Byzantium and the Papacy*, 240 and 235, respectively).

25 George Amiroutzes, who would come to Florence as a Greek *peritus*, writes to Pope Eugenius III in 1435 that "it is now many centuries that the Greeks were cast out of the bosom of the Church" (*PG*, 161:893A).

26 *AG*, 28–29: "Δεῦρο δὴ οὖν, ἁγιώτατε πάτερ, ὑπόδεξαι τὰ σὰ τέκνα μακρόθεν ἐξ ἀνατολῶν ἥκοντα· περίπτυξαι τοὺς ἐκ μάκρου διεστῶτας τοῦ χρόνου, πρὸς τὰς σὰς καταφυγόντας ἀγκάλας."

the actual opening of the council, enjoy a strict right to sit as judges in an ecumenical council. It is doubtless for this reason that the council proceeded simply by means of debate and not by means of votes.[27] It was only by the decree of union in the papal bull *Laetentur Caeli*, of July 6, 1439, that the schism was healed; the Greek bishops, therefore, in signing the decree, at the same time legitimately promulgated it.

The Convocation and Decree: The Latins

Pope Eugenius IV transferred the Council that was meeting in Basel to Ferrara by means of the bull *Doctoris Gentium*, issued on September 18, 1437. Later that year he insisted on this transfer and ordered those conciliar fathers who had not yet done so to come to Ferrara:

> We declare the council of Basel to have been and to be transferred to the aforementioned city of Ferrara, . . . commanding through this present letter by Our apostolic authority that each and everyone who is bound by law and custom to attend an ecumenical council should, in virtue of the oath that they have taken, betake themselves without delay to this council that has been thus transferred.[28]

Since the gathering at Basel had originally been summoned to be an ecumenical council, this summons by itself is in a sense a sufficient convocation of an ecumenical council in Ferrara. Nevertheless, since by this point only a small number of bishops remained at Basel, Eugenius also wrote to the various provinces of the Church to summon bishops to Ferrara. It will be sufficient to quote from one such letter, written to the archbishop of Canterbury, Henry Chichele, on September 19, 1438:

---

27 This is despite Congar's claim that "at Florence, the Greeks sat as fathers of the Council [and] were considered as pastors of the Church just as much as the Latins" ("1274–1974," 364).

28 *EP*, I:112: "Basilense concilium ad praefatam civitatem Ferrariensem fuisse et esse translatum declaramus . . . auctoritate apostolica, per praesentes mandantes omnibus et singulis, qui ad generalia concilia de iure venire tenentur et consueverunt, ad ipsum concilium sic translatum, vigore iuramenti per eos prestititum, quantocius se transferre procurent."

"We charge you to come to the aforementioned ecumenical council as quickly as you are able, and likewise to enjoin and command by Our apostolic authority all and each of your suffragans that they also come."[29] Letters expressed in the same or equivalent terms were sent to the bishops of Italy, and to the dukes of Savoy and Austria, and to the German princes, these temporal rulers being requested to expedite the arrival of bishops from their domains.[30] Universities in France, Spain, Germany, Brabant, Poland, Italy, England, and Scotland were requested to provide masters in theology for the Council.[31] Likewise those synodal fathers who had already assembled in Ferrara in 1438 convoked once again those who had not yet arrived: "This holy synod . . . warns and requires each and all of those who are obliged by law or custom to take part in general councils, to come as soon as possible to this present synod at Ferrara."[32]

While not all the papal letters of convocation appear to have survived,[33] given the letters that are extant together with Eugenius's known will of calling everyone who was "bound by law or custom" to take part in a council, and given too that there is no record of any Catholic province being excluded from the convocation, or of any bishop desiring to attend the council and being refused admittance, it is safe to conclude that the bishops of the Latin Church were summoned in an adequate manner to the Council of Ferrara-Florence.

Although not supposed necessary by divine law, it was customary at the time for certain abbots and heads of religious orders to be summoned to an ecumenical council. This too was done. Letters survive addressed by the pope to the masters-general of the Franciscans, Dominicans, Carmelites, and Camaldolese, and to Cistercian, Cluniac, and Premonstratensian abbots.[34] The author of the *gesta* states that

29 *EP*, I:101: "Mandamus . . . te ad prefatum ycumenicum concilium, quam citius poteris, conferas, et similiter omnibus et singulis tuis suffraganeis . . . auctoritate nostra iniungas et mandes ut se quoque conferat."

30 *EP*, I:101–103, 105.

31 *EP*, I:103.

32 *Decrees of the Ecumenical Councils: From Nicaea I to Vatican II*, ed. Norman Tanner and Giuseppe Alberigo, 2 vols. (Washington, DC: Georgetown University Press, 1990), 1:516–17: "Monet . . . et requirit hec sancta sinodus omnes et singulos, qui in generalibus conciliis de iure et consuetudine interesse tenentur, quatenus ad ipsam presentem Ferrariensem synodum . . . quamprimum se conferre procurent."

33 I have named those included in *EP*.

34 *EP*, I:104–105.

thirty-one abbots were present for the opening ceremonies in 1438.[35] The final decree of union was signed, on the side of the Latins, by the pope, eight cardinals, two patriarchs, eight archbishops, fifty-two bishops, four heads of religious orders, and forty-one abbots.

The Convocation and Decree: The Greeks

We have seen that the common view of the Greeks in the fifteenth century was that an ecumenical council, to be legitimate, must be convoked by the emperor in the manner of the ancient councils, and that the five patriarchates must be represented at it.[36] This aspiration was finally fulfilled by the council of Ferrara-Florence. As mentioned above, from as early as 1422, Emperor John VIII desired to convoke such a council. Early in 1437, the imperial messenger who had been sent to the patriarchs of Alexandria, Antioch, and Jerusalem returned to Constantinople to announce that while the patriarchs themselves were forbidden by the Turks from travelling west, they had appointed proxies. The emperor was persuaded by a Latin envoy, John of Ragusa, that the initial terms of reference for these proxies were too limited and would hinder fruitful discussion; he therefore sent another messenger to the three patriarchs by means of whom new letters of authorization were confirmed.[37]

These three ancient patriarchates were represented throughout the Council, though the proxies themselves did not remain always the same. When the decree of union was signed, Alexandria was represented both by Anthony of Heraclea, the primate of Thrace and Macedonia, and by Gregory Melissenus, the protosyncellus of Constantinople;

---

[35] Joseph Gill, *The Council of Florence* (Cambridge: Cambridge University Press, 1959), 109. The *gesta* is the name given to the most important of the private diaries that treat of the events of the council. Georg Hoffman notes that it is written in the style of a master of ceremonies, and hence could perhaps even be considered a public diary (*Acta Camerae Apostolicae et Civitatum Venetiarum, Ferrariae, Florentiae, Ianuae de Concilio Florentino*, ed. Georg Hoffman, *CFDS* vol. 3/1 [Rome: Pontifical Oriental Institute, 1953], xxii).

[36] There appears at this time to have been no belief among the Greeks equivalent to that which existed among the Latins, that they by themselves could hold a council able to represent the whole Church. This was doubtless due to what John Boojamra calls "the Orthodox belief that Rome continued in some way to be part of the Church, and that Rome could not be considered in heresy since such was never declared by a council" ("The Transformation of Conciliar Theory in the Last Century of Byzantium," *St. Vladimir's Theological Quarterly* 31 [1987]: 215–35, at 235).

[37] Gill, *Council of Florence*, 76.

Antioch was represented by Isidore, metropolitan of Kiev and Russia; and Jerusalem by Dositheus of Monembasia.[38]

Patriarch Joseph II of Constantinople was personally present at the Council from the beginning until his sudden death on June 10, just before its conclusion. At the private Greek discussions at the end of May 1439, he made clear that that he accepted that the "Latin" position on the procession of the Holy Spirit was equivalent to the "Greek" one. According to the Greek *acta*:

> He gave his judgment and accepted [the] Western saints who said that the Holy Spirit is from the Father and the Son, only stipulating that we should not add it to our Creed, but that we should unite with them [the Latins] while preserving all our customs.[39]

In other words, the patriarch of Constantinople accepted the union, though he did not live to sign the decree. While the authenticity of a testament discovered in his room after his death in which he affirmed his acceptance of the Catholic teaching on various disputed questions is a matter of debate,[40] neither side at Florence doubted the final position of the patriarch. Andrea da S. Croce, the author of the so-called Latin *acta* of the council (*Acta Latina Concilii Florentini*) writes of Joseph:

> Before his death he signed with his own hand the above-mentioned draft on the procession of the Holy Spirit, and humbly submitting himself to the rule of holy mother Church, he breathed his last.[41]

---

38 *AG*, 465.

39 *AG*, 432: "Ἐτελείωσε τὴν γνωμὴν αὐτοῦ, καὶ ἔστερξε [τοὺς] ἁγίους δυστικοὺς λέγοντας ἐκ τοῦ Πατρὸς καὶ τοῦ Υἱοῦ τὸ Πνεῦμα τὸ ἅγιον, παραγγείλας μόνον μὴ θήσωμεν αὐτὸ ἐν τῷ ἡμετέρῳ συμβόλῳ, ἀλλὰ τὰ ἔθη ἡμῶν πάντα τηρήσαντες αὐτοῖς ἑνωθησόμεθα."

40 For a full discussion, see Joseph Gill, *Personalities of the Council of Florence, and Other Essays* (Oxford: Blackwell, 1964), 26–32. Though characteristically cautious in his assertions, Gill favors the authenticity of the document.

41 *AL*, 224–25.

That this was the general belief of the Latins is shown by the fact that Joseph was buried with great pomp in the presence of many cardinals inside the Dominican church of Santa Maria Novella; this contrasts with the burial of Dionysius, bishop of Sardis, the previous year, outside the walls of a small church.[42] Nor did the Greeks doubt the attitude of their late patriarch. Mark of Ephesus, who would certainly have exploited any ambiguity in Joseph's position as something favorable to the anti-unionist cause, writes of him:

> With these [the "Latinizers"] the patriarch also voted, he, too, the wretched man being already corrupted and at the same time yearning for his departure from that place, even though destiny was already driving him to his death.[43]

Joseph's successor as patriarch of Constantinople, Metrophanes II, also accepted the union and promulgated it throughout his patriarchate. Metrophanes was elected in May 1440. The following month he wrote to the inhabitants of Methone in the Peloponnese informing them of the union, telling them that they might find full details of what was agreed by studying the decree *Laetentur Caeli*, and adding: "By the grace of God the union of Christians has come about, and between us and the Latins there is now no stumbling block left. Rather we are friends now, and brothers one with another."[44] A month later the patriarch wrote to Crete in the same terms.[45]

Although the Byzantine theory did not explicitly require it, other "metropolitans"—that is, diocesan bishops—were also present at the council. The author of the *gesta* speaks of "twenty archbishops" at the

---

42 Gill, *Council of Florence*, 112.

43 Mark Eugenikos, *Relatio de rebus a se gestis* (*OAU*, 140).

44 *ODM*, 36:46: "Τῇ χάριτι τοῦ θεοῦ γέγονεν ἕνωσις τῶν χριστιανῶν, καὶ μεταξὺ ἡμῶν καὶ τῶν λατίνων οὐδὲν ἔτι σκάνδαλον ἐναπελείφθη, ἀλλ'ἤδη ἐσμὲν ἐν ἀλλήλοις φίλοι καὶ ἀδελφοί."

45 *ODM*, 37:48. While it is not of any great authority, being the letter of a simple Cretan priest, it may be of interest to quote briefly from the letter that one Michael Kalophrenas wrote in reply to his patriarch (recorded here in *ODM*), as it helps to dissipate the myth that the Greeks who did not oppose the union accepted it only sullenly: "When I head the blessed news of the holy union, I danced for joy and cried out, 'Blessed be God!' [Ὅτε τὴν εὐλογημένην φωνὴν ἤκουσα τῆς ἁγίας ἑνώσεως, τὸ δὲ σῶμα ἀγαλλομένῳ ποδὶ χορεύων ἐκραύγαζον· εὐλογητὸς ὁ θεός]."

opening ceremony.[46] He adds that there were "eight abbots and three Staurophoroi, who are called the cardinals of the Constantinopolitan church," as well as many other monks, priests, and lay noblemen, and various royal orators. The total was about seven hundred men.[47] One can understand how Andrew of Rhodes, speaking for the Latins at one of the opening sessions of the Council, was able to say that the pope had gathered together "all the most distinguished men from the Eastern nations—Greeks, Ruthenians, Iberians, Wallachians, and others who come from Pontus and the province of Asia."[48] The final decree of union was signed by the emperor, eighteen metropolitans (three of whom were also acting as patriarchal procurators), one priest acting as a patriarchal procurator, three procurators of absent bishops, five staurophoroi-deacons, and six heads or representatives of monasteries.[49] John Boojamra summarises the facts thus:

> The demands the Greeks had been making for a council *qua* union council were met by Eugenius. The council was held in a convenient location, the Byzantines were more than adequately represented by 700 delegates, the discussion was free and untrammelled by the Latins and within the Greek party itself. The council followed the traditional pattern and made use of patristic sources; and the emperor led the Byzantine party. In addition, the non-Byzantine Orthodox East was well represented by all the patriarchates, as well as the Slav Churches.[50]

---

46 Gill, *Council of Florence*, 109n2.

47 Gill, *Personalities*, 4.

48 *AL*, 38: "Lectissimos quosque Orientalium nacionum, Grecos, Rutenos, Hiberos, Vlachos et alios, qui Pontum et Asiam incolunt."

49 Emmanuel Lanne writes: "The emperor John VIII arrived at Venice with a delegation representative of the Greek Church, which permitted in principle the holding of an ecumenical council according to the norms accepted by the Greek Church itself" ("Uniformité et Pluralisme: les ecclésiologies en présence," in *Christian Unity: The Council of Ferrara-Florence, 1438/39–1989*, ed. Giuseppe Alberigo, Bibliotheca Ephemeridum Theologicarum Lovaniensium 97: International Symposium on the Unity of the Christians 550 years after the Council of Ferrara-Florence, Florence, Italy, 1989 [Leuven: Leuven University Press, 1991], 353–73, at 356).

50 Boojamra, "Transformation of Conciliar Theory," 235.

Testimonies at the Council to Its Ecumenicity

When the Council solemnly opened on April 9, 1438, the bishop of Oporto read to the assembled fathers Pope Eugenius's bull of convocation, *Magnas Omnipotenti Deo*. Dorotheos, Metropolitan of Mitylene, then read the same document in Greek.[51] It contains the following words:

> We decree and declare, in every way and form as best we can, with the assent of the said emperor and patriarch and of all those in the present synod, that there exists a holy universal or ecumenical synod in this city of Ferrara, which is free and safe for all; and therefore it should be deemed and called such a synod by all.[52]

The bull having been read, the Latin delegates at the council replied: "Recipimus et approbamus"—"We accept it and approve it." The Greeks replied: "στέργομεν καὶ ὁμολογοῦμεν"—"We agree and acknowledge it."

While Joseph II of Constantinople was present for much of the Council, he was prevented by illness from attending the opening ceremony, but his consent was read out first in Greek and then in Latin:

> Through this letter of exhortation I grant to the reverend fathers who are delegates of my brothers the holy patriarchs and to all my brothers and co-workers, the metropolitans and other prelates, beloved in the Holy Spirit, to enter upon the present work and to carry out the announcement of the ecumenical council.[53]

---

51 Gill, *Council of Florence*, 111.

52 Tanner and Alberigo, *Decrees of the Ecumenical Councils*, 1:522: "Omni igitur modo et forma, quibus melius possumus, decernimus et declaramus, accedente consensu dictorum imperatoris et patriarche omniumque in presenti existentium synodo, sacram esse universalem seu ycumenicum synodum in hac Ferrariensi civitate omnibus libera et secura, sicque dictam synodum ab omnibus reputari et appellari debere." The key phrase here reads in Greek: "ἀποφαίνομεν καὶ δηλοποιοῦμεν . . . τὴν ἱερὰν οἰκουμενικὴν σύνοδον εἶναι ἐν ταυτῇ τῇ πόλει τῆς Φερραρίας πᾶσιν ἐλευθέρᾳ καὶ ἀσφαλεῖ."

53 *AL*, 30–31: "Per hanc adhortatoriam litteram concedo reverendissimis patribus locumtenentibus sanctissimorum patriarcharum fratrum meorum et omnibus [in] Spiritu sancto dilectis fratribus meis et

Given his future role in sabotaging the union of the churches, it is interesting to note the attitude of Mark Eugenikos, metropolitan of Ephesus, at this early stage. Writing to the pope at the suggestion of Cardinal Cesarini, and having mentioned the various points at issue between East and West, Eugenikos adds: "That which has been said for so long, that there was need of an ecumenical council for these matters, we have today fulfilled."[54] Shortly before the public sessions began, Eugenikos, Isidore of Kiev, and two others spoke to Pope Eugenius on behalf of the Greeks, jointly declaring:

> Because there are present in this [synod] your Holiness and those who are with you, and also the emperor and the patriarch and the delegates of the Eastern patriarchs and the more distinguished section of the Eastern church, for this reason the ecumenical synod is complete and irreproachable.[55]

Speaking at the first of the plenary sessions, the metropolitan of Ephesus explained that he wished to begin by reading the decrees of the first seven ecumenical councils, "for in this way this synod will be harmony with the early synods, with the first and the second and the others."[56]

Similarly, the other principal spokesman for the Greeks, Bessarion, metropolitan of Nicaea, affirmed in his first speech that the bishops have come from all over the earth, "some from the middle of Greece, others from the most northerly and most easterly realms."[57] There is in fact no record of any of the Greek or Latin fathers who participated in

---

coadministratoribus metropolitis et ceteris prelatis ecclesie adire in presentiarum et perficere ycumenici sinodi pronunciationem." The Greek text is not extant.

54 *AG*, 29: "Τὸ πάλαι θρυλλούμενον, ὡς οἰκουμενικῆς συνόδου χρεία τοῖς πράγμασι, σήμερον ἡμεῖς ἐπληρώσαμεν."

55 *SYR*, 304: "Ὅτι μὲν γὰρ πάρεστιν ἐν αὐτῇ [τῇ συνόδῳ] καὶ ἡ μακαριότης σου καὶ οἱ σὺν αὐτῇ, πάρεστι δὲ καὶ οἱ βασιλεὺς καὶ ὁ πατριάρχης καὶ οἱ τοποτηρηταὶ τῶν τῆς Ἀνατολῆς πατριαρχῶν καὶ τὸ κρεῖττον μέρος τῆς ἀνατολικῆς Ἐκκλησίας, κατὰ τοῦτο οἰκουμενική ἐστι τελεία καὶ ἀνελλιπτής."

56 *AG*, 53: "Οὕτω γὰρ ἔσται καὶ ἡ σύνοδος αὕτη ταῖς προηγησαμέναις ἐκείναις ἀκόλουθος, τῇ τε πρώτῃ καὶ τῇ δευτέρᾳ καὶ ταῖς ἑξῆς."

57 *AG*, 43: "Οἱ μὲν ἐκ μέσης αὐτῆς τῆς Ἑλλάδας, οἱ δ᾽ἐκ βορειοτάτων τε καὶ ἀνατολικωτάτων τῆς οἰκουμένης."

the Council denying during the Council itself that it met the criteria for an ecumenical synod.

The status of the Council having been thus generally agreed at the outset, the participants were free to turn to other questions. It was only in the period immediately before the signing of the decree of union that the ecumenicity of the Council, and the consequences of this for the authority of its decisions, again came to the fore. During a series of meetings at the end of May and the beginning of June 1439, the Greeks discussed among themselves whether to declare their acceptance of the *Filioque*. Several speakers emphasized the fact that in the event of an agreement being reached between Greeks and Latins, the Church would be expressing herself in a definitive and infallible way. George Scholarios, one of the three lay *periti* accompanying the Greek delegation, having mentioned his personal belief in the *Filioque*, goes on to express his religious acceptance of whatever the Council determines. "I submit myself to the vote of this, our holy council, or rather, our ecumenical council."[58] A few moments later he repeats the idea with even more emphasis, saying that he is "under a necessity of obeying . . . our council, and, what is more, an ecumenical one."[59] He continues: "For what is worse than that one man, of whatever rank he may be, should resist an ecumenical council, given that such a council represents the whole Church of God?"[60]

Emperor John VIII, speaking on the same occasion, was equally categorical: "I hold this present holy and ecumenical council to be in no

58 *AG*, 430: "'Υποστάττω ἐμαυτὸν τῇ ψήφῳ τῆς ἱερᾶς ταύτης καθ'ἡμᾶς συνόδου, μᾶλλον δὲ τῆς οἰκουμενικῆς ταυτησί." C. Turner remarks of Scholarios at this stage of his career: "It is plain from the 'Discourses' that he felt obliged by the principle of the *consensus patrum* to go beyond his earlier uncommitted position and to accept the Latin dogma as nothing short of the truth revealed by the Holy Spirit himself" ("George-Gennadius Scholarius and the Union of Florence," *Journal of Theological Studies* 18 [1967]: 83–103, at 91). For his later change of mind, see the section "An Invalid Decree?" in ch. 23 ("Denials of the Authority of the Council of Ferrara-Florence").

59 *AG*, 430: "'Υποτάσσω ἔχων πείθεσθαι . . . τῇ ἡμετέρᾳ συνόδῳ καί, ὅ πλέον ἐστι, τῇ οἰκουμενικῇ." Clearly he had never heard that such a council would need to be subsequently received in order to be binding.

60 *AG*, 430: "Τί γὰρ χεῖρον τοῦ ἕνα ὄντα, κὰν ὁπόσου ἀξιώματος ᾖ, θέλειν συνόδῳ οἰκουμενικῇ ἀνθίστασθαι, ἥτις ὅλην τὴν τοῦ θεοῦ ἐκκλησίαν παρίστησι."

way inferior to any of those that has taken place in the past."[61] Even if earlier councils may have had more members present, John avers, yet the matters under discussion are great and divine, and the participants are holy and devout men, and in consequence, its definitions will infallibly declare the truth:

> I consider that holy Church cannot err in any way in [defining] sacred teachings, when she has considered them in a common council. For while it is possible for one man or two or three or even more of those who are now living to be deceived when they consider among themselves, it is entirely impossible for the whole Church to be deceived, concerning which our Lord said to Peter: "Thou art Peter, and upon this rock I shall build my Church, and the gates of Hell will not prevail against it." If it were otherwise, the saving word would have failed, and our faith would have no firm support. But since both these ideas are absurd, the Church of God must needs be infallible, and we must follow her judgment, myself in the first place, who by the grace of God wear the imperial garb.[62]

George Amiroutzes, another of the Greek *periti*, spoke in the same vein, perhaps a few days later.[63] Speaking as if the union had already been decreed, doubtless because he foresaw that it was inevitable, he writes: "I submit myself to the judgment of the Church and obey her in all things. And since she has so decided, I receive it as I do the decisions of

61 *AG*, 432: "Ἐγὼ τὴν παροῦσαν ταύτην ἁγίαν καὶ ὀικουμενικὴν σύνοδον κατ᾽ὀυδὲν ἐλάττω ἡγοῦμαι τῶν προλαβουσῶν ἁπασῶν."

62 AG, 433: "Ἐγὼ νομίζω κατ᾽ὀυδένα τρόπον δύνασθαι πλανηθήναι τὴν ἁγίαν ἐκκλησίαν ἐν τοῖς ἱεροῖς δόγμασι κοινῇ καὶ συνδικῶς σκεπτομένην. ἕνα μὲν γὰρ ἢ δύο ἢ τρεῖς ἢ καὶ πλείονας τῶν νῦν ἀνθρώπων καθ᾽αὐτοὺς σκεπτομένους πλανηθῆναι ἐνδέχεται, πᾶσιν δὲ τὴν ἐκκλησίαν κοινῶς, ὑπερ ἧς ὁ Κύριος εἰπε πρὸς Πέτρον · Σὺ εἶ Πέτρος καὶ ἐπι ταύτῃ τῇ πέτρᾳ οἰκοδομήσω μου τὴν ἐκκλησίαν, καὶ πύλαι ᾄδου οὐ κατισχύσουσιν αὐτῆς, πλανηθῆναι ἀδύνατον ὅλως. Εἰ δε μή, ὅ τε σωτήριος διέπεσε λόγος καὶ ἡ πίστις ἡμῶν ἐπ᾽ἀδρανοῦς βέβηκεν. ἀλλ᾽ἐπεὶ ταῦτα καὶ ἀμφότερα ἄτοπα, διὰ τοῦτο καὶ ἀπλανῆ εἶναι τὴν τοῦ Θεοῦ ἐκκλησίαν ἀνάγκη, καὶ ἡμᾶς ἀναγκαῖον αὐτῇ καὶ τῇ ἀποφάσει αὐτῆς ἕπεσθαι, καὶ πρὸ πάντων ἐμέ, τὸ Βασιλικὸν περικείμενον σχῆμα θεοῦ χάριτι."

63 Gill, *Council of Florence*, 261.

the other councils. For it is impossible for the Church to be mistaken in these matters."[64]

Testimonies after the Council to its Ecumenicity

The conviction of the Greeks that they had taken part in an ecumenical and therefore binding council, "like one of the seven general councils of past times," did not evaporate when they returned to Constantinople, despite what is still sometimes claimed.[65] After the promulgation of the union in July 1439, Gregory Mammas, then the representative of the patriarch of Alexandria, wrote in the same year to Philotheos, the occupant of that see, describing how the emperor had by great exertions brought it about that "an ecumenical council took place in a canonical and legitimate manner."[66] Speaking of the procession of the Holy Spirit, Mammas testifies: "The dogma was investigated with careful enquiry and examination; many conciliar discussions and debates took place, and a great number of interventions were made by either side."[67] The emperor himself, writing the following year to the same patriarch, says that Philotheos may learn of the union that was achieved at Florence "from the definition of the sacred and ecumenical synod."[68]

Philotheos accepted the account that his legate and his emperor both gave him of the great synod in Florence. In response to a letter sent to him from Pope Eugenius, having saluted the Roman pontiff as "most holy, most blessed, most religious, most just, earthly angel and heavenly man," the patriarch continues:

---

64 *ODM*, 32:39: "Ὑποτάσσω δ'ἐμαυτὸν καὶ τῇ κρίσει τῆς ἐκκλησίας καὶ πείθομαι κατὰ πάντα αὐτῇ· καὶ ἐπειδὴ τοῦτο αὕτη ἔκρινεν οὕτω, δέχομαι ὡς τὰς τῶν ἄλλων συνόδων ἀποφάσεις· πλανηθῆναι γὰρ ἐν τούτοις τὴν ἐκκλησίαν ἀδύνατον."

65 For example, by A. Edward Siecienski, *The Filioque: History of a Doctrinal Controversy* (New York: Oxford University Press, 2010), 171.

66 *ODM*, 34:42: "… ἵνα κανονικῷ τε καὶ νομίμῳ τρόπῳ γένηται οἰκουμενική σύνοδος." The date of the letter is unknown.

67 *ODM*, 34:43: "Ἐξητάσθη οὖν τὸ δόγμα μετὰ πολλῆς βασάνου καὶ ἐξετάσεως, καὶ ἐγένοντο πολλαὶ συνοδικαὶ διαλέξεις καὶ διασκέψεις καὶ ἐλαλήθησαν παρ'ἀμφοτέρων τῶν μερῶν πλεῖστα λόγοι."

68 *ODM*, 33:40: "… παρὰ τοῦ ὅρου τοῦ γεγονότος ὑπὸ ταύτης τῆς ἱερᾶς καὶ οἰκουμενικῆς συνόδου."

> We have sufficiently understood the decrees contained in that [letter] concerning the sacred and ecumenical council held with all the fathers representing the holy patriarchs, and with our mighty emperor John Palaiologos, . . . and we know in what way union and peace has been accomplished throughout the Catholic Church by perfect charity, with one soul and one faith and creed, and now that the old schism and enmity have been cast aside, love and peace have been brought back, for a common mystical worship of almighty God.[69]

The patriarch has no doubts about the binding character of a synod thus achieved:

> I have ventured to write to the mighty prince, our Lord Emperor, and to some of the bishops in Constantinople, to point out that anyone who does not accept the things that have been decreed and defined in the holy council should be treated as a tyrant and a heretic, and should not be granted the communion of the holy Catholic Church.[70]

Likewise, when Mark Eugenikos, safely back in Constantinople, sought to undermine the union of the Churches, some Greek bishops and theologians retorted that he could have no right to resist an ecumenical synod. When Eugenikos coined the term "Greco-Latins" to describe those of his fellow countrymen who accepted the union, the aforementioned Gregory Mammas, who from the mid 1440s

69 *ODM*, 38:52: ". . . praecepta illis [sc. litteris] mandata de sacra et ycumenica synodo cum omnibus patribus locatenentibus sanctorum patriarcharum et potentissimo imperatore nostro Ioanne Paleologo . . . satis intelleximus, cognovimusque, quo pacto unio et pax in tota catholica ecclesia celebrata est caritate perfecta, anima una, fide una, ac simbole, abiectoque vetere scismate ac inimicitia in latriam communem ac misticam dei omnipotentis amor et pax revocata sunt." The letter survives only in Latin.

70 *ODM*, 38:53: "Scripsit mea humilitas litteras ad potentissimum principem dominum imperatorem et ad quosdam pontifices Constantinopolim, significans, [ut] si quis ea, que in sacra synodo decreta et diffinita sunt, non recipiat, tam[quam] tyran[n]us et hereticus habeatur, decidatque a communione sancte catholice ecclesie."

would himself become patriarch of New Rome, replied that he did not particularly mind the name, but solemnly warned the bishop of Ephesus:

> One thing only do we know and assert, namely that those who do not accept and follow the decision of an ecumenical council take also to themselves some new name. So the Arians were so called because they adhered not to the decision of the council, but to Arius; and the Eunomians because they adhered to Eunomius, and the Nestorians to Nestorius. But those who adhere to the decision of an ecumenical council receive no new name. And that the council in Florence was an ecumenical one, nobody would deny.[71]

Bessarion, bishop of Nicaea and (with Mark Eugenikos) one of the two principal Greek orators at Ferrara, speaks in similar terms in his letter to one Alexios Lascaris:

> I consider that the very authority of the sacred council is of itself sufficient to convince anyone and to lead him humbly to accept its conclusion, believing it without any contradiction or ambiguity. For one may not believe that the truth was concealed from so great an assembly of men, who were endowed with wisdom, knowledge and all virtue, and to whom one must believe that the Holy Ghost was present.[72]

---

71 *PG*, 160:117A–B: "Ἓν γὰρ μόνον οἴδαμέν τε καὶ λέγομεν, ὅτι οἱ τῆς οἰκουμενικῆς συνόδου τῇ ἀποφάσει μὴ στέργοντες καὶ ἐξακολουθοῦντες, ἐκεῖνοι καὶ ἕτερον ὄνομα λαμβάνουσιν, ὡς Ἀρειανοὶ μὴ στέργοντες τῇ τῆς συνόδου ἀποφάσει, ἀλλὰ τῷ Ἀρείῳ, Ἀρειανοὶ ἐκλήθησαν. Καὶ οἱ τῷ Εὐνομίῳ Εὐνομιανοὶ, καὶ οἱ τῷ Νεστωρίῳ Νεστοριανοί. οὐ μὴν δὲ καὶ οἱ τῇ οἰκουμενικῇ ἀποφάσει στέργοντες ἕτερον ὄνομα λαμβάνουσιν. Ὅτι δὲ καὶ οἰκουμενικὴ σύνοδος ἡ ἐν Φλωρεντίᾳ, οὐδεὶς ἂν ἀρνήσαιτο."

72 Bessarion, Letter to Alexios Lascaris: "Ipsam item auctoritatem sacri concilii simpliciter satis esse puto ad persuadendum quemquam, et inducendum ad eius conclusionem humili corde capessendam, atque credendam sine quacumque contradictione vel ambiguitate, cum tot hominum conventus, qui sapientia, scientia et omni virtute praediti fuisse, quorum in medio adfuisse Spiritum Sanctum ut credamus necesse est, veritatem latuisse

Amiroutzes's testimony at the council has already been quoted. He maintained his position afterward, writing, for example, to the monks of Crete in 1457 that those who do not obey the Florentine definition fall under an anathema, as always happens to those who resist ecumenical (καθολικαῖς) synods.[73] However, of Greek unionist writers whose works survive, John Plousiadenos is perhaps the most insistent about the ecumenical and binding character of the Council of Florence. Plousiadenos was a native of Crete, appointed "head of the churches" on that island by Bessarion some time after April 1463, and later, having taken the name Joseph, bishop of Methone in Greece.[74] In his *Refutatio Marci Ephesi*, he emphasizes the fact that Mark's isolation at Florence is sufficient proof of the falsity of his doctrine. Like Scholarios, he asserts: "It is wholly impossible for one man to be superior to the whole Church gathered in common."[75] Nor does he mince his words. Addressing the bishop of Ephesus directly, he declares: "You, since you separated yourself from the fathers of the sacred council, are also separated from the sacred sheepfold of Christ."[76] Like Mammas, he warns Mark: "The enemies of ecumenical councils receive no other name than that of heretics."[77] In his *Disceptatio pro Concilio Florentino*, Plousiadenos lays down the same principle mentioned by the emperor at Florence, of the impossibility of an ecumenical synod's erring: "Where shall we reckon the Church of Christ and the faith to be, if ecumenical councils can be mistaken? It is not so, not so. For an ecumenical council cannot be mistaken. Rather, it

minime credendun sit" (*PG*, 161:407–48, at 407B; this is Bessarion's own translation into Latin of his original Greek letter to Alexios Lascaris that appears in *PG*, 161:319–406).

73 *PG*, 161:849B. Amiroutzes went into exile in Rome and is buried in the Dominican church of Santa Maria sopra Minerva (*PG*, 161:745–46). He is also known as George of Trebizond, or Trapezuntinus.

74 Louis Petit, "Joseph de Méthone," in *DTC*, 8/2:1526–29. He was killed, cross in hand, during the Turkish massacre in Methone in 1500, and hence may well be called a martyr for the faith (Manoussos Manoussakas, "Recherches sur la vie de Jean Plousiadenos," *Revue des études Byzantines* 17 [1959]: 28–51, at 51).

75 *PG*, 159:1041A: "Πάσης δὲ τῆς Ἐκκλησίας κοινῶς συνελθούσης ἕνα βέλτιστον εἶναι ἀδύνατον παντελῶς."

76 *PG*, 159:1089D: "Σὺ μὲν χωρισθεῖς ἀπο τῶν πατέρων τῆς ἱερᾶς συνόδου, κεχωρισμένος εἶ καὶ τῆς ἱερᾶς τοῦ Χριστοῦ ποίμνης."

77 *PG*, 159:1092A: "Συνόδων ἐχθροὶ οὐκ ἄλλο λαμβάνουσιν ὄνομα, ἢ αἱρετικοὶ ὀνομάζονται."

is heresy to say that it can."[78] And like Mammas, Plousiadenos insists that it is impossible to deny that the council in Florence fulfilled the conditions for ecumenicity:

> It is impossible, certainly, for anyone to say that this council that was held in Florence was not ecumenical. For the pope was there, and the emperor was present, and the patriarchs, and the whole world was represented. And so we say that it was infallible. . . . It is possible that a national council should go astray and fall into heresy. But an ecumenical council cannot be mistaken, as we have often said. If this is so, then since this was an ecumenical synod, how could the Church be found mistaken, she who never goes astray?[79]

Plousiadenos also points out that once an ecumenical council has been completed, no later tergiversations on the part of the conciliar fathers can cause it to become non-ecumenical. Hence, even if some Greek bishops have resiled from the union under popular pressure, nothing is thereby removed from the authority the council of Florence enjoys in the sight of God.[80] After all, it would not be the first time that participants in an ecumenical council had cast their vote in favor of a certain doctrine and had later been cowed into silence or ambiguity. After the great council of Nicaea itself, many a local synod had been

---

78 *PG*, 159:984A: "Ποῦ θήσομεν τὴν τοῦ Χριστοῦ Ἐκκλησίαν καὶ πίστιν, εἰ αἱ οἰκουμενικαὶ σύνοδοι ἐπλανήθησαν; Οὐκ ἔστι τοῦτο, οὐκ ἔστιν. Οὐ γὰρ δύναται οἰκουμενικὴ σύνοδος πλανηθῆναι. Μᾶλλον δ' αἵρεσις ἐστιν εἰπεῖν τοῦτο."

79 *PG*, 159:984C–D: "Ἄλλα ταύτην τὴν ἐν Φλωρεντίᾳ δηλαδὴ γενομένην, οὐ δύναται τις εἴπειν μὴ οἰκουμενικὴν εἶναι. Πάππας γὰρ ἐν αὐτῇ, καὶ βασιλεὺς ὑπῆρχε, καὶ πατριάρχαι, καὶ πᾶσα ἡ οἰκουμένη διὰ τοποτηρητῶν. Διὰ τοῦτο καὶ ἀπλανῆ λέγομεν αὐτὴν εἶναι. . . . τοπικὴν γὰρ δύνατόν ἐστι πλανηθῆναι, καὶ ἀπατηθῆναι ἁιρέσει. οἰκουμενικὴν δὲ ἥκιστα πλανηθῆναι δύναται, ὡς πολλάκις εἴρηται. Εἰ οὖν οὕτω, πῶς ταύτης οἰκουμενικῆς οὔσης, ἡ Ἐκκλησία εὑρέθη ἀπατηθεῖσα, ἢ μηδέποτε πλανηθεῖσα."

80 Many of the Greeks who had welcomed the union at Florence were eventually swayed by such pressure. But at least eight bishops remained faithful, and perhaps more (Joseph Gill, "L'accord gréco-latin au concile de Florence," in *Le concile et Les conciles: contributions à l'histoire de la vie conciliaire de l'Église*, ed. Bernard Botte, Yves Congar, et al. [Paris: Chevetogne, 1960], 183–94, at 193).

held in which some of the 318 fathers had suffered the Nicene Creed to be obscured.[81] But the Creed stood firm for all that:

> The Church, once the synod is over, is not interested in what anyone may say or do or wish. For there in the assembly she receives each one's confession, and this is written in heaven from where no law can erase it. And once he has left the assembly, whatever a man may do, he cannot change that which he confessed in that place.[82]

The reunion of the churches meeting with no opposition from public opinion in the West, it was hardly necessary for Latin authors to stress the ecumenical and binding character of the Florentine synod. Nevertheless, we may quote some testimonies for the sake of completeness. The fifteenth-century Dominican John de Turrecremata begins his commentary on the decree of union with a discussion of the subject. He asserts as a premise that "what has been once defined concerning the faith by unanimous agreement in a universal synod, must be held definitively."[83] He notes that, after the pope, there are four principal patriarchs: the patriarch of Constantinople, who was present in person and gave his consent to what was decreed, and the other patriarchs, who were represented by their delegates.[84] In addition, he here notes: "Beside the representatives of the patriarchs, there were many notable and worthy men from each ecclesial state, that is, both clerics and lay man, who fully represented the Eastern Church." Turrecremata

81 *PG*, 159:993A.

82 *PG*, 159:993A–B: "Ἡ Ἐκκλησία μετὰ τὴν διάλυσιν τῆς συνόδου, οὐδενὸς φροντίζει, τί λέγει, ἢ τί πράττει, ἢ τί βούλεται. ἐκεῖ γὰρ ἐν τῇ συναθροίσει λαμβάνει ἑκάστου τὴν ὁμολογίαν, ἥτις καὶ ἀπογράφεται ἐν οὐρανῷ, ὅθεν ἀπαλειφθεῖναι οὐ θεμιτόν.Ὅταν δὲ ἐξέλθῃ τῆς συναθροίσεως, εἴ τι ἄρα καὶ πράξει, ὅπερ ἐκεῖ ὡμολόγησεν, οὐ δύναται μετατρέψαι."

83 John de Turrecremata, *Apparatus super Decretum Florentinum Unionis Graecorum*, 11: "Quod enim unanimi consensu semel diffinitum est circa fidem in universali synodo, irrectractabilii firmitate tenendum est" (CFDS vol. 2/1. ed. Emmanuel Candal).

84 Turrecremata, *Apparatus super Decretum Florentinum Unionis Graecorum*, 12–13.

is expressing himself somewhat loosely here, as he holds that it is only bishops who are needed to represent the Church in a proper sense at an ecumenical council; when he comments on the word *ycumenicum* at the start of *Laetentur Caeli*, he says, "that is, universal or worldwide, since bishops came together from across the world."[85] Even the emperor's presence and consent was not per se necessary: when he comments on the statement in the preamble to the decree, that it is promulgated by Eugenius, bishop of Rome, "with the agreement of our beloved son, John Palaiologos, illustrious emperor of the Romans [Romeorum]," Turrecremata asks whether this expression implies that no definition of faith could be made by an ecumenical [*universali*] council without the consent and approbation of the emperor. His answer is brief: "We reply, no. This was a particular feature of this case; the consent of the emperor of the Romans to what followed was put at the beginning on account of the division of the Eastern Church from the Roman Church."[86] This somewhat obscure reply perhaps means that since the Greek bishops, in their time of separation from the holy See had had the emperor as the bond of union among themselves instead of the pope, it was therefore natural for John VIII to sign immediately after Eugenius.

Putting these various comments together, we may say that Turrecremata's view is that since the "Eastern" Church was adequately represented at Florence, from both a theological and a sociological point of view, the Council both was and could be clearly seen to be "a true and indubitable and lawful universal council of the Catholic Church."[87]

---

[85] Turrecremata, *Apparatus super Decretum Florentinum Unionis Graecorum*, 21: "Id est, universale sive orbiculare, quia de toto orbe episcopi conveniebant."

[86] See Turrecremata, *Apparatus super Decretum Florentinum Unionis Graecorum*, 13: "Hic surgit questio utrum ex hoc loco vindicare possit imperator ut, absque consensu et approbatione sua, nulla in synodo universali fidei emaneret diffinitio. Respondetur quod non. Hoc enim singulare fuit in hoc casu, ut premitteretur consensus imperatoris Romeorum ad infrascripta, propter divisionem Orientalis ecclesiae ab ecclesia Romana."

[87] Turrecremata, *Apparatus super Decretum Florentinum Unionis Graecorum*, 18: "Verum et indubitatum ac legitimum ecclesie catholice universale concilium."

Latin Archbishop Fantinus Vallaresso of Crete, who was personally present throughout the conciliar discussions, argues along the same lines for the authority of the council. He notes that the emperor and the patriarch of Constantinople had asked the pope for "a universal ecumenical synod from each Church, Eastern and Western," and having numbered the bishops and other senior churchmen present as coming to more than seven hundred on the Latin side and about two hundred on the Greek side, he concludes:

> Any sensible man can thus see how great and how noteworthy was this ecumenical gathering, where so many distinguished fathers came together. We should particularly note this fact, as apt to disconcert the critics.[88]

After all, "for anyone who calls himself a Christian, the authority, faith and reverence of the whole Church, which being gathered together so solemnly in a synodal manner has declared the truth of the Catholic faith, ought to be enough."[89]

To conclude: whether one holds that an ecumenical judgment requires simply a judgment by the pope with some bishops after an ecumenical convocation, or a judgment by the pope with bishops who represent a clear majority of the episcopate, or the agreement of the pope and the four eastern patriarchs—the Florentine definition ranks as ecumenical.

---

88 Archbishop Fantinus Vallaresso, *Libellus de Ordine Generalium Conciliorum et Unione Florentina*, 20: "Potest ergo prudens homo quilibet intelligere, quam magna quamque notabilis fuerit hec ycumenica congregatio, ubi tot notabilissimorum patrum presencia concurrebat, quod ad detrahentium confusionem est singulariter denotandum."

89 Archbishop Fantinus Vallaresso, *Libellus de Ordine Generalium Conciliorum et Unione Florentina*, 24: "Sufficere iam deberet cuilibet qui se Christianum appellat auctoritas, fides ac reverentia totius ecclesiae, que insymul sinodaliter tam sollempniter congregata veritatem Catholice fidei declaravit."

CHAPTER 23

DENIALS OF THE AUTHORITY OF THE COUNCIL OF FERRARA-FLORENCE

Introduction

GIVEN THE AUTHORITY that ecumenical councils are understood to enjoy, it was clearly necessary for those Greeks who wished to remain in a state of separation to deny the ecumenicity of Ferrara-Florence. Although, as remarked in the prior chapter, there is no record of such denials during the Council itself, attempts to disprove its ecumenical character began soon afterward and have continued, unfortunately, for the last almost six hundred years.[1] We may divide these attempts to impugn the authority of the Council into different categories for how they relate to the composition of the council, to the freedom of discussion during it, and to the consensus achieved by it.

[1] Joan Hussey writes of the time between the Council of Florence and the fall of the city in 1453: "in Constantinople there was a sharp rift between unionst and anti-unionist." When the union was finally promulgated in Hagia Sophia on December 12, 1452: "The bull 'Let the heavens rejoice' was accepted, by some in good faith, by others perhaps with 'economy,' and by many not at all" (*The Orthodox Church in the Byzantine Empire*, Oxford History of the Christian Church [Oxford: Oxford University Press, 2010], 201, 281–82). She also notes that "the unionists' chances of success were never really tested, since the political regime supporting them collapsed with the fall of the City" (285).

The Composition of the Council

John Eugenikos, brother of the bishop of Ephesus, wrote an *Antirrhetic* [refutation] *of the Council of Florence* after the union had been achieved.[2] He argues in various ways against its ecumenicity. As an argument against the sufficient composition of the Council, he states that the Latin bishops "lacked power against those who resisted them and against the later council that deposed the one who was in charge."[3] This appears to be an allusion to the Council of Basel, which continued to meet schismatically after it had been transferred by Pope Eugenius to Ferrara, and which in July 1439 claimed to depose the pope, electing in November of that year an anti-pope, "Felix V." If this is John's argument, it is a feeble one. As we have seen, the members of the Council of Basel were formally summoned by Eugenius to Ferrara to participate in the council there. The fact that they did not obey the summons cannot invalidate the Council of Florence, or else it would always be possible for bishops to invalidate a council by refusing to attend it.[4]

In the nineteenth century Nikolay Valerianovich Muraviev also impugned the Council on the grounds that many Greek and Latin bishops neither personally attended nor gave their adhesion to it.[5] In the twentieth century, John Meyendorff made the same claim. With regard to the Greeks, he argued that the emperor's attempt to bring a truly representative delegation of bishops to the Council was only partially successful, since "the bulk of the group was made up of the immediate entourage of the emperor and the patriarch, i.e. an embattled

---

2 John Eugenikos, *Antirrhetic of the Decree of the Council of Ferrara-Florence*, ed. Eleni Rossidou-Koutsou (Nicosia, Cyprus: Research Centre of Kykkos Monastery, 2006). Rossidou-Koutsou argues that the work was composed before 1449 (xliv; further citations of this work will be to page numbers in this edition, rather than to any primary-work sections). Joseph Gill holds that it was written some time after Mark of Ephesus's death in 1453, and "probably long after" (*Personalities of the Council of Florence, and Other Essays* [Oxford: Blackwell, 1964], 219).

3 John Eugenikos, *Antirrhetic*, 11: "ἐκείνων [ἐπισκόπων] δὲ πρὸς τοὺς ἀντιβαίνοντας καὶ τὴν ὕστερον καθηρηκυῖαν σύνοδον, μὴ δυναμένων."

4 The Council of Ephesus, for example, would be invalid because Nestorius and the Antiochene delegation refused to attend when summoned and instead held a separate council.

5 Martin Jugie, *Theologia Dogmatica Christianorum Orientalium ab Ecclesia Catholica Dissidentium*, 5 vols. (Paris: Letouzey et Ané, 1926–1935), 4:515.

remnant of desperate men coming from a surrounded and dying city of Constantinople."[6] But the fact that the emperor and the patriarch were already acquainted with the bishops who came with them to the Council does not seem a particularly strong argument against those bishops having the power to represent the Greek church. Nor did the fact that Turkish troops were encroaching on the imperial city remove the capacity of the bishops for rational thought.[7] The complaint that the Greek church was insufficiently represented is not made by those who were involved in the Council or by their contemporaries, whether or not they were happy with its outcome, as the testimonies quoted in the previous chapter also show.

With regard to the Latins, Meyendorff writes, "practically all the bishops were Italians, with only a few isolated and rather unrepresentative prelates from France, Spain, Ireland, Portugal and Poland."[8] He does not explain in what sense the non-Italian bishops were "unrepresentative." Since the belief in the *Filioque* was universal throughout the West, being professed whenever the Creed was recited at any Mass, it is clear that the bishops who came from these various provinces did in fact represent the belief of all their colleagues on this point of doctrine. While one may freely accept the author's assertion that the Western bishops might have arrived in greater numbers at Florence, one may suspect that had they done so, the resulting vast preponderance of Latins over Greeks would have been made a grievance by later anti-unionist authors. However this may be, two arguments show that the decree of union was not vitiated by the nature of Latin representation. First, the bishops of the West were all invited, and none who wished to attend was excluded. Secondly, as has just been indicated, the beliefs

6 John Meyendorff, "Was There an Encounter between East and West at Florence?" in *Christian Unity: The Council of Ferrara-Florence, 1438/39–1989*, ed. Giuseppe Alberigo, Bibliotheca Ephemeridum Theologicarum Lovaniensium 97: International Symposium on the Unity of the Christians 550 years after the Council of Ferrara-Florence, Florence, Italy, 1989 (Leuven: Leuven University Press, 1991), 153–75, at 164.

7 One might as well argue that the Council of Chalcedon was invalid, because the papal legates came from a city that was being menaced by Attila.

8 Meyendorff, "Was there an encounter?," 164.

of the absent bishops were clear and well-known and were in perfect correspondence with those of the bishops who were present.

The example of England may serve to illustrate the last point. Although summoned by Pope Eugenius, as, for example, by the letter to the archbishop of Canterbury quoted in the prior chapter, no English bishop was present at Ferrara-Florence. Nevertheless, the Council was not rejected by the English Church, either in advance or after the fact. A delegation was appointed by the English authorities, but frightened by the capture and imprisonment by the duke of Burgundy of the very papal envoy who was charged with ensuring their safety, the men chosen for the delegation did not attempt the journey.[9] England was, however, not wholly unrepresented at the great synod, since four Carmelites are known to have attended, two of them in the capacity of *periti*.[10] When news of the bull of union reached London, King Henry VI ordered processions and litanies of thanksgiving. One contemporary witness relates:

> All the clergy and the people went in procession to the churches, the quarters of the city and the public squares according to custom, and returned generous thanks to God with hymns and chants and solemn ceremonies.[11]

The significance of such facts is not that they proved that England "received" the council—since we have already argued in chapter 21 that "reception" as such is not a necessary or even coherent criterion for ecumenicity—but rather that they suggest how the bishops who were present at the Council may be said, at least in an informal sense, to have represented the doctrinal positions of the absent majority.

---

9 Margaret Harvey, "England, the Council of Florence and the End of the Council of Basel," in *Christian Unity: The Council of Ferrara-Florence, 1438/9–1989*, ed. G. Alberigo, Bibliotheca Ephemeridum Theologicarum Lovaniensium 97: International Symposium on the Unity of the Christians 550 years after the Council of Ferrara-Florence, Florence, Italy, 1989 (Leuven: Leuven University Press, 1991), 203–27, at 210.

10 Harvey, "England, the Council of Florence and the End of the Council of Basel," 211.

11 Joseph Gill, *The Council of Florence* (Cambridge: Cambridge University Press, 1959), 299.

Norman Tanner, S.J., has gone even further than Meyendorff, claiming that the Greek Church "was not represented in any proper sense" at the Council of Florence.[12] It would doubtless have greatly surprised the four Eastern patriarchs and the Roman emperor to learn that they were able neither by their personal presence nor by their proxies to achieve any proper representation for the Eastern Church. Tanner's claim is directly contradicted by the bishops themselves who cried out, "στέργομεν καὶ ὁμολογοῦμεν," when the opening decree was read. In all, twenty-five dioceses from across the historic Byzantine territory are represented by the signatures on the final bull of union, *Laetentur Caeli*.[13] It is difficult to understand how so learned an author can make such a claim, given that the Eastern representation at Florence was far greater than Western representation at councils whose ecumenicity he does not dispute, such as Nicaea and Chalcedon.[14]

Freedom of Debate

Those hostile to the Council of Florence have often sought to impugn its authority by claiming that the decree of union was not achieved in a legitimate way. This claim, again, takes several forms. Sometimes it is claimed that the discussion that led to it was not free. At other times it is claimed that the signatures of the Greek bishops were obtained in unworthy ways, either by threats or bribes, or both.

It is not difficult to refute the claim that the Greeks lacked freedom of speech during the Council. The most vehement of the anti-unionists, Mark of Ephesus, was also by far the most prominent Greek in the conciliar debates. He was in fact the only Greek bishop to speak at any length in any of the discussion on the procession of the Holy Spirit.

---

12 Norman Tanner, *The Church in Council: Conciliar Movements, Religious Practice and the Papacy from Nicaea to Vatican II*, International Library of Historical Studies (London: I. B. Taurus, 2011), 170.

13 Including modern-day Greece, Turkey, Bulgaria, and Romania.

14 Francis Sullivan, on the other hand, admitted that "there was a very significant presence of the East" at Florence (*Creative Fidelity: Weighing and Interpreting Documents of the Magisterium* [Eugene, OR: Wipf and Stock, 2003], 75).

Yet at no point in the conciliar *acta* is there any suggestion that the Latins were unhappy that he should be made the chief spokesman for the anti-filioquist position.[15] On the contrary, after John of Montenero had set out the Latin case at length during the twenty-fourth session of the Council, Cardinal Cesarini, who served as intermediary between the pope and the council, was disappointed to find that Mark did not come to the council hall to reply. "We could have wished," Cesarini remarked, "that Ephesus had been present in person, nor do we know for what reason he is absent."[16]

The contemporary Church historian Vlassios Phidas repeats the assertion of the fifteenth-century anti-unionist Silvester Syropoulos that Mark's absence from this twenty-fourth session was by a command of the emperor, issued in order to avoid further arguments, and adds, "after this action by the emperor, all idea of synodal procedure was lost."[17] This contradicts Mark's own statement that his absence on this day was caused by ill health.[18] Even if Syropoulos's assertion were correct, however, Phidas's commentary would be inaccurate. Mark had been given ample time to present his ideas before the conciliar assembly. The whole of the twenty-third session had consisted of a lecture in which he assembled the patristic texts by which he desired to disprove the *Filioque*. The legate of the patriarch of Alexandria wrote to that patriarch that Mark had been "perfectly free in speaking and acting, just as we all were."[19] Had Mark wished

---

15 There was Latin opposition to his desire to begin the plenary sessions by reading and commenting on the decrees of the first seven ecumenical councils, but here too he was allowed to have his way (*AG*, 53).

16 *AL*, 222: "Desideravissemus, ut Ephesinus presentialiter fuisset, et nescimus, qua de causa abfuerit." John Plousiadenos recalls that Mark was canonically summoned to be present at the beginning of the session but had declined to come, alleging illness (*Disceptatio* [*PG*, 159:1064B]; see ch. 24 ["Postscript: Bessarion or Mark of Ephesus?"]).

17 Vlassios Phidas, "Herméneutique et patristique au concile de Florence," in *Christian Unity: The Council of Ferrara-Florence, 1438/9–1989*, ed. G. Alberigo, Bibliotheca Ephemeridum Theologicarum Lovaniensium 97: International Symposium on the Unity of the Christians 550 years after the Council of Ferrara-Florence, Florence, Italy, 1989 (Leuven: Leuven University Press, 1991), 303–23, at 319: "Après cette action de l'empereur, tout sens de procédure synodal a été aboli." Syropoulos's claim is recorded in *SYR*, 394, where he says that Mark was also motivated to renounce discussions on account of the sophistic, argumentative, and obstinate character of the Latins.

18 Mark Eugenikos, *Relatio de rebus a se gestis*: "Μὴ παρόντος ἐμοῦ διὰ τὴν ἀσθένειαν" (*OAU*, 138).

19 *ODM*, 44: "In dicendo et faciendo liberrime, sicut et nos omnes." This part of the document exists only in Latin.

or been able to reply to the Latin rebuttal made by Montenero in the final, twenty-fourth session, he had the opportunity to do so. Some three and a half months passed after this last session before the decree of union was signed, and during this period, the Greeks had many private consultations among themselves in which Mark was present and was granted freedom of speech on terms of perfect equality with the other bishops. During this time he sought to win his colleagues to his way of thinking and failed. Far from Mark of Ephesus having been denied freedom of speech at the Council of Florence, one may say that his was the dominant voice.

Phidas's suggestion that John VIII prevented the Greek bishops from setting out their views adequately is unjust to the memory of that emperor. John sought and achieved a full debate between Latins and Greeks. At the very beginning of the Council, when Eugenikos asked him whether in the discussions on purgatory the Greeks should speak their minds or rather speak "with economy," the emperor answered: "Declare with real contention all our rights."[20] If John VIII saw himself, and was accepted by others, as the head of the Greek delegation, this was only in the traditional sense in which the role of the Roman emperor at an ecumenical council was to ensure the necessary conditions for the bishops to adjudicate the theological matters. He would not of himself end the deadlock between Greeks and Latins that followed the end of the public debates. "I am not master of the synod," he said to Pope Eugenius, "nor will I act tyrannically to bring about the union."[21] Accordingly, he did not seek to bend his delegation in either direction, though at the end of May 1439, once the question of the procession of the Holy Spirit had been thoroughly ventilated both in public and in private, he required his bishops to express a judgment in writing either for or against the Latin position. Joseph Gill explains: "His purpose was clear. It was to make the vacillating come to a decision, which as it

---

20 *SYR*, 280: "Ἀγωνιστικῶς λέγετε πάντα τὰ ἡμέτερα δίκαια." Hussey also denies that the emperor prevented a free discussion (*The Orthodox Church*, 283).

21 *AG*, 418: "Ἐγὼ οὐκ εἰμι αὐθέντης τῆς συνόδου οὐδε τυραννικῶς θέλω ἑνωθῆναι ἡμᾶς."

would be preserved in writing they could not easily go back on, and to discover the majority opinion of the Greek community."[22]

So far from having exerted undue pressure on the Greek bishops to unite to the Latins, the emperor may be considered to have shown some weakness in this regard. When the union was imminent, Mark of Ephesus obtained through John's brother Demetrios an imperial promise that he himself would not be compelled to sign, but might return to Constantinople in freedom.[23] It would have been more in keeping with imperial tradition for a sentence of banishment to have been passed on one refusing to adhere to the definition of an ecumenical council.[24]

Phidas claims that the ecumenical authority of the synod was undermined by the conferences that took place outside the twenty-four official public sessions. The Greek *acta*, for example, report various discussions that took place among the Greek bishops by themselves in the presence of Patriarch Joseph II of Constantinople, who was often too unwell to go out in public; they likewise report discussions between the pope and the emperor and between delegations of cardinals sent from the pope with the emperor or the Greek bishops. From these facts, he draws this remarkable conclusion:

> The authority of the Council existed outside the conference chamber in which the discussions between the representatives of each side took place; this is why the Council of Ferrara-Florence cannot claim to be an authentic successor to the ecumenical councils that were held before the schism. Only the regular participation of the pope and the patriarch would have been able to remedy the deficient organization of the synod.[25]

---

22 Gill, *Personalities*, 121.

23 Gill, *Council of Florence*, 287.

24 Bessarion points out that the pope even paid for the return journey of Mark of Ephesus and his fellow anti-unionist Isaias of Stauropolis (Letter to Alexios Lascaris: "Qui vero concedere noluerunt (fuerunt autem duo, et non plures) . . . sumptibus Romanae Ecclesiae ad propria remearunt" [*PG*, 161:407–48, at 424; this is his own translation into Latin of his original Greek letter that appears in *PG*, 161:319–406]).

25 Phidas, "Herméneutique," 322: "L'autorité du concile existait en dehors de la salle des réunions, dans laquelle

The same author even claims to have discerned from the conciliar acts that, as a result of these private conversations, the council had "the tragic awareness of lacking any authority of its own."[26]

It is not excessive to describe this criticism of the council as absurd. Does our author suppose that no discussions of theological questions were held outside the principal conference chamber at any of the first seven ecumenical councils? Even if, by some moral miracle of universal taciturnity, this should have been true of those councils, it would not alter the facts that twenty-four public sessions were held at Florence, that the pope was present throughout, that the patriarch when unable to be present was kept informed of proceedings, and that there is no record of any bishop protesting that he had been prevented from speaking publicly.

Sometimes it is claimed that the Greeks were bribed into accepting the decree of union. John Eugenikos insinuates this in his *Antirrhetic* when he writes, "the Latin gold was not efficacious with all of us."[27] Even if this charge could be substantiated, it would not annul the decree's authority, since such inducements do not remove moral freedom.[28] In fact, however, the charge lacks a serious foundation. The pope had incurred considerable debts in hosting the Council and was not in a position to distribute large bribes. The anti-unionist chronicler Syropoulos, who was present throughout, states that "no one at all saw florins being handed out there to the signatories or heard either requests or promises."[29] Later he repeats the same assertion even more emphatically: "I call God to witness, who is over all, that there was

se passait le déroulement des discussions entre les représentants des deux côtés; c'est pourquoi le concile de Ferrara-Florence ne pourrait revendiquer le caractère de la continuité authentique des conciles oecuméniques antérieures au schisme. Seule la participation régulière du pape et du patriarche pourrait remédier à l'organisation erronée des travaux du synode."

26 Phidas, "Herméneutique," 322.

27 John Eugenikos, *Antirrhetic*, 11: "Τῶν λατινικῶν στατήρων πρὸς πάντας μὴ ἐξαρκούντων."

28 Theodoret complained in Letter 165 that St. Cyril of Alexandria had made use of his personal fortune to gain acceptance for his doctrine at the Council of Ephesus, but this is not considered as having invalidated that council.

29 *SYR*, 482.

no mention of it made by anyone then, nor was there the slightest hint of a demand by any of ours or of a promise by the Latins."[30] Mark of Ephesus asserts that those among the Greeks who were hesitant to sign were won over by "handsome promises and gifts,"[31] giving no further details. The very vagueness of the charge makes it at once rhetorically effective and historically worthless. Bessarion and Dorotheos of Mitylene were later given pensions of three hundred florins a year each by the pope, but this was a natural token of gratitude to men who had striven generously for the unity of the churches. Dorotheos himself is not especially prominent in the *acta* of the Council, but of the former man Gill remarks: "There is no incident in any contemporary document, not even in the bitter *Memoirs* of Syropoulos, that would suggest that Bessarion acted from any less worthy motive."[32]

A more common charge is that the Greeks were induced to sign not by bribery, but by penury, or at least by the threat of it, since they were dependent on papal money in order to live in Italy and to travel back to Constantinople. In this way the very generosity of Eugenius IV in funding the whole business of the Council is made into grounds for a reproach against him. John Eugenikos in his *Antirrhetic* alludes to this when he claims that the Greeks were compelled to sign "by threats and fear and by various schemes and devices."[33] Eleni Rossidou-Koutsou, the recent editor of the *Antirrhetic*, having quoted this passage, comments: "In the light of this, Gill's view that most of the Greek prelates had freely accepted the Union of Ferrara-Florence, since only a few refused to sign, cannot be maintained."[34] But this is an assertion and not an argument. A reading of the Greek *acta* shows the view that the Greeks signed out of fear is untenable. Gill summarizes the facts thus:

30 *SYR*, 494.
31 Mark Eugenikos, *Relatio de rebus a se gestis*: "Ἐπαγγελίαις λαμπραῖς . . . καὶ δόμασι" (*OAU*, 140).
32 Gill, *Personalities*, 52.
33 John Eugenikos, *Antirrhetic*, 7.
34 John Eugenikos, *Antirrhetic*, 155.

> Till the end of May 1439, i.e. for fifteen months after their arrival in Ferrara, the Greeks were complete masters of their fate, for they still refused point-blank to take part in any more public disputations or to clarify the profession of faith that they had made. Instead, they bluntly told the Latins that it was for them to find some other way of union, because they (the Greeks) had done all that they intend to do. That attitude does not suggest that they were cowed, oppressed or browbeaten by anyone.[35]

If anything, the Greeks appear in the conciliar debates more in the light of accusers than of defendants. They were allowed to make the opening speech, *honoris causa*, and to choose the subject of debate.[36] On the Latin side, Pope Eugenius remarks that far from having been haughtily unwilling to discuss matters of faith, he had, when requested, even given a written statement of faith to the Greeks, something that previously "had always been foreign to the dignity of the Roman Church."[37]

The attitude of John VIII, when desired by a delegation of cardinals in May 1439 to produce a dogmatic statement more precise than what had been offered thus far, was characteristic of Greek self-confidence. "We will write nothing more," replied the emperor of the Romans, "nor say anything more, except for this: if you accept what we have written, we shall unite with you; if not, we will go home."[38] The *acta* show that the agreement reached in the first week of June was achieved not by any fear of poverty or hunger, but by a discussion among the Greeks themselves of the relevant patristic texts, and the growing realization of the principle

35 Gill, *Personalities*, 13.

36 *AG*, 28. Henry Chadwick observes: "Throughout the proceedings, the Latin representatives were asking the Greeks to concede the legitimacy of the western tradition. In effect the Greeks drew up the agenda" ("The Theological Ethos of the Council of Florence," in *Christian Unity: The Council of Ferrara-Florence, 1438/9–1989*, ed. G. Alberigo, Bibliotheca Ephemeridum Theologicarum Lovaniensium 97: International Symposium on the Unity of the Christians 550 years after the Council of Ferrara-Florence, Florence, Italy, 1989 (Leuven: Leuven University Press, 1991), 229–39, at 236).

37 *AG*, 423. Presumably the Pope meant that the Roman church had never done this to those who were doubtful about the orthodoxy of her faith and so wished to scrutinize it, rather than to those who were coming to her as suppliants, asking to be told what to believe.

38 *AG*, 420: "Ἡμεῖς ἄλλον οὐδὲν γράφομεν, οὐδὲ λέγομεν εἰ μὴ ὅτι, ἐὰν δέχησθε ὅσον ἐδώκαμεν, ἑνωθησόμεθα· εἰ δὲ μὴ, ἀπολευσόμεθα."

that the Church Fathers cannot be in conflict with one another on an article of faith. Yet, as late as June 22, 1439, when it seemed that the rights of the Eastern patriarchs would not be recognized to his satisfaction, the emperor told the cardinals, "make arrangements for us to depart, if you would be so kind."[39] Gill concludes:

> Though the Greeks were most anxious to go home as quickly as possible, they refused the easy and sure means of a facile assent to Latin demands for fifteen months and accepted agreement and union only when their own learned theologians put before them arguments they could understand and could not reject. . . . To say that they betrayed their faith because of some not very terrible inconveniences is to condemn them as cowards and to cast an aspersion on the whole of the Greek Church of that day whose highest ecclesiastics, except for two, would have to be said to have accepted what to them was heresy, because the alternative was, not martyrdom or even exile, but a rather protracted absence from home.[40]

Bessarion energetically asserts the freedom that he and his fellow countrymen enjoyed throughout their time in Italy: "We were allowed to act according to our wishes, just as we wanted in all matters. Yet some are not ashamed to say that we suffered violence! As God, who is truth itself, is my witness, it was not so."[41]

The Consensus Reached

If the ecumenical composition and the freedom of the Council cannot be successfully impugned, what of the consensus that it achieved? Here

---

39 *AG*, 452.

40 Gill, *Personalities*, 13–14.

41 Bessarion, Letter to Alexios Lascaris: "In omnibus enim ad libitum nostrum et prout volebamus, ita facere nobis licebat, et tamen non pudet aliquos dicere vim nobis illatam fuisse; quod numquam fuit teste veritate qui Deus est" (*PG*, 161:423A).

again, various arguments have been made. Sometimes it is said that those who needed to give their consent did not do. Here the key question is that of the consent of the patriarchs. Sometimes it is claimed that the consensus that was achieved was based on corrupted patristic texts, and was therefore without value. A more modern claim is that, though consent was given, the two sides did not understand the decree in the same way.

The Consent of the Patriarchs

Of all the Greek bishops present in Florence in July 1439, only two, Mark of Ephesus and Isaias of Stauropolis, refused to sign the decree of union.[42] Those who did sign, as mentioned above, represented twenty-five dioceses from across the historic Byzantine lands and included representatives of all the absent patriarchs. Nevertheless, it has been claimed that true patriarchal consent was lacking. John Eugenikos writes in his *Antirrhetic*:

> The official letters of the patriarchs to their delegates are still preserved with us in their original and genuine state, . . . [saying] that they are not willing to submit themselves to Latin insults or to the unlawful and ridiculous customs of the Latins, nor, as regards the novelty in the Creed must they in any way compromise with them or to accept them. Therefore it is plain from this that the opinion of none of the three was present in accordance with the instructions which they had given.[43]

By the "original and genuine letters," John has in mind those that were revoked before the Council by the emperor at the request of John of

[42] We may contrast this with, for example, the Council of Ephesus, where 198 bishops signed on St. Cyril's side and 43 supported John of Antioch.

[43] John Eugenikos, *Antirrhetic*, 11: "Τὰ μὲν τῶν πατριαρχῶν ἐπιτροπικὰ πρὸς τοὺς σφῶν τοποτηρητὰς γράμματα, ὧν τὰ πρῶτα καὶ γνήσια παρ᾽ἡμῖν εἰσέτι σώζονται . . . ὡς μὴ ἄν ποτε τῇ λατινικῇ λύμῃ καὶ τοῖς ἀθέσμοις καὶ καταγελάστοις σφῶν ἔθεσι καθυπαχθῆναι θελῆσαι, μηδὲ τὴν ἐπὶ τῷ συμβόλῳ καινοτομίαν καὶ ὁπωσοῦν μήτε συγχωρῆσαι τούτοις, μήτε μὴν παραδέξασθαι· δῆλον οὖν πάντως ἐντεῦθεν, ὡς οὐδενὸς ἦν ἐκεῖσε τῶν τριῶν γνώμη, καθότι προσδιοριζόμενοι ἐπιτρέπουσιν."

Ragusa.[44] Since these had been revoked, they cannot establish what the author wishes, though even here one may certainly query whether he is quoting from them *verbatim*. The patriarchal letters that were in force at the time of the Council have apparently not survived. According to Syropoulos, the emperor ensured that they stated that "we are not willing to alter or disturb anything that we have received from the holy and ecumenical councils, and from the saints and teachers of the Church, neither to add anything or take away anything."[45] Accordingly, they were not asked at the council to make any alterations to their creed or liturgy. In any case, the patriarchal "procurators" (that is, delegates) themselves and the other bishops present at Florence must be accepted as the proper judges of the meaning and implication of the authorization received from Alexandria, Antioch, and Jerusalem, and there is no record in the Greek *acta* of anyone suggesting, whether in public session or in a private meeting, that the terms of these letters would preclude the signing of the decree of union. The enthusiastic, indeed ecstatic, letter written by Philotheos, patriarch of Alexandria, to Eugenius IV, shows superabundantly that he did not think that his delegate had misinterpreted his instructions. John Eugenikos's claim that the Florentine synod presented only "the appearance and shadow and image of a council,"[46] not the reality of one, would have been shared by only two of the bishops present in Florence in July 1439.

Nevertheless, in later times and until the middle of the twentieth century, it was generally believed that the patriarchs of Alexandria, Antioch, and Jerusalem met in council in 1443 and condemned the Council of Florence.[47] Even if this were true, it would not imperil the ecumenicity of the Council, since, according to the remark of John

---

44 See the subsection "The Convocation and Decree: the Greeks" under "An Ecumenical Council Was Convoked and Gave Judgment" in ch. 22 ("The Authority of the Council of Ferrara-Florence").

45 *SYR*, 166: " Οὐδὲ γὰρ μεταποιῆσαι τι βουλόμεθα ἤ παρασαλεῦσαι, ἀφ'ὧν παρελάβομεν ἀπὸ τῶν ἁγίων καὶ οἰκουμενικῶν συνόδων καὶ τῶν ἁγίων καὶ διδασκάλων τῆς Ἐκκλησίας, οὐδὲ προσθεῖναι τι τούτοις ἢ ἀφελεῖν."

46 John Eugenikos, *Antirrhetic*, 11: "Σχῆμα τοίνυν μᾶλλονν οἰκουμενικῆς, καὶ σκιὰ καὶ εἴδωλον, ἢ ἔργον ἐγεγόνει."

47 Gill, *Personalities*, 213. The text is reproduced in *ODM*, 45:68–72. Bishop Hilarion Alfeyev repeats this belief in *Orthodox Christianity*, trans. Basil Bush, vol. 1 (Yonkers, NY: St. Vladimir's Seminary Press, 2011), 136.

Plousiadenos already quoted in chapter 22, "the Church, once the synod is over, is not interested in what anyone may say or do or wish."[48] However, since the belief in such a condemnation could in practice be an obstacle to acceptance of Ferrara-Florence, it is worth considering the question.

Gill shows, from both internal and external evidence, that the text purporting to be a copy of a joint patriarchal condemnation of Florence is a late forgery. Some of the internal reasons for denying the authenticity of the document are: the Greek is poor and occasionally incorrect;[49] the patriarchs are named in the wrong order; the Council of Florence is called "the eighth synod," which is the very point that the patriarchs supposedly wish to deny; the Council is said to have "allowed us to sacrifice in unleavened bread and by that means to commemorate the pope";[50] it makes no reference to the fact that each of the patriarchs had been represented at the council by a procurator who signed on his behalf, nor does it contain any repudiation of the procurators' signatures; it states that their very knowledge of the Council came from the report of a certain Arsenios, described as bishop of Caesarea, with no reference to their having received a copy of the decree from the pope or emperor.[51]

The external evidence for the inauthenticity of the document is perhaps even stronger. None of the anti-unionist writers of the fifteenth century shows any awareness of it, even though it would have been a powerful rhetorical argument against the council. Gill remarks:

> Time and again in their writings such an announcement would have been the perfect culmination of long argumentation—and they had to be content with the condemnation of Beccus by the

48 John Plousiadenos, *Refutatio Marci Ephesi* (*PG*, 159:993A).

49 E.g., τῇ πίστει καὶ ὀρθοδοξίᾳ instead of τὴν πίστιν καὶ ὀρθοδοξίαν (*ODM* 45:72).

50 Florence gave no permission to the Byzantines to use unleavened bread and said nothing about the commemoration of the pope.

51 Gill, *Personalities*, 215.

eastern patriarchs, which had taken place as much as a century and a half before, in 1285.[52]

Since the document purporting to be the synodal condemnation by the three patriarchs is the only authority for the very existence of the 1443 synod itself, there is no particular reason to believe that they met in that year. The earliest known copy of the document is in a manuscript of 1648. On the basis of this and some further textual evidence, Gill suggests that the spurious condemnation of 1443 may be the work of the seventeenth-century defender of Orthodoxy George Coresios, who is known to have forged the acts of a "synod of Constantinople of 1450."[53]

Corrupted Texts?

Another argument sometimes heard against the union of Florence is that it was achieved by the use of "corrupted texts" of the Fathers. In his narration of events, Mark Eugenikos says that the quotations used by the Latins to support the *Filioque* were "from apocryphal and unknown books, and at other times from books that had been interpolated and corrupted."[54] Modern admirers of Mark are liable to repeat the charge, even if in more measured tones.[55]

Before considering the charge in detail, we may point out that even if *all* the patristic or conciliar texts adduced by the Latins in favor of the doctrine of the *Filioque* were spurious, which is an extreme hypothesis, this would not in itself invalidate the Florentine definition. Bishops are constituted as an ecumenical council to declare with authority the content of the revelation passed on from the apostles, and whenever they assert that they are doing this, their definitions are endowed with

---

52 Gill, *Personalities*, 216.

53 Gill, *Personalities*, 220–21.

54 Mark Eugenikos, *Relatio de rebus a se gestis*: "Τῶν Λατίνωνν προενεγκόντων ῥητά, τὰ μὲν ἐξ ἀποκρύφων τινῶν καὶ ἀγνώστων βιβλίων, τὰ δὲ ἐκ νενοθευμένων τε καὶ διεφθαρμένων" (*OAU*, 137).

55 For example, Nicholas Constas, "Mark Eugenikos," in *La Théologie Byzantine et Sa Tradition* II (XIII–XIX s.), ed. Vassa Conticello, Corpus Christianorum (Turnhout: Brepols, 2002), 418.

infallibility, and the Christian people must give the assent of divine faith to these definitions. Naturally, the bishops must make use of the normal, human means to ascertain what the content of the apostolic teaching is, if this is disputed, and to do so they will normally have recourse, among other things, to the writings of the Fathers; if they did not so act, they would appear to be "tempting God," relying without necessity on an extraordinary interposition of divine providence. But the infallibility promised to the Church in her teaching means that definitions of faith are not invalidated by any flaws in the arguments used when preparing them, whether these arguments be drawn from the Fathers, from Scripture, from reason, or from some other authority.

This premised, we may respond to the allegation of "corrupted texts." Much of the controversy has centred around some passages in book 3 of St. Basil's *Adversus Eunomium*. The authenticity of these texts has been discussed in chapter 5 of the present volume. It is understandable that commentators should have focused on them, since they were discussed at length during the Council, being the most prominent texts from the eighteenth to the twenty-second sessions. It is quite wrong, however, to assert with Phidas that "this testimony [of St. Basil] was decisive among the Westerners for justifying the theology of the *Filioque*."[56] The time spent on discussing the disputed texts of St. Basil was not due to their having a supreme importance in the minds of the Latins, but simply to the difficulty of the question. When John de Montenero, as the spokesman for the Latins, finally made a full presentation of the Catholic position, he did not even mention these passages. In all, he quoted thirty-two texts from five Greek Fathers (including Didymus of Alexandria under that heading). Of these, four of the six ascribed to Basil are assigned by modern scholars to Didymus, one of the ten

56 Vlassios Phidas, "Herméneutique," 316: "Ce témoignage avait chez les Occidentaux un rôle décisif pour la justification de la théologie du *filioque*." The claim has been repeated more recently by Alexander Alexakis in "The Greek Patristic *Testimonia* Presented at the Council of Florence (1439) in Support of the *Filioque* Reconsidered," *Revue des études Byzantines* 58 (2000): 149–65, at 154n20: "This passage was the basis of the Latin defence of the *Filioque*."

assigned to Athanasius is considered spurious today, and another is unknown. From the Latin Fathers he quoted twenty-nine texts: the authenticity of two (the letter of St. Leo to Turribius and Letter 79 of St. Hormisdas) is a subject of scholarly debate; two others (the letters referred to as "From Damasus to Paulinus" and "From Jerome to Damasus") are considered pseudonymous; the provenance of two others attributed to St. Jerome (an exposition of the Creed and a letter to Augustine and Alipius) is unclear; one other text that is attributed to St. Augustine is considered today to belong to St. Fulgentius, while another ascribed also to Augustine cannot be found in extant versions of the treatise from which John took it. In summary, of sixty-one patristic texts adduced by the provincial of Lombardy in the presence of the gathered bishops, fifty-two are assigned by modern scholarship to thirteen patristic authorities.[57] The claim that the decree of union was brought about by the acceptance of corrupted texts and would not have been brought about without them can therefore not be allowed to stand.

Mutual Incomprehension?

A characteristically modern attempt to deny the binding authority of the Florentine synod is to claim that the two sides were not capable of a dialogue leading to a true consensus, on the ground that their ways of approaching revealed truth were radically different and even incompatible. Nicolas Lossky claims that what took place at Ferrara-Florence was largely "a dialogue of the deaf, which had very little chance of succeeding."[58] Phidas implies the same, claiming that the Latin argumentation at the Council was marked by "deviation toward the method of dialectics of Scholastic theology."[59]

---

[57] Or fourteen, if one includes St. Jerome as the translator of Didymus's *On the Holy Spirit.* See appendix 3 for full details.

[58] Nicolas Lossky, "Climat théologique au Concile de Florence," in *Christian Unity: The Council of Ferrara-Florence, 1438/9–1989*, ed. G. Alberigo, Bibliotheca Ephemeridum Theologicarum Lovaniensium 97: International Symposium on the Unity of the Christians 550 years after the Council of Ferrara-Florence, Florence, Italy, 1989 (Leuven: Leuven University Press, 1991), 241–50, at 243.

[59] Vlassios Phidas, "Herméneutique," 323.

I call this argument "characteristically modern" because it depends on an opposition between "Western theology" conceived as essentially "Scholastic" and "Eastern theology" conceived as essentially "non-Scholastic," an opposition that seems to derive from Slavic theologians of the nineteenth and twentieth centuries.[60] Yet no such opposition is to be found in the discussions of the two principal spokesmen of the council of Florence, Montenero and Mark Eugenikos. Montenero began the first full session of the discussions on the *Filioque* with these words:

> It seems that we must all agree to this, that the witness of Sacred Scripture and the judgments of the holy Fathers whom the holy Church receives are what must be brought forward in these disputations. They are to be considered as being, as it were, the boundary marks of our discussion.[61]

Eugenikos replied that these words "seem good to both sides in common."[62]

True to his principles throughout the following sessions, the Dominican Montenero argued exclusively from authority, principally patristic authority, though more rarely framing an argument directly from Scripture, and occasionally adding a conciliar quotation. Though he was doubtless familiar with the arguments of St. Thomas Aquinas in the *De potentia Dei* and elsewhere by which the Angelic Doctor sought to establish by the light of reason that a hypostatic procession of both the Holy Spirit and the Son from the Father alone would be impossible, he never appeals to such arguments. On one occasion when making a

60 For a general survey, see Marcus Plested, *Orthodox Readings of Aquinas*, Changing Paradigms in Historical and Systematic Theology (Oxford: Oxford University Press, 2012), especially ch. 6, "Readings of Aquinas in Modern Orthodox Thought."

61 *AG*, 252: "Videtur illud oportere inter nos constare sacrae scripturae testimonia sanctorumque patrum, quos ecclesia sancta recipit, sententias in his disputationibus afferendas, habendas veluti terminos quosdam nostrae disceptationis."

62 *AG*, 254: "Συνδοκοῦντα κοινῶς ἀμφοτέροις ἡμῖν."

brief reference to the meaning of "nature," he notes that his definition comes from "your [*sic*] Aristotle, whom I bring into the discussion only because I am obliged to."[63]

The Metropolitan of Ephesus, on the other hand, though also principally interested in patristic texts, on one occasion uses a rather "Scholastic" argument against the *Filioque*. The Holy Spirit, he says, cannot be said to proceed from the substance of the Father and the Son, for then the substance of the Holy Spirit would be distinct from that substance, and therefore something created.[64] While Montenero also discusses the distinction in meaning of "proceeding from the person of the Father," "proceeding from the person of the Son," and "proceeding from the substance of the Father and the Son," this is only in order to elucidate and harmonize the patristic texts on which he is relying, some of which speak of the Holy Ghost as proceeding from the Father, others of which speak of him as proceeding from the Son, and others of which speak of him as proceeding from both. He does not use the somewhat technical language of "person and substance" as the foundation for an *independent* argument for the Catholic doctrine. His Greek interlocutor, on the other hand, uses the same language in order to make a metaphysical case for the opposing doctrine.

In one of his later anti-unionist works, *Syllogisms against the Latins*, Eugenikos again shows himself to be at home with a Scholastic method of argumentation. If the Holy Spirit is said to proceed from the Father and the Son, he states, then this could be understood in three ways: either he proceeds from the two persons; or he proceeds from the essence common to the two persons, or he proceeds from a "spirative power" (προβλητικὴ δυνάμις) common to the two persons. On the first hypothesis, Mark argues, there would be two

63 *AG*, 313: "Aristoteles vester, quem coactus produco."

64 *AG*, 287: "Τὴν κοινὴν οὐσίαν Πατρὸς καὶ Υἱοῦ, ἥτις ἐστὶ μία καὶ ἡ αὐτὴ τῷ ἀριθμῷ, λέγεις αἰτίαν καὶ ἀρχὴν τοῦ ἁγίου Πνεύματος, καθ'ἣν πρόεισιν ἐξ αὐτοῦ τὸ Πνεῦμα· φαίνεται τοίνυν ἐκ τούτων τὴν οὐσίαν τοῦ ἁγίου Πνεύματος αἰτιατὴν εἶναι, κἀντεῦθεν δύο οὐσίας ἐν τῇ ἁγίᾳ Τριάδι συνάγεσθαι καὶ ἀντικειμένας ἀλλήλαις κατὰ τὸ αἴτιον καὶ αἰτιατόν."

first principles in the godhead, which would remove the property of the Father. On the second hypothesis, since a divine person is the essence with certain properties, to proceed from the essence would mean proceeding from the persons, and so one would be faced with the same difficulty as on the first hypothesis. On the third hypothesis, then either the "spirative power" would be the divine essence, which would involve one in the same difficulties as before, or else one would have the absurdity of something completing the divine nature.[65] I quote this argument not in order to explain or analyze it in detail, but simply to show how the chief spokesman for the Greeks at the Council of Florence was perfectly willing to argue his case using technical theological concepts rather than simple appeals to the Fathers or to tradition.[66] On these lines, André de Halleux's summary of the discussions on purgatory in 1438 applies also to the discussions in Florence on the *Filioque*:

> A comparison of the theology of the Latins and the Greeks in the first discussions at Ferrara has revealed no confrontation between a Scholastic, "rational" theology and a monastic, "experiential" theology. Quite the contrary, a basic agreement is noticeable about the respective roles of Scripture, the Fathers and reason in establishing and understanding the truths of the faith.[67]

---

65 *OAU*, 60–62. The argument is summarized by Bessarion in his refutation of Mark Eugenikos (*PG*, 161:142).

66 Bessarion himself replies first that the Holy Spirit proceeds from the spirative power, which is common to the Father and the Son and not really distinct from the divine essence (*PG*, 161:147), then goes on to make the distinction between a principle "from which" and a principle "by which" that was mentioned in the subsection "Can God the Father Be Called 'Sole Trinitarian Principle of the Holy Spirit'?" under "A Preliminary Critique" in ch. 1 ("The 1995 Statement on the *Filioque*").

67 André de Halleux, "Problèmes de méthode dans les discussions sur l'eschatologie au Concile de Ferrare et Florence," in *Christian Unity: The Council of Ferrara-Florence, 1438/9–1989*, ed. G. Alberigo, Bibliotheca Ephemeridum Theologicarum Lovaniensium 97: International Symposium on the Unity of the Christians 550 years after the Council of Ferrara-Florence, Florence, Italy, 1989 (Leuven: Leuven University Press, 1991), 251–301, at 266: "La comparaison des lieux théologiques des Latins et des Grecs dans les premières discussions de Ferrare n'a révélé aucune confrontation entre une théologie scholastique, 'rationelle,' et une théologie monastique, 'experientielle.' On constate, au contraire, un accord foncier sur les fonctions respectives de l'Écriture, des Pères et de la raison dans l'établissement et l'intelligence des vérités de la foi."

For his part, Lossky conversely argues that the theological separation of Greeks and Latins was so great that, without realizing it, they gave different meanings to the final definition of the *Filioque*. The Greeks, he claims, were thoroughly imbued with the Palamite doctrine of a twofold eternal procession of the Holy Spirit, one a hypostatic procession and the other a procession of uncreated spiritual energies, and they simply assumed that it was the latter procession which was being described in the decree of union:

> If for the Latin Fathers of the Council of Florence, this distinction between the unknowable essence and an eternal manifestation [the "energies"] or divine economy with regard to the creature was not a part of their theological awareness, for the "Greeks," it was a part of their heritage and therefore, almost unconsciously, of their mentality. . . . They expected from the "Latins" that these would clarify that in saying of the Holy Spirit that he proceeds from the Father and the Son as from a single principle of divinity, they understood it in regard to the eternal manifestation or divine economy.[68]

The author apparently wishes us to believe that the Greeks convinced themselves that the Latins were speaking of the second, "Palamite" procession of the Holy Spirit, and that this belief of the Greeks induced them to sign the decree. He concludes: "Florence is an example of a 'non-meeting,' where the same words do not signify the same things [to both sides]."[69]

---

[68] Lossky, "Climat Théologique," 249–50: "Si pour les pères latins du Concile de Florence cette distinction entre l'essence incognoscible et la manifestation éternelle, ou l'économie divine vis-àvis de la créature ne faisait partie de leur conscience théologique, pour les 'Grecs,' elle faisait partie de leur patrimoine et donc de leur mentalité de façon presque inconsciente. . . . Ils attendaient des 'Latins' que ceux-ci précisent que lorsqu'ils disent du Saint-Esprit qu'il procède du Père et du Fils comme d'un seul principe de divinité, ils l'entendent dans le plan du rayonnement éternel, ou de l'économie divine."

[69] Lossky, "Climat Théologique," 243: "Florence est un exemple d'une 'non-recontre,' où les mêmes mots ne signfient pas les mêmes choses."

Lossky's argument is without foundation. Throughout the Florentine debates, what was at issue was the hypostatic procession of the Holy Spirit. Montenero made this clear from the first full session in Florence, when he asserted that, in the Blessed Trinity, "to be from another" could mean only "to receive existence from another," and hence that patristic writings that spoke of the Holy Spirit as being "from the Son" asserted that the Holy Spirit had his existence from the Son.[70] Mark Eugenikos denied this linguistic principle precisely because he knew that the hypostatic procession of the Spirit was the subject of debate. The Greeks could not have supposed that the final decree was speaking about another procession, different from that which had been discussed in the council hall. Nor do the fifteenth-century anti-unionist writers suggest that the Greek consent had been obtained by a simple misunderstanding. If they had believed this, they would doubtless have pointed it out, as it would be far less invidious than the suggestion that their fellow countrymen had been induced by bribes or threats into betraying their ancestral faith. Martin Jugie remarks after quoting the crystalline terms of the decree: "By these words, the way was shut to all ambiguities and subterfuges."[71]

An Invalid Decree?

George Scholarios, having been converted into an anti-unionist by the death-bed appeal of Mark Eugenikos, sought to undermine the authority of Florence by a battery of arguments.[72] Some have already been considered: the allegations of bribery, the claim that the decree of union was signed only from a desire to save Constantinople, the

---

70 *AG*, 288.

71 Jugie, *Theologia Dogmatica*, 2:349.

72 Summarized in Jugie, *Theologia Dogmatica*, 4:516, and Gill, *Council of Florence*, 407–408. For Scholarios, see subsection "Testimonies at the Council to Its Ecumenicity" under "An Ecumenical Council Was Convoked and Gave Judgment" in ch. 22.

hardships and homesickness of the Greeks. But Scholarios also gives three reasons why the final decree was not promulgated in a proper manner: the Council of Florence did not put the Creed before its definition like the other councils; it did not confirm the preceding synod, the Second Council of Nicaea; the decree was promulgated as a definition of the pope, not a definition of the synod.

The first two of these objections are simple cavilling. There was not the slightest ambiguity about whether the bishops present at Florence professed the Nicene-Constantinopolitan Creed, since all of them recited it liturgically, and the debated point was precisely about a word inserted into that creed. Likewise, there was not the slightest doubt that all the bishops present recognized Nicaea II. To claim that a conciliar decree, in order to be binding, must begin with an explicit confirmation of the previous ecumenical council, even when this council has been peacefully recognized by all parties for more than six hundred years, is to introduce an arbitrary and unreasonable criterion of ecumenicity.[73]

Scholarios's third argument is more interesting. He correctly notes a difference between the Florentine decree and that of the first seven councils. *Laetentur Caeli* begins with these words:

> Eugenius, bishop, servant of the servants of God, for a perpetual remembrance. With the consent to what is written below of our most dear son John Palaiologos, illustrious emperor of the Romans, and of the procurators of our venerable brothers the patriarchs and the other representatives of the Eastern Church.[74]

---

73 One may add that the definitions of the first seven councils were in fact read at Florence by Mark of Ephesus in full assembly, on October 16, 1438 (*AG*, 68–86).

74 *AG*, 459: "Eugenius episcopus, servus servorum dei, ad perpetuam rei memoriam. Consentiente ad infrascripta carissimo filio nostro Iohanne Paleaologo romaeorum imperatore illustri, et locatenentibus venerabilium fratrum nostrorum patriarcharum, et ceteris orientalem ecclesiam repraesentantibus."

Likewise, the strictly defining part of the decree begins:

> In the name, then, of the Holy Trinity, Father, Son and Holy Spirit, with the consent of this sacred universal Florentine council, we declare and define that this truth of the faith is to be believed and accepted by all Christians.[75]

The "we" in this sentence can only refer to Pope Eugenius himself: the council is said to consent to the definition, rather than to define.[76] The first seven councils, on the other hand, issued their definitions as coming from the assembled multitude of the bishops.

Since the pope himself was not personally present at any of those councils of the first millennium, there was no other for way for them to have phrased their definitions. It is, though, interesting to speculate how they would have phrased them had the Roman pontiff been present. It is possible that the phrasing of *Laetentur Caeli* corresponds to a characteristic Western mentality in which the plenary power of the pope tends to loom larger than the plenary power of a council.[77] However this may be, as an argument against the validity of the decree, Scholarios's observation fails. The bishops did not sign like notaries, as mere witnesses to a papal act, but as being themselves satisfied with its correctness. Thus the Greek bishops added to their names and offices the words στοιχήσας ὑπέργραψα, "satisfied, I subscribe."[78]

---

75 *AG*, 462: "In nomine igitur sanctae trinitatis, patris et filii et spiritus sancti, hoc sacro universali approbante Florentino concilio, diffinimus ut haec fidei veritas ab omnibus christianis credatur et suscipiatur."

76 Yet the Greek text has, for *approbante*, the term ἐπιψηφιζομένης, which is arguably stronger, as literally meaning "confirming or decreeing by vote." See appendix 1 for the full text.

77 The phrase *sacri approbatione concilii*, which emphasizes the supreme power of the pope rather than that of the pope and council considered as one, first appears in 1179 at the Third Lateran Council (Yves Congar, "1274–1974: Structures ecclésiales et conciles dans les relations entre Orient et Occident," *Revue des sciences philosophiques et théologiques* 58 [1974]: 355–90, at 360).

78 This is the formula found on the original bull of union, photographically reproduced in Gill, *Council of Florence*, 295. The Greek *acta* contain the different but equivalent formula ἀρεκτὸς ὑπέργραψα (*AG*, 465–66).

Conclusion

Now that we have considered the way in which the council of Ferrara-Florence fulfilled the criteria for an ecumenical council and responded to its ancient and modern opponents, what conclusion should be drawn? I suggest this one. In the sense in which St. Athanasius wrote that "the word of the Lord by the synod of Nicaea stands firm for ever," one may also say: "The word of the Lord by the synod of Florence stands firm for ever."

CHAPTER 24

POSTSCRIPT: BESSARION OR MARK OF EPHESUS?

THUS FAR I HAVE ARGUED for the ecumenical and binding character of the Council of Florence by considerations directly relevant to the subject—the convocation, composition, procedure, and consensus of the council. To complement this defense, I shall attempt a more delicate task: a moral comparison of the two principal Greek theologians of the time, as revealed by their activities during and after the Council. I suggest that this comparison offers an indirect confirmation of the validity of the Florentine decree.

Bessarion and Mark Eugenikos were both taken from the monastic life and consecrated as bishops in order to raise the level of theological learning among the Greek episcopate, partly in view of the approaching reunion Council with the Latins.[1] Bessarion was the younger man, having been born in 1403, while Mark was born in 1394.[2] They appear

1 Joseph Gill, *Personalities of the Council of Florence, and Other Essays* (Oxford: Blackwell, 1964), 46.

2 Gill, *Personalities*, 46, 231.

from the outset as the chief spokesmen for the Greeks. Both were chosen to belong to the small group that took part in the informal discussions on eschatology at Ferrara in 1438. At the public sessions themselves, so far as one can judge from the Greek *acta*, they were the only Greek bishops to make a significant contribution to the debates. Likewise, both of them had made the journey from Constantinople to Italy with the determination of upholding the rights of their own Church. "On arrival in the west, Mark Eugenikos was not obviously either more pro- or more anti-Latin than Bessarion."[3]

Mark, in his letter to Eugenius IV, written in Ferrara, asserts that the Pope can bring about the union of the churches simply by suppressing the *Filioque* and abolishing the "dead sacrifice" of unleavened bread used as the matter for the Holy Eucharist. Bessarion began by protesting equally clearly, though with greater civility, about the so-called "addition" to the Creed. "We wish your reverence to know," he tells Cardinal Cesarini, "that we deny this freedom [of adding a word to the Creed] to every church and to every synod, even to an ecumenical synod, and not only to the Roman Church."[4] In the treatise written many years later to Alexios Lascaris, Bessarion frankly admits the natural preference for the opinions of his own nation that he had brought to the great council: "I for my part loved our people, as was right, and I could have wished that our cause had been the stronger one, had that been possible; yet the truth had to be loved and preferred to all else."[5] This candid spirit was in evidence from the beginning of the public sessions in Ferrara. In his first speech, he tells the Latin Fathers that they, the Greeks, have come to Italy "desiring only to find the truth, preferring even to possess

---

3 Michael Angold, "Byzantium and the West 1204–1453," in *Eastern Christianity*, ed. Michael Angold, Cambridge History of Christianity 5 (Cambridge: Cambridge University Press, 2006), 53–78, at 74.

4 *AG*, 159: "Εἰδέναι βουλόμεθα τὴν αἰδεσιμότητα ὑμῶν ὅτι ταύτην ἡμεῖς τὴν ἄδειαν ἀπὸ πάσης ἀφαιροῦμεν ἐκκλησίας τε καὶ συνόδου, καὶ αὐτῆς τῆς οἰκουμενικῆς, ἀλλ᾽οὐκ ἀπὸ μόνης τῆς ῥωμαϊκῆς ἐκκλησίας."

5 Bessarion, Letter to Alexios Lascaris: "Amabam equidem nostros homines ut par erat, nostramque causam, si fieri potuisset, optassem esse meliorem; sed amanda in primis ac praeferenda veritas fuit" (*PG*, 161:319–20; as noted in a previous chapter, this is his own Latin translation of his Greek original found immediately prior in the same *PG* volume). This sentence occurs in the dedication addressed to Pope Paul II, with which the letter was accompanied.

this and be beaten, while disdaining to miss it and be victorious."[6] The confidence with which he told Cesarini a month later that no one had any power to alter the Creed of Nicaea-Constantinople shows that, at the beginning at least, he was not expecting the Greeks to be "beaten."

As late as April 1439, Bessarion still tended to believe that the Latins had been wrong to place the *Filioque* in the Creed without reference to an ecumenical council. In his crucial *Oratio Dogmatica de Unione*, delivered to the Greek delegation alone, he asserts that the Eastern Church had until now been right to separate themselves from the Latins, for these men had committed the fault of "judging of common things privately." Now that they had remedied their fault by meeting in a common synod, however, the Greeks must beware lest they in their turn become guilty:

> For now that they are free from the fault in question, having of their free will assembled in a general council, and declared that they will do whatever can be shown to be reasonable, and have made themselves as a result clear of all blame, we too must make proof of great zeal and forethought, so that we may do our duty carefully and sensibly, lest the charge which until now we have been accustomed to cast upon the Latins might return upon ourselves, and we might end by being judged guilty of that which once we alleged against them. For if, as we have been accustomed to say, the Latins were to be blamed for having decided a matter of faith on their own judgment alone before a general council had been called, now that what we sought has been done, and we have all gathered together, we must seriously strive and make great efforts in order that we may go from here without fault.[7]

---

6 *AG*, 38: "Τὴν δ᾽ἀλήθειαν ἀνευρεῖν προθυμούμενοι μόνον, καὶ μετὰ μὲν ταύτης ἀγαπῶντες καὶ τὸ νικᾶσθαι, ταύτης δὲ ἄνευ καὶ τὸ νικᾶν ἀπωθούμενοι."

7 *ODDU*, 7–8. My English translation is made from Bessarion's own Latin version of his speech; the original speech, of course, was made in Greek.

At some point after this speech, even this restrained criticism of the Latins faded, and he accepted the phrase in the decree of union that the word *Filioque* had been added to the Creed "lawfully and reasonably" (*licite et rationabiliter*).

As for the truth of the doctrine, as opposed to the manner in which it had been placed in the Creed, Bessarion's mind had already changed at the time of the *Oratio*. A remark of his recorded only in the Latin *acta* shows that, at the start of the council, he accepted the Photian belief in procession from the Father alone. Commenting on the phrase "from the Father and the Son," he says that it could be false either because the Holy Spirit does not proceed from the Father or because he does not proceed from the Son, and adds, "and this latter [proposition] we say to be true, and you say to be false."[8] The change was made possible by his openness to the testimony of the Fathers. Having heard the Dominican provincial of Lombardy, John of Montenero, set out the Catholic case from patristic sources, he told the other Greek bishops: "We will do our duty as children, paying a proper attention to our fathers, submitting our own will to them and receiving seeds [of truth] from them."[9] This, after all, was how previous councils had proceeded, following not syllogistic reasoning but the bare assertions of earlier doctors.[10] His later description of the effect of Montenero's words suggests not only an intellectual conviction but also a spiritual conversion:

> When I saw and heard those [authorities], then suddenly I left behind me all spirit of strife and contradiction, and I gave in to the authorities of those who had thus spoken. . . . Not only did I give in, but I also gave thanks to our Savior, that he had granted me to hear and understand things that I had never previously heard.[11]

---

8 *AL*, 49: "Una earum [orationum] est falsa sive: 'non procedit a patre,' alia: 'non procedit a filio'—et hanc veram nos esse dicimus, vos contra."

9 *ODDU*, 14–15.

10 *ODDU*, 12.

11 Bessarion, Letter to Alexios Lascaris: "Cum enim vidissem et audivissem eas [auctoritates], subito omni contentione et contradictione postposita, acquievi auctoritati dicentium . . . non solum acquievi verum etiam gratias egi Salvatori nostro qui mihi donavit, et audivisse et intellexisse, quae numquam ante audivi" (*PG*, 161:425A).

Those who did not wish to accept the union had only two options left, he told his fellow Greeks. On the one hand, they could declare that the Fathers had erred about the Holy Spirit. But no one will accept this view unless he wishes to overturn all the foundations of our faith, the mysteries of the Church, and all truth.[12] Alternatively he could claim that the patristic passages that support the *Filioque* were all interpolations, and not authentic. But such a course is absurd, particularly as applied to the Latin Fathers:

> It is the plainest folly, if we say that their books have been corrupted, changed and interpolated by some rash and daring act, since they exist in so great a number and were written by so many doctors, since they are found in so great a number of texts and volumes, some of them in particular of very great age and scattered and multiplied across the face of the earth, and since the argument in them is developed in a logically coherent way: they make the truth as clear as can be.[13]

Bessarion is urgent with his confrères that they should not shrink from acting in accordance with the truth that has emerged from the debate, but should rather bear in mind their future judgment: "What reply will we make to God about why we remained separated from our brothers, when he descended from heaven, was incarnated and crucified in order that he might unite us and bring us into one sheepfold?"[14] He even ventures by way of peroration to remind them of his own integrity as a motive of credibility:

---

[12] *ODDU*, 68: "Nec vos a[p]probatis, nisi quis omnia fidei nostrae fundamenta, ecclesie mysteria, et omnem veritatem evertere velit."

[13] *ODDU*, 68–69: "Apertissima ignavia est, si tot eorum libros, tot eorum opera doctorum, tot eorum labores, tot volumina—praesertim antiquissima manu nonnulla eorum conscripta, et per totum orbem terrarum sparsa, et multiplicata, per ipsum item sequentium ad praecedentia connexum et convenientiam, ipsam veritatem luce clarius ostendentia—temerario ausu corrupta, mutata et superadditata esse dicemus."

[14] *ODDU*, 71: "Que nobis relinquetur apud deum responsio, quare a fratribus divisi fuerimus, quos ut uniret, et ad unum ovile redigeret, ipse descendit de celis, incarnatus et crucifixus est?"

> I call to witness God, and all you who are present, and all our posterity, that from the beginning even to this day, I have always taken thought for and spoken what things have seemed to me true, just, useful, and helpful to us and to our salvation, without passion or deceit. I have not been silent out of fear—lest anyone should think me influenced by the Latins. I have not preferred my own safety to the common utility. No: commending myself and all I have to God and submitting it to his divine will, he who from my earliest years has always ruled and governed my life better than I could have chosen for myself, I have set the common good for my goal, and looking to this alone, I have done and said whatever I have either done or said, seeking at once both the truth of the faith as far as I could and also that our people might attain bodily safety.[15]

His fervor, though, is unmarred by fanaticism, and the speech ends on a note of pathos that almost six centuries later is still moving:

> You, however, have free will, and you must do whatever seems good to yourselves. May the better and healthier cause prevail with you also, by the will of heaven. But if the worse one should triumph, which may God forbid, let the whole human race, and every age, rank and condition know this—for I must declare it once more—that I am innocent of this evil, of this bitter schism. I have never held, nor do I now hold, that we should be divided without any reason from the Latins. I do not persuade myself that they judge wrongly concerning the faith, nor that they believe

[15] *ODDU*, 72: "Ego quidem summum deum, et vos omnes presentes, et cunctos posteros nostros testor, quod sine passione et fraude, quae vera, quae iusta, quae utilia, quae conducentia nobis et nostre saluti mihi visa sunt, a principio usque ad hunc diem non cessavi dicere, non omisi consulere, nec timore deterritus (ne quis me Latinis affectum putet) tacui, nec propriam securitatem communi utilitati preposui: sed me et mea omnia Deo commendans, et eius divine voluntati subiciens, qui totam mihi vitam ab ineunte etate melius quam optassem, direxit atque rexit, commune bonum mihi, ut finem, proposui, et ad hoc solum respiciens, et feci et dixi, quaecumque vel feci vel dixi, simul et fidei veritatem quoad potui, et corporalem salutem ut nostri adipiscantur, conatus."

> differently from the saints of East and West. Nor am I ignorant what dangers, what disasters, what ruin awaits us and our country. I have foreseen it and I have predicted it, and as far as I could, I have prevented it. And if I shall not have been able to succeed, then not with me lies the blame, but with them who hear me.[16]

Appropriately enough, Bessarion was chosen to read the decree of union in Greek in the cathedral of Florence at the ceremony of July 6, 1439, that marked the end of the schism.

Twenty-four years later, writing to the people of Constantinople as both their lawful patriarch and a cardinal of the Roman church,[17] he says of the disputed word: "If you are willing to consider it rightly, it was not an addition, but an exposition, an explanation, a declaration";[18] if the doctrine had not been true, it would have been right to avoid the word, but "if it is true, and in accord with the faith of the saints, we are now 'fearing a fear where there is no fear,' and serving superstition rather than piety."[19] As he had made a testimony to the other bishops a quarter of a century earlier, so now he offers a last testament to his fellow-countrymen suffering under the Turkish yoke:

> I do not think that you will say that I have erred from ignorance or from incompetence, since you know that from my earliest

---

[16] *ODDU*, 73: "Vos, vero, cum libera sit vobis voluntas, quodcumque agendum videatur, id agatis. Vincant autem nutu divino etiam apud vos, quae meliora et saniora sunt. Quod si (quod absit) peior sententia superabit, hoc tamen omne genus humanum, omnis etas, omnis ordo atque conditio sciat (protestandum enim rursus est) quod innocens ego sum ab hoc malo, hoc acerbo schismate; nec huius umquam sententiae fui, nec sum, preter omnem rationem a Latinis dividi. Nec enim mihi persuadeo, non recte et vere de fide eos sapere, et eadem que sanctos doctores, tam Orientales quam Occidentales, non credere eos. Nec ignoro, quae hinc nos et nostram rempublicam sequentur pericula, que calamitates, quae excidia. Sed previdi, predixi, et ne fiant, providi. Quod si proficere non potui, non mei dicentis, sed audientium culpa est [εἰ δὲ μὴ ἐδυνέθην ἀνύσαι, οὐ τοῦ εἰπόντος, ἀλλα τῶν μὴ πεισθέντων τὸ ἔγκλημα]."

[17] In 1455 he was almost elected pope. A contemporary witness, writing to the Duke of Milan, observed that "if the Greek cardinal had exerted himself more the tiara would have been his" (quoted in N. Paxton, "Cardinal Bessarion of Nicaea," *Eastern Christian Journal* 10, no. 1 [2003]: 9–24, at 18).

[18] Bessarion, Encyclical to the Greeks: "Si recte considerare volueritis, non additio fuit sed expositio, sed explanatio, sed declaratio" (*PG*, 161:481–90, at 487C; this is his own Latin translation of his Greek original found in the same *PG* volume).

[19] Bessarion, Encyclical to the Greeks: "Quod si verum est, et fidei sanctorum consonans, ibi timemus timorem, ubi non est timor, et superstitioni magis quam pietati indulgemus" (*PG*, 161:487C).

youth I have spent all my time in the study of letters, and studied the dogma about which we are speaking with great toil and diligence. What could a man choose who from his youth lived in lowliness and obedience, forgoing his own will, and who, if it may be said without boasting, has read, heard and written much about the vanity of the world, about progress in morals, about eternal rewards and punishments, than to nourish his mind with true and right thoughts, and to embrace the truth once he has found it?

This truth I hold so much the dearer now than before, as my age weighs the more heavily upon me, and the growing infirmity of my body daily puts me in mind of my death and makes me grow weary of life. I know well, my Fathers, and brothers, and my sons, dearly beloved in Christ, that not much life remains to me, and that the time of my dissolution is at hand, when, as the wise say, men begin to conceive a fear of things of which they had previously no fear. For they see the day draw near when they will have to give an account of all their past life. But the closer death comes to me, the more the integrity of my faith consoles me. For I hope that the truth of my faith may make up for what I lack from good works for my soul's salvation. For the sake of faith I turned my back on all those honourable positions which I had among you, and which were neither few nor trifling, and I followed the truth of this faith with my whole heart. . . .

Just as I did not set great store by the honours which I had among you, so also, as God is my witness, I set as little store by those which I have now. Indeed, if I had even more than I do, I should cast them all aside and go over to you with the greatest haste, if it were not that I am conscious of having chosen the better part, and if I did not know for sure that this holy and

Catholic Church believes and transmits and teaches the things that lead to life eternal.[20]

By the time this appeal was sent by the exiled patriarch, Mark Eugenikos was already dead.[21] Unlike Bessarion he had experienced no conversion at the Council of Florence, nor afterwards. Although he stated that he accepted the principle that the Latin fathers were reliable guides in matters of faith, he was unmoved by Montenero's exposition of their thought. The texts quoted by the Dominican taught the *Filioque*—therefore they must be corrupt. In vain did Bessarion exclaim: "If we remove all such words from the books—whole homilies, commentaries on the Gospels, complete treatises on Trinitarian theology—there will be nothing left but blank pages."[22] Mark laid down an a priori principle that made discussion impossible: "To the extent that the writings of Western saints are in accord with the letter of St. Maximus to Marinus, I take them to be genuine; to the extent that they disagree with it, I do not accept them."[23]

It is, unfortunately, impossible to acquit the metropolitan of Ephesus

---

20 Bessarion, Encyclical to the Greeks: "Neque me ex ignorantia, vel imperitia a veritate, ut arbitror, dicetis aberrasse, cum me sciatis a teneris annis omne vitae meae tempus in litterarum studiis consumpsisse, summaque opera ac diligentia huic, de quo loquimur, dogmati incubuisse, et quantum fieri potuit investigasse veritatem. Quid enim aliud eligere sibi potuit homo, qui ab ineunte aetate propria abdicatus voluntate in humilitate atque obedientia vixerit, et (qui sine iactantia dictum sit) multa de vanitate mundi, de emendatione morum, de praemiis, vel poenis aeternis legerit, audierit, scripserit, quam rectis verisque sententiis alere animam, et inventam fidei veritatem amplecti? Quam certe eo pluris quam antea in praesentia facimus, quo magis ingravescente iam aetate, multiplicati corporis morbi mortem mihi quotidie minantur, et vitam taedio esse faciunt. Scio certe Patres, et fratres, et scio in Christo filii dilecti, non multum esse quod nobis superest vitae, et iam tempus nostrae resolutionis instat, quo, ut sapientes aiunt, advenit hominibus timor earum rerum, quasi antea formidare non solebant. Vident enim appropinquare diem, quo omnis anteactae vitae reddenda est ratio. Me quidem quo magis vicina est mors, eo magis consolatur integritas fidei. Spero enim id, quod ex operibus ad salutem animae meae deerit, fidei veritate posse suppleri. Ob hanc causam spretis et contemptis honoribus, ii quos apud vos habui (habui autem nec parvos nec paucos) totus hanc fidei veritatem sum secutus . . . et quae apud vos habebamus non magni fecimus, et quae nunc habemus testem invocamus Deum, aeque parvifecissemus, quin potius spretis, contemptisque omnnibus, etiam si multa plura haberemus, ad vos quam celerrime defecissemus, nisi nobis essemus conscii elegisse meliora, nisi exploratum haberemus hanc sanctam et catholicam Ecclesiam illa credere, illa tradere, et docere, quae ad vitam aeternam iter faciunt" (*PG*, 161:486B–87B).

21 He died on June 23, 1444 (Sophron Pétridès, "La mort de Marc d'Ephèse," *Echos d'Orient* 13 [1910]: 19–21, at 19).

22 *AG*, 401.

23 *SYR*, 394: "Ὅσα τῶν δυστικῶν ἁγίων ῥητά εἰσι σύμφωνα τῇ πρὸς Μαρῖνον ἐπιστολῇ τοῦ ἁγίου Μαξίμου, δέξομαι ὡς γνήσια· ὅσα δὲ διαφωνοῦσιν, οὐ παραδέξομαι." We have seen in the first part of the present volume that there is no need to hold St. Maximus's doctrine incompatible with the Latin understanding of the *Filioque.*

of the charge of bad faith. His assertion that it was illicit to add any word to the Creed was based on the declaration of the Council of Ephesus, and he continued to make the same assertion though it was pointed out to him that that Council had explicitly referred to the original creed of Nicaea and not to the longer creed of Constantinople that was in liturgical use in both East and West. His assertion that the *Filioque* was false was based, in Florence, on a few scriptural and patristic texts that admitted of either a Catholic or a non-Catholic interpretation.[24] Having failed to attend Montenero's exposition of the Catholic case, he dismissed without study all the Latin texts that told against him as inauthentic.

As we have seen, in his later defense of his behavior at Florence, Eugenikos did not scruple to accuse his fellow bishops of having been won over by bribery; the patriarch himself had been "corrupted."[25] This is in striking contrast to Bessarion's generous appeal to his colleagues: "You must do whatever seems good to yourselves." Having previously spoken approvingly to Pope Eugenius of the latter's convocation of the council, Mark now declares that it had always been unnecessary:

> We did not have an incomplete faith until now, nor were we in need of a council or a definition in order that we might learn something new, being the sons and disciples of the ecumenical councils and of the fathers who shone in the councils and afterwards.[26]

---

24 In the first part of this work, I looked at those he drew from the Fathers under consideration. See the section on *Contra Sabellianos* in ch. 3 (St. Athanasius); the subsection "Disputed Readings" under the *Adversus Eunomium* and the section on Homily 24 in ch. 5 (St. Basil); the sections "An Eternal Procession and Reception" and "The Son as Breather and Fount of the Holy Spirit" in ch. 6 (St. Epiphanius); the section "The Holy Spirit is Consubstantial with the Son" in ch. 11 (St. Cyril of Alexandria); and the section on Theodoret in ch. 12 ("Roots of Anti-Filioquism in the Patristic Era").

25 Mark Eugenikos, *Relatio de rebus a se gestis*: "῞Ουτοις δὲ καὶ ὁ πατριάρχης ἐπεψηφίσατο, προδιεφθαρμένος ἤδη καὶ οὗτος" (*OAU*, 140). See the subsection "The Convocation and Decree: the Greeks" under "An Ecumenical Council Was Convoked and Gave Judgment" in ch. 22 ("The Authority of the Council of Ferrara-Florence").

26 Mark Eugenikos, Letter to a Monastic Superior on Mount Athos: " Οὐδὲ γὰρ ἐλλιπῆ τὴν πίστιν εἴχομεν ἄχρι τοῦ νῦν, οὐδε συνόδου καὶ ὅρου πρὸς τὸ μαθεῖν τι καινότερον ἐδεόμεθα οἱ τῶν οἰκουμενικῶν συνόδων καὶ τῶν ἐν ταύταις καὶ μεταξὺ τούτων διαλαμψάντων πατέρων υἱοί τε καὶ μαθηταί" (*OAU*, 170).

In his anxiety to deny the binding character of the Florentine synod that he had once declared to be ecumenical, he comes close to denying the very idea of a living, teaching Church. "No one lords it over our faith, not an emperor, nor a high priest, nor a false synod, nor anyone else, but only God."[27] He does not hide his isolation from the other bishops at Florence. Recalling the crucial meeting at which the patriarch declared his adhesion to the *Filioque*, he writes: "From then on, I was divided from them, and left by myself."[28] Continuing division from the Latins is justified by their times of fasting, their rites of baptism and their unleavened bread,[29] and also by their ridiculous habit of shaving.[30] In a crude if spirited pun, he declares that the unionist bishops have defined the *Filioque* "in their ὅρος or rather in their ὀρρός."[31]

While none of Bessarion's contemporaries deny his integrity,[32] the same cannot be said for Eugenikos. Gregory Mammas, patriarch of Constantinople from the mid 1440s and delegate of the patriarch of Alexandria during the Council of Florence, suggests in his *Responsio ad epistolam Marci Ephesini* that Eugenikos's intransigent attitude towards the union was due in part to disappointed expectations. He quotes Mark's charge that his fellow bishops signed the decree from a desire to make money, and after having first pointed out that Mark himself received the same expenses from the Pope as everyone else, he recalls that Mark had had a portrait painted of Pope Eugenius and had

---

27 Mark Eugenikos, Letter to a Monastic Superior on Mount Athos: "Οὐδεὶς κυριεύει τῆς ἡμῶν πίστεως, οὐ βασιλεύς, οὐκ ἀρχιερεύς, οὐ ψευδὴς σύνοδος, οὐκ ἄλλος οὐδείς, ὅτι μὴ θεὸς μόνον" (*OAU*, 170).

28 Mark Eugenikos, *Relatio de rebus a se gestis*: "Ἐγὼ δὲ χωρισθεῖς αὐτῶν ἔκτοτε καὶ ἐμαυτῷ σχολάσας" (*OAU*, 140).

29 Mark Eugenikos, Encyclical to all Orthodox Greeks (*OAU*, 142–43).

30 Mark Eugenikos, Letter to George, a priest of Methone, against the rites of the Roman Church (*OAU*, 165). In the same place, Mark also finds fault with Latin churches for having no bishop's throne and accuses Latin priests of throwing the ablutions on to the ground when cleansing the chalice after Holy Communion, and of standing on their own altars. I do not know what the last accusation can refer to.

31 Mark Eugenikos, Encyclical to all Orthodox Greeks (*OAU*, 456–57). The former word means "definition"; the latter is defined in the Greek dictionary as "the end of the *os sacrum*."

32 John Meyendorff, however, suggests that he was a secret pagan! This is on account of his having been a pupil and friend of Gemistos Plethon, who was accused of the same charge (*Byzantine Theology: Historical Trends and Doctrinal Themes*, 2nd rev. ed [New York: Fordham University Press, 1983], 113). Vojtech Hladky points out that John and Mark Eugenikos were also pupils of Plethon, and states that it is impossible to doubt the firm Christian faith of any of the three (*The Philosophy of Gemistos Plethon: Platonism in Late Byzantium, between Hellenism and Orthodoxy* [Burlington, VT: Ashgate, 2014], 207).

written a letter to him in which he wrote among other things: "Father Abraham, lift up your hands and bless your children who have come to you from the East." Was it because he was disappointed to receive no money from the Pope for doing this, Mammas wonders, that he is now accusing others of avarice?[33]

Even though Sylvester Syropoulos's *Memoirs* were written to justify those Greeks who had resiled from the union, its portrait of Mark of Ephesus suggests a considerable element of vanity in that bishop's character. When Mark learned that he has been appointed procurator for Antioch, he complained that this was an indignity: since as a simple monk he had been a procurator for Alexandria, he should not represent only Antioch now that he is a bishop.[34] When he first entered the council chamber, he abused the simple monk who, having been chosen to represent Alexandria, was seated at a higher position than himself, so that the monk, to avoid conflict, left his appointed seat and took another one at random.[35] Syropoulos also relates that, according to Bessarion, Mark was inconsistent in his opposition to the *Filioque*. The metropolitan of Nicaea affirms that, having opposed the doctrine during the public sessions, Eugenikos promised in a private audience that they both had with the pope and the emperor that he would finally accept it, given time.[36]

Joseph Plousiadenos gives us a similar impression of the character of the metropolitan of Ephesus, as marred by vanity and by either inconsistency or a lack of straightforwardness. In his *Responsio* addressed directly to Eugenikos, even though the latter was now dead, he says: "You thought that the Latins were inexperienced in learning, and that you would thus persuade them to yield to you. But you found things there to be other than you had expected."[37]

---

33 *PG*, 160:132C.
34 *SYR*, 248.
35 *SYR*, 248, 252.
36 *SYR*, 422.
37 Joseph Plousiadenos, *Refutatio Marci Ephesi*: "Σὺ μὲν γὰρ ᾤμου τοὺς Λατίνους ἀπείρους εἶναι σοφίας, καὶ οὕτω πείσειν αὐτοὺς ὡς ἀμαθεῖς ὑπακοῦσαι σοι. Ἐκεῖ δὲ ἄλλως εὗρες ἢ ὡς σὺ ἤλπιζες" (*PG*, 159:1028D).

The bishop of Methone also gives a curious account of Mark's failure to appear for the final session of the Council, when Montenero set out the Catholic case at length. We have already seen how Syropoulos claims that the emperor had forbidden him to attend lest he cause trouble, while Mark in his memoirs attributed his absence to ill health. Plousiadenos rhetorically reminds Mark of the nature of the malady:

> The council once more sent a messenger to call you. Those who were sent found you raving and crying out with broken phrases. When they invited you to the council, you replied: "I cannot come; for last night some cardinals took the roof off my house and came in, and scourged my limbs with fiery rods—and do they now invite me to the council? I cannot come. Do you not see the wounds yourselves?" And showing your limbs you said: "See, how I am black and blue all over." They understood what kind of sickness you were suffering from and returned to tell the sacred council that you could not come because you were unwell.[38]

When Mark learned that the synod was minded to force him to appear before it to answer for his failure to subscribe, Plousiadenos relates, he went to the emperor to ask to be saved from a public humiliation, but in such a way that John VIII was led to think that Mark would submit to the union once they had returned to Constantinople:

> Do not [Plousiadenos quotes him as saying to the emperor] insult my grey hairs, so that I should have to appear foolish and ignorant to the Italians. My Lord Emperor, prepare some excuse for me. Let some little time go by. I think it would be a great disgrace for me to give my signature in this place.[39]

38 Joseph Plousiadenos, *Refutatio Marci Ephesi* (*PG*, 159:1068B–C).

39 Joseph Plousiadenos, *Disceptatio pro Concilio Florentino*: "Μή μου τὴν πολίαν ὑβρίσητε, καὶ φανῶ τοῖς Ἰταλοῖς

Plousiadenos adds that when Mark got off the ship in Constantinople and found himself cheered by a crowd, he took heart and resolved again to oppose the union.[40]

One would gladly avoid mentioning a final detail recorded by the bishop of Methone; yet it seems generally unknown, and for a Catholic it presents a terrible, symbolic significance. Having recalled how Mark described the old patriarch, Joseph II, as having been "corrupted" at Florence, even though, according to Plousiadenos, he would not have dared to say so if the patriarch had been still alive, "or if you had so much as seen his shadow," the author goes on to contrast the manner of their deaths. Patriarch Joseph II, having gladly accepted the union and professed his faith in the Holy Spirit, in purgatory, and in the Roman pontiff, knelt down, raised his hands to heaven, and died giving thanks.

> But you, who so insolently abuse him and those who were with him, did not so die, but rather, you breathed forth your soul along with the filth of the latrine. The whole city knows it. For the justice of God knows how to pay back each one for the faith which he has, just as once happened with Arius, that byword for madness. For he sent forth his bowels beneath him, while you expelled the filth upwards.[41]

St. Anastasius I of Antioch taught that when the Holy Spirit is called in the Psalms the "breath of his mouth," the "mouth" represents the

μωρός τε καὶ ἀμαθής. Φρόντισον, κύριε βασιλεῦ, ἀπολογίαν δοῦναι ὑπὲρ ἐμοῦ. Ἄφετε παρελθεῖν ὀλίγος καιρός. Ἀισχύνην μεγίστην ἡγοῦμενος τὴν ὑπογραφήν μου ἀποδοῦναι ἐνταῦθα" (*PG*, 159:992B–C).

40 Joseph Plousiadenos, *Disceptatio pro Concilio Florentino* (*PG*, 159:992B–C).

41 Joseph Plousiadenos, *Refutatio Marci Ephesi*: "Σὺ δὲ ὁ ἀναιδῶς συκοφαντών αὐτὸν καὶ τοὺς μετ᾽αὐτοῦ, οὐχ οὕτως, ἀλλ᾽ὁμοῦ σὺν τῇ κόπρῳ τοῦ ἀφεδρῶνος ἐξέπνευσας· μαρτυρεῖ τοῦτο ἡ πόλις. Οὕτως οἶδεν ἡ θεῖα δίκη ταλαντεύειν ἕκαστον κατὰ τὴν ἑαυτοῦ πίστιν, ὡς πάλαι τὸν τῆς μανίας ἐπώνυμον Ἄρειον, ὅς κάτω τὰ ἔγκατα ἔπεμψεν, σὺ δὲ ἄνω τὴν κόπρον" (*PG*, 159:1088B). A similar account is given by Hubertin Pusculo, an Italian who was in Constantinople at the time. The second stanza of Pusculo's poem *Constantinopolis* describes Eugenikos's copremesis at some length, and also draws the analogy with Arius (Pétridès, "La mort de Marc d'Ephèse," 20).

only-begotten Son.[42] Is it possible to see in this wretched end of Mark Eugenikos, notorious throughout Constantinople, a sign of heaven's displeasure with one who had so determinedly denied to the divine mouth the honor of breathing forth the consubstantial Spirit, and who has passed on this denial to his posterity?

---

42 Anastasius of Antioch, *De Sanctissima Trinitate* (*PG*, 89:1324D).

APPENDIX I

The Florentine Definition of the Procession of the Holy Spirit*

Ἐν τῷ ὀνόματι τοίνυν τῆς ἁγιάς τριάδος, τοῦ πατρὸς καὶ τοῦ ὑιοῦ καὶ τοῦ ἁγίου πνεύματος, ταύτης τῆς ἱερᾶς καὶ οἰκουμενικῆς τῆς ἐν Φλωρεντείᾳ ἐπιψηφιζομένης συνόδου ὁρίζομεν, ἵνα αὕτη ἡ τῆς πίστεως ἀλήθεια ὑπὸ πάντων τῶν χριστιανῶν πιστευθείη τε καὶ ἀποδεχθείη, καὶ οὕτω πάντες ὁμολογῶσιν, ὅτι τὸ πνεῦμα τὸ ἅγιον ἐκ τοῦ πατρὸς καὶ τοῦ υἱοῦ ἀιδίως ἐστί, καὶ τὴν ἑαυτοῦ οὐσίαν καὶ τὸ ὑπαρτικὸν αὐτοῦ εἶναι ἔχει ἐκ τοῦ πατρὸς ἅμα καὶ τοῦ ὑιοῦ, καὶ ἐξ ἀμφοτέρων ἀιδίως ὡς ἀπὸ μιᾶς ἀρχῆς καὶ μοναδικῆς προβολῆς ἐκπορεύεται.

Διασαφοῦντες, ὅτι τοῦθ’ὅπερ οἱ ἅγιοι διδάσκαλοι καὶ πατέρες ἐκ τοῦ πατρὸς διὰ τοῦ υἱοῦ ἐκπορεύεσθαι λέγουσι τὸ πνεῦμα τὸ ἅγιον, εἰς ταύτην φέρει τὴν ἔννοιωαν ὥστε διὰ τούτων δηλοῦσθαι, καὶ τὸν υἱὸν εἶναι κατὰ μὲν τοὺς γραικούς, αἰτίαν, κατὰ δὲ τοὺς λατίνους, ἀρχὴν τῆς τοῦ ἁγίου πνεύματος ὑπάρξεως, ὥσπερ καὶ τὸν πατέρα.

Καὶ ἐπεὶ πάντα ὅσα ἐστὶ τοῦ πατρός, αὐτὸς ὁ πατὴρ τῷ μονογενεῖ αὐτοῦ υἱῷ ἐν τῷ γεννᾶν δέδωκε, πλὴν τοῦ εἶναι πατέρα, τοῦτ’αὐτό, ὅτι τὸ πνεῦμα τὸ ἅγιον ἐκ τοῦ υἱοῦ ἐκπορεύεται, αὐτὸς ὁ υἱὸς παρὰ τοῦ πατρὸς ἀιδίως ἔχει, ἀφ’οὗ ἀιδίως γεγέννηται.

In nomine igitur sancte Trinitatis, Patris, Filii, et Spiritus Sancti, hoc sacro universali approbante Florentino concilio, diffinimus ut hec fidei veritas ab omnibus christianis credatur et suscipiatur, sicque omnes profiteantur, quod Spiritus sanctus ex Patre et Filio eternaliter est, et essentiam suam suumque esse subsistens habet ex Patre simul et Filio, et ex utroque eternaliter tanquam ab uno principio procedit, declarantes quod id, quod sancti doctores et patres dicunt, ex Patre per Filium procedere Spiritum sanctum, ad hanc intelligentiam tendit, ut per hoc significetur Filium quoque esse, secundum Grecos quidem causam, secundum Latinos vero principium subsistentie Spiritus sancti, sicut et Patrem.

Et quoniam omnia, que Patris sunt, Pater ipse unigenito Filio suo gignendo dedit, praeter esse Patrem; hoc ipsum, quod Spiritus sanctus procedit ex Filio, ipse Filius a Patre eternaliter habet, a quo etiam eternaliter genitus est.

In the name of the holy Trinity, Father, Son and Holy Spirit, we define, with the approval of this holy and universal council of Florence, that the following truth of faith shall be believed and accepted by all Christians and thus shall all profess it: that the Holy Spirit is eternally from the Father and the Son, and has his essence and his subsistent being from the Father together with the Son, and proceeds from both eternally as from one principle and a single spiration. We declare that when holy doctors and fathers say that the Holy Spirit proceeds from the Father through the Son, this bears the sense that thereby also the Son should be signified, according to the Greeks indeed as cause, and according to the Latins as principle of the subsistence of the Holy Spirit, just like the Father.

And since the Father gave to his only-begotten Son in begetting him everything the Father has, except to be the Father, so the Son has eternally from the Father, by whom he was eternally begotten, this also, namely that the Holy Spirit proceeds from the Son.

---

* Text taken from *Decrees of the Ecumenical Councils: From Nicaea I to Vatican II*, ed. Norman P. Tanner and Giuseppe Alberigo, vol. 1 (Washington, DC: Georgetown University Press, 1990; copyright Sheed & Ward, an imprint of Bloomsbury Publishing Plc.), 526–27.

APPENDIX 2

Acts of Ecumenical Councils Approving by Name Certain Teachers of the Faith

Acts of the First Session of the Council of Chalcedon, October 8, 451[1]

The most glorious judges and the whole senate said, "Let each one of the most reverend bishops of the present synod hasten to set forth how he believes, writing without any fear, but placing the fear of God before his eyes, knowing that our divine and pious Lord believes according to the ecthesis of the three hundred and eighteen holy fathers at Nicaea, and according to the ecthesis of the one hundred and fifty after them, and according to the canonical epistles and ectheses of the holy Fathers Gregory [Nazianzen], Basil, Athanasius, Hilary, and Ambrose, and according to the two canonical epistles of Cyril, which were confirmed and published in the First Council of Ephesus, nor does he in any point depart from the faith of the same."

[1] Mansi, 6:935D–38A: "Gloriosissimi iudices et amplissimus senatus dixerunt: Unusquisque reverendissimorum episcoporum praesentis sancti concilii, quomodo credit, in scriptis sine ullo metu, Dei timorem ante suos oculos ponens, exponere festinet, cognoscens, quoniam divinissimus et piissimus dominus noster secundum expositionem in Nicaea congregatorum trecentorum decem et octo sanctorum patrum, et secundum expositionem qui post eos fuerunt, centum quinquaginta, et secundum canonicas epistolas et expositiones sanctorum patrum, Gregorii, Basilii, Athanasii, Hilarii, Ambrosii, et Cyrilli duas canonicas epistolas in Ephesina prima synodo publicatas et confirmatas, credit, nullo modo ab earum fide recedens." All translations in this appendix will be my own.

From the Letter of Emperor Justinian I Read at the First Session of the Second Council of Constantinople, May 5, 553[2]

We follow in every way the holy fathers and doctors of the holy Church of God: Athanasius, Hilary, Basil, Gregory the theologian, and Gregory Nyssa, Ambrose, Theophilus, John of Constantinople [Chrysostom], Cyril, Augustine, Proclus, and Leo, and we receive all the things that have been written and produced by these men concerning the true faith and for the condemnation of heretics.

From the Statement of Faith Approved at the Third Session of the Second Council of Constantinople, May 9, 553[3]

We follow in all respects also the holy fathers and doctors of the Church: Athanasius, Hilary, Basil, Gregory the theologian, and Gregory Nyssa, Ambrose, Augustine, Theophilus, John of Constantinople, Cyril, Leo, and Proclus, and we receive all that they have set forth concerning the true faith and for the condemnation of heretics.

---

2 Mansi, 9:183AB: "Sequimur autem in omnibus sanctos patres et doctores sanctae Dei ecclesiae, id est, Athanasium, Hilarium, Basilium, Gregorium theologum, et Gregorium Nissenum, Ambrosium, Theophilum, Ioannem Constantinopolitanum, Cyrillum, Augustinum, Proculum, Leonem, et omnia quae ab his de fide recta et ad condemnationem haereticorum conscripta et expolita sunt suscipimus."

3 Mansi, 9:201D–2A: "Sequimur per omnia et sanctos patres et doctores ecclesiae, id est, Athanasium, Hilarium, Basilium, Gregorium theologum, et Gregorium Nissenum, Ambrosium, Augustinum, Theophilum, Ioannem Constantinopolitanum, Cyrillum, Leonem, Proculum, et suscipimus omnia quae de recta fide et condemnatione haereticorum exposuerunt."

APPENDIX 3

Patristic Testimonies Claimed by John de Montenero in Addressing the Council of Florence at the Seventh and Eighth Public Sessions in March 1439

(with Judgments on Authorship from *Clavis Patrum Graecorum* and *Clavis Patrum Latinorum*)*

Latin Testimonies

1. Leo, Sermon for Pentecost (*PL*, 54:402A; authentic)
2. Leo, Letter to Turribius (disputed)
3. Damasus, Letter to Paulinus (inauthentic)
4. Hilary, *De Trinitate* 7.20 (*PL*, 10:250C–51B; authentic)
5. Hilary, *De Trinitate* 3.29 (*PL*, 10:69A–70A; authentic)
6. Jerome, Letter to Damasus (inauthentic)
7. Jerome, Letter to Augustine and Alipius (unknown)
8. Jerome, Exposition of the Nicene Creed (inauthentic)
9. Ambrose, *De Spiritu Sancto* 1.11 (*PL*, 16:732C; authentic)
10. Ambrose, *De Spiritu Sancto* 2.12 (*PL*, 16:771B–C; authentic)
11. Ambrose, *De Spiritu Sancto* 1.15 (*PL*, 16:739A–B; authentic)
12. Ambrose, *De Spiritu Sancto* 1.4 (*PL*, 16:718B; authentic)
13. Augustine, Letter, "On the faith to Peter," no. 1 (*PL* 65: 674A; by St. Fulgentius of Ruspe)
14. Augustine, Letter, "To Orosius against the Priscillianists and Origenists" (*PL*, 42:669–78; treatise authentic, but John's quotation not found)

* The text of John's speeches is given in full in the account of the seventh and eighth sessions in *AL*, 200– 222. The *Greek Acts* summarise the speeches briefly in *AG*, 396– 98, where they are described as occurring in the eighth and ninth sessions. The difference is due to the fact that the *Greek Acts* describe as the first Florentine session a preliminary meeting in February 1439 at which no doctrinal discussions took place (*AG*, 239).

15. Augustine, *Contra Maximinum* 2.14 (*PL*, 42:770–71; authentic)
16. Augustine, *Contra Maximinum* 2.14 (*PL*, 42:771; authentic)
17. Augustine, *In Iohannis Evangelium tractatus* 16.99 (*PL*, 35:1888–89; authentic)
18. Augustine, *De Trinitate* 4.20 (*PL*, 42:908; authentic)
19. Augustine, *De Trinitate* 5.14 (*PL*, 42:921; authentic)
20. Augustine, *De Trinitate* 15.25 (*PL*, 42:1092; authentic)
21. Hormisdas, Letter 79 (*PL*, 63:514B; authentic, though passage quoted disputed)[1]
22. John the Deacon, *Vita Sancti Gregorii Magni* 2.2 (*PL*, 75:87B–88A; authentic)
23. Gregory the Great, *Dialogi* 2.38 (*PL*, 66:204B; authentic)
24. Gregory the Great, *Moralia in Iob* 1.22 (*PL*, 75:541B; authentic)
25. Gregory the Great, *Moralia in Iob* 2.56 (*PL*, 75:598B; authentic)
26. Gregory the Great, *Moralia in Iob* 30.4 (*PL*, 76:533D–534A; authentic)
27. Boethius, *De Trinitate* 1 (*PL*, 64:1249C, 1254C; authentic)
28. Boethius, *De Trinitate* 1 (*PL*, 64:1254C; authentic)
29. Isidore, *Etymologiae* 7.3 (*PL*, 82:268C; authentic)

Greek Testimonies

1. Basil, *Contra Eunomium* 5 (*PG*, 29:724C; authenticity of book 5 is disputed, strong arguments favor Didymus as the author)
2. Basil, *Contra Eunomium* 5 (*PG*, 29:724C; see entry 1)
3. Epiphanius, *Ancoratus* 73 (*PG*, 42:153B; authentic)

[1] The passage quoted is, however, disputed. It is relegated to a footnote in O. Guenther, ed., *Avellana Collectio*, vol. 2, Corpus Scriptorum Ecclesiasticorum Latinorum 35 (Vienna: F. Tempsky, 1898).

4. Epiphanius, *Adversus haereses* [*Panarion*/Πανάριον] 3.74 (*PG*, 42:493B; authentic)
5. Didymus, *De Spiritu Sancto* 36 (*PG*, 39:1064C; authentic, but extant only in Jerome's version)
6. Didymus, *De Spiritu Sancto* 37 (*PG*, 39:1065D–66A, authentic, but extant only in Jerome's version)
7. Athanasius, *Orationes adversus Arianos* 3.22 (*PG*, 26:376A; authentic)
8. Athanasius, *Orationes adversus Arianos* 1.50 (*PG*, 26:118A–B; authentic)
9. Athanasius, work described by John as "a certain letter" (exact place not found, but bears similarities to parts of the *Epistolae ad Serapionem*)
10. Athanasius, *Epistolae ad Serapionem* 4.2 (*PG*, 26:640A; authentic)[2]
11. Athanasius, *Epistolae ad Serapionem* 3.1 (*PG*, 26:625A–B; authentic)
12. Basil, *Contra Eunomium* 5 (*PG*, 29:732A; see entry 1)
13. Basil, *Contra Eunomium* 5 (*PG*, 29:725A; see entry 1)
14. Athanasius, *Epistolae ad Serapionem* 1.21 (*PG*, 26:580B; authentic)
15. Athanasius, *Epistolae ad Serapionem* 1.20 (*PG*, 26:580A; authentic)
16. Athanasius, *Epistolae ad Serapionem* 1.14 (*PG*, 26:565B; authentic)
17. Athanasius, *De Incarnatione Verbi Dei* (inauthentic)
18. Athanasius, *De decretis Nicaenae Synodi* (presumably taken from the account of the acts of the Council ascribed to "Gelasius Cyzicenus" but not found in existing versions)

[2] As noted in chapter 1, I use the older division into four rather than three letters, as found in *The Letters of Saint Athanasius concerning the Holy Spirit*, trans. C. R. B. Shapland (London: Epworth, 1951).

19. Cyril of Alexandria, Letter to Nestorius (*PG*, 77:105Cff.; authentic)
20. Cyril of Alexandria, Letter to John of Antioch (*PG*, 77:173A; authentic)
21. Cyril of Alexandria, Letter 55 (*PG*, 77:316D; authentic)
22. Cyril of Alexandria, *De Trinitate dialogi* 2 (*PG*, 75:721D; authentic)
23. Cyril of Alexandria, *De Trinitate dialogi* 3 (*PG*, 75:844A; authentic)
24. Cyril of Alexandria, *Thesaurus de Trinitate* 34 (*PG*, 75:581C; authentic)
25. Cyril of Alexandria, *Thesaurus de Trinitate* 33 (*PG*, 75:573C; authentic)
26. Cyril of Alexandria, *Thesaurus de Trinitate* 34 (*PG*, 75:589A; authentic)
27. Cyril of Alexandria, *Thesaurus de Trinitate* 34 (*PG*, 75:600D; authentic)
28. Cyril of Alexandria, *Thesaurus de Trinitate* 34 (*PG*, 75:585A; authentic)
29. Cyril of Alexandria, *Thesaurus de Trinitate* 34 (*PG*, 75:603A–B; authentic)
30. Basil, *De Spiritu Sancto* 18 (*PG*, 32:152B; authentic)
31. Basil, *Contra Sabellianos et Arium et Anomoeos* (*PG*, 31:609B; authentic)
32. Cyril of Alexandria, Commentary on the 9th anathema (*PG*, 76:308D–9A; authentic)

APPENDIX 4

Greek and Latin Traditions regarding the Procession of the Holy Spirit

(by the Pontifical Council for Promoting Christian Unity) *

Preamble

The Holy Father, in the homily he gave in St. Peter Basilica on 29 June in the presence of the Ecumenical Patriarch Bartholomew I, expressed a desire that "the traditional doctrine of the Filioque, present in the liturgical version of the Latin Credo, [be clarified] in order to highlight its full harmony with what the Ecumenical Council of Constantinople of 381 confesses in its creed: the Father as the source of the whole Trinity, the one origin both of the Son and of the Holy Spirit." What is published here is the clarification he has asked for, which has been undertaken by the Pontifical Council for Promoting Christian Unity. It is intended as a contribution to the dialogue which is carried out by the Joint International Commission between the Roman Catholic Church and the Orthodox Church.

The Clarification

In its first report on "The Mystery of the Church and of the Eucharist in the light of the Mystery of the Holy Trinity," unanimously approved

* Ed. note: This is the document published in 1995 by the Pontifical Council for Promoting Christian Unity, discussed at some length at the beginning of this book. The English is as presented in Pontifical Council for Promoting Christian Unity, "Traditions regarding the Procession of the Holy Spirit, " *Eastern Christian Journal* 2, no. 3 (1995): 35–46.

in Munich on 6 July 1982, the Joint International Commission for Theological Dialogue between the Roman Catholic Church and the Orthodox Church had mentioned the centuries-old difficulty between the two Churches concerning the eternal origin of the Holy Spirit. Not being able to treat this subject for itself in this first phase of the dialogue, the Commission stated: "Without wishing to resolve yet the difficulties which have arisen between the East and the West concerning the relationship between the Son and the Spirit, we can already say together that this Spirit, which proceeds from the Father (Jn 15:26) as the sole source in the Trinity and which has become the Spirit of our sonship (Rom 8:15) since he is also the Spirit of the Son (Gal 4:6), is communicated to us particularly in the Eucharist by this Son upon whom he reposes in time and in eternity (Jn 1:32)" (*Information Service* of the Secretariat for Promoting Christian Unity, n. 49, p. 108, I, 6).

The Catholic Church acknowledges the conciliar, ecumenical, normative and irrevocable value, as expression of the one common faith of the Church and of all Christians, of the Symbol professed in Greek at Constantinople in 381 by the Second Ecumenical Council. No profession of faith peculiar to a particular liturgical tradition can contradict this expression of the faith taught and professed by the undivided Church.

On the basis of Jn 15:26, this Symbol confesses the Spirit "τὸ ἐκ τοῦ Πατρὸς ἐκπορευόμενον" ("who takes his origin from the Father"). The Father alone is the principle without principle (ἀρχὴ ἄναρχος) of the two other persons of the Trinity, the sole source (πηγή) of the Son and of the Holy Spirit. The Holy Spirit therefore takes his origin from the Father alone (ἐκ μόνου τοῦ Πατρός) in a principal, proper and immediate manner.[1]

The Greek Fathers and the whole Christian Orient speak, in this regard, of the "Father's monarchy," and the Western tradition, following St. Augustine, also confesses that the Holy Spirit takes his origin from the Father *principaliter*, that is, as principle (*De Trinitate* XV, 25, 47, *PL* 42, 1094–1095). In this sense, therefore, the two traditions recognize that the "monarchy of the Father" implies that the Father is the sole Trinitarian Cause (ἀιτία) or principle (*principium*) of the Son and of the Holy Spirit.

This origin of the Holy Spirit from the Father alone as principle of the whole Trinity is called ἐκπόρευσις by Greek tradition, following the Cappadocian Fathers. St. Gregory of Nazianzus, the Theologian, in fact, characterizes the Spirit's relationship of origin from the Father by the proper term ἐκπόρευσις, distinguishing it from that of procession (τὸ προϊέναι) which the Spirit has in common with the Son. "The Spirit is truly the Spirit proceeding (προϊόν) from the Father, not by filiation, for it is not by generation, but by ἐκπόρευσις (*Discourse* 39, 12, *Sources chrétiennes* 358, p. 175). Even if St. Cyril of Alexandria happens at times to apply the verb ἐκπόρευσθαι to the Son's relationship of origin from the Father, he never uses it for the relationship of the Spirit to the Son (Cf. *Commentary on St. John*, X, 2, *PG* 74, 910D; *Ep* 55, *PG* 77, 316 D, etc.). Even for St. Cyril, the term ἐκπόρευσις as distinct from the term "proceed" (προϊέναι) can only characterize a relationship of origin to the principle without principle of the Trinity: the Father.

That is why the Orthodox Orient has always refused the formula τὸ ἐκ τοῦ Πατρὸς καὶ τοῦ Υἱοῦ ἐκπορευόμενον and the Catholic Church has refused the addition καὶ τοῦ Υἱοῦ to the formula τὸ ἐκ τοῦ Πατρὸς ἐκπορευόμενον in the Greek text of the Nicene-Constantinopolitan Symbol, even in its liturgical use by Latins.

The Orthodox Orient does not, however, refuse all eternal relationship between the Son and the Holy Spirit in their origin from the Father. St. Gregory of Nazianzus, a great witness to our two traditions, makes this clear in response to Macedonius who was asking: "What then is lacking to the Spirit to be the Son, for if nothing was lacking to him, he would be the Son?—We say that nothing is lacking to him, for nothing is lacking to God; but it is the difference in manifestation, if I may say so, or in the relationship between them (τῆς πρὸς ἄλληλα σχέσεως διάφορον) which makes also the difference in what they are called" (*Discourse* 31, 9, *Sources chrétiennes* 250, pp. 290–92).

The Orthodox Orient has, however, given a happy expression to this relationship with the formula διὰ τοῦ Υἱοῦ ἐκπορευόμενον (who takes his origin from the Father by or through the Son). St. Basil already said of the Holy Spirit: "Through the Son (διὰ τοῦ Υἱοῦ), who is one, he is joined to the Father, who is one, and by himself completes the Blessed Trinity" (*Treatise on the Holy Spirit*, XVIII, 45, *Sources chrétiennes* 17 *bis*, p. 408). St. Maximus the Confessor said: "By nature (φύσει) the Holy Spirit in his being (κατ᾽ουσίαν) takes substantially (οὐσιωδῶς) his origin (ἐκπορευόμενον) from the Father through the Son who is begotten (δι᾽ Υἱοῦ γεννηθέντος)" (*Quaestiones ad Thalassium*, LXIII, *PG* 90, 672 C). We find this again in St. John Damascene: "(ὁ Πατὴρ) ἄει ἦν, ἔχων ἐξ ἑαυτοῦ τὸν αὐτοῦ λόγον, καὶ διὰ τοῦ λόγου αὐτοῦ ἐξ ἑαυτοῦ τὸ Πνεῦμα αὐτοῦ ἐκπορευόμενον)," in English: "I say that God is always Father since he has always his Word coming from himself, and through his Word, having his Spirit issuing from him" (*Dialogus contra Manichaeos* 5, *PG* 94, 1512 B, ed. B. Kotter, Berlin 1981, p. 354; cf. *PG* 94, 848–49 A). This aspect of the Trinitarian mystery was confessed at the seventh Ecumenical council, meeting at Nicaea in 787, by the Patriarch of Constantinople, St. Tarasius, who developed the Symbol as follows: "τὸ Πνεῦμα τὸ ἄγιον, τὸ κύριον καὶ ζωοποιόν, τὸ ἐκ τοῦ Πατρὸς διά τοῦ Υἱοῦ ἐκπορευόμενον" (Mansi, XII, 1122 D).

This doctrine all bears witness to the fundamental Trinitarian faith as it was professed together by East and West at the time of the Fathers. It is the basis that must serve for the continuation of the current theological dialogue between Catholic and Orthodox.

The doctrine of the *Filioque* must be understood and presented by the Catholic Church in such a way that it cannot appear to contradict the Monarchy of the Father nor the fact that he is the sole origin (ἀρχή, αἰτία) of the ἐκπόρευσις of the Spirit. The *Filioque* is, in fact, situated in a theological and linguistic context different from that of the affirmation of the sole Monarchy of the Father, the one origin of the Son and of the Spirit. Against Arianism, which was still virulent in the West, its purpose was to stress the fact that the Holy Spirit is of the same divine nature as the Son, without calling in question the one Monarchy of the Father.

We are presenting here the authentic doctrinal meaning of the *Filioque* on the basis of the Trinitarian faith of the Symbol professed by the second Ecumenical Council at Constantinople. We are giving this authoritative interpretation, while being aware of how inadequate human language is to express the ineffable mystery of the Holy Trinity, one God, a mystery which is beyond our words and our thoughts.

The Catholic Church interprets the *Filioque* with reference to the conciliar and ecumenical, normative and irrevocable value of the confession of faith in the eternal origin of the Holy Spirit, as defined in 381 by the Ecumenical Council of Constantinople in its Symbol. This Symbol only became known and received by Rome on the occasion of the Ecumenical Council of Chalcedon in 451. In the meantime, on the basis of the earlier Latin theological tradition, Fathers of the Church of the West like St. Hilary, St. Ambrose, St. Augustine and St. Leo the Great, had confessed that the Holy Spirit proceeds (*procedit*) eternally from the Father and the Son.[2]

Since the Latin Bible (the Vulgate and earlier Latin translations) had translated Jn 15:26 (παρὰ τοῦ Πατρὸς ἐκπορεὺεται) by "qui a Patre procedit," the Latins translated the ἐκ τοῦ Πατρὸς ἐκπορευόμενον of the Symbol of Nicaea-Constantinople by "ex Patre procedentem" (Mansi VII, 112 B). In this way, a false equivalence was involuntarily created with regard to the eternal origin of the Spirit between the Oriental theology of the ἐκπόρευσις and the Latin theology of the *processio*.

The Greek ἐκπόρευσις signifies only the relationship of origin to the Father alone as the principle without principle of the Trinity. The Latin processio, on the contrary, is a more common term, signifying the communication of the consubstantial divinity from the Father to the Son and from the Father, through and with the Son, to the Holy Spirit.[3] In confessing the Holy Spirit "ex Patre procedentem," the Latins, therefore, could only suppose an implicit *Filioque* which would later be made explicit in their liturgical version of the Symbol.

In the West, the *Filioque* was confessed from the fifth century through the *Quicumque* (or *Athanasianum*, DS 75) Symbol, and then by the Councils of Toledo in Visigothic Spain between 589 and 693 (DS 470, 485, 490, 527, 568), to affirm Trinitarian consubstantiality. If these Councils did not perhaps insert it in the Symbol of Nicaea-Constantinople, it is certainly to be found there from the end of the eighth century, as evidenced in the proceedings of the Council of Aquileia-Friuli in 796 (Mansi XIII, 836, D, ff.) and that of Aachen of 809 (Mansi XIV, 17). In the ninth century, however, faced with Charlemagne, Pope Leo III, in his anxiety to preserve unity with the Orient in the confession of faith, resisted this development of the Symbol which had spread spontaneously in the West, while safeguarding the truth contained in the *Filioque*. Rome only admitted it in 1014 into the liturgical Latin version of the Creed.

In the Patristic period, an analogous theology had developed in Alexandria, stemming from St. Athanasius. As in the Latin tradition, it was expressed by the more common term of procession (προϊέναι) indicating the communication of the divinity to the Holy Spirit from the Father and the Son in their consubstantial communion: "The Spirit proceeds (προεῖσι) from the Father and the Son; clearly, he is of the divine substance, proceeding (προϊὸν) substantially (οὐσιωδῶς) in it and from it" (St. Cyril of Alexandria, *Thesaurus*, *PG* 75, 585 A).[4]

In the seventh century, the Byzantines were shocked by a confession of faith made by the Pope and including the *Filioque* with reference to the procession of the Holy Spirit; they translated the procession inaccurately by ἐκπόρευσις. St. Maximus the Confessor then wrote a letter from Rome linking together the two approaches—Cappadocian and Latin-Alexandrian—to the eternal origin of the Spirit: the Father is the sole principle without principle (in Greek ἀιτία) of the Son and of the Spirit; the Father and the Son are consubstantial source of the procession (τὸ προϊέναι) of this same Spirit. "For the procession they [the Romans] brought the witness of the Latin Fathers, as well, of course, as that of St. Cyril of Alexandria in his sacred study on the Gospel of St. John. On this basis they showed that they themselves do not make the Son Cause (αἰτία) of the Spirit. They know, indeed, that the Father is the sole Cause of the Son and of the Spirit, of one by generation and of the other by ἐκπόρευσις—but they explained that the latter comes (προϊέναι) through the Son, and they showed in this way the unity and the immutability of the essence" (*Letter to Marinus of Cyprus*, *PG* 91, 136 A–B). According to St. Maximus, echoing Rome, the *Filioque* does not concern the ἐκπόρευσις of the Spirit issued from the Father as source of the Trinity, but manifests his προϊέναι (*processio*) in the consubstantial communion of the Father and the Son, while excluding any possible subordinationist interpretation of the Father's Monarchy.

The fact that in Latin and Alexandrian theology the Holy Spirit proceeds (προεῖσι) from the Father and the Son in their consubstantial communion does not mean that it is the divine essence or substance that proceed in him, but that it is communicated from the Father and the Son who have it in common. This point was confessed as dogma in 1215 by the Fourth Lateran Council: "The substance does not generate, is not begotten, does not proceed; but it is the Father who generates, the Son who is begotten, the Holy Spirit who proceeds: so that there is distinction in persons and unity in nature. Although other (*alius*) is the Father, other the Son, other the Holy Spirit, they are not another reality (*aliud*), but what the Father is the Son is and the Holy Spirit equally; so, according to the orthodox and catholic faith, we believe that they are consubstantial. For the Father, generating eternally the Son, has given to him his substance (. . .) It is clear that, in being born the Son has received the substance of the Father without this substance being in any way diminished, and so the Father and the Son have the same substance. So the Father, the Son and the Holy Spirit, who proceeds from them both, are one same reality" (DS 804–5).

In 1274 the Second Council of Lyon confessed that "the Holy Spirit proceeds eternally from the Father and the Son, not as from two principles but as from one single principle (*tamquam ex uno principio*)" (DS 850). In the light of the Lateran Council, which preceded the Second Council of Lyon, it is clear that it is not the divine essence that can be the "one principle" for the procession of the Holy Spirit. The *Catechism of the Catholic Church* interprets this formula in n. 248 as follows: "The eternal order of the divine persons in their consubstantial communion implies that the Father, as the 'principle without principle' (DS 1331), is the first origin of the Spirit, but also that as Father of the only Son, he is, with the Son, the single principle from which the Spirit proceeds (Second Council of Lyons, DS 850)."

For the Catholic Church, "at the outset the Eastern tradition expresses the Father's character as first origin of the Spirit. By confessing the Spirit as he 'who proceeds from the Father' ("ἐκ τοῦ Πατρὸς ἐκπορευόμενον": cf. Jn 15:26), it affirms that he comes from the Father through the Son. The Western tradition expresses first the consubstantial communion between Father and Son, by saying that the Spirit proceeds from the Father and the Son (*Filioque*). [. . .] This legitimate complementarity, provided it does not become rigid, does not affect the identity of faith in the reality of the same mystery confessed" (*Catechism of the Catholic Church*, n. 248). Being aware of this, the Catholic Church has refused the addition of καὶ τοῦ Υἱοῦ to the formula τὸ ἐκ τοῦ Πατρὸς ἐκπορευόμενον of the Symbol of Nicaea-Constantinople in the Churches, even of Latin rite, which use it in Greek. The liturgical use of this original text remains always legitimate in the Catholic Church.

If it is correctly situated, the *Filioque* of the Latin tradition must not lead to a subordination of the Holy Spirit in the Trinity. Even if the Catholic doctrine affirms that the Holy Spirit proceeds from the Father and the Son in the communication of their consubstantial communion, it nonetheless recognizes the reality of the original relationship of the Holy Spirit as person with the Father, a relationship that the Greek Fathers express by the term ἐκπόρευσις.[5]

In the same way, if in the Trinitarian order the Holy Spirit is consecutive to the relation between the Father and the Son, since he takes his origin from the Father as Father of the only Son,[6] it is in the Spirit that this relationship between the Father and the Son itself attains its Trinitarian perfection. Just as the Father is characterized as Father by the Son he generates, so does the Spirit, by taking his origin from the Father, characterize the Father in the manner of the Trinity in relation to the Son and characterizes the Son in the manner of the Trinity in his relation to the Father: in the fullness of the Trinitarian mystery they are Father and Son in the Holy Spirit.[7]

The Father only generates the Son by breathing (προβάλλειν in Greek) through him the Holy Spirit and the Son is only begotten by the Father insofar as the spiration (προβολή in Greek) passes through him. The Father is Father of the One Son only by being for him and through him the origin of the Holy Spirit.[8]

The Spirit does not precede the Son, since the Son characterizes as Father the Father from whom the Spirit takes his origin, according to the Trinitarian order.[9] But the spiration of the Spirit from the Father takes place by and through (the two senses of διά in Greek) the generation of the Son, to which it gives its Trinitarian character. It is in this sense that St. John Damascene says: "The Holy Spirit is a substantial power contemplated in his own distinct hypostasis, who proceeds from the Father and reposes in the Word" (*De Fide orthodoxa* I, 7, *PG* 94, 805 B, ed. B. Kotter, Berlin 1973, p. 16; *Dialogus contra Manichaeos* 5, *PG* 94, 1512 B, ed. B. Kotter, Berlin 1981, p. 354).[10]

What is this Trinitarian character that the person of the Holy Spirit brings to the very relationship between the Father and the Son? It is the original role of the Spirit in the economy with regard to the mission and work of the Son. The Father is love in its source (2 Cor 13:13; 1 Jn 4:8,16), the Son is "the Son that he loves" (Col 1:14). So a tradition dating back to St. Augustine has seen in the Holy Spirit, through whom "God's love has been poured into our hearts" (Rom 5:5), love as the eternal Gift of the Father to his "beloved Son" (Mk 1:11; 9:7; Lk 20:13; Eph 1:6).[11]

The divine love which has its origin in the Father reposes in "the Son of his love" in order to exist consubstantially through the Son in the person of the Spirit, the Gift of love. This takes into account the fact that, through love, the Holy Spirit orients the whole life of Jesus towards the Father in the fulfilment of his will. The Father sends his Son (Gal 4:4) when Mary conceives him through the operation of the Holy Spirit (cf. Lk 1:35). The Holy Spirit makes Jesus manifest as Son of the Father by resting upon him at Baptism (cf. Lk 3:2–22; Jn 1:33). He drives Jesus into the wilderness (cf. Mk 1:12). Jesus returns "full of the Holy Spirit" (Lk 4:1). Then he begins his ministry "in the power of the Spirit" (Lk 4:14). He is filled with joy in the Spirit, blessing the Father for his gracious will (cf. Lk 10:21). He chooses his Apostles "through the Holy Spirit" (Acts 1:2). He casts out demons by the Spirit of God (Mt 12:28). He offers himself to the Father "through the eternal Spirit" (Heb 9:14). On the Cross he "commits his Spirit" into the Father's hands (Lk 23:46). "In the Spirit" he descended to the dead (cf. 1 Pt 3:19), and by the Spirit he was raised from the dead (cf. Rom 8:11) and "designated Son of God in power" (Rom 1:4).[12] This role of the Spirit in the innermost human existence of the Son of God made man derives from an eternal Trinitarian relationship through which the Spirit, in his mystery as Gift of Love, characterizes the relation between the Father, as source of love, and his beloved Son.

The original character of the person of the Spirit as eternal Gift of the Father's love for his beloved Son shows that the Spirit, while coming from the Son in his mission, is the one who brings human beings into Christ's filial relationship to his Father, for this relationship finds only in him its Trinitarian character: "God has sent the Spirit of his Son into our hearts, crying Abba! Father!" (Gal 4:6). In the mystery of salvation and in the life of the Church, the Spirit therefore does much more than prolong the work of the Son. In fact, whatever Christ has instituted—Revelation, the Church, the sacraments, the apostolic ministry and its Magisterium—calls for constant invocation (ἐπίκλησις) of the Holy Spirit and his action (ἐνέργεια), so that the love that "never ends" (1 Cor 13:8) may be made manifest in the communion of the saints with the life of the Trinity.

Endnotes [by the Pontifical Council]

1 These are the terms employed by St. Thomas Aquinas in the *Summa Theologica*, Ia, q. 36, a. 3, 1um and 2um.

2 It is Tertullian who lays the foundations for Trinitarian theology in the Latin tradition, on the basis of the substantial communication of the Father to the Son and through the Son to the Holy Spirit: "Christ says of the Spirit: 'He will take from what is mine' (Jn 16:14), as he does from the Father. In this way, the connection of the Father to the Son and of the Son to the Paraclete makes the three cohere one from the other. They who are one sole reality (*unum*) not one alone (*unus*) by reason of the unity of substance and not of numerical singularity" (*Adv. Praxean*, XXV, 1–2). This communication of the divine consubstantiality in the Trinitarian order he expresses with the verb *procedere* (ibid., II, 6). We find this same theology in St. Hilary of Poitiers, who says to the Father: "May I receive your Spirit who takes his being from you through your only Son" (*De Trinitate*, XII, *PL* 10, 471). He remarks: "If anyone thinks there is a difference between receiving from the Son (Jn 16:15) and proceeding (*procedere*) from the Father (Jn 15:26), it is certain that it is one and the same thing to receive from the Son and to receive from the Father" (*De Trinitate*, VIII, 20, *PL* 10, 251A). It is in this sense of communication of divinity through procession that St. Ambrose of Milan is the first to formulate the *Filioque*: "The Holy Spirit, when he proceeds (*procedit*) from the Father and the Son, does not separate himself from the Father and does not separate himself from the Son" (*De Spiritu Sancto*, I, 11, 120, *PL* 16, 733 A = 762D). St. Augustine, however, takes the precaution of safeguarding the Father's monarchy within the consubstantial communion of the Trinity: "The Holy Spirit proceeds from the Father as principle (*principaliter*) and, through the latter's timeless gift to the Son, from the Father and the Son in communion (*communiter*)" (*De Trinitate*, XV, 25, 47, *PL* 42, 1095). St. Leo, *Sermon* LXXV, 3, *PL* 54, 402; *Sermon* LXXVI, 2, ibid. 404.

3 Tertullian uses the verb *procedere* in a sense common to the Word and the Spirit insofar as they receive divinity from the Father: "The Word was not uttered out of something empty and vain, and he does not lack substance, he who proceeded (*processit*) from such a [divine] substance and has made so many [created] substances" (*Adv. Praxean*, VII, 6). St. Augustine, following St. Ambrose, takes up this more common conception

of procession: "All that proceeds is not born, although what is born proceeds" (*Contra Maximinum*, II, 14, 1, *PL* 42, 770). Much later St. Thomas Aquinas remarks that "the divine nature is communicated in every processing that is not *ad extra*" (*Summa Theologica*, a, q. 27, a. 3, 2um). For him, as for all this Latin theology which used the term "procession" for the Son as well as for the Spirit, "generation is a procession which puts the divine person in possession of the divine nature" (ibid., a, q. 43, a. 2, c), for "from all eternity the Son proceeds in order to be God" (ibid.). In the same way, he affirms that "through his procession, the Holy Spirit receives the nature of the Father, as does the Son" (ibid., a, q. 35, a. 2, c). "Of words referring to any kind of origin, the most general is procession. We use it to indicate any origin whatever; we say, for instance, that the line proceeds from the point; that the ray proceeds from the sun, the river from its source, and likewise in all kinds of other cases. Since we admit one or another of these words that evoke origin, we can therefore conclude that the Holy Spirit proceeds from the Son" (ibid., a, q. 36, a. 2, c).

4 St. Cyril bears witness here to a Trinitarian doctrine common to the whole school of Alexandria since St. Athanasius, who had written: "Just as the Son says: 'All that the Father has is mine' (Jn 16:15), so shall we find that, through the Son, it is all also in the Spirit" (*Letters to Serapion*, III, 1, 33, *PG* 26, 625B). St. Epiphanius of Salamis (*Ancoratus*, VIII, *PG* 43, 29 C) and Didymus the Blind (*Treatise on the Holy Spirit*, CLIII, *PG* 34, 1064A) link the Father and the Son by the same preposition ἐκ in the communication to the Holy Spirit of the consubstantial divinity.

5 "The two relationships of the Son to the Father and of the Holy Spirit to the Father oblige us to place two relationships in the Father, one referring to the Son and the other to the Holy Spirit" (St. Thomas Aquinas, *Summa Theologica*, Ia, q. 32, a. 2, c).

6 Cf. *Catechism of the Catholic Church*, n. 248.

7 St. Gregory of Nazianzus says that "the Spirit is a middle term (μέσον) between the Unbegotten and the Begotten" (*Discourse* 31, 8, *Sources chrétiennes* 250, p. 290). Cf. also, in a Thomistic perspective, G. Leblond, "Point of view on the procession of the Holy Spirit," in *Revue Thomiste*, LXXXVI, t. 78, 1978, pp. 293–302.

8 St. Cyril of Alexandria says that "the Holy Spirit flows from the Father in the Son (ἐν τῷ Υἱῷ)," *Thesaurus*, XXXIV, *PG* 75, 577A).

9 St. Gregory of Nyssa writes: "The Holy Spirit is said to be of the Father and it is attested that he is of the Son. St. Paul says: 'Anyone who does not have the Spirit of Christ does not belong to him' (Rom 8:9). So the Spirit who is of God [the Father] is also the Spirit of Christ. However, the Son who is of God [the Father] is not said to be of the Spirit: the consecutive order of the relationship cannot be reversed" (Fragment *In orationem dominicam*, quoted by St. John Damascene, *PG* 46, 1109BC). And St. Maximus affirms in the same way the Trinitarian order when he writes: "Just as the Thought [the Father] is principle of the Word, so is he also of the Spirit through the Word. And, just as one cannot say that the Word is of the voice [of the Breath], so one cannot say that the Word is of the Spirit" (*Quaestiones et dubia*, *PG* 90, 813B).

10 St. Thomas Aquinas, who knew the *De Fide orthodoxa*, sees no opposition between the *Filioque* and this expression of St. John Damascene: "To say that the Holy Spirit reposes or dwells in the Son does not exclude his proceeding from the Son; for we say also that

the Son dwells in the Father, although he proceeds from the Father" (*Summa Theologica*, a, q. 36, a. 2, 4um).

11 St. Thomas Aquinas, following St. Augustine, writes: "If we say of the Holy Spirit that he dwells in the Son, it is in the way that the love of one who loves reposes in the loved one" (*Summa theologica*, la, q. 36, a. 2, 4um). This doctrine of the Holy Spirit as love has been harmoniously assumed by St. Gregory Palamas into the Greek theology of the ἐκπόρευσις from the Father alone: "The Spirit of the most high Word is like an ineffable love of the Father for this Word ineffably generated. A love which this same Word and beloved Son of the Father entertains (χρῆται) towards the Father: but insofar as he has the Spirit coming with him (συνπροελθόντα) from the Father and reposing connaturally in him" (*Capita physica* XXXVI, *PG* 150, 1144D–45A).

12 Cf. John Paul II, Encyclical *Dominum et Vivificantem*, nn. 18–24, *AAS* LXXVIII, 1986, 826–31. Cf. also *Catechism of the Catholic Church*, nn. 438, 689, 690, 695, 727.

Bibliography

PRIMARY SOURCES: SACRED SCRIPTURE

Biblia Sacra, Iuxta Vulgatam Versionem. Edited by Bonifatius Fischer and Robert Weber. 4th edition. Stuttgart: Deutsche Bibelgesellschaft, 1994.

The Greek New Testament. Edited by Kurt Aland and Barbara Aland. Stuttgart: Deutsche Bibelgesellschaft, 1994.

The Holy Bible. Revised Standard Version. 2nd Catholic edition. San Francisco: Ignatius Press, 1994.

PRIMARY SOURCES: MAGISTERIAL

Acta Apostolicae Sedis. Rome: Vatican Press: 1909–.

Catechism of the Catholic Church. London, England: Geoffrey Chapman, 1994.

Code of Canons of the Eastern Churches. Washington, DC: Canon Law Society of America, 1992.

Codex Iuris Canonici Auctoritate Ioannis Pauli PP. II Promulgatus. Vatican City: Libreria Editrice Vaticana, 1983.

Conciliorum Collectio Regia Maxima. 12 vols. Edited by Jean Hardouin. Paris: Typographia Regia, 1714–1715.

Decrees of the Ecumenical Councils: From Nicaea I to Vatican II. Edited by Norman Tanner and Giuseppe Alberigo. 2 vols. Washington, DC: Georgetown University Press, 1990.

Denzinger, Heinrich. *Compendium of Creeds, Definitions and Declarations on Matters of Faith and Morals*. 43rd Latin–German edition. Edited by Helmut Hoping and Peter Hünermann. Latin–English edited and translated by Robert Fastiggi and Anne Englund Nash. San Francisco: Ignatius Press, 2012.

Magnum Bullarium Romanum, ab Leone Magno usque ad S.D.P. Clementem X. Lyons: P. Borde and J. and P. Arnaud, 1692.

Sacrorum Conciliorum et decretorum nova et amplissima collectio. Edited by John Mansi. 53 vols. Leipzig: H. Welter, 1759–1927.

The Decrees and Canons of the Seven Ecumenical Councils. Edited by Henry Percival in *NPNF2* vol. 14.

PRIMARY SOURCES: COLLECTIONS OF PATRISTIC AND MEDIEVAL WORKS.

Clavis Patrum Graecorum [listing authors and works for *CCSG*, with authenticity rating]. Edited by M. Geerhard. 6 vols. Turnhout: Brepols, 1974–2003.

Clavis Patrum Latinorum [listing authors and works for *CCSL*, with authenticity rating]. Edited by E. Dekkers and A. Garr, 3rd edition. Steenbrugge: Brepols, 1995.

Concilium Florentinum: Documenta et Scriptores [*CFDS*]. 11 vols. Rome: Pontifical Oriental Institute, 1940–1976.

CFDS vol. 1: *Epistolae Pontificiae ad Concilium Florentinum Spectantes*. Edited by Georg Hoffman.

CFDS vol. 2/1: *Apparatus Super Decretum Florentinum Unionis Graecorum,* by John de Turrecremata. Edited by Emmanuel Candal.

CFDS vol. 2/2: *Libellus de Ordine Generalium Conciliorum et Unione Florentina,* by Fantinus Vallaresso. Edited by Emmanuel Candal.

CFDS vol. 3/1: *Acta Camerae Apostolicae et Civitatum Venetiarum, Ferrariae, Florentiae, Ianuae de Concilio Florentino*. Edited by Georg Hoffman.

CFDS vol. 3/2: *Orientalium Documenta Minora*. Edited by Georg Hoffman.

CFDS vol. 4/1: *Tractatus Polemico-Theologicus de Graecis Errantibus,* by Andreas de Escobar. Edited by Emmanuel Candal.

CFDS vol. 5: *Quae Supersunt Actorum Graecorum Concilii Florentini*. Edited by Joseph Gill.

CFDS vol. 6: *Acta Latina Concilii Florentini,* by Andreas de Santacroce. Edited by Georg Hoffman.

CFDS vol. 7/1: *Oratio Dogmatica de Unione,* by Bessarion. Edited by Emmanuel Candal.

CFDS vol. 9: *The Memoirs of Sylvester Syropoulos on the Council of Florence*. Edited by Vitalien Laurent.

CFDS vol. 10: *Opera Anti-Unionistica,* by Mark Eugenikos. Edited by Louis Petit.

Corpus Christianorum, Series Graeca [*CCSG*]. Turnhout: Brepols, 1953–.

Corpus Christianorum, Series Latina [*CCSL*]. Turnhout: Brepols, 1953–.

Nicene and Post-Nicene Fathers of the Christian Church, 1st and 2nd series [*NPNF*1/2]. Edited by Philip Schaff and Henry Wace. Edinburgh: T. & T. Clark; New York: Christian Literature Company, 1899.

Patrologia Graeca [*PG*]. 162 vols. Edited by Jacques Migne. Paris, 1857–66.

Patrologia Latina [*PL*]. 221 vols. Edited by Jacques Migne. Paris, 1844–64.

Patrologia Orientalis [*PO*]. Edited by René Graffin, François Nau, François Graffin, et al. Paris: Firmin-Didot. 1904–.

PRIMARY SOURCES I: PATRISTIC AND ANCIENT

Ambrose. *De Isaac et anima*. Columns 527–60 in *PL* vol. 14.

———. *De Spiritu Sancto*. Columns 731–850 in *PL* vol. 16.

———. *Letters*. Columns 913–1642 in *PL* vol. 21.

———. *Expositio in Lucam*. Columns 1607–944 in *PL* vol. 15.

———. *On the Holy Spirit*. Translated by H. de Romestin. Pages 91–158 in *NPNF*2 vol. 10.

———. Letters and Hymns. Translated by H. de Romestin. Pages 411–73 in *NPNF*2 vol. 10.

Ammianus Marcellinus. *History: Books XIV–XIX*. Translated by J. Rolfe. London: W. Heinemann, 1935.

Anastasius of Antioch. *De Sanctissima Trinitate*. Columns 1309–30 in *PG* vol. 89.
Aristotle. *Parts of Animals*. Translated by A. Peck. Cambridge, MA: Harvard University Press, 1955.
Athanasius. *Apologia contra Arianos*. Columns 239–410 in *PG* vol. 25.
———. *Contra Sabellianos*. Columns 95–122 in *PG* vol. 28.
———. *De decretis Nicaenae Synodi*. Columns 415–76 in *PG* vol. 25.
———. *De synodis*. Columns 681–794r.
———. *Epistola ad Afros Episcopos*. Columns 1029–48r.
———. *Epistolae ad Serapionem*. Columns 529–676 in *PG* vol. 26.
———. *Historia Arianorum*. Columns 691–796 in *PG* vol. 25.
———. *Orationes adversus Arianos* 1–3. Columns 11–467 in *PG* vol. 26.
———. Selected Works and Letters. Translated by Archibald Robertson. *NPNF*2 vol. 4.
———. *The Letters of Saint Athanasius concerning the Holy Spirit*. Translated by C. R. B. Shapland. London: Epworth, 1951.
———. *Letters to Serapion on the Holy Spirit*. In *Works on the Holy Spirit: Athanasius's Letters to Serapion on the Holy Spirit and Didymus's On the Holy Spirit*. Translated by Mark DelCogliano, Andrew Radde-Gallwitz, and Lewis Ayres. Popular Patristics Series 43. Yonkers, NY: St. Vladimir's Seminary Press, 2011.
Augustine of Hippo. *De fide et Symbolo*. Columns 181–96 in *PL* vol. 40.
———. *De Trinitate*. Columns 819–1098 in *PL* vol. 42.
———. Letters. Columns 61–1094 in *PL* vol. 33.
———. Selected Works. Translated by Arthur Haddan. New edition. *NPNF*1 vol. 3.
———. Selected Works. Translated by J. Pilkington and J. Cunningham. *NPNF*1 vol. 1.
Basil of Caesarea. *Adversus Eunomium*. Columns 497–670 in *PG* vol. 29.
———. *Against Eunomius*. Translated by Mark DelCogliano and Andrew Radde-Gallwitz. Fathers of the Church 122. Washington, DC: Catholic University of America Press, 2011.
———. *Contre Eunome*. Edited by Bernard Sesboue and Georges-Matthieu de Durand. Paris: Cerf, 1982.
———. *De Spiritu Sancto*. Columns 87–218 in *PG* vol. 32.
———. Homilies and Sermons. Columns 163–618 in *PG* vol. 31.
———. *Letters 1–58*. Translated and edited by Roy Deferrari. Loeb Classical Library 190. Cambridge, MA: Harvard University Press, 1926.
———. *On the Holy Spirit*. Translated by David Anderson. Crestwood, NY: St. Vladimir's Seminary Press, 1980.
———. Selected Works. Translated by Blomfield Jackson. *NPNF*2 vol. 8.
———. *Sur Le Saint-Esprit*. Translated by Benoît Pruche. *Sources Chrétiennes* 17 *bis*. Paris: Cerf, 2002.
Cassiodorus. *Historia tripartita*. Columns 879–1214 in *PL* vol. 69.
Cyril of Alexandria. *Apologeticus contra Theodoretum*. Columns 385–452 in *PG* vol. 76.
———. *De adoratione in spiritu et veritate*. Columns 133–1126 in *PG* vol. 68.
———. Letters. Columns 9–390 in *PG* vol. 77.
———. *Explanatio in Lucae Evangelium*. Columns 475–950 in *PG* vol. 72.
———. *Explicatio XII capitum*. Columns 295–312 in *PG* vol. 76.
———. *Expositio in Ioannem*. *PG* vol. 73 and columns 9–756 in *PG* vol. 74.
———. *Expositio in Ioel*. Columns 327–408 in *PG* vol. 71.

———. *Thesaurus de Sancta et Consubstantiali Trinitate*. Columns 9–656 in *PG* vol. 75.
———. *Commentary on St. John's Gospel*. Translated by H. Liddon. 2 vols. London: Walter Smith, 1885.
———. *Letters 1–50*. Edited by John McEnerney. Washington, DC: Catholic University of America Press, 2007.
Cyril of Jerusalem. Catechetical Lectures. Translated by Edwin Hamilton Gifford. In *NPNF2* vol. 7, pt. 1.
Didymus. *On the Holy Spirit*. In *Works on the Holy Spirit: Athanasius's Letters to Serapion on the Holy Spirit and Didymus's On the Holy Spirit*. Edited and translated by Mark DelCogliano, Andrew Radde-Gallwitz, and Lewis Ayres. Popular Patristics Series 43. Yonkers, NY: St. Vladimir's Seminary Press, 2011.
Epiphanius. *Ancoratus*. Columns 11–236 in *PG* vol. 43.
———. *Ancoratus*. Translated by Young Richard Kim. Fathers of the Church 128. Washington, DC: Catholic University of America Press, 2014.
———. *Panarium*. Columns 155–1200 in *PG* vol. 41.
———. *The Panarion*. Translated by Frank Williams. Leiden: Brill, 2013.
———. *The Panarion of St. Epiphanius, Bishop of Salamis: Selected Passages*. Translated by Philip R. Amidon. New York: Oxford University Press, 1990.
Eusebius of Caesarea. *De vita Constantini*. Columns 905–1230 in *PG* vol. 20.
———. *Church History*. Translated by Aarthur McGiffert. Pages 73–404 in *NPNF2* vol. 1.
———. *Prolegomena on Constantine the Great*; *Life of Constantine*; *Constantine's Oration to the Assembly of the Saints; Oration in Praise of Constantine*. Translated by Ernest Richardson. Pages 411–610 in *NPNF2* vol. 1.
Evagrius. Selected Works and Letters. Pages 41–202 in *Evagrius Ponticus*. Edited with introduction by Augustine Casiday. New York: Routledge, 2006.
Fulgentius Ferrandus. Letters and Opuscala. Columns 887–956 in *PL* vol. 67.
Gregory Nazianzen. *Carmina*. Columns 397–1600 in *PG* vol. 37.
———. Orations. Columns 395–1252 in *PG* vol. 35; columns 11–664 in *PG* vol. 36.
———. *Discours 32–37*. Edited by Claudio Moreschini. Paris: Cerf, 1985.
———. Selected Orations. Translated by Charles Browne and James Swallow. Pages 203–435 in *NPNF2* vol. 7.
Gregory of Nyssa. *Adversus Graecos de communibus notionibus*. Columns 175–86 in *PG* vol. 45.
———. *Contra Eunomium*. Columns 243–1122 in *PG* vol. 45.
———. *De Oratione Dominica*. Columns 1109–10 in *PG* vol. 46.
———. *De Spiritu Sancto adversus Macedonianos*. Columns 1301–34 in *PG* vol. 45.
———. *Gregory of Nyssa: The Letters*. Translated by Anna Silvas. Supplements to *Vigiliae Christianae*. Leiden: Brill, 2007.
———. Letter 35, "to Peter his own brother on the divine *ousia* and hypostasis." Pages 247–59 in *Gregory of Nyssa: The Letters*, trans. Silvas. Attributed to Basil as Letter 38, "to Gregory his Brother, on the difference between substance and person," pages 196–227 in *Letters 1–58* (trans. Deferrari). Translated also by Blomfield Jackson in *NPNF2*, 8:137–41, with Basil's letters.
———. *Oratio catechetica magna*. Columns 9–116 in *PG* vol. 45.
———. *Quod non sit tres dii*. Columns 115–36 in *PG* vol. 45.

———. Selected Works and Letters. Translated by William Moore and Henry Wilson. *NPNF2* vol. 5.

Gregory the Great (Pope Gregory I). Letters. Columns 441–1328 in *PL* vol. 77.

———. *Homiliae in Evangelia*. Columns 1075–314 in *PL* vol. 76.

———. *Vita S. Benedicti*. Columns 126–204 in *PL* vol. 66.

———. *Moralia in Iob*. Columns 515–1162 in *PL* vol. 75; columns 9–782 in *PL* vol. 9–782.

———. *Moralia in Iob*. Translated by John Henry Parker. London: J. G. F and J. Rivington, 1844.

———. *Moralia in Iob*: Libri XXII–XXXV. Translated by Marc Adriaen. *CCSL* vol. 143B.

———. *The Book of Pastoral Rule and Selected Letters*. Translated by James Barmby. *NPNF2* vol. 12, pt. 2.

Hilary of Poitiers. *De Trinitate*. Edited by P. Smulders. *CCSL* vols. 62 and 62A.

———. *De Trinitate*. Columns 25–472 in *PL* vol. 9.

———. *Ex opere historico fragmentum*. Columns 627–724 in *PL* vol. 10.

———. *On the Trinity*. Translated by L. Pullan and E. Watson. Pages 40–234 in *NPNF2* vol. 9, pt. 1.

———. *On the Trinity*. Translated by Stephen McKenna. Fathers of the Church 25. Washinton, DC: Catholic University of America Press, 1954.

———. *Preface to His Opus Historicum*. Translated by P. Smulders with commentary. Supplements to *Vigiliae Christianae* 19. Leiden: Brill, 1995.

Hormisdas. Letters. Edited by O. Guenther in *Avellana Collectio* vol. 2. *Corpus Scriptorum Ecclesiasticorum Latinorum* vol. 35. Vienna: F. Tempsky, 1898.

Irenaeus. *Contra Haereses*. Columns 437–1224 in *PG* vol. 7.

Isidore of Seville. *Etymologiae*. Columns 73–728 in *PL* vol. 82.

John Damascene. *Adversus Constantinum Cabalinum*. Columns 309–44 in *PG* vol. 95.

———. *De fide orthodoxa*. Columns 789–1228 in *PG* vol. 94.

———. *De hymno Trisagio*. Columns 21–62 in *PG* vol. 95.

———. *De Sancta Trinitate*. Columns 9–18 in *PG* vol. 95.

———. *Dialogus contra Manichaeos*. Columns 1505–84 in *PG* vol. 94.

———. *Oratio II de Imaginibus*. Columns 1283–318 in *PG* vol. 94.

———. *On the Orthodox Faith*. Translated by S. Salmond. *NPNF2* vol. 9, pt. 2.

Justinian I. *Novella ad religionem pertinentes*. Columns 921–1054 in *PL* vol. 72.

Leo I (Pope). Letters. Columns 593–1218 in *PL* vol. 54.

———. Sermons. Columns 141–468 in *PL* vol. 54.

———. Letters and Sermons. Translated by C. Feltoe. *NPNF2* vol. 12, pt. 1. London: Parker, 1895.

Leo II (Pope). Letters. Columns 387–420 in *PL* vol. 96.

Maximus the Confessor. Disputatio cum Pyrrho. Columns 287–354 in *PG* vol. 91.

———. Letters. Columns 1–45 and 363–650 in *PG* vol. 91.

———. Opuscula theologica et polemica ad Marinum. Columns 9–286 in *PG* vol. 91.

———. *Quaestiones ad Thalassium de Scriptura*. Columns 1–65 and 243–786 in *PG* vol. 90.

———. *Quaestiones et dubia*. Columns 1–78 and 785–856 in *PG* vol. 90.

———. *Quaestiones et dubia*. Edited by J. H. Declerck. *CCSG* 10.

———. *Opuscules théologiques et polémiques*. Edited by Jean-Claude Larchet and Emmanuel Ponsoye. Paris: Cerf, 1998.

———. *Questions à Thalassios*. Tome 3, *Questions 56 à 65*. Translated by Françoise Vinel. Paris: Cerf, 2015.

Nicephoros I. *Apologeticus pro sacris imaginibus*. Columns 533–832 in *PG* vol. 100.

Sixtus III. Letters and Decrees. Columns 583–618 in *PL* vol. 50.

Socrates Scholasticos. *Church History*. Translated by A. Zenos. Pages 1–178 in *NPNF2* vol. 2.

———. *Historia Ecclesiastica*. Columns 29–842 in *PG* vol. 67.

Sozomen. *Church History*. Translated by A. Zenos. Pages 239–427 in *NPNF2* vol. 2.

———. *Historia Ecclesiastica*. Columns 843–1630 in *PG* vol. 67.

Stephanos Diakonos. *Vita S. Stephani Iunioris*. Columns 1069–186 in *PG* vol. 100.

Theodore Abu Qurrah. *Theodore Abu Qurrah*. Translated by J. Lamoreaux. Library of the Christian East 1. Provo, UT: Brigham Young University Press, 2005.

Theodore of Mopsuetia. *Commentarium in Evangelium Ioannis*. Columns 727–86 in *PG* vol. 66.

Theodore of Mopsuetia [attribution uncertain]. *Expositio symboli depravati*. Columns 1015–20 in *PG* vol. 66.

Theodore of Stoudios. Letters. Columns 903–1670 in *PG* vol. 99.

Theodoret. Letters. Columns 1173–494 in *PG* vol. 83.

———. *Historia Ecclesiastica*. Columns 881–1280 in *PG* vol. 82.

———. *Interpretatio in epistolas S. Pauli*. Columns 35–878 in *PG* vol. 82.

Victorinus, Marcus. *De Trinitate hymni*. Columns 1139–46 in *PL* vol. 8.

Vigilius of Thapse. *Contra Eutychen*. Columns 95–154 in *PL* vol. 62.

Vita et acta Maximi. Anonymous. Columns 67–172 of *PG* vol. 90.

Zeno of Verona. *Tractatus*. Columns 253–528 in *PL* vol. 8.

PRIMARY SOURCES II: MEDIEVAL AND EARLY MODERN

Amiroutzes, George. *De processione Spiritus S. et de una Ecclesia*. Columns 829–68 in *PG* vol. 161.

———. *De unione Ecclesiarum ad Eugenium IV*. Columns 889–94 in *PG* vol. 161.

Aquinas, Thomas. *Commentary on the Gospel of John 9–21*. Translated by Fabian Larcher, O.P. Latin/English Works of St. Thomas Aquinas 36. Lander, WY: Aquinas Institute for the Study of Sacred Doctrine, 2013.

———. *Quaestiones disputatae de potentia Dei*. Edited by Raymundo Spiazzi. Turin: Marietti, 1953.

———. *Scriptum super libros sententiarum Petri Lombardi*. Edited by Pierre Mandonnet and Maria Fabianus Moos. 4 vols. Paris: Lethielleux, 1929–1947.

———. *Summa theologiae*. Edited by Institutum Studiorum Medievalium Ottaviensis. 5 vols. Ottawa: Studium Generalis Ordo Praedicatorum, 1941.

Bessarion. Letter to Alexios Lascaris. Columns 319–406 in *PG* vol. 161.

———. Letter to Alexios Lascaris [his own translation into Latin]. Columns 407–48 in *PG* vol. 161.

———. Encyclical to the Greeks. Columns 449–80 in *PG* vol. 161.

———. Encyclical to the Greeks [his own translation into Latin]. Columns 481–90 in *PG* vol. 161.

———. *Oratio Dogmatica de Unione* [with his own translation into Latin]. Columns 543–614 in *PG* vol. 161; *CFDS* vol. 7/1.

———. *Refutation of Mark of Ephesus*. Columns 11–244 in *PG* vol. 161.

Bellarmine, Robert. *De conciliis*. Pages 189–406 in *Omnia Opera* vol. 2. Paris: Vives, 1870.

Calvin, John. *Institutes of the Christian Religion*. Edited by John Thomas McNeill. Philadelphia: Westminster, 1960.

Cano, Melchior. *De Locis Theologicis*. Edited by Juan Belda Plans. Madrid: Biblioteca de Autores Cristianos, 2006.

Eugenikos, John. *Antirrhetic of the Decree of the Council of Ferrara-Florence*. Edited by Eleni Rossidou-Koutsou. Nicosia, Cyprus: Research Centre of Kykkos Monastery, 2006.

Eugenikos, Mark. *Epistola ad Georgium presbyterum Methonensem contra ritus Romanae Ecclesiae*. Pages 470–74 in *PO* vol. 17 (1923).

———. *Epistola ad Georgium Scholarium*. Pages 460–64 in *PO* vol. 17.

———. *Epistola ad moderatorem Monasterii Vatopedii in Monte Atho*. Pages 477–79 in *PO* vol. 17.

———. *Epistola encyclica contra Graecos-Latinos*. Pages 449–59 in *PO* vol. 17.

———. *Oratio ad Eugenium Papam Quartam*. Pages 336–41 in *PO* vol. 17.

———. *Relatio de rebus a se in Synodo Florentina Gestis*. Pages 444–49 in *PO* vol. 17.

———. *Testimonia quibus probata Sanctum Spiritum a Patre solo procedere*. Pages 342–67 in *PO* vol. 17.

Innocent III (Pope). Letters. Columns 9–1612 in *PL* vol. 215; Columns 9–1174 in *PL* vol. 216.

Kabasilas, Neilos. *De dissidio Ecclesiarum*. Columns 683–700 in *PG* vol. 149.

Mammas, Gregory. *Responsio ad epistolam Marci Ephesini*. Columns 111–204 in *PG* vol. 160.

Moghila, Peter. *La confession orthodoxe de Pierre Moghila*. Translated by A. Malvy and M. Viller. *Orientalia Christiana* 10, no. 39. Rome: Pontificium Institutum Orientalium Studiorum, 1927.

Plousiadenos, Joseph. *Canon in Synodum Florentinam*. Columns 1095–102 in *PG* vol. 159.

———. *Disceptatio pro Concilio Florentino*. Columns 959–1024 in *PG* vol. 159.

———. *Pro Concilio Florentino*. Columns 1109–394 in *PG* vol. 159.

———. *Refutatio Marci Ephesi*. Columns 1023–94 in *PG* vol. 159.

Sales, Francis de. *The Catholic Controversy*. Translated by Henry Mackey. London: Burns & Oates, 1909.

Scholarios, George. *Responsio ad epistolam Marci Ephesi*. Pages 464–70 in *PO* vol. 17.

Turrecremata, John de. *Summa de Ecclesia*. Venice, 1561.

MODERN REFERENCE AND LINGUISTIC RESOURCES

A *Greek–English Lexicon: With a Revised Supplement*. Edited by Robert Scott and Henry Liddell. 9th ed. Oxford: Clarendon, 1996.

A Patristic Greek Lexicon. Edited by G. W. H. Lampe. Oxford: Oxford University Press, 1969.

Dictionnaire de théologie catholique [*DTC*]. 15 vols. Paris: Letouzey et Ané, 1907–1951.

Goodwin, William Watson, and John H. Betts. *A Greek Grammar*. London: Bristol Classical Press, 1997.

The Oxford Dictionary of the Christian Church. Edited by Frank Cross and Elizabeth Livingstone. 3rd revised ed. Oxford: Oxford University Press, 2005.

Turner, Nigel. *Grammar of New Testament Greek*. Vol. 3, *Syntax*. Edinburgh: T. & T. Clark, 1963.

SECONDARY AND MODERN SOURCES

Afanasieff, Nikolai. "Le concile dans la théologie orthodoxe russe." *Irenikon* 3 (1962): 316–39.

Alberigo, Giuseppe, ed. *Christian Unity: The Council of Ferrara-Florence, 1438/39–1989*. Bibliotheca Ephemeridum Theologicarum Lovaniensium 97: International Symposium on the Unity of the Christians 550 years after the Council of Ferrara-Florence, Florence, Italy, 1989. Leuven: Leuven University Press, 1991.

Alexakis, Alexander. "The Greek Patristic *Testimonia* presented at the Council of Florence (1439) in Support of the *Filioque* reconsidered." *Revue des études Byzantines* 58 (2000): 149–65.

Alexopoulos, Theodoros. "The Eternal Manifestation of the Spirit 'Through the Son' (διὰ τοῦ Υἱοῦ) according to Nikephoros Blemmydes and Gregory of Cyprus." Pages 65–86 in *Ecumenical Perspectives on the Filioque for the 21st Century*. Edited by Myk Habets. London: Bloomsbury Academic, 2014.

Alfeyev, Hilarion, archbishop of Voloklamsk/Podolsk. *Orthodox Christianity*. Translated by Basil Bush. Vol. 1. Yonkers, NY: St. Vladimir's Seminary Press, 2011.

———. *Orthodox Christianity*. Translated by Andrew Smith. Vol. 2. Yonkers, NY: St. Vladimir's Seminary Press, 2012.

———. "The Reception of the Ecumenical Councils in the Early Church." *St. Vladimir's Theological Quarterly* 47 (2003): 413–30.

Alivisatos, Hamilcar. "Les conciles oecuméniques IVème, Vème, VIIème et VIIIème." Pages 111–23 in *Le concile et Les conciles: contributions à l'histoire de la vie conciliaire de l'Église*. Edited by Bernard Botte, Yves Congar, et al. Paris: Chevetogne, 1960.

Angold, Michael. "Byzantium and the West 1204–1453." Pages 53–78 in *Eastern Christianity*. Edited by Michael Angold. Cambridge History of Christianity 5. Cambridge: Cambridge University Press, 2006.

Ayres, Lewis. *Nicaea and its Legacy: An Approach to Fourth-Century Trinitarian Theology*. Oxford: Oxford University Press, 2004.

Bailleux, Emile. "L'Esprit du Père et du Fils chez saint Augustin." *Revue thomiste* 77 (1977): 5–29.

Beckwith, Carl. *Hilary of Poitiers on the Trinity: From De fide to De Trinitate*. Oxford Early Christian Studies. New York: Oxford University Press, 2008.

Behr, John. *The Nicene Faith*. Vol. 2. Crestwood, NY: St. Vladimir's Seminary Press, 2004.

Bermejo, Luis M. *Infallibility on Trial: Church, Conciliarity and Communion*. Westminster, MD: Christian Classics, 1992.

Berthold, George. "Cyril of Alexandria and the *Filioque*." *Studia Patristica* 19 (1989): 143–47.

———. "Maximus the Confessor and the *Filioque*." *Studia Patristica* 18 (1985): 113–17.

Betti, Umberto. "Relations entre le pape et les autres membres du collège épiscopal." Pages 791–803 in *L'Eglise de Vatican II*. Edited by Guilherme Barauna and Yves Congar. Vol. 3. Unam Sanctam 51c. Paris: Cerf, 1966.

Billot, Louis. *Tractatus de Ecclesia Christi sive Continuatio Theologiae de Verbo Incarnato*. Vol. 1. Rome: Giachetti, 1909.

———. *De Deo Uno et Trino: Commentarius in Primam Partem S. Thomae*. Rome: Gregorian University Press, 1926.

Boguslawski, Steven C., and Robert L. Fastiggi, eds. *Called to Holiness and Communion: Vatican II on the Church*. Scranton, PA: University of Scranton Press, 2009.

Bois, J. "Constantinople, 1er concile de." Columns 1227–31 in *DTC* vol. 3.

Boojamra, John. "The Transformation of Conciliar Theory in the Last Century of Byzantium." *St. Vladimir's Theological Quarterly* 31 (1987): 215–35.

Botte, Bernard, Yves Congar, et al., eds. *Le concile et les conciles: contributions à l'histoire de la vie conciliaire de l'Église*. Paris: Chevetogne, 1960.

Bouyer, Louis. *The Church of God, Body of Christ and Temple of the Spirit*. Chicago: Franciscan Herald, 1982.

Boyle, John P. *Church Teaching Authority: Historical and Theological Studies*. Notre Dame, IN: University of Notre Dame Press, 1995.

Brachet, Jean-Yves, and Emmanuel Durand. "La réception de la *Clarification* romaine de 1995 sur le *Filioque*." *Irénikon* 78, no. 1–2 (2005): 47–109.

Bebis, George. "Tradition in the Orthodox Church." Pages 53–63 in *A Companion to the Greek Orthodox Church*. Edited by Fotios Litsas. New York: Greek Orthodox Diocese of North and South America, 1984.

Bulgakov, Sergei. *The Comforter*. Translated by Boris Jakim. Grand Rapids, MI: Eerdmans, 2004.

———. "Is Orthodoxy Infallible?" (1926). *Eastern Christian Journal* 7, no. 1 (2000): 73–86.

Camelot, Pierre-Thomas. "Les conciles oecuméniques des IVème et Vème siècles." Pages 45–73 in *Le concile et Les conciles: contributions à l'histoire de la vie conciliaire de l'Église*. Edited by Bernard Botte, Yves Congar, et al. Paris: Chevetogne, 1960.

Campbell, Theodore. "The Doctrine of the Holy Spirit in the Theology of Athanasius." *Scottish Journal of Theology* 27 (1974): 408–40.

Chadwick, Henry. *East and West: The Making of a Rift in the Church, from Apostolic Times until the Council of Florence*. Oxford: Oxford University Press, 2005.

———. "The Theological Ethos of the Council of Florence." Pages 229–39 in *Christian Unity: The Council of Ferrara-Florence, 1438/39–1989*. Edited by Giuseppe Alberigo. Bibliotheca Ephemeridum Theologicarum Lovaniensium 97: International Symposium on the Unity of the Christians 550 years after the Council of Ferrara-Florence, Florence, Italy, 1989. Leuven: Leuven University Press, 1991.

Chesterton, G. *K. Orthodoxy*. London: John Lane, 1909.

Clément, Olivier. "Liminaire [editorial]." *Contacts*, no. 48 (1964): 241–42.

Congar, Yves. *After Nine Hundred Years: The Background of the Schism between the Eastern and Western Churches*. New York: Fordham University Press, 1959.

———. "Conclusion." In *Le concile et Les conciles: contributions à l'histoire de la vie conciliaire de l'Église*. Edited by Bernard Botte, Yves Congar, et al. Paris: Chevetogne, 1960.

———. *Diversity and Communion*. North American edition. Mystic, CT: Twenty-Third Publications, 1985.

———. *I Believe in the Holy Spirit*. Vol. 3, Milestones in Catholic Theology. New York: Crossroad, 1997.

———. "Quatre siècles de désunion et d'affrontement." *Istina* 13 (1968): 131–52.

———. "La 'réception' comme réalité ecclésiologique." *Revue des sciences philosophiques et théologiques* 56 (1972): 369–403.

———. "1274–1974: Structures ecclésiales et conciles dans les relations entre Orient et Occident." *Revue des sciences philosophiques et theologiques* 58 (1974): 355–90.

———. "Bulletin d'ecclésiologie: conciles et papauté." *Revue des sciences philosophiques et théologiques* 60 (1976): 281–308.

———. "Quelle idée s'est-on faite du concile entre Nicée I et Nicée II?" *Revue des sciences philosophiques et théologiques* 63 (1979): 429–34.

Constas, Nicholas. "Mark Eugenikos." In *La théologie byzantine et sa tradition*. Vol. 2. Edited by Vassa Conticello. Corpus Christianorum. Turnholt: Brepols, 2002.

Costelloe, M. "Nestorian Church." Pages 343–47 in *New Catholic Encyclopedia*. Washington, DC: Catholic University of America Press, 1967.

Cunningham, Mary, and Theokritoff Elizabeth, eds. *The Cambridge Companion to Orthodox Christian Theology*. Cambridge Companions to Religion. Cambridge: Cambridge University Press, 2008.

Davis, Leo Donald. *The First Seven Ecumenical Councils (325–787): Their History and Theology*. Collegeville, MN: Liturgical, 1990.

Décarreaux, Jean. *Les Grecs au Concile de l'Union*. Paris: Picard, 1969.

Daley, Brian. "Revisiting the *Filioque*, Part Two: Contemporary Catholic approaches." *Pro Ecclesia* 10, no. 2 (2001): 195–212.

Demacopoulos, George E., and Aristotle Papanikolaou, eds. *Orthodox Readings of Augustine*. Crestwood, NY: St. Vladimir's Seminary Press, 2008.

Doerfler, Marie. "Entertaining the Trinity Unawares: Genesis XVIII in Western Christian Interpretation." *The Journal of Ecclesiastical History* 65, no. 3 (2014): 485–503.

Drecoll, Volker, and Margita Berghaus, eds. *Gregory of Nyssa: The Minor Treatises on Trinitarian Theology and Apollinarism. Proceedings of the 11th International Colloquium on Gregory of Nyssa*. Leiden: Brill, 2011.

Dulles, Avery. *Magisterium: Teacher and Guardian of the Faith*. Naples, FL: Ave Maria University Press, 2007.

Durand, Georges-Matthieu. "Un passage du IIIe livre contre Eunome de s. Basile dans la tradition manuscrite." *Irenikon* 54 (1981): 36–52.

Dvornik, Francis. *The General Councils of the Church*. London: Burns and Oates, 1961.

———. *Byzantium and the Roman Primacy*. New York: Fordham University Press, 1966.

———. "Which Councils Are Ecumenical?" *Journal of Ecumenical Studies* 3 (1966): 314–28.

Evans, Gillian. "The Council of Florence and the Problem of Ecclesial Identity." Pages 177–85 in *Christian Unity: The Council of Ferrara-Florence, 1438/39–1989*. Edited by Giuseppe Alberigo. Bibliotheca Ephemeridum Theologicarum Lovaniensium 97: International Symposium on the Unity of the Christians 550 years after the Council of Ferrara-Florence, Florence, Italy, 1989. Leuven: Leuven University Press, 1991.

Fedwick, Paul. *A Study of the Manuscript Tradition, Translations and Editions of the Works of Basil of Caesarea*. Vol. 3, Corpus Christianorum. Bibliotheca Basiliana Universalis. Turnhout: Brepols, 1997.

Forget, Jacques. "Conciles." Columns 647–76 in *DTC* vol. 3.

Fortescue, Adrian. *The Orthodox Eastern Church*. London: Catholic Truth Society, 1920.

———. *The Orthodox Eastern Church before the Schism*. Whitefish, MT: Kessinger, 2010 (repr.).

Fourneret, P. "Diocèse." Columns 1362–63 in *DTC* vol. 4.

Fritz, G. "Nicée, Deuxième Concile de." Columns 417–41 in *DTC* vol. 11/1.

Gaillardetz, Richard R. *Teaching with Authority: A Theology of the Magisterium in the Church*. Theology and Life Series 41. Collegeville, MN: Liturgical, 1997.

Galot, Jean. "L'origine éternelle de l'Esprit Saint." *Gregorianum* 78, no. 3 (1997): 501–22.

Garrigues, Jean-Miguel. "A la suite de la clarification romaine: Le *Filioque* affranchi du 'Filioquisme.'" *Irenikon* 69 (1996): 189–212.

———. "A la suite de la clarification romaine sur le *Filioque*." *Nouvelle revue theologique* 119 (1997): 321–34.

———. *L'Esprit qui dit* "Père!": *l'Esprit-Saint dans la vie Trinitaire et le problème du* Filioque. Croire et Savoir 2. Paris: Téqui, 1982.

———. *Le Saint-Esprit sceau de la Trinité*. Cogitatio Fidei 276. Paris: Cerf, 2011.

Gavin, Frank. *Some Aspects of Contemporary Greek Orthodox Thought*. 2nd ed. London: Morehouse, 1936.

Geanakoplos, Deno. "A New Reading of the Acta, Especially Syropoulos." Pages 325–51 in *Christian Unity: The Council of Ferrara-Florence, 1438/39–1989*. Edited by Giuseppe Alberigo. Bibliotheca Ephemeridum Theologicarum Lovaniensium 97: International Symposium on the Unity of the Christians 550 years after the Council of Ferrara-Florence, Florence, Italy, 1989. Leuven: Leuven University Press, 1991.

Gibson, Edgar C. S. The Thirty-Nine Articles of the Church of England. 3rd revised ed. London: Methuen, 1902.

Gill, Joseph. *The Council of Florence*. Cambridge: Cambridge University Press, 1959.

———. *Personalities of the Council of Florence, and Other Essays*. Oxford: Blackwell, 1964.

———. *Byzantium and the Papacy, 1198–1400*. New Brunswick, NJ: Rutgers University Press, 1979.

———. "L'accord gréco-latin au concile de Florence." Pages 183–94 in *Le concile et Les conciles: contributions à l'histoire de la vie conciliaire de l'Église*. Edited by Bernard Botte, Yves Congar, et al. Paris: Chevetogne, 1960.

Grégoire, José. "La relation éternelle de l'Esprit au Fils d'après les écrits de Jean de Damas." *Revue d'histoire ecclésiastique* 64 (1969): 713–55.

Groot, Joannes de. *Summa Apologetica de Ecclesia Catholica ad Mentem S. Thomae Aquinatis*. 2 vols. Regensburg: G. J. Manz, 1890.

Grumel, Venance. "Quelques témoignages byzantins sur la primauté romaine." *Echos d'Orient* 30 (1931): 422–30.

Guretzki, David, "The *Filioque*: Reviewing the State of the Question." Pages 40–63 in *Ecumenical Perspectives on the* Filioque *for the 21st Century*. Edited by Myk Habets. London: Bloomsbury Academic, 2014.

Habets, Myk, ed. *Ecumenical Perspectives on the* Filioque *for the 21st Century*. London: Bloomsbury Academic, 2014.

Halleux, André de. "Pour un accord oecuménique sur la procession de l'Esprit Saint et l'addition du *Filioque* au symbole." *Irenikon* 15 (1978): 451–69.

———. "Cyrille, Theodoret et le *Filioque*." *Revue d'histoire ecclésiastique* 74 (1979): 597–625.

———. "Problèmes de méthode dans les discussions sur l'eschatologie au Concile de Ferrare et Florence." Pages 251–301, in *Christian Unity: The Council of Ferrara-Florence, 1438/39–1989*. Edited by Giuseppe Alberigo. Bibliotheca Ephemeridum Theologicarum Lovaniensium 97: International Symposium on the Unity of the Christians 550 years after the Council of Ferrara-Florence, Florence, Italy, 1989. Leuven: Leuven University Press, 1991.

Harvey, Margaret. "England, the Council of Florence and the End of the Council of Basel." Pages 203–27 in *Christian Unity: The Council of Ferrara-Florence, 1438/39–1989*. Edited by Giuseppe Alberigo. Bibliotheca Ephemeridum Theologicarum Lovaniensium

97: International Symposium on the Unity of the Christians 550 years after the Council of Ferrara-Florence, Florence, Italy, 1989. Leuven: Leuven University Press, 1991.

Hefele, Charles-Joseph. *Histoire des conciles d'après les documents originaux*. Translated and annotated by Henri Leclercq et al. 19 volumes. Paris: Letouzey et Ané, 1907–1938.

Hladky, Vojtech. *The Philosophy of Gemistos Plethon: Platonism in Late Byzantium, between Hellenism and Orthodoxy*. Burlington, VT: Ashgate, 2014.

Hussey, Joan. *The Orthodox Church in the Byzantine Empire*. Oxford History of the Christian Church. Oxford: Oxford University Press, 2010.

Lanne, Emmanuel. "La *Processio* dello Spirito Santo nella tradizione occidentale." *Nicolaus* 24, no. 1/2 (1999): 245–60.

———. "Uniformité et pluralisme: les ecclésiologies en présence." Pages 353–73 in *Christian Unity: The Council of Ferrara-Florence, 1438/39–1989*. Edited by Giuseppe Alberigo. Bibliotheca Ephemeridum Theologicarum Lovaniensium 97: International Symposium on the Unity of the Christians 550 years after the Council of Ferrara-Florence, Florence, Italy, 1989. Leuven: Leuven University Press, 1991.

Jaeger, Lorenz. *The Ecumenical Council, the Church and Christendom*. London: Geoffrey Chapman, 1961.

Jugie, Martin. *De Processione Spiritus Sancti*. Rome: Facultas Theologica Pontificii Athenaei Seminarii Romani, 1936.

———. *Theologia Dogmatica Christianorum Orientalium ab Ecclesia Catholica Dissidentium*. 5 vols. Paris: Letouzey et Ané, 1926–1935.

———. *Le schisme Byzantin: aperçu historique et doctrinal*. Paris: Lethielleux, 1941.

———. "Constantinople IV." Columns 1273–307 in *DTC* vol. 3.

———. "Primautée dans les églises separées d'oriente." Columns 344–91 in *DTC* vol. 13/1.

———. "Schisme byzantin." Columns 1312–468 in *DTC* vol. 14/2.

Khomiakov, Alexei. *L'Eglise Latine et le Protestantisme au point de vue de l'Eglise d'Orient*. Lausanne: Benda, 1872.

Krauthauser, Carl. "The Council of Florence Revisited." *Eastern Christian Journal* 4, no. 1 (1997): 141–54.

Ku, John Baptist. *God the Father in the Theology of St. Thomas Aquinas*. American University Studies Series VII, Theology and Religion 324. New York: Peter Lang, 2013.

Ladaria, Luis. *El Espiritu Santo en San Hilario de Poitiers*. Madrid: Eapsa, 1977.

Laurent, Vitalien. "Mélanges." *Revue des études byzantines* 17 (1959): 190–200.

Leemans, Johan. "Logic and the Trinity." Pages 111–30 in *Gregory of Nyssa: The Minor Treatises on Trinitarian Theology and Apollinarism. Proceedings of the 11th International Colloquium on Gregory of Nyssa*. Edited by Volker Drecoll and Margita Berghaus. Leiden: Brill, 2011.

Levering, Matthew. *Engaging the Doctrine of the Holy Spirit: Love and Gift in the Trinity and in the Church*. Grand Rapids, MI: Baker Academic, 2016.

L'Huillier, Peter. *The Church of the Ancient Councils: The Disciplinary Work of the First Four Ecumenical Councils*. Crestwood, NY: St. Vladimir's Seminary Press, 1996.

Likoudis, James, ed. *Ending the Byzantine Greek Schism*. 2nd ed. New Rochelle, NY: Catholics United for the Faith, 1992.

Lohn, Ladislaus. "Doctrina S. Basilii de processionibus divinarum Personarum." *Gregorianum* 10 (1929): 329–64, 461–500.

Lossky, Nicolas. "Climat théologique au Concile de Florence." 241–50 in *Christian*

Unity: The Council of Ferrara-Florence, 1438/39–1989. Edited by Giuseppe Alberigo. Bibliotheca Ephemeridum Theologicarum Lovaniensium 97: International Symposium on the Unity of the Christians 550 years after the Council of Ferrara-Florence, Florence, Italy, 1989. Leuven: Leuven University Press, 1991.

Louth, Andrew. "The Use of the Term Ἴδιος in Alexandrian Theology from Alexander to Cyril." *Studia Patristica* 19 (1989): 198–202.

Manoir, Hubert du. *Dogme et spiritualité chez saint Cyrille d'Alexandrie*. Paris: Vrin, 1944.

Manoussakas, Manoussos. "Recherches sur la vie de Jean Plousiadenos." *Revue des études byzantines* 17 (1959): 28–51.

Margerie, Bernard de. "L'analogie dans l'oecuménicité des conciles: notion clef pour l'avenir de l'oecuménisme." *Revue thomiste* 84 (1984): 425–46.

———. "Vers une relecture du concile de Florence, grâce à la reconsidération de l'Ecriture et des pères grecs et latins." *Revue thomiste* 86 (1986): 31–81.

Marot, Hilaire. "Note sur la pentarchie." *Irenikon* 32 (1959): 436–42.

Maspero, Giulio. "The Fire, the Kingdom and the Glory: The Creator Spirit and the Intra-Trinitarian Processions in the *Adversus Macedonianos* of Gregory of Nyssa." Pages 229–76 in *Gregory of Nyssa: The Minor Treatises on Trinitarian Theology and Apollinarism. Proceedings of the 11th International Colloquium on Gregory of Nyssa*. Edited by Volker Drecoll and Margita Berghaus. Leiden: Brill, 2011.

Meredith, Anthony. *Gregory of Nyssa. The Early Church Fathers*. London: Routledge, 1999.

Meyendorff, John. *Orthodox Church: Its Past and Its Role in the World Today*. Translated by J. Chapin. 3rd revised ed. Crestwood, NY: St. Vladimir's Seminary Press, 1981.

———. *The Byzantine Legacy in the Orthodox Church*. Crestwood, NY: St. Vladimir's Seminary Press, 1982.

———. *Byzantine Theology: Historical Trends and Doctrinal Themes*. 2nd revised ed. New York: Fordham University Press, 1983.

———. *Rome, Constantinople, Moscow: Historical and Theological Studies*. Crestwood, NY: St. Vladimir's Seminary Press, 1996.

———. "What is an Ecumenical Council?" *St. Vladimir's Theological Quarterly* 17 (1973): 259–73.

———. "Was There an Encounter between East and West at Florence?" Pages 153–75 in *Christian Unity: The Council of Ferrara-Florence, 1438/39–1989*. Edited by Giuseppe Alberigo. Bibliotheca Ephemeridum Theologicarum Lovaniensium 97: International Symposium on the Unity of the Christians 550 years after the Council of Ferrara-Florence, Florence, Italy, 1989. Leuven: Leuven University Press, 1991.

Newman, John Henry. *Certain Difficulties Felt by Anglicans in Catholic Teaching*. London: Longman & Green, 1908.

———. Tract 90. 1841. Rep. N.p: Ulan Press, 2012.

Nichols, Aidan. *Rome and the Eastern Churches: A Study in Schism*. Edinburgh: T. & T. Clark, 1992.

———. "The Reception of St. Augustine and His Work in the Byzantine-Slav Tradition." *Angelicum* 64 (1987): 437–52.

Norris, Frederick W. *Faith Gives Fullness to Reasoning: The Five Theological Orations of Gregory Nazianzen*. Supplements to *Vigiliae Christianae* 13. Leiden: Brill, 1990.

North American Orthodox–Catholic Theological Consultation. "'The *Filioque*: A

Church-Dividing Issue?' An Agreed Statement." *St. Vladimir's Theological Quarterly* 48 (2004): 93–123.

Ott, Ludwig. *Fundamentals of Catholic Dogma*. Cork: Mercier, 1960.

Papandreou, Damaskinos. "Via Synodica." Pages 353–73 in *Christian Unity: The Council of Ferrara-Florence, 1438/39–1989*. Edited by Giuseppe Alberigo. Bibliotheca Ephemeridum Theologicarum Lovaniensium 97: International Symposium on the Unity of the Christians 550 years after the Council of Ferrara-Florence, Florence, Italy, 1989. Leuven: Leuven University Press, 1991.

Parys, Michel van. "Quelques remarques à propos d'un texte controversé de Basile au concile de Florence." *Irenikon* 40 (1967): 6–14.

Passaglia, Carlo. *De conciliis oecumenicis: theses Caroli Passaglia de conciliis deque habitu quo ad Romanos pontifices referuntur*. Edited by Heribert Schauf. Rome: Herder, 1961.

Patriarchs of the Eastern Churches. "Encyclical of the Eastern Patriarchs, 1848: A Reply to the Epistle of Pope Pius IX, 'to the Easterns.'" Orthodox Christian Information Center. orthodoxinfo.com/ecumenism/encyc_1848.aspx.

Paxton, N. "Cardinal Bessarion of Nicaea." *Eastern Christian Journal* 10, no. 1 (2003): 9–24.

Penido, Mauxilio Texeira-Leite. "Gloses sur la procession d'amour dans la Trinité." *Ephemerides theologicae lovanienses* 14 (1937): 33–68.

Peri, Vittorio. "Le pape et le concile oecuménique." *Irenikon* 56 (1983): 163–93.

Pesch, Christian. *Praelectiones Dogmaticae*. Vol. 1. Fribourg: Herder, 1903.

Petit, Louis. "Joseph de Méthone." Columns 1526–29 in *DTC* vol. 8/2.

Pétridès, Sophron. "La mort de Marc d'Ephèse." *Echos d'Orient* 13 (1910): 19–21.

Phidas, Vlassios. "Herméneutique et patristique au concile de Florence." Pages 303–23 in *Christian Unity: The Council of Ferrara-Florence, 1438/39–1989*. Edited by Giuseppe Alberigo. Bibliotheca Ephemeridum Theologicarum Lovaniensium 97: International Symposium on the Unity of the Christians 550 years after the Council of Ferrara-Florence, Florence, Italy, 1989. Leuven: Leuven University Press, 1991.

Plested, Marcus. *Orthodox Readings of Aquinas*. Changing Paradigms in Historical and Systematic Theology. Oxford: Oxford University Press, 2012.

Pontifical Council for Promoting Christian Unity. "Traditions regarding the Procession of the Holy Spirit." *Eastern Christian Journal* 2, no. 3 (1995): 35–46.

Popescu, Dumitru. "Il problema del *Filioque*: ekporeusis e processio." *Nicolaus* 26, no. 1–2 (1999): 261–69.

Pusey, Edward. *A Letter to Richard, Lord Bishop of Oxford, on the Tendency to Romanism Imputed to Doctrines Held of Old, as Now, in the English Church* [1840]. N.p.: General Books, 2010.

Ramsey, Boniface. *Ambrose. The Early Church Fathers*. London: Routledge, 1997.

Régnon, Théodore de. *Études de théologie positive sur la Sainte Trinité*. Vol. 1. Paris: V. Reteaux, 1892.

Sieben, Hermann Josef. *Studien zum Ökumenischen Konzil: Definitionen und Begriffe, Tagebücher und Augustinus-Rezeption*. Paderborn: Ferdinand Schöningh, 2010.

Siecienski, A. Edward. *The Filioque: History of a Doctrinal Controversy*. New York: Oxford University Press, 2010.

Sullivan, Francis. *Magisterium: Teaching Authority in the Catholic Church*. New York: Paulist, 1983.

———. *Creative Fidelity: Weighing and Interpreting Documents of the Magisterium*. Eugene, OR: Wipf and Stock, 2003.

Swete, Henry Barclay. *On the History of the Doctrine of the Procession of the Holy Spirit: From the Apostolic Age to the Death of Charlemagne*. Cambridge: Deighton and Bell, 1876. Repr., n.p.: Nabu, 2014.

Tanner, Norman. *The Councils of the Church: A Short History*. New York: Crossroad, 2001.

———. *The Church in Council: Conciliar Movements, Religious Practice and the Papacy from Nicaea to Vatican II*. International Library of Historical Studies. London: I. B. Taurus, 2011.

Toom, Tarmo. "Hilary of Poitier's *De Trinitate* and the Name(s) of God." *Vigiliae Christianae* 64, no. 5 (2010): 456–79.

Torrance, Thomas F. *The Trinitarian Faith: The Evangelical Theology of the Ancient Catholic Church*. Edinburgh: T. & T. Clark, 1988.

Turner, C. "George-Gennadius Scholarius and the Union of Florence." *Journal of Theological Studies* 18 (1967): 83–103.

Vannier, Anne-Marie. "L'apport de la Clarification sur le *Filioque*." *Revue des sciences religieuses* 75, no. 1 (2001): 97–112.

Vatican Council II. Vol. 1, *The Conciliar and Post-Conciliar Documents*. Edited by Austin Flannery, O.P. New revised edition. Dublin: Dominican Publications; New York: Costello, 1975.

Wilhelm, Joseph. "Councils, General." Pages 423–35 in *Catholic Encyclopedia*. New York: Encyclopedia Press, 1913.

Zizioulas, John. *Being as Communion: Studies in Personhood and the Church*. Contemporary Greek Theologians 4. Crestwood, NY: St. Vladimir's Seminary Press, 1985.

———. "One Single Source: An Orthodox Response to the Clarification on the *Filioque*." Orthodox Research Institute. orthodoxresearchinstitute.org/articles/dogmatics/john_zizioulas_single_source.htm.

Index